STARBOUND

STARBOUND

Gordon *and* Nina Stuermer

David McKay Company, Inc.
New York

Library of Congress Cataloging in Publication Data
Stuermer, Gordon.
Starbound.

1. Starbound (Ketch) 2. Voyages around the world.
I. Stuermer, Nina, joint author. II. Title.
G420.S88S87   910′.41 [B]   77-9983
ISBN 0-679-50778-7

10 9 8 7 6 5 4 3 2 1
Manufactured in the United States of America

This book is dedicated to
our parents, who gave us the dream . . .
our son, Ernie, a fine seaman and companion . . .
and all the yachties; may they have fair winds and tranquil seas.

Contents

Annapolis to Panama: The Caribbean   1

CHAPTER   1   Seven-Year Shakedown Cruise:
                   The First Six Years   3

           2   Seven-Year Shakedown Cruise:
                   The Last Year   27

           3   Bermuda—The Hard Way   39

           4   Bermuda Scramble   55

           5   The Leewards   63

           6   Through the Windwards
                   and Make a Right Turn   77

           7   To Panama via Curaçao and Cartagena   89

           8   The Panama Canal—A Piece of Cake   103

Galapagos to Tonga: The Eastern Pacific   113

CHAPTER   9   A Taste of the Pacific—
                   Galapagos to the Marquesas   115

          10   Polynesian Paradise   127

          11   The Tuamotus and Tahiti   143

          12   *Iles Sous le Vent*   161

          13   Cruisers, Tenders, Anchors—and Samoa   169

Fiji to Cocos: The Western Pacific 179

CHAPTER 14 Tonga and Fiji 187

15 New Zealand, Aotearoa 195

16 The Ship's Log: Across the Tasman Sea 209

17 Inside the Great Barrier Reef 219

18 Coup d'Etat in Dili 241

19 Bali: Temples and Rice Paddies 259

South Africa to Annapolis: The Indian and Atlantic Oceans 273

CHAPTER 20 Across the Indian Ocean to South Africa 275

21 The Dark Continent 287

22 Home Are the Sailors 303

APPENDIX A Food, Stores, and Galley Equipment 315

B Tools 325

C Spares 329

D Passages 333

Glossary of Nautical Terms 337

PART I

Annapolis
to
Panama

The Caribbean

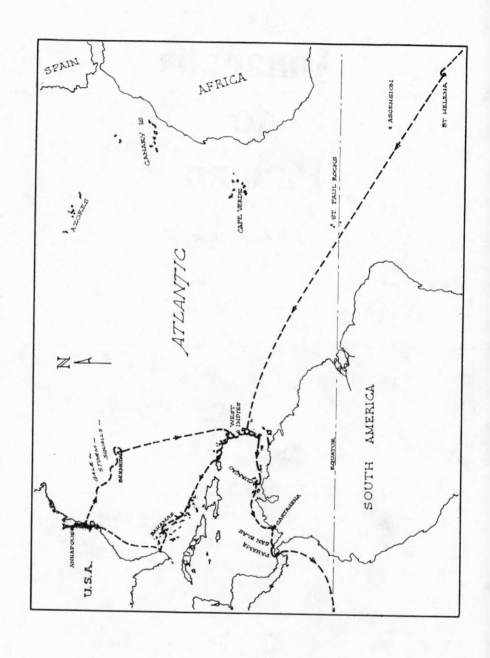

1

Seven-Year Shakedown Cruise: The First Six Years

"By God, we're going to sea!" I exulted. "This is the year. We must go to Bermuda this summer, and don't argue that we're not ready—we'll be ready. We've got to have a shakedown cruise."

Nina looked at me. "Gordon, do you really trust that poor old engine? What if it gives out when we really need it? I'm worried about it."

"Don't worry," I assured her. "Nothing will go wrong with the engine. It's running fine—besides, we can't afford a new one till next winter. It'll be O.K. We're going!"

We borrowed a life raft and a radio telephone from Dick and Ricky Clover. We borrowed a small package motor-generator from Frank Baldwin, whose son, Greg, was going with us. We loaded up our lockers with food and spent our evenings studying charts.

We coordinated our departure date from Annapolis with members of the Arundel Yacht Club, three of whom were going with us. Eight other members of the club had chartered a 45-foot cutter and were departing at the same time as we. We were ready!

Starbound once again hustled down the Chesapeake Bay bound for Norfolk, Virginia. It was June 24, 1972—sixteen months before the departure date for our long-planned world cruise. We were to arrive in Little Creek in two days' time, fill our fuel and water tanks, and check the weather. Tropical storm Agnes had passed up Chesapeake Bay just a few

3

days before and had dumped a huge amount of rain on the East Coast. The rivers were over their banks to the north of us, and we knew that a large amount of debris would be carried down the bay behind us. We wanted to be on our way.

Seven people were on board. Besides Nina, me, our sixteen-year-old son, Ernie, and Ernie's friend Greg Baldwin, there were Bob Leal, Bill Ellsworth, and Jeanne Miles—all good sailors and members of the Arundel Yacht Club. Jeanne's husband, Harry Miles, was skipper of the cutter which was accompanying *Starbound*. Originally, both Harry and Jeanne were going to crew on *Starbound*, but last-minute problems left the cutter without a qualified skipper, so Harry had to fill the gap. Being a good friend, he asked Jeanne to go with *Starbound* and give us a hand. I was glad she was there; Jeanne's an experienced blue water sailor.

Two days in Little Creek, Virginia, had us impatient to leave. The wind was still light and variable, but Weather Central promised westerlies on the following day, so we started the diesel and motored out of the bay and toward the Chesapeake Light in a flat calm.

Starbound motored along at about 4 knots. We weren't pushing her because we wanted to economize on fuel. I could hear the engine revolutions surge once in a while but thought nothing of it, assuming that the old worn governor was the contributing factor.

By dark we had a light reaching breeze out of the southwest. We secured the engine and began to sail. What a marvelous night—the breeze was warm and fair, the stars were shining, and we were on our way to our first tropical island.

At noon the next day our meridian altitude shot combined with a morning sun line put *Starbound* a few miles north of her rhumb line to Bermuda. At sunset the atmosphere changed very suddenly and became muggy. The horizon was misty and the sea water dipped up by a bucket was much warmer than it had been that afternoon. We were in the Gulf Stream. The sky was cloudy but there were no signs of the thunder squalls we had been told might be prevalent.

The sun rose on the third morning but we only knew it because of the lightening sky. The cloud cover was thick. In the late afternoon the wind had backed to the southeast, and I decided to start the engine and motor-sail in order to hold our course. The cloud cover was breaking but not enough for a sun shot. Towering thunderheads appeared to the southeast, and we knew that we were approaching the eastern edge of the Gulf Stream. As the sky grew dark with approaching night, all hands were on the lookout for a possible squall. I tuned the radio to a Norfolk station and learned that a weak cold front had left the coast that afternoon. A quick calculation showed that it would probably catch up with us about midnight. At 2200 the wind started to pick up speed. Happily for *Starbound,* it also began to haul fair—but I was being very cautious. That cold front had me worried. Remembering my meteorology courses, I knew that a southwest wind would precede the front by a few hours. I turned *Starbound* into the wind and waves, and the crew dropped the main-topsail and then the mainsail. With the big boom secured in its crutch, Bob, Bill, and Ernie started furling the sail tightly and putting on extra gaskets.

I turned *Starbound* off the wind and secured the engine once again. I was starting to worry about that engine. While running under load, the arhythmic surge I had noticed earlier could be detected more and more frequently. I kept thinking about what might happen if the governor on the engine failed completely. I was sure that was what the problem was, and I remembered brief bits of terrible stories I had heard about runaway diesel engines. Well, I reasoned, I could always just shut off the fuel and the engine would stop. I put the problem out of my mind. *Starbound* was sailing on course, although I thought we might be north of our rhumb line by a few miles. We had the big yankee jib and the mizzen sail pulling well and I felt that the sail area was small enough to preclude danger from sudden gusts. Anyway, with the mainsail secured, we could drop the rest of the sails in a hurry. My innocence was touching—at least to me. Other people have found it amusing, or even shocking.

The front was catching up fast. We could see lightning backlighting clouds to the south and west of us now, almost continuously. I decided we'd better drop the sails, but we were sailing so nicely. We could wait a bit longer. A few drops of rain fell—then with a smashing roar the squall drove into *Starbound* with total violence. We had been caught with too much sail up.

Shakedown cruise? Shakeup is more the word. Lightning was a continuous muted flicker through horizontal sheets of rain. Thunder rumbled incessantly but was barely heard over the scream of wind which in a few seconds had climbed a sirenlike scale to an ear-piercing intensity, and *Starbound* heeled and heeled. As the deck fell out from under my feet, I grabbed for the mizzen mast and held tightly.

I could see Bill at the helm holding onto the wheel with one hand and clutching the big varnished binnacle with his whole upper body; and looking below me (good God, *below* me?) Bob lay grinning up from the scuppers where he had landed—and stayed, thanks to high solid bulwarks. What the hell is he smiling about, I wondered? When Bill and Bob, friends of ours from the Arundel Yacht Club, volunteered to act as crew on our cruise to Bermuda, they certainly couldn't have had any idea they'd end up in a situation like this one. In the next flash of lightning I could see the port tip of the 40-foot yard grazing the foam-streaked black water, and in that calm way sometimes visited upon one when under great stress. I thought, "That's much too far over!"

I called to Bill to fall off and at the same instant I heard a strange sound like the twang of a bowstring releasing an arrow, and felt the mizzenmast vibrate under my arms. An instant later something hard, heavy, and writhing fell on my head and shoulders. I grabbed at the thing and realized it was the mizzen topmast weather shroud. Oh, great, I thought—but is the boat falling off? I reached for the wheel and helped Bill turn her off the wind. The deck leveled and *Starbound* raced off downwind, pulled by the big yankee jib which I was wishing to hell I had doused an hour before in favor of the small fore-staysail.

The morning sun sparkled against a cobalt blue sea flecked with friendly small crests of white foam which were being driven before a light northerly breeze. The entire ship's company was topside examining the mizzen shroud which had dropped on my head at the height of the squall, and which we had managed in the dark to coil in great round loops and tie to the rail and chain plates. The decks were drying quickly in the sun and wind and everyone's outlook was cheerful—excepting the captain's. The wire shroud had pulled right out of the fitting at the mizzenmasthead and I had to know why. After studying the end of the wire, I knew the answer. Whoever had made up the fitting had cut away the internal six strands of the 1×19 wire shroud to make the fit-up easier and in so doing had reduced the strength of the fitting. What about the other shrouds? I didn't know and I was worried. Another similar failure could mean the possible loss of the mizzenmast. But putting that problem out of mind was easy—a much worse problem was becoming very evident. I had started the engine that morning and found that the propeller wasn't turning. Bob and I started investigating. The shaft was free—I could turn it by hand. And the engine was running well with no more of that surging noise I had been worrying about. Bob and I looked at each other and said, "The transmission!"

We worked on the machinery all day. By nightfall, sweaty and tired, we admitted defeat. The old gearbox had given up the ghost and couldn't be fixed at sea. The clutch plates were completely worn away and had only been driving the shaft intermittently—which accounted for the surging engine revolutions.

I called the crew together and told them that I intended heading back to the coast. Everyone was disappointed but agreed with my reasoning. I knew that parts for the ancient transmission would be unavailable in Bermuda because they were unavailable anywhere. Also, the wind had been busily veering around to head us once again and looked as if it would keep going right around to become the prevailing southwest breeze. By heading for Cape May, New Jersey, we would be on a port tack, relieving the strain on the mizzenmasttop due to the missing starboard shroud. I would rather have headed for the mouth of the Chesapeake Bay, back the way we came, but the wind from the southwest wouldn't allow that course. Our newest sun shots put us 20 miles north of our original rhumb line.

Three days later at 0400 we picked up the Cape May light. By 0900 we were sailing between the huge stone jetties of Cape May Harbor with the start of the flood tide helping us along. We managed to make the left-hand fork at the end of the jetty into the harbor mouth before the wind quit on us entirely. *Starbound* turned a full 360 degrees right in the middle of the channel as the tidal current washed us into the harbor. As the Coast Guard Training Station docks came abreast of us, I noted we were on the edge of the channel and called to Ernie to drop the anchor. We swung to the tide and began dropping the limp sails. It was very hot and humid. Two coastguardsmen idled at the end of their dock and watched us.

"Good morning," I called. "Our engine is out of commission. Can you get a cutter to give us a tow to the yacht club anchorage?" They looked at each other and broke into a trot toward their office. By 1000 *Starbound* was securely anchored in front of the Cape May Yacht Club and I was sitting in their snack bar with a cold beer in one hand and a telephone in the other.

That night, Jeanne flew to Bermuda to join her husband and help bring the cutter home. By the next morning, Bill's girlfriend had driven up from Annapolis and then departed with Bob and Bill.

For the next week, Ernie and Greg exploited the fun to be had in Cape May and Nina and I tried to find a way to get *Starbound* home.

I found an expert on marine transmissions and induced him to come out and look at *Starbound's* "innards." Ten minutes of investigation verified the worst. The transmission couldn't be fixed without removing it and taking it to a machine shop—a major job which involved making parts. Nina and I started looking for a tow.

One week later we were back at our dock in Annapolis. We had contracted with a fisherman and his boat to help us up the Delaware Bay, through the Chesapeake and Delaware Canal, and down the Chesapeake Bay to Annapolis. The boat was a 16-foot fiberglass cruiser with a 140 hp outboard attached. I think the fisherman did it for a bet. God knows we didn't pay him much.

The end of the summer of 1972 was at hand. Our "vacation" was over and *Starbound* needed a new engine.

We had one year left before departing on a world cruise.

Nina and I had bought *Starbound* in December 1966, had moved aboard the same day, and had been walking around grinning at our friends, somewhat like kids who have a secret. We became experts in the care and feeding of a large wooden boat, and began fitting her out for our dream of dreams, a cruise around the world. Let me take another look at those words. A CRUISE AROUND THE WORLD! Can any phrase sound more exciting to a sailor? We planned to sail from the Chesapeake in October 1973, with Bermuda as the destination of our first leg, thence to the West Indies, through the Panama Canal, and into the South Pacific (more magic words).

A glossary of nautical terms defines *shakedown cruise* as meaning "one for the purpose of adjusting machinery and instruments, and familiarizing a crew with a new vessel." And that's what we did for seven years—in addition to making rather substantial payments to various lending institutions.

After selling our four-bedroom house in the suburbs of Washington, D.C., and moving to a small apartment, we tramped over and through hundreds of boatyards and boats. It's the same old story—everything we liked was out of financial reach and everything we could afford wasn't worth buying. Then we found *Starbound* through a series of implausible circumstances. When Nina first saw the vessel sitting quietly in the water at the Smith Creek dock near the mouth of the Potomac River, tears came to her eyes. She leaped from the dock to the broad sweep of teak deck, stretched her arms out to embrace the mast, and cried, "For this boat, I'll go back to work!"

I laughed and replied, "Hell, for this boat you'll *have* to go to work."

We fell in love with *Starbound* at first sight and bought her by the skin of our financial teeth. She is large and livable: 35 tons of seagoing ketch with a traditional gaff rig, a long bowsprit, and a diesel auxiliary. Her beam is 17 feet, length on deck 50 feet, and draft 6 feet 6 inches. When we purchased her she also had peeling paint and rotten sails and frayed running rigging. Her diesel was on its deathbed and her other mechanical systems were suffering from lack of maintenance. As I went over her with the marine surveyor, my brain kept ringing up a series of dollar signs like the cash register in a supermarket. Her hull was sound except for some soft frame heads on either side, and her bottom was copper-sheathed.

I stood in the last light of the sunset that cold December evening looking at *Starbound* on the marine railway. The surveyor had left for his home and fireside and I was alone with my ship. I looked at her confusing assortment of running rigging, let my eyes travel up her 65 feet of mainmast, and said aloud to myself, "Well, boy, you've really done it! So now what?" And I answered myself, "Now the shakedown cruise starts!"

Our immediate task was to move *Starbound* to Annapolis, about 60 miles up the Chesapeake Bay.

December weather in the Chesapeake can sometimes be soft and warm, but not for us on that third day of the month. A big high-pressure system was moving across Delaware. The barometer stood at 30.41 inches of mercury (1030 millibars). A northerly was being funneled right down the bay at 15 to 20 knots. At 0800 the sky was a brilliant blue, achingly bright to the eyes. I glanced at the big Centigrade thermometer I'd suspended from the mizzen boom with a string the night before. It stood at minus 6 degrees (about 21 degrees Fahrenheit).

I had on thermal underwear, heavy jeans, a wool sweater, a heavy-lined waterproof coat, and fur-lined gloves and boots. The wind found the chinks in my armor and I shivered.

In retrospect I should have gone below, laced my hot coffee with rum, snuggled up to the big kerosene heater, and relaxed for a few days. But I hadn't yet acquired the patience a good cruising sailor must have. I said firmly, "O.K., crew. Let's go!"

My friend George, who had volunteered to help us get the boat to Annapolis, gazed at me with a skeptical eye, sniffed the biting wind, and asked mildly, "Sure you don't want to wait a day or two?" "No," I replied. "With this temperature the Annapolis creeks might freeze and then I don't know when we could get in."

"O.K.," said George. "Let's try to swing the compass before we get out of the river."

We tried but weren't too successful, what with the wind and the chop. We did determine that our northerly course had little or no variation, so we ignored it. After all, a nice day's run—we would surely be in by sunset. And the sun was shining; the day would most likely warm up considerably. George had a date with a very sexy blonde that evening and I assured him we'd be into port in plenty of time. Poor George.

At 0200 the next morning, an exhausted, frozen crew crawled over the 1-inch layer of ice on the decks forward and with various hammers started chipping ice off the anchor, chain, and winch. I put *Starbound*'s bowsprit close to the retaining wall of the U.S. Navy facility on the north shore of the Severn River at Annapolis, then, stopping her forward way, went forward over the ice-glazed decks on hands and knees to put the big anchor over the side. *Starbound* fell back on her chain and when we felt her check herself, we tumbled below for big steaming mugs of hot buttered rum and fell into our bunks with scarcely a word to each other.

At 0900 I awoke to the sound of boat engines. Lying in my bunk and listening, it seemed as if two or three boats were motoring around and around us. When *Starbound* began rocking from their wakes I jumped up, threw on some clothes, and went topside to find out what was going on. Sure enough, two boats were circling us and taking photographs. The reason for this was immediately apparent. The entire forward half of the boat was encased in glittering ice. I had known the night before that the spray tossed up by *Starbound*'s bow as we smashed into the waves had frozen on her gear, but we couldn't see how much, and we'd been so exhausted we'd ignored it. The mainmast, shrouds, and running rigging for

15 feet up from the deck were coated with a heavy layer of white ice. The ship's bell, clad in dripping icicles, was unrecognizable. The fife rail with its belaying pins and coils of line looked like a squat monster crouched at the foot of the mast. The anchor winch and catheads were faintly familiar lumps, and the decks had turned to treacherous glacial slopes as far aft as the mizzenmast.

Another day of brilliant blue sky and bright sun reflected scintillating flashes from our icy decorations as *Starbound* rolled gently from the wakes of the boats circling us. I stood there with my mouth open. *Starbound* was beautiful! I called Nina, Ernie (then eleven years old), and George on deck to see. Our big black poodle, Prancer, preceded them. He had spent the trip huddled in a corner and braced against the motion of the ship. Now, at the sound of my voice, he bounded topside and trotted forward, slipping and sliding on the ice. The beauty of the scene didn't interest him at all. I guess he felt that twenty-six hours without a tree was as much as he could take. He hoisted his leg on the fife rail and kept it propped there for a long time. The expression on his furry face had us all laughing, then we broke out our cameras and took pictures of ice-laden *Starbound.*

After breakfast, we hooked up the washdown pump and managed to clear the decks and anchor winch of their icy glazes. We raised the anchor and motored around Horn Point and into Spa Creek, hooting our horn for the bridge to open. Scooting through the narrow slot we saw the boatyard ahead of us on the east bank of the creek and managed to work *Starbound* into a big berth at the end of the dock. For the time being this would be home.

Two days later the big high-pressure system pushing all the cold air down from the north moved out to sea and the temperature went up to 70 degrees. A warm southerly wind set in and blew steadily for the next three days. I sniffed the warm air and smiled at Nina.

She smiled back and said, "Let's not ever do that banging into the waves again if we can avoid it by waiting. O.K.?"

"O.K.," I replied.

Boatyards, yacht yards, marinas—where do the live-aboard people keep their boat-homes? It was a big problem in 1967 and the problem hasn't gone away during the years we've lived aboard.

We knew that we would remain in the Annapolis area of the Chesapeake Bay until Ernie graduated from high school. So we looked for a berth for *Starbound.*

Our parking spot in Spa Creek was for the winter only, since it was the summer berth of a big "gold-plated" diesel cruiser. We were happy to find any slip, even temporarily, that would accommodate our 17-foot beam. We had electrical power of sorts. The dock wiring was strung from poles situated about every 20 feet along the dock and suspended by ancient ceramic insulators. Each entire dock of approximately 20 slips was fused for only 30 amperes. Any two resistance-type electrical devices could not be employed without blowing the fuses for the dock. This eliminated our use of handy devices like electric heaters, stoves, coffee pots, frying pans, and pressing irons—that is, unless just one device at a time was used, and no one else on the dock plugged something of like capacity in while the *Starbound* folks were happily ironing a shirt or perking some coffee or soldering an electrical terminal.

During the winter in latitudes which have freezing weather, live-aboard people have another problem—keeping water tanks full. At our first boatyard, along with the scarcity of electricity, we had to go through a two-hour exercise to fill *Starbound*'s water tanks. The water pipes under the docks which supply the slips with water all summer long are turned off and drained shortly after Labor Day to preclude their possible freezing and subsequent bursting. One lonesome sill cock was left active and jutted out from the side of one of the yard buildings. To reach that faucet from the farthest slip meant laying 500 feet of garden hose down the dock and around the pierhead, or else spanning the water between the odd-angled docks with a lesser amount of hose, perhaps 200 feet. Well, we had only 200 feet of hose. So we'd uncouple each separate roll and hook them together. Then we'd break out the heaving line and one of us would walk down the dock, turn left around the pierhead and left again beside the old shop building, then out on the beat-up rickety pier which had an A-frame for pulling masts jutting up from its end pilings. With luck, an accurate and strong heave of the line would just allow the yellow ball to be caught by the recipient whose body was usually cantilevered over the water while hanging onto the rusty A-frame with one hand. A boat hook helped. The female coupling end of the hose would have the heaving line bent to it and the hose would be pulled across to the old dock. Then while the end was walked down to the shop building, the main body of the hose would form a long catenary into the water and out again. Finally the hose would be screwed to the sill cock and the water turned on. We'd let the water run a few minutes to flush out the hose lengths, then stuff the end in the tank filler opening. On the coldest days, water spilled on the teak decks would immediately freeze into a thin, slick film. The water pressure was so low that we always expected the water to freeze inside the hose before it came trickling out the end. It would take two hours to satisfy *Starbound*'s 300-gallon capacity. Then, we would quickly turn off the sill cock, disconnect the hose, and haul it aboard *Starbound* as fast as possible. We'd thoroughly drain each length before ice formed inside, then roll the lengths up, couple each hose on itself, and restow them in the lazarette; water for another two weeks was aboard.

Keeping warm that first winter was a constant job. Since electrical heat couldn't be used, we elected to try kerosene heaters. We bought two of the very good, English-made, high-stack heaters. They burn with a clean blue flame and put out 5,000 BTU's each. We could also heat hot water on their tops, or even cook on them. Since all hot water had to be heated in a kettle, we were assured of a constant small supply without using the propane stove. Of course, as with all heaters of this type, the heat would rise and our faces would be hot while our feet remained cold.

As soon as we were settled into this first berth, we began looking for another which we hoped would have a few more amenities, like adequate electrical power, and water outlets closer to the boat. New Year's Eve we moved to a big marina adjacent to the Annapolis Yacht Club. Again we were using the slip belonging to a large cruiser wintering in Florida. But we had a place until April—with 30-ampere and 50-ampere receptacles on the dock for each slip, and a water tap 20 feet away. And, seeming like a late Christmas present, a clothes washer and dryer were available for our use.

Three months of winter passed by in a rush and suddenly the willows were a cloud of green against the winter-brown banks of the creeks. We could extinguish the kerosene heaters now during the days while we hustled into the District of Columbia to work. In the evenings we'd clean the heater burners, fill the tanks with fuel, and relight them. The boat always smelled of kerosene. Our clothes became saturated with the faint reek of the fuel and caused a few comments at work. We decided to install some sort of proper heating system as soon as possible and stepped up our research on the subject.

Good friends of ours owned an ancient 65-foot power boat. She had been built by Consolidated Yachts in the 1920s and was originally a rumrunner but had been converted to a pleasure yacht following repeal of prohibition. Dave and Lyn Westergard had bought her in New Jersey and had lived on her with their children for a time during which Dave had installed a very workable heating system. He recommended it to me for *Starbound* and I explored his boat carefully to see if I could adapt the system to ours. The basics of the system were a small package hot water boiler, fueled with diesel and ignited electrically with 115 volts AC, and a pump which pushed hot water through "baseboard" heaters mounted in strategic locations through the boat. The word *package* when applied to boilers means that all of the items necessary for its operation are attached directly to the boiler— things like the fuel pump, blower, blower motor, hot water circulating pump, and electrical relays. Our boat has a walk-in engine room with enough space for the installation, so we bought one of these marvelous gadgets. At Dave's advice we ordered a unit which had a "tankless coil" installed in its boiler. One line of our domestic water supply ran into the coil. The line coming out connected to the hot water faucets. This arrangement gave us all the hot water we could use, with a very low expenditure of electrical power. We hooked up two loops of copper tubing to the boiler water outlets. One loop ran aft and one forward from our amidships engine room. The loops were suspended from the floors just below the cabin sole. What a delightful feeling it was when we triggered the switch for the first time and the boiler lit off with a quiet rumble and commenced to operate smoothly and efficiently. Even more delightful was the luxury of hot showers, and being able to walk about below on a warm cabin sole during nippy spring nights with the cabin temperature at a comfortable 70 degrees.

By the first day of April we had surveyed most of the Annapolis water-front looking for a permanent home for *Starbound*. The list of things in the must-do-immediately category was growing longer and longer and we had to find a suitable location where we could work on the boat. Finally we found a section of the tee end of a dock in a small boatyard at the mouth of Back Creek. The owner, Dick Vosbury, seemed to be an amenable guy who claimed to be tolerant of what he called "do-it-your-selfers" and "live-aboarders."

We brought *Starbound* back around Horn Point, which juts into the Severn River and separates Spa Creek from Back Creek. We eased up to the big tee dock, and, with the eyes of most of the people in the yard watching us, made a perfectly terrible landing. I was at the helm and was so wrapped up in my approach that I didn't notice that the square yard had not been cockbilled sufficiently. The tip of the yard caught the shrouds of the ancient 8-meter yacht laying on one arm of the tee and swung our big bowsprit right into the dock pilings. Thank God we were moving very slowly. As our sprit shrouds hit the high dock pilings, the tip of the square yard twanged loose from the 8-meter's shrouds. The vibration broke the rotten whippings on the wooden shroud rollers of the old boat and all of the roller halves leaped from the shrouds and fell into the water. Cursing to myself, I backed *Starbound* off the pilings, and with full left rudder and a short burst of the engine managed to swing her big stern into the dock clear of the bow of the 8-meter. Many willing hands took our dock lines and secured us. I felt as if the dock people were saying to themselves, "Let's tie this son of a bitch up fast so he can't hit something else." With a red face and mumbled apologies, I fished the wooden roller halves out of the creek with a boat hook, and later on that day I went aboard the 8-meter, which thankfully was deserted, and whipped the gear back on to the shrouds.

We had a home dock now. We didn't know it at the time, but we were to live at that dock for the next five years.

I kept, and still keep, a little pocket memorandum book with me at all times. I started doing this on the day we bought *Starbound*. We found it impossible to remember everything we needed when going into town for boat supplies. With the book, we could also develop priority lists and keep our thoughts organized so that the truly staggering amount of work we had to do could proceed more efficiently.

Prying into my files the other day, I found the very first of our pocket memo books started the day after we had bought *Starbound*. What fascinating lists it contains. Our only restrictions on boat work that first year were due to lack of money. We were so badly strapped after our initial outlay of cash, with the added burden of a big bank payment each month, that there wasn't much money left for boat "things." Luckily we were well supplied with tools. I am a good mechanic and a fair carpenter, and Nina is an expert with a paintbrush.

Nina tackled the paint jobs from the deck up, while I gritted my teeth and started making some headway on the hull topsides. *Starbound*'s hull had been painted black when she was built and kept that color until her previous owner had slapped on a single coat of white enamel right on top of the black. The paint was chipping and peeling, and the heat absorption of the black paint, even through the white top coat, was high enough to cause her seams to pop. The compound on the bow seams protruded one-eighth inch through the white paint in ugly black lines.

I borrowed a high-speed industrial disc sander from a friend and commenced to wood down the hull from rub rail to the copper sheathing 6 inches above her water line. Loose seams were reefed and caulked. Then I painted her with two coats of white primer and two coats of semigloss white enamel. Nina sanded and painted the house sides white and changed the color of the spars from a horrible pinkish shade of buff to a light ivory cream.

Nights after work, Nina made curtains and new covers for the cushions while I tried to make sense out of the Frankenstein laboratory I found in the engine room. We raked enough muck from the bilges to pollute a good portion of the Chesapeake, but being environmentally minded people, we set Ernie to carrying bucket after bucket of sludge up to the trash bin in the yard.

After we had the creeping deterioration to the painted topsides somewhat arrested, we started working on deck leaks. The teak decks are 2 inches thick and caulked with a polysulfide rubber compound. But many deck plugs were loose and the caulking had been allowed to "stand proud" and be loosened by shuffling feet. The deck leaks were many, and when the spring rains thundered down we had to cover the house top with tarpaulins to avoid a soaking below. All the worst leaks were directly over our bunks, which seems to be a standing rule for deck leaks.

During lunchtime at my Navy office I would get on the telephone and start finding where needed items were and how much they would cost. We had to let the old rotten nylon sails stay on the booms for another year, but the frayed running rigging had to be replaced lest a failure bring down a heavy boom on someone's head. The old tarred Italian hemp lanyards were removed one at a time and new five-eighths-inch nylon was rove through the big lignum vitae deadeyes. We couldn't afford Dacron or nylon for the halyard tackles, so we replaced the old brittle sisal with new yellow manila, promising ourselves some nice soft Dacron when we could afford it.

Our ship was starting to look good. We found ourselves standing on the dock admiring her pretty paint job and new running rigging. By the end of May her old diesel had a new lease on life and we were frantic to go for a sail. The first weekend in June promised beautiful weather and fulfilled the promise. Instead of working at the dock while all the boats in the creek sailed out for the weekend, we dropped our dock lines and joined them. What fun! Our own boat—and she was sailing! We were so happy we were silly, laughing and singing. We were realizing our dream.

It was August before we went sailing again. More deck work, more rigging, more engine work; all of this and more kept us tied to the dock on weekends. A beautiful day for sailing is also a beautiful day for working on the boat.

In December we put *Starbound* into the biggest yacht yard in Annapolis for repairs to the frame heads, which the marine surveyor had told us needed replacing. The best shipwrights in the area worked for that yard and did a very fine, albeit expensive, job replacing frame heads, sheer strake, and rub rail between the main and mizzen chain plates on the port side.

While in the yard, Nina, Ernie, and I busied ourselves with additional renewal of running rigging. Ernie was working on the bowsprit on the third day we were in the yard and stopped to climb back on deck. "Dad," he said, "there's a big soft spot in the wood of the bowsprit where the martingale fitting through-bolts to it."

Oh, boy, I thought—just what I need! I climbed out on the sprit and started probing—my pocket knife blade, although turned across the grain, sunk right to the hilt into the wood. We let go the mainstay from the bowsprit and loosened the topmast stay. Then we let go the bobstay and removed the martingale stay and shrouds. We took off the martingale and its foundation plates, knocking out the 10-inch-long stainless bolts holding them in place. I started chiseling, and cursed myself for excluding the spars from the survey before we bought the boat.

The bowsprit is 12 × 12 inches at the butt tapering to 6 × 6 inches at the tip and is shaped hexagonally. It is over 17 feet long from butt to tip. By the time I had finished chiseling out the soft wood in the sprit, I had a hole 7 inches wide by 1 foot long completely through the spar. I knew that rot spores would be in the grain even further than where I had stopped cutting. I started pricing repairs against a new sprit. A new sprit was $800. Repairs at the yard were estimated at $600. We didn't have it—after paying for the work on the frame heads we would be lucky to have money for groceries. We decided to repair it ourselves.

By the time we had made our decision, the rest of the work had been completed by the yard and we motored *Starbound* to her berth in Back Creek and secured her lines. The next morning I grabbed a handsaw, and with Nina and Ernie tending halyards attached to the 9-foot outer end of the bowsprit, I sawed through the thin pieces of good wood left in the center of the sprit following my chiseling operation. We swung the front section over to the dock, reattached the halyard to the butt of the spar, unbolted the gammon irons, and, with some industrious prying and swearing, soon had both pieces layed out on the dock tee. The weather was cold, but we started work. Luckily, there was very little snow that winter, and many days had a temperature over 60 degrees. We hand-cut 3-foot vee scarf joints in each section of bowsprit. We laminated together five pieces of beautiful clear-grained fir. We cut the ends of the new built-up piece to fit the two original pieces and glued them all together with the best structural-grade epoxy glue we could find. We through-bolted the pieces so they'd hold their position and for additional strength, and we drilled a 1-inch-diameter hole at the apex of each vee joint and drove in a hardwood dowel soaked in epoxy and capped with a plug at each end. When the glue had set, we took turns with adze, draw knife, and plane and slowly shaped the new center piece to match the tapered hexagonal of the original. It was the end of March before the bowsprit was put back on *Starbound*. Twenty friends besides ourselves were involved in swinging that 500-pound spar back into place and securing it. I poured a lot of drinks that day, and we spent the afternoon toasting *Starbound*'s regained beauty with the return of her long slim nose.

The summer came upon us fast: the summer of 1968. We had managed to find a new mainsail and mizzen sail for a price we could afford. We called them our intermediate sails and had them sewn from 7.5-ounce Dacron. The cut wasn't entirely satisfactory and the material was too light, but they allowed us to experiment with the set and methods of attachment. The sails tracked onto the booms, brailed onto the gaffs, and parreled onto the masts. Parrels are made up of lignum vitae or nylon "beads" strung onto wire rope. They encircle the mast and shackle onto the luff of the sail. They take the place of the wooden hoops which are still in use on many gaff-rigged boats, and they are supposed to be an improvement. Sometimes we wondered about this as we tried to raise or lower sail in a smooth fashion.

In the fall of 1968 we decided to invite several friends to come on board and go sailing with us on Chesapeake Appreciation Day. Each year the high point of the day is the skipjack race. The skipjacks are the last boats still working under sail in America, and when a stiff wind is blowing they are really something to see as they come charging down the bay with their big leg-of-mutton sails pulling them along. We anchored in good position to see the race while drinking our hot buttered rum. It was a chilly, windy day. After the race was over we waited for some of the smaller craft around us to haul up their anchors and clear the area. I started the engine and we weighed anchor. After the tackle was secured, we put all fore and aft sail on her and started sailing back toward the Chesapeake Bay Bridge, which was just a few miles south of us. We had just come onto our course and I was about to secure the engine when a loud, expensive-sounding clanking began emanating from the engine room. I idled the engine down, gave the helm to Nina, and jumped below. The engine itself was making that terrible noise! It sounded like a broken connecting rod, but I couldn't be sure. I stopped the engine and we sailed. We had a fine fair breeze right to the entrance of Back Creek and then the wind went fluky as it usually does in creeks with high banks. We dropped all sail, and with trepidation and a dry mouth, I started up the clanking engine. We thumped, hammered, and banged along at a very slow pace into the creek and layed *Starbound* up to her dock. As we secured the engine I thought to myself, Well—that's the last sail this year. That clanking engine sounds like a winter's work. It was.

The flowers of spring were blooming before the engine repairs were complete. We were still debating putting in a completely new engine before leaving on our world cruise, but in the meantime our budget would only allow us to repair the old Hercules diesel.

Nineteen sixty-nine was a fine year for *Starbound*. As soon as the engine was running smoothly again, we went sailing every weekend and holiday. We discovered that we could work on many of the needed jobs as well away from our dock as tied to it. We would sand and paint, scrub bilges, and do rigging work while anchored in some pretty creek on the eastern shore of the bay. From that time on it was a rare cruise when we didn't complete one project or another. The year of 1969 was our Chesapeake Bay goof-off year. We could almost see the end of the "big" jobs. The deterioration of the ship had been arrested and was now being reversed. We kept making her better and better. Each cruise would expose some fault which we then undertook to remedy. And we were more financially solvent now, since Nina's and my salaries had both increased substantially since we had bought *Starbound.* We were starting to be able to put more money into her. Halyards and sheets were changed from hard, splintery manila to soft Dacron, and various leads of the running rigging were changed to make for easier handling. The sails were recut for a better fit, and we started to design new sails and to investigate the best way to buy them.

We prowled all over the Chesapeake Bay that year. *Starbound* had her long nose stuck into every creek and river we could reach on a long weekend—sometimes extended by a day or two of annual leave from our government jobs. We had many parties on board that year. We didn't plan them—they would just happen. We'd roll into Saint Michaels, one of our favorite ports, and find three boats full of friends already there, and it was instant party time. We'd raft up in the inner harbor, make drinks, and send a delegation ashore for two or three buckets of steamed crabs.

We sailed until the weekend before Christmas, then stripped the sails and running rigging from her and put on the ancient, threadbare tarpaulins we used for winter covers.

We started working on the decks that winter. We'd determined to eliminate all topside leaks. Quite an order—there are well over a half-mile of polysulfide seams in her deck and house top, and over 3,000 teak plugs covering the deck fastenings. We replaced every teak plug and resecured every fastening. We used many, many tubes of polysulfide liquid rubber merely to replace portions of the deck seams which had been loosened. Late spring of 1970 was upon us before we were finished, but oh, did the decks look beautiful. And in the first big rainstorm, they didn't leak a drop.

The best teak decking is layed with square sections; that is, if the plank is 2 inches wide, it is also 2 inches thick. Then when they're bent to the curve of the deck they won't warp or pull up on the edge. The best seam compound is polysulfide rubber that has been applied in its liquid state at least one-quarter inch deep over a strip of caulking cotton which has been rolled, not hammered, into the caulking bevel. Before the seam compound is used, the seam must be primed with the primer recommended by the manufacturers of the polysulfide rubber. The primer we use looks like thinned-down rubber cement. If the primer is used, the compound will stay in the seam; if not, the rubber will soon break loose from the seam at its edges and eventually will get scuffed loose. After the seam compound has cured completely, the seam should be worked down flat with the teak decking. We found a high-speed disc sander equipped with about 60-grit paper to be essential for this purpose. When using a high-speed sander, a delicate touch is the only way to avoid a scarred deck. With a little practice, we quickly learned how to flatten the seams and at the same time cut down the new projecting deck plugs, each set in its little puddle of epoxy glue, without removing any appreciable amount of teak from the deck. It's a back-breaking job, but it's the only way we've found to get a really nice finish on an old teak deck.

As the summer of 1970 approached, we decided to start our vacations from our respective jobs on the July Fourth weekend—and to make our first circumnavigation—of the Del-Mar-Va Peninsula. This peninsula is formed by the eastern shore of the Chesapeake Bay and is bounded on the west by the bay itself, on the east by the Atlantic Ocean, on the south by the Chesapeake Bay entrance at Norfolk, Virginia, and on the north by the

Delaware Bay, Delaware River, and Chesapeake and Delaware Canal. It's a nice little 500-mile jaunt and would give us our first opportunity to take *Starbound* into a real ocean.

All our sails were in order. We had rigged the square sail and raffee to be handled from the deck. The raffee is a triangular sail on *Starbound,* which is set flying and sets above the square yard from three points: the yard ends and the truck of the main-topmast.

To become a devotee of square rig sailing, it is only necessary to try it once. I can't think of a nicer way to sail off the wind. We can put 1,200 square feet of nylon up before the wind and let *Starbound* sail virtually unattended.

On July 5 we left Annapolis for Norfolk. Six people were aboard. Nina, Ernie, and I, Nina's sister Betty, our friend Bob Bopp, and Ernie's friend Jim McMartin. We had supplies stacked in our storage spaces and charts by the score, and we considered ourselves ready for anything.

We spent two marvelous days sailing down the Chesapeake before a light northwest breeze. Just off Thimble Shoal Channel a few miles north of Norfolk the wind died completely and by noon of the third day we were rolling on a glassy bay, going nowhere, with the air temperature about 95 degrees and the humidity very high. I decided to start the engine and it merely grunted at me. The batteries were high. I tried again. No results. Bob and I checked out the whole starting circuit. Everything was fine. The transmission and shaft were free. Nothing was jammed. Bob and I crouched in the engine room dripping sweat, replacing it with beer, and looking at each other.

Bob said he thought the only thing it could be was a hydraulic lock due to water in the cylinders.

I checked the oil stick and found the sump chock full of a salt water and oil emulsion. I pulled the injectors, and salt water ran freely out of the number 4 cylinder, then slowed to a trickle and stopped. Bob and I looked at each other again, muttered some profanities, and went topside to get another cold beer.

"We gotta pull the head, Bob."

"Yep."

"I'll work on one side and you work on the other."

"O.K."

In one hour we had the head off and found the trouble. Corrosion had lowered a section of the block between the cylinder and a water passage. We had a disgusting little water channel in the flat-milled surface of the block. I had a spare head gasket of soft annealed copper, so we peened the block on either side of the channel, coated gasket cement on all the right surfaces, replaced the head, and torqued all the bolts down to the best of our ability with an undersize torque wrench. We pumped the water and oil

mixture out of the sump and replaced it with oil. The engine started and
ran beautifully.

We pulled into a fuel dock in Little Creek, Virginia, at sunset. We could
see the Chesapeake Bay Bridge Tunnel from the dock and congratulated
ourselves on our mechanical abilities. I decided to change the engine oil
again to get rid of the last of the salt water in the sump and found it full of
the nasty gray emulsion again. Number 4 cylinder was full of salt water
again.

Bob gazed on the mess taciturnly.

"Well, Gordon, let's tear it down again and check the flatness of the
head. The head is corroded in the same area as the block and it might be
warped too." We did and it was.

The fuel dock was one of the facilities of Cobb's Marina in Little Creek,
and I trudged up to the office to ask the manager if we could stay on the
end of the fuel dock for a day. Mrs. Cobb was still in the office that evening
and when I had explained our problem she agreed to let us stay at the dock
for a day if we moved to the very end of the tee. She also suggested I check
in with her in the morning and she would find out where to take the head
for repairs.

The next day was one of those beautiful days everyone deserves once in a
while to offset the bad days. The sun was bright, and a cool breeze was
blowing from the northwest, which meant we wouldn't have left the bay to
go north anyway. We wanted to wait for the prevailing southwest wind to
take us up the coast. Mrs. Cobb offered me the keys to her new station
wagon and told me where to find a good machine shop. By midafternoon
the head had been milled flat and we had found a new head gasket and had
borrowed a high-capacity torque wrench. By 1700 the head was installed,
the engine had been run and checked out with no leaks, and the torque
wrench had been returned.

That evening we stood on the dock with tall, cool drinks in our hands and
noticed that the wind was veering and might be fair by the next afternoon.

We went to sea on the tenth of July. By sunset we had cleared the first of
the big sea buoys off the Virginia and Maryland coasts. We turned
Starbound to the north-northeast with all of our fore and aft sails drawing
and started to really move. The wind was off the port quarter and the waves
were dead aft. Night came upon us quickly and a gibbous moon dove in
and out of the clouds scudding along overhead. We planned to stop in
Ocean City, Maryland, for a few days. Ocean City is a nice little resort town
with a protected harbor and a narrow inlet from the sea that can give a
sailor nightmares. The maximum current at both flood and ebb approaches
5 knots. Slack water before flood would be at 0730 the next morning and
that's when we planned to arrive.

I stayed on the wheel that night and felt *Starbound* surge forward on the big swells coming up astern. The wind had piped up to about 20 knots. We were 2 or 3 miles east of the line of buoys stretching up the coast and could easily pick up their flashes, each with a different characteristic. It was simple piloting. As each buoy came abeam we noted the time on the chart.

I had always figured *Starbound*'s hull speed at a little better than 8 knots, but between midnight and 0300 we had averaged 9.3 knots over the ocean bottom. The wave action and a favorable current were really boosting us along. It looked like a very early arrival off the inlet unless we slowed her down. We started the engine, came about into the seas, and for the first time appreciated how really hard the wind was blowing. The main came down easily and we fell off onto a port tack again, proceeding north at a more sedate pace.

The wind fell off as the sky lightened and by 0700 we were sailing due west toward the direction our RDF was giving us, with about one-mile visibility. The atmosphere was full of mist and we couldn't see where the sky ended and the sea started. A big blue water tower swam out of the haze ahead of us with huge letters painted on it—OCEAN CITY. There was the inlet. We were right on course. We could see the waves breaking on the southernmost jetty as we approached the entrance buoy. I checked my watch. It was 0730, on schedule for the tide.

I lined up the buoys and started the engine. Pushing the throttle forward increased the engine speed to 2,000 RPM and we rapidly approached the narrow entrance.

Nina thrust her head and shoulders up the companionway and yelled, "Gordon, the engine is making a terrible noise and smoke is pouring out of the engine room, and the light over the chart table is getting dim."

I dove below, looked and listened, jumped back topside, and spun the wheel to the right as I brought back the throttle to idle. I called to Ernie to raise the main-staysail quickly. That sail went up faster than ever before and started drawing to get us off the beach which lay just 100 yards off the port beam. We cleared the buoy marking the northernmost shoal area. Turning the wheel over to Bob, I jumped below again and pulled the panel away from the engine compartment on the galley side. The big starter motor was smoldering and sending up an evil-smelling cloud of dense white smoke. A terrible-sounding noise was emanating from it. I had to stop the engine. I called up to Bob to pull back the fuel shut-off. The engine stopped and the electric lights brightened instantly. I grabbed a fire extinguisher and gave the starter motor and relay a big shot of carbon dioxide. It stopped smoking and I went topside to check the situation. We were sailing slowly up the Ocean City coastline with the beach a few hundred yards off the port beam with the wind light and fair off the port quarter. I tried to start the engine again. Nothing happened.

Once again Bob and I sat beside the old diesel and stared at it with consternation. We had the problem solved in a very short while. The starter relay had meshed the starting gear with the flywheel gear, but had not retracted it after the engine started. The big flywheel had caused the starter motor to spin at a very high speed and had burned out the entire starting circuit including relay and wiring. We could only guess what the starter motor itself looked like inside. In any case, there was no way to start the engine. We were now a genuine sailing vessel, and sailing vessels don't sail into Ocean City inlet.

We didn't have a radio-telephone on board. If we had, I would have immediately called the U.S. Coast Guard. In retrospect what I should have done was to take Nina's suggestion and light off a distress signal. An orange flare would have been easily visible to the Coast Guard station just off the inlet entrance. Instead, I reasoned that we weren't really in distress. We would sail toward Cape May inlet, about 30 miles up the coast, and if I couldn't fix the starter, we would sail inside the breakwater there and anchor.

My decision was based on a faulty premise—the weather. We sailed north about 15 miles and were about 2 miles off the beach when the wind fell to nothing. We had been watching thunderstorms making up in the southwest and when they started rolling toward us we said, "Aha, now we'll get some wind." We did, but only in a few vagrant puffs. Then the black cloud would be over us and dump down heavy rain for a few minutes, then pass on to the northeast. This went on for two hours. Finally I looked at my watch, then at the beach. It seemed nearer. I took out the azimuth circle, placed it on the big steering compass, and shot some bearings. The damned beach was only about a mile away now! We sat there with *Starbound* rolling in a swell. Worry lines were creasing brows; everyone kept sneaking looks at me.

Nina said, "Damn it, honey, I think we ought to shoot off a flare or something."

She helped me make up my mind.

"O.K.," I said, "break 'em out." We had red parachute flares and orange smoke flares layed out on the quarter berth with the big war-surplus 50mm Navy flare gun.

A light plane flew over quite high up. I shot the red flare up where I thought he might see it. The plane kept flying south in a straight line. Nothing. Damn! I went below to study our position on the chart and to see what the coastal pilot book had to say about currents.

Nina yelled from topside, "There's a helicopter coming. Maybe it's the Coast Guard." I leaped for the companionway, scooping up an orange smoke flare from the quarter berth as I jumped. There it was—coming from the north. I leaned over the taffrail on what I hoped was the lee side and used the striker provided with the flare to ignite it. I was totally unprepared for the huge billowing mass of bright orange smoke that came from that flare! I nearly dropped it in surprise.

Nina called, "He's coming this way! He sees us! Yay!" The helicopter circled us twice. I threw the flare into the water well away from the boat. Another surprise; it floated and kept putting out orange smoke. Well, I thought, those are very nice gadgets—I'll buy some more.

The helicopter was about 100 yards off the water now, and on his second circle around, a crewman stood in the open hatch of the fuselage and held up a big sign on which was printed "WHAT IS YOUR TROUBLE?"

I pointed down at the screw, made circular motions with my hand, and shook my head negatively—all at the same time.

The crewman nodded and ducked inside as the helicopter circled again. Another big sign was held out to us: "COAST GUARD CUTTER IS ON WAY."

Nina yelled, "Whee! We're saved, we're saved! Let's everybody have a drink." That's my wife—a practical thinker.

The cutter showed up within thirty minutes and passed us a heavy towline. After some discussion, we talked them into hauling us back to Ocean City. Bob was instrumental in this decision. Ocean City was much closer to Annapolis by car than was Cape May, New Jersey, the next nearest place we could get into. Also, Bob knew people in Ocean City and that meant transportation which we might need. "Also," he added casually, "Ocean City is a fun town and we'll be docked right in the middle of it."

We were tied to the dock at one of the major fishing marinas in Ocean City within two hours. Being towed into the inlet with the tide coming out was something I don't want to do again. But the grayhaired cox'n on that cutter babied us through the swells and the cross currents, and around the dog-leg channel, without even changing the catenary of the towline. He layed *Starbound* up to the dock with a 5-knot current running and we didn't even rub the creosote off the pilings. Then he held us in position till our lines were all secured. What an expert! When he came aboard to get the necessary data from us, we thanked him in a manner reflecting the best traditions of the sea.

Bob and I found a rarity—a master mechanic. He also happened to be the General Motors dealer for marine engines in Ocean City. He found a used starter relay like mine and rebuilt it. Then he found a rotor for the starter in New Jersey. It arrived in Ocean City one day later by Greyhound bus. He rebuilt the starter motor and checked the whole system out. It was beautiful. I put it back on *Starbound,* rewired the starting circuit, and we were ready to go.

We left at the stand of the tide before ebb, early next morning, a week after our ignominious arrival. Our southerly had started blowing again and we raised square sail and raffee and sailed up to the entrance of the

Delaware Bay, then up the bay to where it becomes the Delaware River. We arrived at the Delaware end of the Chesapeake and Delaware Canal in the dark, and just in time to catch the 3-knot ebb down into the Chesapeake Bay. The canal is lit up like the Los Angeles Freeway with big mercury lights spaced evenly down either bank. We felt like we were flying through—with the current helping we were motoring at 9 knots.

We sailed the rest of the night and by 1000 the following morning tied up to our home dock. We were tired and thankful to be home safely after our adventure. Our first circumnavigation—in a very small way.

We spent the fall of 1970 making lists. Although there were many gaps in *Starbound*'s inventory, we knew what those deficiencies were. Primary goals were to obtain a new main engine for trouble-free motoring, a motor-generator to provide us with 115 volts of alternating current, and new sails which must include a big "yankee" headsail. We also needed a good yacht tender—something better than our little 9-foot fiberglass peapod which we hung on the davits aft—rather a stable, nonsinkable ship's boat with which we could, if necessary, lay out a second heavy anchor in rough weather and in which we could carry a big load of supplies from shore to ship. We needed a new radio-telephone and an inflatable life raft. Most of these items we knew must wait until our last year before the great adventure. Lack of money was still our big problem.

We decided to concentrate immediate energies on making *Starbound* as good a sailer as we could expect from her type of boat. A cod-headed, mackerel-sterned, gaff-rigged ketch has never been noted for windward ability under sail. After many hours of research and study, we determined that her sail plan should include the biggest headsail that we could fit on her. A yankee jib with a 50-foot luff and a high clew which would sheet inboard was the answer. I designed one which we felt would answer our needs. A new gaff mainsail with horizontally sewn panels and a flat-cut new main-topsail were also in order. And after much analysis which left the cabin sole in the main saloon strewn with tracing paper, we decided to do away with the mizzen gaff and to make the mizzen sail a leg-of-mutton shape—commonly called a "Marconi" sail, although this term more properly applies to the mast on which the sail sets.

We sent out a dozen letters to sailmakers in the United States, Great Britain, Australia, and Hong Kong asking for quotes based on our specifications. Wintertime found us comparing samples of sailcloth and prices. A decision was easy to reach. The sailmaker in Hong Kong quoted us prices much lower than the other sailmakers we solicited. The fabric samples of Japanese Tetoron were of a superior weave to most of the other cloth we inspected, and the Hong Kong sailmaker could furnish the fabric in the red-brown color we wanted—called "tanbark" in some areas of the world.

The fabric we chose was 10-ounce (American weight) fabric of a very tight weave. We pulled with all our strength on the bias of the 6-inch sample piece and could not induce a "bag" into the fabric. The small distortion we could put into the piece disappeared immediately when we released the strain. Most of the samples we were sent failed this simple test. We ordered our new sails for spring delivery. We wanted to order our storm sails too—a main-trysail and a small storm jib—but the money just wasn't there.

We hoped to take a cruise to Bermuda in 1971 and try out our new sails while bolstering our confidence in our slowly growing sea knowledge. But as spring weather slowly rolled up the Chesapeake Bay country, we perused our notebooks, counted our money, and decided it would have to wait for another year. We hadn't yet purchased even the mandatory equipment to make an ocean cruise feasible.

We spent that entire year gunkholing with friends. My mother and father went vacationing with us for a ten-day cruise of the eastern shore and we had a fine time. We nosed *Starbound* aground into the soft Chesapeake mud twice. We clogged the fuel filters once and had to sail into a tricky harbor without benefit of auxiliary power. My mother brought her four little dogs with her—with our big poodle, Prancer, that made five dogs—and we still had a good time. We learned how to shorten sail fast as the violent Chesapeake thundersqualls approached; we learned how to heave *Starbound* to, which she does nicely. We put in some unexpected practice at piloting our ship into a safe anchorage in a heavy fog—a rarity in the Chesapeake. Best of all, we finally had *Starbound* sailing well. Downwind sailing is effortless for her. The square sail and raffee need no tending. If the weather blew up, we would drop the raffee. Going to weather we found that she would foot along very well with her bow about 55 degrees off the true wind. We could bring her up to 45 degrees with the sails still drawing, but she would slow to a crawl and our leeway would increase until she almost appeared to be sailing sideways. At 55 degrees her leeway would be about 8 degrees, so we learned quickly that if we made good 60 to 65 degrees on each board, we were doing really well. Of course, we wanted her to point like a 12-meter sloop; but—compromise, compromise. We were finally satisfied that we were getting everything out of her that a boat of her type can give. Anyway, we rationalized, cruising is 98 percent downwind, isn't it?

2

Seven-Year Shakedown Cruise: The Last Year

One year! One year to go!

When the decision has been made to embark on a world cruise in a sailing boat, the prospective world cruisers cannot say: We'll leave when the boat and ourselves are ready. If they do, they'll never go. That's because they'll never be ready. A strange thing to say? It's true! Trepidation is always breathing cold wind on one's neck and hampering those several more tasks that are always present and that must be accomplished. Even if you've worked for seven years on a boat, as we have done, those "must-do" jobs continue to generate. It's so easy to delay leaving the dock until just those "few more" jobs are done.

Two important dates. Ernie would graduate from high school in June 1973, and I would be forty-three years old on the tenth day of October. A good day for departure, a day which we had pinned down within a month after buying *Starbound.* We would keep the date.

Our "shakedown" thus far had shown us that our most urgent requirement was a new engine—a major financial investment. Sad experience on our two longest cruises had laid on two basic requirements: we needed an engine that was as reliable as could be built, and it must be one for which spare parts could be obtained anywhere.

We studied the specifications and prices of every diesel engine on the American market. We knew we needed all the power we could get in a package which would fit in the space to be evacuated by our old Hercules engine. A 6-cylinder in-line diesel had to be the choice. A hydraulic transmission and a fresh-water cooling system would eliminate two problems which poor old Hercules had continuously bestowed on us. We wanted new instrumentation, since the ancient gauges on the control panel aft only occasionally reflected Hercules's faltering performance. New and simplified engine controls must replace the nightmare assemblage of pipes, pivots, and push rods which directed Hercules to go forward or back, to speed up or slow down.

We carefully measured the distance between engine stringers, the clearance fore and aft, the drop between the top of the stringers and the propeller shaft, and we studied engine horsepower and revolutions and torque curves.

We finally decided to buy the 6-cylinder engine whose basic block is manufactured by Ford Motor Company of England. The Osco Motor Corporation located in Souderton, Pennsylvania, is one of three different U.S. companies which "marinize" that basic block and market it for marine use. After extensive correspondence with them we made arrangements to have the engine delivered to the Trumpy and Sons' boatyard in Annapolis, Maryland. Osco's representative, Tom Cooper, was very cooperative. The new engine had everything we wanted. Engine components were standard, which in case of failure could be replaced at most places around the world. How different from poor old Hercules!

We unbolted Hercules from his bed and removed every piece that could be unbolted, including the defunct transmission. We stripped out the old mechanical controls and pulled yards of copper tubing and old wiring from under the cabin sole, some of which led to nothing. Each evening, after having worked all day for the government, we would put in another six hours for *Starbound* and topple exhausted into bed at midnight.

On the day before *Starbound* was to be towed around Horn Point and into the boatyard, we took time off from our jobs and removed the refrigerator, cabinets, and galley counter from their location above the engine enclosure. We stacked the main saloon high with galley components and arranged a passageway through the chaos to the stove and sink. Our "living" was done in the master stateroom and meals were eaten while sitting on our bunks. With the refrigerator upside down on the deck we knew those meals would be spartan for several days.

Next morning the yard tug chugged up to *Starbound,* took a towline and put-putted out of our creek with *Starbound* trailing behind like a big docile St. Bernard following a dachshund.

Ten days later the same little tug landed us back against our home dock pilings, and we were $1,800 more in debt, not including the cost of the new engine! The yard had done a good job. The engine had been set in place and bolted to solid mounts on the engine stringers, with the propeller shaft carefully aligned. While we were out of the water the bottom was painted. We also had all of the topside hull seams reefed out and replaced with white seam compound. When *Starbound* was built her hull seams had been filled with a dark compound and her hull painted black. Even after I had taken her topsides down to wood, and repainted her with a "system" of two coats of white primer and three coats of white semigloss enamel, those seams gave us trouble. The old dark compound would absorb heat right through the paint, expand, and crack through the new white coating.

"Gotta get rid of that ol' black compound, boy" was the verdict of the few good shipwrights left in the area. We decided that we might as well take care of the problem once and for all. Having all those seams reefed and refilled added a lot to our yard bill, but we reasoned that if the hull gave us problems caused by the heat of a Chesapeake Bay summer, the problems would surely multiply in an equatorial climate. Each seam was carefullly cleaned out, then filled with a flexible white compound. The hull was sanded smooth and fair, and two coats of primer were put on. We added the finish coats ourselves after *Starbound* was back in the water—no small feat considering the wake from the boats speeding past our dock.

Now our evenings were spent in rebuilding the part of the galley we had torn out. The cabinets and counter and refrigerator had to be reinstalled. But before putting the refrigerator back in place I decided to check the insulation. To my disgust I found that it was rock wool instead of the much more efficient polyurethane foam insulation which is used in all modern units. Another decision—should we change it? We decided it would be a long time before that stainless steel box would be upside down in the main saloon again. We had noticed that during the hot summers the efficiency of the refrigerator would noticeably drop, and we hoped this operation would solve that problem, which was sure to become worse in tropical weather. I bought the "foam-in-place" canisters necessary for the operation and tackled the messy job, managing to spray only a small amount around the cabin and in Nina's hair. Finally the box was back in place with the trim rebuilt around its face, the motor purring away making the beer cold.

Next, the new instrument panel had to be mounted in its box on the afterdeck and a bundle of wires threaded down through the afterdeck, under the lazarette bulkhead, along the cabin sole stringers, and into the engine room. New terminal blocks were installed on the engine room bulkhead and wiring from all the sensing devices for the engine were led to it. Electrical continuity to each gauge and meter was checked and rechecked. The new engine controls were installed beside the binnacle. Mounts and clamps had to be revised to fit peculiar spaces. Salt water piping had to be rerouted to the new heat exchangers, and the big bronze exhaust duct needed some expensive brazing work before it would mate smoothly with the new engine exhaust flange.

November had settled its frosty mornings on the creek before we raised our weary heads from the engine compartment, straightened our aching backs, and heaved a sigh of completion. We checked the oil and water levels, bled the fuel filters, primed the pumps, and started the engine. It caught immediately with a throaty roar and idled back to a smooth rumble. What a beautiful sound! A few adjustments to the throttle linkage made the new tachometer read just what it should. Oil pressure and water temperature were right on the marks proclaimed by the instruction manual as optimum. I slipped the control lever one notch forward and *Starbound* surged against her spring lines as creek water kicked back from her propeller. Back to neutral! Then, as the lever was pulled back to the reverse detent, the propeller reversed its direction and we saw the water swirl forward along the hull.

We cast off the lines and went for a motor boat ride. Sheer delight! Our high hopes were realized as we motored up and down the creek and waved to friends on the docks. We were careful to follow break-in procedures and kept the engine load light for several hours. When we were finally able to run the engine at full operating speed, *Starbound* moved through the water as she never had before while under power. We were satisfied.

We went back to perusing our work lists. I had been spending my lunch hours at work researching and designing storm sails. We finally decided to buy a small storm jib with large hanks which could be snapped onto the mainstay, and a heavy storm trysail which could be brailed onto the mainmast. We ordered them from our Hong Kong sailmaker.

We consulted the tattered pages of our pocket notebooks and made over the list of remaining items which we had to purchase outright. The list included the following items:

> Automatic battery charger
> Radio-telephone
> Auto-pilot
> Life raft
> Large dinghy and outboard motor
> Scuba gear
> Signal flags
> Radar reflector
> Medical kit

In addition we worked up lists of supply items we must have on board such as paints for the bottom, hull, and spars; engine oil; spare parts for the main engine, motor-generator, outboards, refrigerator, stove, and all electrical devices; line and wire for new halyards, sheets, downhauls, and lazy jacks; and extra blocks, shackles, and thimbles.

The work remaining to be done included regalvanizing the 400 feet of half-inch anchor chain; installing fiddles around all work surfaces, particularly in the galley; making an afterdeck awning; constructing a man-overboard pole and buoy apparatus; cutting new foam mattresses for the forecastle bunks; and building lockers in the lazarette to securely contain the numerous cans of paint and engine oil that we must carry with us.

There was work to do in town too. We had to begin our investigations into the mysteries of passports and visas. Hundreds of charts and dozens of sailing directions need to be ordered. We went to our bank and talked at length with the officers there about the best way to have our funds readily available while cruising. Appointments were made with our doctor and dentist so as to preclude medical problems while at sea. (Nina and I had to undergo periodontal work at a cost of about $1,800 over the next ten months—something we hadn't counted on at all.)

With the incredible mass of work stacked up in front of us, we had to learn a basic lesson: how to turn off our mental switches to future problems so as to concentrate on current jobs. We set up priority lists on top of our priority lists and started to tackle one job at a time.

We found a 3-kilowatt diesel motor-generator at a sizable discount in price, and a contractor friend managed to buy a large marine converter for us at another discount. Now we could charge our batteries and have 115 volts of alternating current available for use at the same time. It is a lovely thing to be able to use power tools aboard a boat without having to depend on shore current.

Just before the Federal Communications Commission put the new law into effect regarding radio-telephones, we bought a 75-watt AM set which satisfied our desire for some electronic means of communication. We would have liked to install a small VHF-FM set and one of the big single-sideband outfits, but a check of price tags stopped us from any further conjecture in that direction.

We counted our money nervously and ordered a four-man life raft, not the most expensive make. At the same time, we found a suitable dinghy at Sears Roebuck and Company, an 11-foot fiberglass boat intended for fishing. It has positive flotation and bait wells and is light enough to be picked up by two men. The boat stows upside down on *Starbound*'s big house top and is brailed down to four eye bolts.

An old discarded Evinrude 5.5 horsepower outboard came to light in the corner of the marina engine shop. We bought it for $25 and repaired it. A 6-gallon fuel tank and hose completed the outfit and gave us a very satisfactory ship's tender.

Extensive modifications would have been needed to fit a self-steering wind vane apparatus to *Starbound*'s stern. The mizzen boom would have interfered with the vane. Therefore, we wanted an auto-pilot and came to acquire one in a rather unusual fashion. In early winter a big (65 feet LOA) schooner had tied up in a marina in Spa Creek and I met one of the co-owners of the boat in a local hardware store in Annapolis. He was tall and tanned, had a wild look in his eye, and was barefoot. His fisherman's sweater was old and smelly and his shorts were ragged and dirty. It was cold, about 50 degrees outside. I offered him a lift back to his boat, was invited aboard, and met the rest of the crew. There were three or four women and three or four other men; I couldn't seem to get an accurate count. There were also a number of small children scattered here and there about the boat. These people stated their intention to go cruising and "live off Mother Nature's bounty." They would work wherever and at whatever they could for the small amount of money they claimed to need. The crew came from New England, where they had purchased the schooner for $15,000 (I could smell the rot in her), and were headed down the inland waterway for Florida. Then they were going "to the islands, where the food can be picked off the trees." First they tried to sell me the old 4-cylinder diesel engine. I carefully explained that they would need it for motoring down the waterway.

"Motoring? Oh, no!" They looked radiant. "We're going to *sail* down the waterway. We don't *like* mechanical things. We'll use the *wind* to go where we want."

I explained that it was against the law to sail in the inland waterway canals, that they would have to motor, and that if they wanted to sell the engine, perhaps Florida would be a better place to do so.

Finally and reluctantly, they agreed that perhaps they hadn't investigated the problem thoroughly. Then the big guy I had picked up, evidently the acting captain, said, "Well, O.K., but that's one thing we're going to get rid of." He jabbed a large thumb at what looked like an auto-pilot compass head.

"What?" I asked, "The auto-pilot?"

"Damn right!"

"Why? It's a handy thing to have."

"Don't want no damn mechanical or electrical crap. Just a lot of damn trouble."

"What do you mean, 'get rid of it'?" I asked hopefully.

"Anybody takes it out of the ship can have it!" He folded his arms. "I've already ripped some of it out." He hooked his thumb at a scrambled heap of paraphernalia. He had torn the wires loose from the compass head and stuffed them in a snarled coil in the corner of a bunk. I stood up slowly, my mind racing, and said, "I'll be right back with my tools."

Four hours later, Ernie and I were happily assembling the components of a Wood-Freeman auto-pilot on the cabin sole of *Starbound*'s saloon. Evidently the previous owner of the old schooner had been a methodical man, and the manuals for the mechanism were fortunately still on board. We laid out the wiring diagrams on the chart table and carefully traced the circuits. We hooked up all the wiring and when everything seemed in order applied the 12-volt power source to the input terminals. Holding our breath, we switched on the set. The motor started to run and the compass head began to orient itself. When it came onto our heading at the dock, the rays clicked and the motor stopped running. We had an auto-pilot!

Scuba gear is an absolute necessity for a cruising boat, at least for a boat as large as *Starbound.* Diving under her hull with just the breath in our lungs was possible, of course, but we couldn't stay down long enough to do any meaningful work. I bought a used, good make of regulator and two air tanks; we already had masks and fins. Then I lined up a qualified instructor and had myself checked out with the gear. I have never regretted the acquisition or the training.

Nina priced a set of signal flags. The cheapest usable ones (made of cloth, not plastic) were over $110. Nina stopped by the sailmaker's trash bin and salvaged scrap pieces of spinnaker nylon in all the needed colors, then made a set of patterns and commenced to cut and sew. Within a few weeks we had a beautiful set of signal flags which continue to be the envy of other cruising boats.

We were not convinced of the necessity of a radar reflector for ocean cruising in the tropic belt. However, cruising people we'd met all mentioned their trusty radar reflector. So we found a large lifeboat-type folding reflector made of a metal mesh. We mounted this on a hefty wooden pigstick and ran it to the mizzen top. Next time we were out cruising on the bay, a power-boating friend with a very expensive radar set aboard checked out our reflection and declared that *Starbound* did indeed put a bright pip on his screen. I have to assume the reflector is worthwhile—if a radar watch is being kept on the ship which might be bearing down, and if the radarman isn't goofing off, and if they see you in time to change course.

When we started cruising with *Starbound* on the Chesapeake Bay, our medical kit consisted of a tin box of Band-Aids, tweezers, and a tube of antibacterial ointment. Over the slave-labor years we had added niceties such as burn ointment, gauze, bandages, adhesive tape, and various disinfectants. Now we were embarking on a world cruise and must do some serious thinking about medicine.

We had recently purchased two books which should be in every ocean cruiser's library: *First Aid Afloat* by Paul B. Sheldon, M.D., and *Advanced First Aid Afloat* by Peter F. Eastman, M.D. Both these books contain all the information needed to outfit and use a comprehensive medical kit while voyaging to anywhere. Prescriptions for the needed drugs can be obtained from the family doctor. If a friend is available who is a doctor and also a sailor, he can be a big help.

Dick Clover, M.D., a good friend of long standing, outfitted a good part of our medical kit out of his own stores. This was a big savings to us over buying the supplies from a prescription counter. Nina's doctor, John Hedeman, wrote prescriptions for the things we still needed, and advised us about what special items he felt might be helpful. We managed to stow everything we needed in a heavy plastic airline bag, one of those big white ones with lots of flaps, compartments, and zippers. About 2 cubic feet handled all, and we stowed the bag in the driest, coolest, and most accessible place on the boat—the bottom of Nina's hanging locker.

I had been working as a naval architect for the Naval Ship Systems Command in Washington, D.C. In all, eighteen years of government service were stacked up in my personnel folder. My future career took up a lot of my thinking time. An early retirement is always an attractive prize, but the earliest age at which I might retire was 50 years. And that only if the government decided to lower the hiring ceiling, as is periodically done, and offered an inducement toward early retirement. Otherwise the normal early retirement age is fifty-five years with at least twenty years of service completed. At the age of forty-three, the contemplation of working for at least seven more years before cruising the world was enough to put me into a short mental depression. I refused to contemplate it.

I sat down with my boss, who is also a good friend, on a day about nine months before our planned departure date.

"Paul," I said, "I've been wanting to have a talk with you regarding my future plans."

Paul looked inquisitive.

"You've been aboard our boat and I suppose you've guessed that we didn't buy something like her just to piddle around the Chesapeake Bay."

"No," he said, "I've always supposed that you'd make a long cruise one day."

"Right," I said. "We're taking her around the world, and we plan on leaving Annapolis on October tenth of this year. I wanted to let you know as soon as our plans were firm."

I walked out of Paul's office feeling as if I'd dynamited the pass behind us. A new feeling slowly came over me. I wanted to throw everything on board and leave immediately. I kept thinking of how fast the world changes, and how if we didn't soon see the beautiful, wild, and lonesome parts of it we'd never see them.

With six months to go we became more and more aware of a triple-barreled and interrelated problem which kept cropping up with increasing frequency: what was our sailing schedule to be; that is, when did we want to be in what places? Since that schedule would be based purely on the world's weather patterns, would it be flexible enough to allow us more time in places we liked, or in which we had to work to replenish the strongbox? Who would go with us—how long would they be on board—how much should they contribute to the boat while aboard? We had, of course, been thinking of and discussing these questions for some time.

We sat down in a welter of books and pilot charts and began to clarify on paper the sailing route we had talked and thought about for many months. We found the pilot charts to be the best cruise-planning guide of all the documents we possessed. As we actually started putting dates down in writing, some of our problems began solving themselves.

This is the way it worked: First, we had a total of three years in which to sail the world—primarily based on future career considerations and available funds. Second, there are places in the world which a cruising yacht generally finds untenable at certain times of the year. These places, along our loosely defined route were the North Atlantic in winter, the Caribbean in summer, the Southwest Pacific in "down under" summer (November to April), the Tasman Sea in "down under" winter, Indonesian waters from October to April, and the Cape of Good Hope anytime. However, January is considered the best time of year to sail around that "Cape of Storms."

"It's starting to make sense now," Nina said, as she continued to draw red pencil lines on the charts. "We leave the Chesapeake before November, spend the winter in the West Indies, get to the Panama Canal by mid-February, and play around in the South Pacific till October, by which time we should leave Suva, Fiji, for New Zealand."

"Right," I said. "Then we'll work in New Zealand during their summer, and by April of 1975 we'll be on our way across the Tasman Sea to Sydney and then go north up the Australian coast inside the Great Barrier Reef."

"Yeah! and follow Captain Cook's route of exploration with *Endeavor;* then to Thursday Island and around the top of Australia to Darwin; from there to Bali and the rest of Indonesia; out of Indonesia by September and down to South Africa by Christmas, probably at Durban; then around the Cape in January, work in Capetown a few months, leave in March and sail a slant across the South Atlantic back to the West Indies."

Nina asked what we would do for three and a half months in the Indian Ocean. I didn't know yet, but the Seychelles, Madagascar, Mauritius, and the east coast of Africa were all there and we would surely find them fascinating places to visit.

We made up our sailing schedule and based it on departure dates from each port. Arrival dates depended on how fast we might sail and were too nebulous to contemplate. It would be interesting to compare our actual departure dates from each port with the originally planned dates.

Now to our last problem; who would go with us? For the first part of the voyage, the problem resolved itself. All our friends wanted to go! It's relatively inexpensive to fly to the West Indies and back, so it would be a fine winter vacation for anyone. Harry and Jeanne Miles wanted to join us in Norfolk, Virginia, and make the first bold essay across the 600 miles of North Atlantic to Bermuda. Pete Nevins and his attractive girlfriend, Janelle, wanted to join us in Bermuda and make the eight-day trip to Antigua. Don and Keren Dement, who lived near us aboard their fiberglass Columbia 45, wanted to island-hop with us down the Leeward Islands to Martinique. Bob and Edna Zahn, both fine sailors, agreed to join us in Martinique, explore the Windward Islands with us, and then take the four-day hop to Dutch Curaçao behind our big square sail and raffee. Ray Kukulski, our bachelor friend, would join us in Curaçao and wanted to stay with us for three months—all the way to Tahiti.

From Tahiti onward we would let the situation take care of itself. It's very hard to see as far as eight months ahead. Also, the air fare to Tahiti gave the financial cold shudders to most of our friends; but not to Betty, Nina's sister, who decided to join us in Tahiti for about two weeks.

We told everyone wanting to go with us what it would cost. It came to $250 per month per person. We had put in a lot of study to arrive at that figure. We knew what our food would cost and what our consumption rate would be. We also knew what it cost per year to keep *Starbound* in good shape. We felt the charge to be equitable. Subsequent study of receipts showed us that we were right. We eat and drink very well on our ship and we hate to scrimp on stores.

With three months left before October 10, we had all of our stores and supplies lists completed. Nina concerned herself solely with food and habitability items. I busied·myself with lists of spare parts, tools, and bosun's stores. (See the Appendix. The lists show the items we had omitted through ignorance and later found necessary and also those we should have omitted to begin with.)

We drew an exaggerated outline sketch of *Starbound* showing all of her stowage areas. Then we spent a lot of time figuring out where to put what. *Starbound* has a big midships galley, a separate engine room, and a large aft lazarette, all in her favor. She also has a wet bilge and big deep frames, both liabilities when striking down stores. Large wooden bins had been constructed under the master stateroom cabin sole which were used for the exclusive purpose of storing canned goods and keeping them above any bilge seepage, that is, away from the hull planking. All of the many cases of canned goods were stored there. All other food items were stored in the galley lockers. The galley and head lockers also had to absorb an amazing amount of soap, toothpaste, toilet paper, deodorant, and assorted other potions, lotions, and gadgetry.

Tools were stowed under a transom seat in the main saloon, where they would stay dry and could be gotten to easily. Spare parts went on the engine room shelf and under the quarter berth and they took up a lot of space. The lazarette contained engine oil, paint, hoses, scuba gear, and rolls of spare line and wire for our rigging. It also held many odds and ends we didn't want to throw away and still had to put somewhere.

Starbound's waterline crept up her hull, and finally, with three inches of her copper sheathing still showing, we were finished. We stood with our weight on one leg and then the other, making small noises like, "Well, now" and "Ah" and "Hum."

Work at our respective jobs was finally completed a few weeks before departure date, and our co-workers threw noisy, friendly farewell parties for us. Suddenly we were on our own. In those last few weeks I put a final finish coat on *Starbound*'s hull and spars. After a trip to New York I returned home to *Starbound* full of thoughts and plans of final things to do. We tackled the remaining jobs. Ernie and I restowed the lazarette once again and finally managed to get everything securely in place and clear of the steering cables. We made a man-overboard pole and fastened it to our life ring and flashing light. All of the fourteen shroud lanyards were set up again and our standing rigging stood taut with the masts well in line. We climbed around the tophamper like monkeys, inspecting every block, shackle, swivel, and cotter pin. A dab of paint was added here and there.

The last load of ship's stores arrived. A small panel truck drove into the marina yard with the springs well compressed. Ernie ran a dolly stacked with cases up and down the dock and I wrestled the cases below. Nina had the tough job; she listed each item on a card, then stowed it all away.

I've always thought that those often written words, "on the threshold of a great adventure," were somewhat trite. Now that it was our turn, however, those words exactly reflected our feelings. We dashed around town on our last few days and picked up items on our dwindling "must-get" lists. Many small pieces of paper with scribblings in pen and pencil were taped to the bulkhead over the chart table and fluttered in the hatchway breeze. They were scratched off one at a time as we hurried up the companionway ladder on another trip to town.

And then it was October 10, 1973. We topped off our water tanks, made farewell phone calls, and talked endlessly to a constant stream of friends and well-wishers. Quite a crowd came down to see us off. The drinks and talk flowed easily while our internal excitement welled higher and higher.

In the late evening hours the gentle tidal flow up the bay slowed and stopped and then, imperceptibly at first, reversed itself and was noticed only by the captain. I got to my feet from my place of repose on the deck, set my drink down, and rumbled the main engine into life.

I smiled at the crowd. "O.K., you drunks! Gentlemen, shake hands; ladies may kiss us. Everyone ashore to let go our dock lines. Wave good-by, and no tears!"

3

Bermuda—The Hard Way

Cheers (and tears after all) came from our champagne-filled friends as they pushed *Starbound* away from the dock at 2200 hours. We idled out of Back Creek into the Severn River and powered out of the river into the bay—a misty calm bay. Within an hour, with Thomas Point Light abeam of us, the mist thickened and we abandoned the plan to sail all night. A turn to starboard into South River and then another put us into Harness Creek, for the past seven years one of our favorite gunkholes. Our big double bunk felt particularly welcome after the farewell excitement. We were tired but still lay awake for a while letting our racing thoughts deaccelerate. Ray Kukulski had come with us for the trip down to the Southern Virginia boatyard where *Starbound* would get her bottom prettied up. We could hear him buzzing away in the quarter berth. We finally slept.

Harness Creek glittered in the early morning sunlight. We waved good-by to the blue heron standing on the fallen tree trunk, and were on our way to Fishing Bay on the Piankatank River for our final haul-out. The Chesapeake gave us a beam wind and sunny skies. *Starbound* romped down to Solomon's Island, curled into the northern mouth of the Patuxent River, and decided she'd gone far enough for one day. Nina had an aromatic "something" dripping juice into an oven pan. I pressed the starting button on the diesel and powered toward the anchorage as Ernie and Ray dropped and furled the sails. The big hook went down and found a soft mud bottom and the chain was checked at that fortunate combination of sufficient scope and swinging room.

A hail from a fat-duck fiberglass boat anchored near us followed the demise of our diesel rumble and there, waving, stood our friend Pete Nevins, the intrepid aviator. He and his friend Janelle would eventually join *Starbound* in Bermuda and become part of the crew to Antigua.

Solomon's Island is a fair anchorage—anyway, it still was in the fall of 1973—but it's being built up rapidly, evidently in the name of progress. Standing on the deck of our ship and turning our gaze shoreward, that progress bore a striking resemblance to a fungicidal growth crawling up the pretty Virginia countryside. Two or three years ago in this anchorage we would wake with a fall sunrise to the soft conversation of migrating birds rafted on the water. Now the primary sounds are the snarl of outboard engines and the hiss-thunk of pile drivers slamming down the underpinnings of pier, dock, restaurant, bar, or retaining wall—any and all detrimental to the bay ecology.

We started our engine with the first streaks of dawn light showing above the eastern shore. The gray water around us reflected the shoreline like a mirror as we idled out of the small bay. We kept it quiet, not wanting to disturb people still sleeping, but a black-hearted fisherman in a big twin diesel cruiser defeated our purpose by winding up both engines in an ear-splitting roar before yelling instructions to his crewman to let go his dock lines. He surged past us dragging a hole in the water about 3 feet deep, calculated to rock every anchored sailor right out of his bunk. We shrugged and advanced our engine throttle, hoping to turn the corner before heads came out of hatches and perhaps identified *Starbound* as the culprit. A fair wind ruffled up the Chesapeake and flickers of gold on the water announced the rising sun. Our red-brown sails went up just as we reached the southernmost buoy at the entrance of the Patuxent River, and the unexpected easterly breeze presented us with a nice reach for all of half an hour, then veered to the south. We motored all day with the light southerly pushing on *Starbound*'s nose, and finally arrived at the mouth of the Piankatank River just after 1700 hours. We ran into Fishing Bay around the long spit of land reaching out from the town and, turning north at the end of the spit, had a fair wind for the first time in eleven hours. Thirty minutes later *Starbound* was tied to a dock at Deagle's Marine Railway Company. The yard was closed for the day and we turned into our bunks early.

The next morning, Cap'n Lee Deagle, now in his seventies, greeted me at the office with, "How ya, boy—whar's that good-lookin' wife a' yours?"

"She's down on the boat, Cap'n Lee. She'll be up to say hello in a while. How's everything with you—going to Florida again this year?"

"Oh, Lord, yes! Can't take this terrible old cold and snow and damp around here in the winter. I'll be headin' down that way next month. Got me a little house down there now, ya know."

"That's fine, Cap'n Lee—well, we'll probably beat you to the warm. Soon as we get the bottom painted we'll be on our way around the world."

"Round the world? Good Lord, boy—you all really gonna do it, huh?"

"Yeah—well, you know, Cap'n Lee—we've been planning it now for a lot of years, and the time has come. My son is out of high school and the boat is paid for and we've got a few bucks in the bank. We can't figure how there's a better time—so we quit our jobs and we're going."

"Land's sake, that's somethin'. Hey, Bug, here's Gordon come back with *Starbound*—says he's goin' round the world. When we gonna haul him?"

"Bug" Deagle, Cap'n Lee's younger brother, came out of the back office and said, "Hi! Good to see you. Round the world, hey? That's a mighty long way. Let's see now, this here's Saturday and we don't work this afternoon, a' course, but I guess we can haul ya out on Monday. That O.K.?"

"Yup," I said, "that's fine. All I want is to get a good scrub job on her bottom and as soon as she's dry—put on the paint. I brought my own paint and it works well, so I'm going to keep using it."

We talked a while longer about the yard, the workmen, the weather, and our trip. Than I strolled back down to *Starbound* and organized our day's work.

Ray and I fell to on the starboard bulwark. A short section of planking around the big closed chock needed replacing. Ernie wrestled the ancient small dinghy off its stern davits and onto the dock, and began sanding it down, inside and out. Nina stayed below and worked on one job after another in our personal disaster area. What a lot of stores to stow!

The next day was Sunday, but not a day of rest for us. We continued the jobs begun the day before. The bulwark planking was cursed and grunted into place and primer painted. Ernie had the small dinghy glowing with renewed beauty.

As the sun dropped below the trees lining the shore of the bay, we broke out our charcoal hibachi and broiled steaks. Nina made a huge tossed green salad, and the refrigerator cooled several six-packs of beer. It was a fine evening and a good dinner. Talk of our sailing plans filled *Starbound*'s saloon.

Our ship was back in the water in two days and her crew had blisters on their hands, paint on their skins, and notable lower back pains. *Starbound* had a new propeller shaft, new zincs, and a fresh coat of bottom paint. Our only problem had been the weather. The air temperature remained very cool and the vinyl paint we were using refused to flow smoothly. We experienced some sagging of the paint skin that left us with arms waving, and calling for the scraper and a fresh brushful of paint. But time was pressing us and we could do nothing about the weather. After rolling down the railway and back into her natural element, *Starbound* went back at the tee of the old dock for two more days. More topside jobs had to be finished and we couldn't do them at the yacht club docks in Norfolk. We wanted to be at the Hampton Yacht Club by Friday noon, so we worked toward leaving very early Friday morning.

By Thursday evening our work on *Starbound* was complete. We turned into our bunks early in the evening and set the alarm for 0100.

Friday morning at 0130 we were battling our way out of the river mouth into a short cold chop set up by a stiff northeast wind. Then the mischievous gods of the sea taught me a lesson.

The big yankee jib, still in its bag, was lost over the side. I had placed it, as I often did, into the bow netting so that once in the bay fairway we could hank it onto the main-topmast stay. I hadn't tied the bag to the netting, thinking it would be secure enough. *Starbound* stuck her nose into a big wave and the buoyancy of the bag lifted it up, aft, and over the back edge of the net. The channel was too dark, rough, and confined to allow a search. We had to go on. We tried a few circles trying to spot the bag with our searchlight but with no luck. Hoping it would stay afloat until it hit the beach, we took careful note of our position, the wind direction, and the apparent current set. We would drive up from Hampton and look for it, but in the meantime there was *Starbound* to consider. A river mouth at night is no place to run in circles. We powered our way out of danger. It was a relief to clear the entrance buoy marking the shallows east of the river mouth and to turn south onto our course for Norfolk. We set our sails using the flying jib and staysail in lieu of the lost yankee. Hampered by heavy coats and fingers aching with cold, we thought about the tropic islands waiting for us over the southern horizon.

The northeaster didn't ease with the daylight—it whooped with glee as it made us shorten our sail area. *Starbound* raced down York Spit Channel, picked up the long line of buoys marking Thimble Shoal Channel pointing the way into Hampton Roads, and then nuzzled her broad bow up the tight channel of the Hampton River.

The Hampton Yacht Club expected us, and the dockmaster directed *Starbound* into a secure berth and took her lines. I plugged our shore electric line into the dock receptacle and cut our heating system into the circuit. Then I went topside for a good look at the high cirrus clouds whisking over the hard blue sky. A weather check was the original reason for our stop our second reason was to meet Harry and Jeanne Miles, our first set of additional crew. Now we had a third mission—we must try to find our lost jib!

Ray had driven down and had been waiting for us at the club. We secured the ship and within an hour Nina and I were in his car heading north for the south shore of the Piankatank River. I had the chart on my lap and a road map on top of it, and contemplated all the possible pieces of shoreline on which the big nylon bag full of Dacron might have drifted.

Six hours later we looked at the darkening sky and turned the car south. We had driven and walked many miles of beach. We had notified the police, the Coast Guard, and every boatyard and fishing dock in the area and offered a sizable reward for the return of the sail. We'd pinned up notices in every little country store in the area, with Ray's home address and phone number added for a contact. Our guess was that the bag had sunk before reaching shore and that some fisherman would dredge it up with his oysters sometime during the winter and end up with a very nice cover for his boat.

As soon as we were back on *Starbound* I sat down at the typewriter and ordered a new jib from Hong Kong. I had copies of our original order, so the process was simplified. The next morning I mailed the letter at the post office and walked back to *Starbound* comtemplating the problems of picking up the new sail in Bermuda—or Martinique—or Curaçao.

Hampton Yacht Club is a very nice place, with a concrete building and good docks, a nice dining room and a passable bar. The old club house had recently been torn down and replaced with the new "modern" structure, which was, no doubt, the nth degree in efficiency and "now" architecture, but somehow, I preferred the old wooden club house with its verandas and relaxed, informal atmosphere. I also preferred the traditional yacht club way of greeting visiting boats, a way which has disappeared in the Hampton area. Even though we were affiliated with a Lloyd's registered yacht club we were informed that we would be charged 15 cents per foot per day, including the first day, which even the most mercenary yacht clubs usually extend without charges. This was hospitality with the hand outstretched—palm up!

The morning dawned fair and cool with the northeast wind still prevailing at 15 knots. The barometer was high.

Harry and Jeanne arrived in the midmorning. Ray picked them up at the airport and brought them to the club with their duffle. Harry's first words, of course, were "All right, let's get this bucket underway!"

The weather report was good. I had levered the phone number for the Navy's Fleet Weather Central from my friends in Washington, D.C., and had been checking with them daily. There resided somewhere in the Norfolk area a nice cooperative "duty" lieutenant who sat at a desk correlating all the weather data from the Navy's ships at sea. The latest weather satellite photos were pinned on the wall in front of his desk. No other man could give me a more complete weather picture. I was told by this sage of sages that the winds would shift to the northwest overnight and then hold from the west for the next several days. Perfect! We started getting ready to leave for Bermuda in the morning—a Sunday.

Someone should have told us about Takaroa, the Polynesian god of the sea. Takaroa had long ago decreed that departure on a Sunday would bring bad luck to foolhardy sailors. But we didn't know. In the morning the winds were still northeast, making a liar out of the weatherman, and backing up Takaroa. The barometer was still high, though, and we figured that the wind would probably back around to the northwest later in the day. This was corroborated by a last-minute call to Fleet Weather Central.

We motored to the fuel dock at 0730 and took aboard 118 gallons of diesel oil to complete our full load of 300 gallons. At 0800 we swung the compass in the river mouth. The deviation was so slight as to be negligible. At 0900 *Starbound* pushed her nose down the river.

An hour later we were in Thimble Shoal Channel heading for the Chesapeake Bay Bridge Tunnel. The wind was still northeast at 20 knots. It was very cold, and Nina was both seasick and very angry. The head seas were short and lumpy and I wasn't feeling too well myself—and I haven't been seasick since I was ten years old. The diesel hammered away, shoving us into the short chop, and Nina's slightly green countenance appeared out of the hatchway, directed an awful glare at me, and spoke: "You *promised* me we'd *never* do this again when we didn't *have* to!" She kept the glare working for a few seconds, then disappeared below.

I thought about it. Then I turned the helm over to Harry and went below to tune in the noon weather forecast. "Northeast and fresh for the next two days," the man predicted. Oh, Fleet Weather Central, what have you done to me!

We were approaching the bridge and the wind was blowing harder than ever as it funneled its way into the entrance of the Chesapeake. I looked to the right and could see the entrance buoys to Little Creek in the distance. I gritted my teeth, cursed not so silently, and wheeled *Starbound* to the right. Harry turned to the left, jammed his hands in his pockets, and stared at the bridge opening leading out of the bay. Harry was disgusted; he wanted to go to sea!

We tied up to the fuel dock at Cobb's Marina, our old standby spot for our two previous ventures out of the Chesapeake. I called up Fleet Weather Central from the marina office. They verified the local forecast we had picked up on the radio; northeast to east winds for several days. We made arrangements to hole up in Little Creek for the time being and then sat down with the crew to talk over our immediate plans.

I decided to take the bus up to Washington early next morning. There were a few business errands I could complete. Harry and Jeanne returned to Annapolis to await my call.

I flew back down to Norfolk on Tuesday morning with impatience boiling in me. I wanted to get going! The weatherman continued his week-long policy of bad reports, and I walked the docks, worked on small jobs, and bitched at everyone.

Friday, October 26 dawned bright and clear with the wind backed to the northwest. I ran up the dock while Nina was fixing breakfast and called Fleet Weather Central; they knew me by now.

"Well, skipper—looks like tomorrow would be a fine time for you to shove off. We're going to have northwesterlies backing to west and you ought to have a sleigh ride all the way to Bermuda. Couldn't be better!"

I placed a call to Annapolis to Harry and Jeanne and told them to be down by nightfall and we'd get under way in the early morning hours. The evening was spent in furious activity making ready for sea.

Breakfast was eaten in the dark next morning and at 0700 we flipped off our dock lines and headed into the sunrise. The wind was northwest as advertised and at 0815 *Starbound* shoved her nose past the Chesapeake Bay Bridge and encountered the Atlantic swells. At last!

Then we found what a shrew the north Atlantic could be. The wind dropped off in the afternoon and we motor-sailed to get as far to sea as fast as we could. Sunday morning dawned with the wind right on our nose. By evening it was blowing SSE at 30 knots. Where were the promised westerlies? The seas were big and we had to motor-sail far north of our rhumb line to keep the ship moving. We were disgusted with meteorologists in general, but reserved our really choice comments for Fleet Weather Central. Monday dawned on a discouraged, cold crew. The seas continued big and from the wrong direction and the wind continued to blow hard, also from the wrong direction.

A gusty midnight squall had badly torn one of our old jibs and we had to put it below. It was the lightweight roller furling jib and we shouldn't have been carrying it, but we kept trying to keep *Starbound* steadied on some semblance of her course, and found it very hard to do so without our big yankee headsail. Monday night rolled across *Starbound* like a black cloud of evils straight out of Pandora's box. The wind increased to gale force as the barometer dropped to 29.72 inches, then to 29.68, finally to 29.64. The flying jib lost its clew roping at 2200 hours and Ernie crawled forward with his safety line locked into the bowsprit shrouds and handed it alone. The main-staysail and flying jib had been the last headsails left except for the storm jib, still in its bag. I still felt that we could carry the staysail. Everything looked secure for the time being and I went below to get some rest.

Ernie woke Nina and me for our 0100 watch, and I could tell from the motion of the ship that the weather had not improved. If anything it had deteriorated even more. I braced myself against the bunk and crawled into my foul-weather gear. Then I strapped on my heavy safety harness and made my way aft, followed by Nina. I thought again how relatively quiet it was below when I knew that the wind was shrieking outside. I left the top sliding hatch closed and opened the lower companionway door to crawl out on the afterdeck. Harry had the wheel and Ernie brushed by me on his way below.

"Goodnight, Dad," he said, and dived down the hatch. I didn't blame him for hurrying. It was wet below but warm, and—more important—quiet! It was strange how wearing the noise could be after a time at the wheel. The rush and crash of the water and the constant scream of the wind through the rigging worked on the nerves like a mean woman.

I peered at Harry in the heavy dark, his face faintly reflecting the red glow from the binnacle, and felt for the mizzenmast to steady myself against the roll of the ship. My eyes needed some time to gain their night vision and the salt spray didn't help. When I had the mizzenmast in my grasp I could feel the heavy texture of Dacron wrapped all around it in lumpy folds with line overlapping the cloth in crosshatched ridges.

"Hey, Harry!" I yelled over the wind. "What the hell happened to the mizzen?"

"The outhaul and track let go, ripped right off, screws and all! But we're lucky—the sail looks O.K. Ernie got it in fast. It was whipping around so we couldn't haul it down all the way, but we managed to get it strapped in tight to the mast and it's secure for the time being. Ernie did a damn good job!"

I agreed, even while I thought, God—all we've got left is the main and staysail!

While I've never considered myself a praying man, that black, blowing morning I did some praying. So did Nina. I was at the helm, and Nina sat braced in the windward seat, both of us with our safety lines secured. The big seas rolled up from the quarter and we could see their white tops pass by on either side of *Starbound*.

"How big would you say those waves are?" Nina asked.

"Oh, twenty to twenty-five feet, with an occasional thirty-footer," I speculated.

"I was afraid of that." She got up to give the bilge pump a few strokes.

Thirty minutes later the line securing the mizzen sail to the mast came adrift and Nina crouched down on the deck to resecure it. By the time the job was finished the lightweight foul-weather gear she was wearing was soaked through. She vowed, with some sailor-type curses, to buy a heavy duty set of gear when we made Bermuda.

Morning finally came to us, bringing gifts: a partly cloudy sky, big seas, and a veering wind. Maybe there's something to this prayer business. Of course, there's nothing like a storm at sea for giving people a little religion. When a sailor looks around at that wind-whipped water and feels the power in those huge waves, he doesn't much feel like cursing the Almighty.

Instead he tends to ponder back over all those mistakes he's made in his life and wish there hadn't been quite so many.

By 1900 that Tuesday night our light westerlies had turned into mean line squalls—mean, but still from the west! Our staysail gave up the ghost when the third squall hit us and ripped three panels beyond our repair. We finally set the storm jib and within the next forty-five minutes five of the meanest squalls we had yet seen successively clobbered *Starbound*. We were heading on a southeasterly course, but with each squall we would swing the ship off to due east and let the squall wallop *Starbound* on her tail. Our strategy worked fine although there were times when the ship felt as if she was only hitting the tops of the waves on her way downwind. The wind during the highest gusts was touching a velocity of 60 knots. Those gusts were of short duration but that sudden screaming blast is what does the damage. Luckily everything held together. Anyway, we were lucky for a short time. Harry and Jeanne went back on watch in time to catch a last squall. Nina and I had just gone below when a wail of wind and a loud crash bounced us back topside, both of us yelling, "What was that?"

Harry laconically said, "Our port mizzen shrouds just carried away. I'm putting her up to relieve the strain."

"Oh, God," I thought, "why now?" I quickly looked over the damage. The two lower shrouds were connected to a stainless steel flounder plate which had been welded to a mast tang. The flounder plate had failed at the weld and the two shrouds, still connected to the plate, had whipped the plate to the deck and had taken a chunk of teak 3 inches long and a half-inch deep out of the edge of the house top deck edge. It had just missed Jeanne, and I thought, "What if it had hit her head?"

Harry held *Starbound* into the wind while I loosed the mizzen halyard and shackled its end to a husky padeye bolted through a port side frame head. Then Nina and I cranked the halyard in and stabilized the lower mizzenmast. Harry put the helm up and *Starbound* fell off and began making headway again. Nina and I watched her for a while and, finally satisfied, staggered below to our bunk.

Eventually the squalls seemed to get weary and went away to bother some other piece of ocean, and the wind settled down to a relaxing 20 knots from the west. *Starbound* started working her way back toward her rhumb line.

Wednesday's morning light brought a relatively smooth ocean with the waves and wind still from the west. Best of all, the day stayed partly cloudy and gave us a chance to dry out our soggy living quarters and clear our soggy minds. All of the mattresses went topside; blankets and pillows festooned the rigging, and we started to congratulate ourselves on our fine seamanship and the end of our problems. Bermuda was just over the next bunch of waves.

By the next afternoon we knew we had been hasty in our predictions. The wind was fair—if we had been on our rhumb line. But our noon sights showed us to be 100 miles further north than we wanted to be! We tried to hold our course as southerly as we could but *Starbound* just didn't want to move that far into the wind without proper headsails. We were getting a southwest fresh breeze at 25 knots by sunset, and the sky appeared to be clearing. As full night rolled over us, a crescent moon showed its blade to a 6-foot sea.

We ran the engine constantly to try to get back our southing. The safe way to approach Bermuda from the west is around the southerly end of the island, but now it looked as if we would be going around the northern reef whether we wanted to or not. We kept checking the fuel level of our tanks, peering at the wet end of the dip stick, and assuring each other that we still had plenty of fuel and there was nothing to worry about—and then the engine stopped! I went below and checked the fuel filters and found them full of salt water. Now we had something to worry about. A morning sun line advanced to a noon latitude sight had put us due north of Bermuda, and the wind was still southwest. What now?

I cleaned the fuel filters, bled the fuel system, went topside, and pushed the starter button. The relay hammered out a staccato of sound, but the engine wouldn't start. It was getting dark, the barometer was high, and everything was fine as far as weather was concerned, except we knew we didn't have a hope of putting *Starbound* to windward with no jibs and no engine. I thought about it, then started Ernie at repairing the flying jib, the only headsail we had left that might be repaired. Nina and I went below and started working on the starter. Things started to come together. Ernie had the jib sewn up and flying in about three hours. Nina and I were nauseated from lying flat on the galley deck with our heads down next to the engine, but the starter was repaired. Salt water had splashed from the bilge onto the lower starter housing, in spite of the big copper pan under our engine, and had liberally dosed the starter gear shaft with its corrosive properties. The sliding gear was partially frozen onto the shaft but various magic sprays which come in aerosol cans loosened up the rust. Some diligence with fine-grit "wet or dry" sandpaper, a little more magic spray, and a touch of good machine grease finished our job. We bolted the starter back onto the engine, connected up the battery leads, and went topside to start the engine. We stood there a moment (another prayer) and touched the button. The engine roared to life without hesitation. That called for a drink. We turned *Starbound* as far south as we could put her and still have the sails drawing, and then had a very late dinner (*and* a drink).

By morning, a sunny Saturday, I had cleaned the fuel filters once again and discovered that we had not only salt water in our fuel, but also an inordinate amount of black sludgy scale. The terrific bouncing around that

Starbound had gotten from the November North Atlantic had loosened up all of the hard black residue that for twenty-three years had been slowly building up on the inner walls of her tanks. I hadn't even thought of having them cleaned before leaving on our trip.

We turned on the radio telephone to see if we could pick up Bermuda Harbor Radio. We had never really used our radio except to check it out before departure, so when the station came in loud and clear on 2182 kHz, Nina and I were as delighted as if we'd invented the thing.

Harry's grumble reached our ears: "Good thing something on this bucket works."

We listened to Bermuda Harbor Radio transmitting to several boats. And then, as if by special arrangement, we heard *Shearwater* begin to check in with them. We were delighted! *Shearwater* is a 72-foot staysail schooner and Jim Shearston, her skipper, is a good friend of ours. His location as given to BHR was 100 miles to the west of Bermuda. Since our latest position was reckoned to be 90 miles to the northeast of the island, we calculated we were at least 200 miles from *Shearwater.*

I picked up the mike and tried to compose the words I should use. As soon as Jim signed off, I called, "Bermuda Harbor Radio, this is yacht *Starbound;* over."

"Yacht *Starbound,* this is Bermuda Harbor Radio. What can we do for you, *Starbound?*"

We looked at each other! My God, it works! I nearly said, "Great Zot! I've invented radio!" Instead, I kept my cool and said in my best radio-techniques voice, "Bermuda Harbor Radio, this is yacht *Starbound.* Our approximate position is 90 miles northeast of Bermuda. We've been through some rough weather in the last few days and have torn up our headsails to the point where we find it impossible to go to windward. We have salt water in our fuel tanks and can't seem to keep the engine running for longer than fifteen minutes at a time. Can you give us any indication of what kind of weather we can expect in the next day or two? Over."

A very English-sounding voice answered.

"Ah, *Starbound,* ah, this is Bermuda Harbor Radio. What is your destination? Over."

How embarrassing! "Bermuda Harbor Radio, this is yacht *Starbound.* Our destination is Saint George, Bermuda. Over."

"*Starbound,* Bermuda Harbor Radio. Can you please monitor this frequency for a short while? We'll contact the meteorological people and get you a forecast for this area."

"Bermuda Harbor Radio, this is *Starbound.* Thank you, we'll stand by. *Starbound* clear and monitoring."

"Bermuda Harbor Radio clear."

We were elated! We felt as if now we had someone else watching over us.

The wind was still blowing from the southwest. I decided to check with Bermuda when they came back on the air and see if they could put a radio direction finder on our signal and give us a bearing to the island. It would serve as a check on our navigation.

Within half an hour, Bermuda had confirmed our position—we were northeast of the island. Another sun line put us 90 miles out. They also told us that a weak cold front would come through about 0300 the next morning and would bring northwest breezes for the next twenty-four hours. Northwest winds would allow us to reach southwest. I thanked them and we all went topside and studied the sky and our sails. We wanted to stay where we were until the front came through. The breeze was quite light from the southwest. First we tried to heave to, but *Starbound* rolled the wind right out of her sails and the gear slammed around in a horrible fashion. We finally dropped all the sails and lay ahull, something we had never tried at sea before. And *Starbound* rolled and rolled. All night long she rolled! No one slept much. All our bedding was wet and the motion made it an effort just to stay in our bunks. Nina and Ernie finally found somewhat stable diagonal positions on our big double bunk. Harry and Jeanne curled up on the transom seats in the main saloon and tried to rest. I stayed topside and studied the ship's action until my eyes started closing of their own accord, then went below and looked longingly at the big quarter berth. It resembled a swamp! Being located partially under the main hatch, it had received frequent dollops of rain and spray. I mentally resolved to do something to protect that berth—I wasn't sure what.

Digging out the afterdeck seat cushions from where we had stuffed them at the foot of the quarter berth, I staggered with them into the master stateroom where Ernie and Nina lay sleeping. They looked as if they were clinging to the bunk with their fingers and toes. I shoved the seat cushions under the bunk overhang, crawled in after them, scrooched the cushions around into a layer between the deck and me, and fell face down. I think I slept. I know I was up more than down. I kept sliding back the main hatch and peering out at the black sea and the drizzle of rain and wondering when that cold front would arrive, and allow us to set sail again and put an end to this blasted rolling.

About 0330 a change in the ship's motion indicated that our front was coming through. By the time we had light to see, the wind had switched to northwest and the sky was clearing. We shook the sleep from our heads and started the business of putting sail on the ship. It was wonderful to feel a controlled motion again. In a short time, good smells wafted up from the galley. A hot breakfast put us all in fine humor—and we were on a straight course for Bermuda.

By nightfall I knew I had made another mistake. I hadn't studied the pilot chart or sailing directions, which would have indicated a southerly setting current. Worst of all, I hadn't believed the RDF. As full night closed about our particular piece of ocean, we could see the faint reflection of a glow against the clouds: Bermuda—almost due north of our postion.

Ernie looked at me with an eighteen-year-old's disdain, unfortunately warranted. "I *told* you the RDF was right, Dad!"

"O.K., O.K.," I muttered. "Let me talk to Bermuda and see if they can help us. But not until morning. It's almost flat calm now, so let's drop the sails and just lay here for the night. I'll take the first watch."

Starbound drifted under a blue sky and was making bare steerageway on a blue sea. The wind was very light from the northwest. Ocean swells let her rise and fall but so gently as to be scarcely noticeable. We were monitoring Bermuda Harbor Radio constantly. At 0800 I had asked them to see if they could round up someone willing to give us a tow into Saint George, a bare 15 miles to the north. The brightly shining sun was warming the crew's spirits as it dried bedding and clothes. Sea birds circled *Starbound* and we envied them their easy grace and speed.

I managed to start the diesel again and *Starbound* started plugging along at 4 knots. We sounded the fuel tanks, trying to get an idea of how much salt water and sludge we might be able to drain off. We finally surmised that of the 8 inches of moisture showing on the sounding stick, at least 4 inches were composed of stuff that shouldn't be there at all. I wondered why the engine would even start, much less run. The excellent fuel-filtering system was the answer. Big primary strainers composed of fine mesh screening pulled most of the sludge from the incoming fuel, and the secondary cartridge filters were picking up the sludge residue and salt water. Of course, the filter reservoirs were not designed to hold much over a cup and as soon as they filled, water was pulled into the injectors and the engine would snort a few times and quit running. Salt water must taste awful to a palate accustomed to clean diesel fuel.

"*Starbound,* this is Bermuda Harbor Radio. Do you read me? Over."

I took two jumps. The first to the engine controls to shut off the diesel, the second down the companionway to the radio-telephone. "Bermuda Harbor Radio, this is yacht *Starbound.* I read you loud and clear. Over."

"*Starbound,* Bermuda Harbor Radio. We have contacted a large motor-sailer who is willing to give you a tow to the harbor. She is presently in Saint George waiting for clearance. Since the customs and immigration people are on strike, she cannot clear immediately and has informed us that she is willing to give you a hand. Is that understood? Over."

"Bermuda Harbor Radio, this is yacht *Starbound.* We read you fine and understand your message. Does the motor-sailer know how big we are? We weigh 35 tons. Does she have sufficient power to tow us? Over."

"*Starbound,* Bermuda Harbor Radio. Our understanding is that the yacht is a 70-footer with twin diesel engines. Her name is *Kanaloa* but you cannot

contact her since only her VHF-FM set is in service at this time. We can
talk to either of you and pass any necessary information. Over."

"Bermuda Harbor Radio, this is *Starbound.* Sounds fine to us! Please
send her along with our blessings and thanks. Our estimated position is due
south of Saint George at approximately fifteen miles out. Over."

"*Starbound,* Bermuda Harbor Radio. We read you as being fifteen miles
south of Saint George. Can you give us a slow count to twenty, please, and
we will take a bearing. Over."

"Bermuda Harbor Radio, *Starbound* starting to count: one thousand, two
thousand, three thousand, four thousand . . . twenty thousand. Bermuda
Harbor Radio, this is *Starbound.* Did that work out O.K. for you? Over."

"*Starbound,* Bermuda Harbor Radio. Yes, we have your bearing as 178
degrees from us. We will direct *Kanaloa* to proceed to your location. Please
describe your yacht. Over."

I gave them a complete description, right to the 40-foot square yard on
the mainmast, the red-brown sails, and the long bowsprit.

At 1100 I was in the engine room cleaning engine filters again and heard
Ernie call, "Hey, I think I see her coming!"

I ran topside to check. A speck was growing on the northern horizon. I
jumped back below and finished the now familiar job. Back topside the
engine started immediately and we headed north to meet our helper.

A big sleek white yacht with varnished topsides swung around us in a
wide circle, came up from astern, and matched our speed. "Ahoy there,
Starbound! Where bound?" "Could you use a tow?" "How about a cold
beer?" These and other like questions were hurled across the water to us.
We grinned back at them as the monkey's fist carried our heaving line over
their bow and wrapped itself neatly around their lifeline. We payed out the
big anchor warp as *Kanaloa* moved into position ahead of us. The one-inch-
diameter plaited nylon slowly straightened its catenary, and shining water
droplets were wrung from its length as it took the strain. We were under
tow!

Three hours later the towline was passed to a harbor tug and we were
towed past the entrance buoys and started through Town Cut, the narrow
rock lined passage into Saint George Harbor. *Starbound* was flying the
Arundel Yacht Club burgee from her mainmasthead, the Bermuda flag
from her starboard crosstree spreader, the American Yacht Ensign from her
stern staff, and just for a brave display, the United States ensign from her
mizzen top. This last ensign measures 10 feet on the fly and was a gift to
Ernie from a friend. It was reputed to have been a battle flag from one of
our World War II battleships; a brave display indeed!

We saw *Kanaloa* go into the harbor ahead of us and dock at the big
wharf where the cruise ships usually lay. By then I had the filters cleaned

again and the engine tested, so as we approached Government Island I called to the tug to cast us off, which they finally did after I convinced them our engine would run for a short time. Ernie hauled in our towline at top speed while I started the diesel. *Starbound* came about in a sharp circle and in three minutes time we were tying up to the wharf directly behind *Kanaloa.*

The feel of the solid concrete wharf under our feet was strange as we walked to *Kanaloa* to express our thanks. With everybody talking at once, we had drinks thrust into our hands and met our rescuers in person. Charley Forsyth, the skipper, laughed about our 40-foot square yard. "I thought Bermuda Harbor was kidding me," he said, grinning. "Who in hell ever hears of a square yard nowadays? But there it was!"

Charley and I got into a corner by ourselves while he explained to me about the strike by government workers which was in effect. "Only the chief customs officer is working," he said, "and we'll just have to wait our turn. It could be two or three more days because he has to clear the cruise ships which come into Hamilton."

"Well, hell!" I asked, "Can't we at least dock our boats at the Dinghy Club? I don't like laying on this big wharf."

"Don't know if we can or not. We got in just this morning and I haven't had time to investigate. We're supposed to stay with our boats till they clear us."

"Well, they haven't told me that yet, so I'll play dumb Yank and trot over to the Dinghy Club to see if there's dock space." I walked across the wharf down the fence and through the wide open gates which nobody seemed to be guarding, then up to the road and started downhill toward the narrow harbor formed by the town and Government Island. I started to ask people for the harbor master and they finally directed me to a small shop selling English wool products.

"Yes, he owns this shop," I was told, "but he is not here right now. If you'll go down to the Dinghy Club dock, we will send him along." I left my name and strolled back to the dock area. Five yachts were rafted up to the concrete quay on the town side of the little harbor. I walked across the 100-foot-long bridge which forms the end of the harbor and found myself on Government Island. A few small fishing boats were scattered loosely along the quay nearest the bridge, and up further near the mouth of the harbor were the government tug berths.

"Let's see now," I thought. "If that one fishing boat would move forward, I could lay *Starbound* right in there with a 180-degree turn in front of the bridge."

"Mr. Stuermer?" I turned to greet a polite, stocky gentleman with gray hair.

Ten minutes later I was running down the wharf to *Starbound* and yelling to Charley Forsyth, "Crank her up Charley—if we go now they'll have a berth for us!"

Charley decided to let us go in first and then back *Kanaloa* in and lay outboard of us. Ernie had the diesel running and one spring line remaining to the wharf when I leaped to the taffrail and onto the afterdeck. The breeze pushed our bow around and I eased the throttle forward, praying that the engine wouldn't stop for the five minutes I needed. Around the end of Government Island we flew, then up the narrow harbor at 3 knots. I held her starboard side in close to the yachts rafted up there. The yard was cockbilled very high so I wouldn't foul any rigging, but even so heads popped out of hatches and viewed *Starbound's* 17-foot beam with alarm. A young woman on the last boat we passed exclaimed, "You're going to hit me!"

"No I'm not, lady," I said in a conversational voice. "See, I missed you by a whole foot." I swung the wheel three full turns to the left and *Starbound* started to pivot on a point just aft of her mainmast. Faster and faster she swung. The tip of the bowsprit arced by the bridge with 10 feet to spare, then swung over the fantail of the tiny fishing boat nearest the bridge. A young blond boy cleaning fish on the fantail looked at the big sprit swinging over his head and smiled at us. As *Starbound's* headway began carrying her starboard bow into the concrete quay, I brought back the shifting lever and reversed the screw. Her stern swung to starboard as I knew it would, her bows drifted to port exactly right, and she nuzzled her fenderboard up to the quay just as her forward way stopped. The crowd on the quay gave a few mild cheers as they made our lines fast. I tried hard to look nonchalant after completing the best landing I'd ever made.

"O.K., crew, we're here! Let's go find the pub!"

4

Bermuda Scramble

Somers Pub on the Square nestles itself into the ground floor of a block of eighteenth-century buildings which lies on the north side of a large segment of pavement called King's Square in Saint George. A well-thrown shackle pin from *Starbound*'s afterdeck could be bounced off the heavy oak door of the pub.

Charley Forsythe and I sat in the pub on the curve of the bar near the door and drank cool English lager out of fat pint mugs. After three hours of conversation and beer we knew each other fairly well. Our crews were in and out, but Charley and I just kept pushing our empty mugs to the bartender for another refill.

Charley moved down the bar to the telephone on the paneled wall and started putting through a call to his boss in New York. I sat forward and started making lists in my pocket notebook. The beer was getting to me but the list was easy to write because I refused to contemplate the dollar amounts I'd eventually have to add at the right-hand edge of the page. It read:

> Get water aboard
> Arrange to get tanks cleaned
> Fill fuel tanks
> Sails to sailmaker tomorrow
> Take mizzen tangs to welder
> Find new outhaul tracks for mizzen and main-staysail
> Ditto mizzen boom track
> Fix anchor damage to bulwark
> Hamilton for spare parts, *good* foul-weather gear, and stores
> Have Ernie overhaul rigging and check over top hamper
> Have Nina make new mast boot for mizzen

Sometime during the evening, two very polite English bobbies eased in the front door and spied Charley and me.

"Good evening. Are you the captains of the two American yachts?"

We assured them that we were.

"The customs and immigration officer will be down in the morning about ten o'clock to clear your boats. He has requested us to ask you to keep your crew members in the vicinity of the yachts, if you will, since you've not been officially cleared."

"Fine, fine! said Charley, who had been here before. "Can we assume that the pub is 'in the vicinity'? We can assure you that our crews will be on the yachts, in the pub, or en route from one to the other. How's that?"

"I suppose that will be all right, sir. Our chief concern is that the crews do not start touring about the island until C and I has had their go."

"O.K.!" I said. "We'll handle it. Is the government workers' strike still on?"

"Yes, sir. It is still on and might be for some time. The gentleman coming tomorrow is the chief customs inspector and he is doing all of the work himself. As you can imagine, he is very busy."

"Yeah, we can imagine. Can we buy you fellows a drink?"

"Not while we're on duty, sir, but we'll catch you up another time, thanks awfully." And off they went—smart, neat, and polite. Only the cream of the crop of English bobbies draw Bermuda duty.

I vaguely remember getting aboard *Starbound* sometime in the early morning. I woke up with the sun, feeling well. Our customs officer showed up at 0900 and cleared us with a minimum of fuss.

I went up the street and rented one of the little motorbikes which, it seems, three-quarters of the island's population uses to get around. After a cautious five minutes I had control of the beast and set out on my hunt for "bits and pieces."

The local Shell Oil representative helped me find a man to clean our fuel tanks and I turned him over to Nina and Ernie with instructions to clean the tanks and fill them with fresh diesel fuel. Ernie started on a hunt for fresh water, which needed to come to the dock in a tank truck, and Nina began questioning the dock committee about laundry facilities.

I cranked up my two-cycle motorbike and started down the curving, narrow, rock-and-tree-lined roads for the main city of Hamilton. The wicker saddle baskets were full of broken shroud tangs and twisted outhauls. The little bike buzzed me down Mullet Bay Road and across the bridge to Kindley Field Road which runs parallel to the U.S. Naval Air Station. Across the causeway I found Blue Hole Hill and a right turn put me onto Shore Road. The left-hand driving scared hell out of me, I couldn't look at the beautiful scenery because my eyes were frozen on the narrow traffic lane ahead. Small English cars leaped at me from corners and

Nina at the helm during a Chesapeake Bay shakedown cruise. *Courtesy of L. John Larsen*

Getting the galley ready for
active use after the
installation of refrigeration
equipment.

Starbound underway,
viewed from aloft.

Starbound gets the sandwich treatment at the crowded Dinghy Club, St. George, Bermuda.

Loading up and taking inventory before the voyage. Nina and Ernie.

Anchorage at Dominica in the Leewards.

Heading into Panama, with Gordon and Nina on watch.

In one of the Panama Canal's locks, *Starbound* shares
space with a huge tanker.

While knuckling through the Canal, Gordon at the
helm receives instruction from pilot Bill Boyland.

Heading toward the Pacific, *Starbound* locks through
behind the super-tanker *Nefeli,* which fills the lock,
wall to wall.

Almost into the Pacific, *Starbound* at Tobaga Island
with *Topaz,* seen over the bow of *Eolus,* right.

Topaz underway is reminiscent of the Great Days of Sail.

Good friends gather—the *Topaz* crew poses for a group portrait.

An anchorage in the San Blas Islands.

A native family in the San Blas Islands.

motorbikes snarled by from fore and aft with their riders crouching ferociously over the handlebars. Slowly I began to relax my grip on the bike and take more interest in the surroundings. It was nicely nostalgic seeing tropical flowers and trees again. Little black children were scattered all over the countryside and their shrill cries were accompanied by the barking of large numbers of assorted dogs. The population explosion hasn't bypassed Bermuda. Hamilton City traffic, both vehicular and pedestrian, was thick on Front Street. I found the big P and W store right on the waterfront and parked the motorbike in a cluster of its own kind on the harbor side of the street.

The Bermuda tourist trade stores have a remarkably efficient machinery for removing a maximum number of tourist dollars from pockets. My shock at the prices displayed in shop windows was reinforced by the tags appended to marine fittings in the P & W emporium. And there were no fittings heavy enough for *Starbound.* I showed my broken outhaul track to several clerks. Oh, no sir, we wouldn't have anything like that—doubt if you'll find it in Bermuda, sir. You might try the marine shop just three blocks down.

Four motorbike parkings, lockings, and walks later, I was given a name: Albert Darrell, Harbor Road, Warwick Parish. Oh, yes, sir, old Darrell has all kinds of heavy fittings out in that rigging loft of his. I looked at my watch. 1500 hours. Too late today to get to Warwick Parish. I rode around Hamilton until I found Trott Road and a sailmaker called Skip Tatum. He and his assistant, John Harries, agreed to come that night to look at our damaged headsails and make me a quote for repairs. I thought about a cold beer in the dark pub, got on the motorbike, and headed back to Saint George.

Ernie and Nina had made progress. Seven buckets of sludge had been removed from our fuel tanks. The tanks were clean and filled with diesel. The water truck had arrived with 2,000 gallons and *Starbound* took 300 of them. *Kanaloa* took the rest, a very thirsty boat.

Skip and John arrived at dusk, and fingering ripped Dacron, hummed and clucked, and shook their heads sadly. Flying jib: $100; main-staysail: $100; roller furling jib: $90; mizzen: $35. I helped load the bags into their panel truck and watched them drive away. Hands in my pockets and head down, I walked back across the square to the pub, thinking. Clean fuel tanks: $100; fill tanks with diesel: $100. It had been an expensive day. And I still had to find outhauls and track. I needed a drink. Like scotch. Yeah! Scotch!

Next morning I watched Albert Darrell paw through his third or fourth box of junk and pull out an old Merriman outhaul track. Nicked and dinged and dark brown with the patina of age, it was an exact copy of our damaged gear.

"Well, you can buy that one from me, but I don't have another. Now what kind of sail track do you need?"

"Seven-eighths extruded bronze."

"Well, go look in that big bundle of stuff in the rack on the wall over there, and pick out what you want. I'll see how soon we can fix those tangs for you. Stainless, are they?"

"Yeah, I think they're 316L alloy." I found two lengths of fairly new sail track and put them beside the tangs. Sunshine came through the windows in dusty beams and lightened the gloom overhead. I could see old masts and booms lying across the bottom beams of the wooden trussing up there. A big ship's wheel was being repaired on a workbench running down one wall of the shed. The leavings of a thousand boats were hung, stacked, and binned in that shed. I saw some blocks I wanted to buy, but a ship's name on a tag said they belonged to somebody.

Mr. Darrell came back into the rigging loft. "Have 'em for you in two days."

"O.K.! Can I pay for these things now?"

"No, no! Just take 'em along and if you can use 'em you can pay me when you pick up the tangs."

"Well, how much are they?"

"I don't know just now. I'd have to find my catalogs and look up the prices. Just take 'em along."

It was the only game in town, so I took 'em along.

Three days passed by in a blur of hard work. Harry and Jeanne came down to say good-by. They were flying back to the States the next morning. I was doing a balancing act with my feet on the taffrail and setting track screws on the mizzen boom with a brace and screwdriver bit. Harry watched me for a while and then said softly, "Damn it, Gordon. You're really busting your ass keeping this lash-up together, aren't you?" What could I say? I mumbled some platitude. After Harry and Jeanne walked away to the taxi stand I thought about his words. Yeah, I guess I was "busting my ass" to keep the lash-up together. But I don't know any other way to do it. If you don't work hard at it when necessary, your dream can go to hell in a hurry, and this cruise had been my dream for many years.

After some confusion with telegrams which was finally resolved by a telephone call, we knew when Pete and Janelle would join us for the eight or nine-day hop to Antigua. It would work out well. They would arrive about the time *Starbound* would be ready to leave. I asked Pete to buy another outhaul track for me and bring it with him. Everything else was shaping up, but our budget was in stinking shape. We had spent nearly $1,000 making good the storm damage and resupplying the boat. I remembered that old saying: Yacht cruising is the most expensive way in the world to go third class.

How do parties start? The best ones seem to just happen. We started drinking gin and tonic with Charley and his girlfriend on Saturday afternoon. Our two bobbie friends, Frank and Stan, joined us, coming aboard with another bottle under arm. Stan brought his girlfriend. We had a sort of open house going with lots of people wandering through *Starbound,* most of them interested strangers. The eastern sky was lightening before we got to bed.

We were planning to leave for Antigua the following weekend, so Nina, Ernie, and I started working ten hours each day on *Starbound* to finish up all of the jobs we had listed in our notebooks. We repainted *Starbound*'s bow, which looked pretty scruffy after our rough Atlantic passage. We overhauled the halyard blocks all around, and carefully checked the entire tophamper, right down to the last cotter pin. Then I started sweating it out in the engine room, changing the sump oil and filters for the main engine and auxiliary generator. And I overhauled our bilge pumps. Ernie broke out the handy-billy and took up on the lanyards, setting all fourteen shrouds up taut. Nina made and installed a new mast boot on the mizzen and then repainted some dinged areas on the booms and bowsprit. Of course, all these jobs were done while being kibitzed by our new neighbors, who generally came over with a can of beer in each hand, "one for me and one for you."

Pete and Janelle flew in on Friday and came driving out the quay in a taxi, waving and yelling hellos. We spent the afternoon in our favorite pub regaling each other with adventurous tales, us telling about our terrible trip to Bermuda and them telling about the on-again, off-again airline strike under the auspices of which they were taking their union-enforced leave of absence.

We went to bed about midnight and I lay awake thinking of the underwater check I needed to do the next day on the propeller, the shaft bearing, the rudder, and the fathometer transducer. A loud crash topside brought me sitting straight up in bed. Then there were heavy footsteps overhead and another clattering crash. I got up, walked aft, and put my head out the main hatch just in time to observe one of the young mariners from the boat next door tripping over the lifelines and falling aboard his own boat. Then he staggered to his feet, battered but not beat, and fell head first down the main hatch. I went back to bed and Nina asked sleepily, "What the hell was all that?"

"That was one of the lads from next door coming home with a full load."

"Just call him twinkle-toes," Nina remarked, and she turned over and went back to sleep.

Next morning I rose up through the water under *Starbound*'s stern with the bubbles floating upward past my face mask. I hooked one arm over the top of the big "barn-door" rudder and shoved my mask upward on my forehead as I broke through the surface of the water. I spit out the scuba mouthpiece. How the devil did all the gasoline get into the water? Undulating rainbows spread their spectra all around the harbor and I could taste the horrible stuff.

A timid voice called to me from the quay. "Gordon, could you do us a big favor? Could you dive down here just aft of your boat and see if my motorbike is down there? I think I remember riding it off into the water last night." It was Twinkletoes.

Of course! That's where the gasoline was coming from. I took the end of a line from him, adjusted my mask, bit down on the mouthpiece, and swam down to the bottom 25 feet below. There was the bike, looking very forlorn in the clear water. I tied a bowline around the gooseneck supporting the handlebars, then swam slowly to the surface and gave the boys a thumbs-up sign. Twinkle-toes and friends pulled the dripping machine to the quayside and I climbed the boarding ladder to *Starbound*'s afterdeck. I started to slip the scuba straps off my shoulders when another hung-over sailor confronted me. "Uh, I don't suppose you'd consider looking for another one?"

"Another one? You mean you followed suit?"

"Uh, yeah. I think mine's up forward of your bowsprit somewhere. I'd sure appreciate it if you could have a look."

Wearily, I cracked a can of beer and washed the taste of gasoline out of my mouth. I refastened the scuba harness and rolled over the taffrail back into the rainbowed water. The second submarine motorbike was laying on its side 40 feet down and a full boat length forward of *Starbound,* tucked well under the transom of an old fishing trawler. I could see the keel floating way up there over my head. I tied another line around another pair of handlebars, like roping a steer by the horns, and surfaced. It had taken twenty minutes to find the second machine and I was tired and cold.

I took a hot shower and thought about the cutlass bearing at *Starbound*'s stern. It seemed overly worn and allowed the shaft a bit of play. I decided to replace it in Antigua, and with that decision made, I climbed out of our big stainless tub and made wet footprints into the master stateroom.

While I was dressing, I heard the galloping put-put of a two-cycle engine starting. By the time I got topside, the boys from next door had both of the wet motorbikes running; not well, but running. Pretty fair mechanics. After the bikes were well dried out they took them back to the rental agency and complained that they weren't running too well and traded them in on a fresh pair, probably for use in another sounding operation.

We went back to work making ready for sea, and by the end of the day had so completed our tasks that we decided to take our departure in the morning.

We had a noisy farewell party in Somers Pub that evening and next morning, Sunday, November 18, we cleared customs for Antigua. On the way to Town Cut we paused to swing our compass on Saint Davids light, then headed out of the cut for "Spit" buoy, with Janelle standing at the helm, gripping the spokes and staring fiercely at the compass while the rest of us put up sail after sail.

5

The Leewards

I could feel the rhythmic tremor transmitted through oak and pine and teak to the soles of my sea boots as the ship pounded her bluff bow into the short steep chop. Three things had me worried: the black night, the driving rain, and the lee shore. *Starbound* was hard on the wind with the sails trimmed flat as practicable, and the engine was turning at 1,500 revolutions per minute to help her claw her way to windward. The presence of the huge reef to leeward was a tangible thing, and I kept checking our course by the reddish glow backlighting the big Kelvin-White compass. She was holding her own and when the taffrail log turned its pointer just ten more nautical miles I'd be able to ease her to starboard a few spokes and let her make better speed and less leeway.

"Everything's fine," I silently told *Starbound.* "Just keep pushing into it for a little while longer and we're home free. After all, eight days of good sailing under sunny skies—one lousy night can't hurt us."

The rain stopped again and a few stars appeared between the black clouds I knew were there. Off the starboard bow about 15 miles lay the shoreline of the island of Barbuda, and off our beam was the extensive north reef of that island. I stared hard into the gloom, hoping to see something, anything. And then I saw the completely unexpected: a flare arced its way upward! A white flare! So white it appeared greenish blue in the rain clouds which reflected its glare. It burned brightly through its entire arc, upward and downward, then was swallowed by the night which seemed even more black by contrast. I held onto the wheel tightly, my mouth suddenly dry. Someone must be on the reef! Hell, I thought, we can't go over there. We'd be on the coral in nothing flat. I edged around the wheel and, holding a spoke with one foot, leaned forward and shoved open the sliding hatch. "Nina! Come on deck!"

Within two minutes, Nina had the wheel and was peering out at the night from under the hood of her foul-weather gear.

I warmed up the transmitter and checked the time—0045. I exercised my radio technique for one full hour and then fifteen minutes longer. No one answered. No one. Neither Barbuda, nor Antigua, nor English Harbor, nor any ship. At 0200 I switched off the radio-telephone and went back topside.

The night was clearing. We spotted the loom of town lights from both Barbuda and Antigua. We had made our easting, so we brought *Starbound* four points to starboard and secured the engine. The needle of the speed log slowly swung up to seven.

I heard a noise below. Pete had gotten up and was bolting the shaft brake down. When he came topside I explained to him what I'd seen.

"A white flare? Usual procedure for distress is a red flare."

"I know, Pete. But someone shot off a white one, and it was near as dammit to that reef. All I can think to do is report it to whatever authorities are available when we get into English Harbor."

"Yeah. Makes you appreciate American waters and the U.S. Coast Guard, doesn't it?" It sure did!

Starbound tore down the windward side of Antigua on a broad reach and as Willoughby Bay opened up, we started sheets and fell off for English Harbor. The entrance appeared with a suddeness which surprised us. We rounded the reef which extends out from the southern headland and lined up the marks on the hill sloping up from the far side of the harbor.

What a great hurricane hole! As we sailed by the fort perched high on the steep cliff to our left, the entire harbor opened up before us and we could see dozens of big masts projecting up from the quay which lined the waterfront of Nelson's Dockyard. When we looked back, we saw that the harbor was entirely landlocked. Not a ripple of ocean swell could leak into this snug haven.

We anchored off the quay with the Q flag flying from the starboard mizzen spreader, and within fifteen minutes a boatload of authorities were aboard and perusing our papers. Everything was in order, they assured us. Then came the *mordida,* the bite. "Just a little donation for the Boys' Club, sar!"

I gave them five American dollars, and after they'd gone Nina gave me hell! Two British West Indies dollars would have been generous enough. British West Indies dollars are called BWI dollars, pronounced "beewee," and were worth about 55 cents U.S. in November 1973.

We weighed the anchor and, letting it hang from its chain on the fairlead, motored over to the impressive array of yachts lined up along the quay, their bows out and sterns in. We reset the hook well out from a vacant spot we'd noticed. Then we took a long stern line ashore with the dinghy and secured it to one of the big black bollards made from a buried cannon barrel. With a large expenditure of "Swedish steam" we warped *Starbound*'s stern into the slot between two 60-foot schooners, letting out chain from the anchor winch as she moved aft. We crossed two more lines from our stern to the quay and then set out our second anchor well to windward of the first. When all our lines were adjusted, *Starbound* lay with her transom just 6 feet away from the concrete quay. Looking down, we could see the coral sand bottom just 4 feet below the deepest part of her keel. The water was clear as gin.

Lord Jim was there, her long blue hull gleaming in the tropical sun. And the charter windjammer *Flying Cloud,* taking her famous name from the old tea clipper. The big charter schooner *Harvey Gamage,* loaded with people, backed her way into a slip shortly after we arrived.

We wandered up and down the quay, admiring the fleet. Pete, Ernie, and I also admired the profusion of bikinis.

I found myself trying to talk coherently about *Starbound* to a girl about eighteen or nineteen. She had curly auburn hair and a lot of silky smooth, golden tanned skin. Her bikini was something that any self-respecting spider could have woven in three minutes. I managed to convey the information that we didn't really need another cook aboard for our trip down the islands. As she strolled down the quay, I tore my eyes from the stern view with reluctance and faced Pete who stood there grinning, with his eyes slightly glazed. "Damn, that was an offer I found hard to turn down," I grumbled.

We'd had a good sail down from Bermuda with lots of sunshine, fair winds, and fun. I'll always remember Pete standing behind the binnacle, entirely nude, with one foot on the wheel, *Starbound* heeled to a tradewind, a driving tropical rain shower coming down, singing a raunchy song at the top of his voice, and trying to work up a lather with a bar of soap faster than the rain could wash it off.

After dark that evening we sat on the afterdeck listening to one of the truly lovely sounds of the West Indies, a steel band. We followed the enchanting sounds to the Admiral's Inn and found a large group of men and boys, all of them black, swinging their individualized mallets with seemingly wild abandon at a large collection of battered-looking oil drums whose heads had been dished, tempered, thinned, and tuned with what must have been extraordinary skill and patience.

We danced the night away under the spreading branches of tropical trees, with the scent of frangipani blossoms drifting by in an unseen cloud.

Pete and Janelle had to fly back to the United States. The airline strike was finally settled and they had to begin flying the big jets again. Nina and I helped them pack their gear, and we scoured *Starbound* for this and that small item which was sure to be left behind.

Pete really wanted to stay in Antigua for a few more days but Janelle, without coming right out with it, seemed to have had enough of the cruising life for a while. She had been constantly seasick for the entire eight days at sea from Bermuda. Not hanging-over-the-taffrail sick, but the lying-down-feeling-bad sick which perhaps is the worst kind.

In the afternoon of the morning Pete and Janelle flew away, Ernie and I were in the dinghy putting some finishing touches on the topside paint. A hail came across the water and we saw Don Dement sitting in a launch grinning at us from beneath a beat-up Scandinavian sailing cap which I think he dug out of the forecastle of a Mariehamn Cape Horner.

"Hey," I yelled. "Where did you come from? We didn't expect you for a few more days. Come aboard."

I took the launch painter from his hand and tied it off to the end of the bowsprit. The stern of the launch swung in under the martingale shrouds and Don clambered up to the foredeck while explaining. "We flew in a few days ago and we're staying at the hotel right around the point across the bay. Keren is over there now and I thought I'd come see if *Starbound* was in yet."

So here was our crew to Martinique.

There are some men who can do almost anything well. Such a man is Dement. He's tall and slender with light brown hair and long sensitive hands which he can employ with facility to almost any task. His field is electronics, the very advanced, exotic kind—but I had heard him play a clarinet, and many times a piano, with artistic skill and professional competence.

Keren is a big, beautiful woman. She's tall, and her sparkling green eyes can look into mine from the same level, if I stand up very straight.

Don and Keren live in Annapolis aboard their Columbia 45 sloop to which they've applied their many talents, turning it from an impersonal lump of white plastic containing a few panels of teak-faced plywood into a comfortable and versatile floating home. As Don says, "It's nothing that imagination, talent, and money can't accomplish."

Ernie took the launch around the point to the hotel, collected Keren, and brought her back to *Starbound.* A few people wandered over from neighboring boats and Nina started mixing interesting combinations in her electric blender consisting of various local fruits, ice, and lots of Antigua rum.

Just so do the better parties start. I remember that much later in the evening we went for a motor boat ride to rescue a vagrant bottle of scotch imprisoned in the Dement's hotel room. I also remember diving off the hotel dock into the water fully clothed: wallet, traveler's checks, notebook and all. When the rum has been consumed, I should never, never start on the scotch.

We had completed most of the ship's work by the weekend and decided to spend Saturday and Sunday doing some tourist-type sightseeing, an activity I despise but which I somehow feel obligated to do.

We wanted to be on our way by Tuesday morning, giving me Monday to replace the worn cutlass bearing on the main shaft. I put the job out of my mind for the time being and decided to enjoy myself.

Don, Keren, Nina, and I arranged to take a taxi into St. Johns, the capital city of Antigua. The town has a population of 20,000 inhabitants, approximately one-third of the island's population, of which 99 percent are black.

Our taxi cost $20 BWI for a dusty, sweaty ride across incredibly bad roads to the northwest corner of the island on which is spraddled the most unattractive town of any in the West Indies, St. Johns. Dirty, hot, and ugly as it was, we hurried to buy some very fine rum at very good prices and got ourselves back to Nelson's Dockyard. The countryside we passed through made some of the poorer depressed areas of Mexico appear bright and cheery by comparison.

So we learned why all of the boating people stayed at the dockyard and seldom ventured into town. For us, the dockyard is the heart of the island. It's an attractive, clean sort of outdoor museum which is beautifully maintained by the Society of English Harbor. The yacht chartering offices and wharves of V. E. B. Nicholson and Sons are within the dockyard compound and can arrange to supply almost anything a visiting boat might need.

I spent two hours underwater on Monday—one hour in the morning removing the propeller and bronze housing containing the worn cutlass bearing, and one in the afternoon putting the stuff back on. In between my scuba trips I took a short ride in the launch across the harbor to the establishment of Antigua Slipways Limited and managed to talk the manager into releasing one of his busy mechanics long enough to press the old bearing out of its housing and press the new one in.

In the late afternoon I rounded up a cooperative taxi driver who took me for a ten-minute ride to a big gas works where I had my two scuba tanks refilled for $1 each.

While I was so employed, Ernie and Don filled our water tanks, a procedure which must be arranged with the "water man" who pumps the stuff from big stone reservoirs constructed in Nelson's time. We were charged 6 cents BWI per gallon.

I paid our dockage charges at the office. They came to 5 cents BWI per foot per day, which seemed reasonable in return for the amenities of the dockyard we'd enjoyed.

At 0700 next morning our anchors came aboard and we motored out the pass. Setting all fore and aft sail, we turned left for the island of Guadeloupe, whose mountains we could see in the distance.

From the British West Indies to the French West Indies, in eight hours. By 1500 our anchor dropped into the water of Anse Deshayes, a beautiful little cove with some very arid scenery surrounding the blue water.

We'd planned to make fairly good time through the rest of the Leeward Islands. Don and Keren had only a few weeks to spend with us and some of that time we wanted to spend in Fort-de-France, Martinique. So we didn't plan to dawdle unless the anchorage and scenery really warranted a longer look.

We would have liked to explore the ports of Gosier, Saint Anne, and Saint Francis, but they lay to windward. On the other hand, the Iles des Saintes looked like a clear reaching sail for us and a good harbor when we got there. We relegated Guadeloupe proper to our "next time" list and next morning set out with the sunrise for Des Saintes.

There are actually eight little Saint Isles, all of them dependencies of Guadeloupe, but just two of them are lived on—Terre de Haute and Terre de Bas.

We experienced our first real "cape effect" with the trades as *Starbound* sailed past the southern tip of Guadeloupe's Basse Terre. The northeast tradewind bent around the cape and commenced to head us until we were well into the channel. The "moderate" trades were blowing 25 to 30 knots and we cranked up the diesel to reduce our leeway to a minimum. After two tacks we found ourselves with the harbor dead to windward and still one mile away, so we dropped all sail and hammered into the wind and current, inching our way along for the protection of the bay at Terre de Haute. At 1600 hours the hook went down and we all collapsed on the afterdeck with a rum punch in hand to aid our recovery rate. The strong trades made the swell push into the bay and *Starbound* rolled a bit more than usual but we all agreed we could live with it for a day or two.

We went ashore for dinner and found a small French restaurant with good prices. Nina and Keren practiced their French for the amusement of the proprietor while we proceeded to demolish several delicious chicken halves and four liters of a most excellent white wine.

The morning light brought us a shock. I had climbed topside and stood in my jockey shorts on the side deck, making a brave stream into the harbor water, when I heard a clunking sound forward. I leaned further over the lifeline and saw that our big launch, which we had boomed out to the end of the bowsprit, was upside down—motor and all. I leaped for the foredeck before I'd finished my first task and succeeded in wetting on my foot. Cursing, I ran to the forward bulwark and by hauling hard on the stern painter managed to turn the launch right side up.

Evidently the launch had been tripped over by the anchor chain catching on the lower housing of the outboard motor when the wind had swung the ship's bow off to one side. The removable seat tops were missing and, worse yet, the outboard motor cowling. The fuel tank was floating alongside the launch at the extent of, and fastened by, the fuel hose.

I dashed below and scooped up a pair of pants, struggling into them on the way back up. I dropped into the launch with a plastic bucket in one hand and started bailing. When the launch was mostly dry I retrieved the fuel tank, said a quick prayer, and pulled the starting cord. The outboard started right away, ran rough for a minute, then smoothed out to its normal snarl. Thanks, Mr. Evinrude!

I let go the painter and roared away downwind. After an hour's search I found the seat tops washed up on the rocks about a half-mile to leeward. The cowling must have sunk. We never found it. Now, where in hell was I going to find a cowling for an eight-year-old Evinrude? Well, anyway, it still ran O.K.

We decided to have lunch ashore, then explore the island. We had heard that Terre de Haute had an entirely white population and that Terre de Bas was entirely black. Our information must have been very dated. We saw many blacks on Terre de Haute, and they were obviously living there. We did notice that most of the white population were fair-haired and blue-eyed, a legacy from their Breton and Norman ancestors. We also noticed that, except for the village children, the people seemed faintly hostile and were barely civil. Of course, that might have been because of our communication problem. We found that they speak a kind of Creole there, not French.

The small seaside village is called Bourg des Saintes, and it looks like a charming place. Its charm took an abrupt downturn after we had eaten lunch at a small open-air restaurant. We had chosen to eat langouste, or crayfish, after quite a lengthy negotiation with the fat, mustachioed proprietress as to cost. When our bill was presented it was over twice the amount agreed upon. Keren was so angry I thought she was going to belt the old broad with a wine bottle. We finally paid part of the bill, still much more than was originally agreed upon, and on the spot decided to get under way in the morning. Our first taste of the French West Indies was giving us ptomaine poisoning.

The anchor was weighed at 0930 and *Starbound* blew through the southwest pass of the Saints at 7 knots. Dominica lay dead ahead with Morne Diablotin rising 4,747 feet above the blue Caribbean sea.

Dominica is the kitchen garden for the rest of the islands in the Leeward-Windward chain. Bananas are the island's chief crop but it also exports all varieties of citrus fruits, and coconuts, cacao, vanilla, pineapple, mangoes, avocados, as well as every vegetable that I'd ever seen and some that I'd never even heard of before. The rainfall that makes everything grow so well varies from 45 inches per year on the coast to 350 inches in the rain forest. At last, a lush, rich tropical island!

On the northwest coast, a small projection juts out into the sea and there is a deep curving indentation behind it. On the island chart that indentation is named Prince Rupert Bay. We decided to check it out as a possible anchorage.

When *Starbound* rounded the end of that small projecting cape, the whole crew stood on the deck, mouths agape, and stared at a perfect example of a tropical paradise. I think it is the beach which first catches the eye. The contrast of that sweeping crescent of black sand caught between trees and water was startling to our northern eyes. The water is a clear, achingly bright blue of that particular shade that Scripto ink used to be (remember that ink in the fat little clear-glass bottles?). A myriad of coconut palms lined the shore and draped their fronds over the black sand beach like a dark green roof. A blue hulled yawl lay quietly at anchor close into the beach, her reflection bearing witness to the calmness of the little bay.

I brought the engine control handle on the binnacle side back to the Idle Forward detent and let *Starbound* ease her way toward the beach. Nina watched the fathometer, calling out the numbers designated by the flickering neon bulb. When I heard her say 8 feet I pulled the handle to Idle Reverse and watched the water moving aft alongside the hull slow to a stop, then, imperceptibly at first, start moving forward. Ernie was standing forward with the big Herreshoff anchor balanced on the cap rail waiting for my thumbs-down signal. I gave it to him and he tipped the 130-pound hook over the side. Down through the clear water it went, and he watched it land on the bottom, turn over to the pressure of the stock, and bite into the firm sand with the down-pointing fluke. The chain whirled across the wildcat and rattled out the hawse. When the painted links designating 10 fathoms of chain flew over the side he spun the winch brake wheel clockwise and the free-wheeling wildcat slowed, then stopped. The catenary of the chain straightened as our sternway set the hook firmly in the bottom. I had already put the control lever to neutral, so I pulled the fuel shut-off lever back and the engine went silent. Then I switched the starting key to its off position before the low-oil-pressure buzzer disturbed the new silence. None of us said anything for a few minutes; we were too busy drinking in the beauty of the bay.

I broke the silence. "Gin and tonic?"

Far down the beach we could see a wooden dock and signs of a town. We checked the chart again. It was Portsmouth. After our drink I ran the launch down to the dock and turned it over to four little black boys who insisted on watching it for me. I found the police station and turned over two crew lists, which were stamped and one copy returned. Our entry was completed. I ransomed the launch for the price of four Cokes and headed back to *Starbound* for another gin and tonic.

We noticed that the blue yawl was *Bloodhound.* We had seen her the previous summer in Annapolis and again in Bermuda, where we made the casual acquaintance of her young American crew. There were no signs of life aboard.

Just visible among the palm trees girding the beach was what appeared to be a woven palm frond fence, about 5 feet high and 100 feet long. Beside a break in the fence and attached to it there was a small board sign. Our ten-power binoculars made the small lettering readable: SPOTLIGHT RESTAURANT.

"Now, what do you suppose that is?" we all wondered. "Do you think it's actually a restaurant?"

We had an answer very quickly. A stocky black man came through the break in the fence and walked down to the beach, shading his eyes to look out at *Starbound.* Then he walked back up under the palms and reappeared dragging a small wooden dinghy behind him. We waited with interest while he rowed out and came alongside, backed his oars, and smiled up at our five attentive faces. His teeth were large and very white in a most amiable dark face. He wore a green aloha shirt imprinted with red tropical flowers, and a pair of khaki slacks.

"Good afternoon, ladies and gentlemen; may I speak to the captain?"

"Good afternoon," we all replied.

"I'm the captain," I said.

"I am Bruno, sar—the owner of the Spotlight Restaurant. It is there, sar, on the beach." He gestured with a hand. "Your friends from the other boat are now sitting at my bar drinking the most delicious rum punch. They noticed your approach and suggested that I come out and invite you all to dinner at the restaurant, sar. It will be the most delicious dinner, sar—all served in the family style. They from the other boat will be there also."

"Well, Bruno, that sounds fine, but how much does dinner cost?" I asked.

"Seven dollars American for each person, sar. But—" he went on hurriedly, noting the expression on my face—"it is the most delicious dinner, sar, with all the foods from Dominica. There will be large lobsters, sar, grilled over the open fire; and mountain chicken, sar, of the most delicious taste; and palm heart salad; and so many, many other delicious foods, sar—and also with the meal"—he lowered his voice conspiratorially—"all the wine you can drink! Oh, sar, there will be so many delicious foods that you will not be able to eat it all!" He gave the oars a few short strokes to keep his boat in position.

We talked it over quickly. Why not? Seven bucks a head was not too bad. Hell, how many places like this are there in the world?

"All right, Bruno, you'll have five more for dinner. Seven o'clock?"

Bruno grinned. "That will be just right, sar. Then you will have time for our famous rum punch before dinner. The first one is complimentary." He started rowing to the beach and his deep voice with the Carib lilt floated back to us, "Until this evening, my friends."

When I am an old, old man, sitting with my memories on the afterdeck of my boat, I will still remember that dinner. When the conversation with friends comes around to gastronomical delights I will always be able to say, "Well, now, the Blue Fox in San Francisco is pretty good, but have you ever been to Bruno's Spotlight Restaurant in Prince Rupert Bay, Dominica?"

The floor was hard-packed earth. The roof was woven palm fronds suspended between live coconut palms. The tables were long trestle-type platforms with benches on either side. The decor was pure Caribbean with kerosene lanterns in colorful shades. A four-man steel band made some of the loveliest sounds in the world while we drank and danced and ate—and ate some more.

Bruno was right: we couldn't eat it all, but we made a damn good try. The huge grilled lobster halves hung over both ends of the platter and dripped butter on the white tablecloth. The "mountain chicken" legs, frog legs to the uninitiated, looked like they came from a turkey and tasted like they came from heaven. For the first time in our lives, we ate our fill of palm heart salad. And there were delicious Carib concoctions made from plantain and dasheen and tania and breadfruit. And a beautiful dessert, a combination of island fruits, soursop and mango and pineapple and pawpaw. And the wine flowed like water.

I slept late the next morning and awoke listening to a joyful splashing outside the port over our bunk. Nina brought me a steaming cup of hot coffee and I got that down, then went topside and dove over the side and joined the rest of the crew frolicking in the delightful blue water.

We talked while we swam and decided to get underway for the town of Roseau just 18 miles down the coast. We'd heard the Anchorage Hotel had free moorings for yachts and we thought that it would be a good place from which to arrange an island tour.

We left Prince Rupert Bay with Bruno waving good-by to us from the beach and sailed the 18 miles, picking up a mooring at the hotel by 1400.

A quick recon of the hotel facilities revealed some very high prices for food and drink, and the fact that the hotel manager expected our patronage. We had a few expensive drinks served indifferently at the hotel bar and picked up a brochure at the front desk listing the tours that could be arranged through the hotel. Their cost was back-breaking: about U.S. $14 each, for a limited tour which would include the Emerald Pool—a recently discovered "sacred place" of the ancient Carib tribes. We wanted a tour, but not at those prices.

Ernie decided to prowl around the hotel grounds, so we other four took a taxi to the Fort Young Hotel. Now here was a hotel, an imaginative blend of antiquity lightly overlaid with modern facilities. The bar was excellent, and expensive. We checked a menu and the right-hand column made us decide to eat aboard *Starbound.*

Our taxi driver, taking us back to the Anchorage Hotel, was an enterprising and pleasant islander named Conrad. He listened to us discussing tour prices and offered to take all five of us on a six-hour tour for $30, which would include the Emerald Pool and part of the windward side of the island. His automobile was clean and pleasant, and Conrad was soft-spoken and polite and seemed well educated. We looked at one another and agreed to meet him near the hotel at 0900 next morning.

What a grand tour we had! We picked bananas, oranges, and cacao pods directly from the trees and ate them. We walked the beautiful beaches on the east coast and watched the canoe builders work at hewing out the huge logs in the old way. When we were thirsty, Conrad stopped the car and picked green drinking nuts from the coconut palms and opened them with a wicked-looking machete he carried in the trunk. But the highlight of the day was the Emerald Pool. It is a magically beautiful place discovered by a government survey team while trekking through the rain forest in the center of the island. There are no signposts, concrete walks, or beer stands, and damn few tourists.

Conrad pulled the car off the road in a muddy wide spot and we followed him through a barely discernible opening in the trees.

We jumped from log to log which had been laid across the muddy path like an old corduroy road. Finally emerging on a drier part of the trail, we climbed, slid, jumped, and scrambled through the rain forest for about a mile.

Keren's voice was continually ringing through the woods behind us, "Dammit, wait for me!"

A last steep descent brought us to a beautiful stream running swiftly over and around rocks and trees. The tropical forest closed so tightly overhead that only occasionally did a ray of sunlight reach through to light our way. We were in a continual green-hued twilight until we emerged suddenly from the gloom into a bowl-shaped grotto of astonishing beauty. A fairy-lace waterfall plunged 35 or 40 feet into what was truly an emerald pool. Rays of sunlight drove down from above and lent an ethereal atmosphere to the place. No wonder the old Caribs called it a sacred place. Long streamers of liana vines hung from the tree limbs above and moss grew on the surrounding rocks. Varicolored birds and butterflies carved erratic trails through the misty air. We all just sat on the rocks and gazed. There was no need to speak.

Don and I noticed that the water had carved out a deep hollow behind the fall itself. We managed to work our way behind the veil of water and take some photographs from there while carefully shielding our cameras from the moisture.

We stayed for a while, then climbed back up the slippery trail to the car. That product of Detroit looked rather unreal, sitting there by the road, after where we'd been.

Back at the hotel, we paid Conrad, thanked him gratefully, and slipped him an additional tip when we found out how many children he had at home.

The pleasant afterglow of our tour was doused by the hotel management. The young woman at the desk hailed me and told me that we would have to pay U.S. $5 per day for using their mooring. Since I was in possession of a brochure which the hotel had distributed throughout the islands advertising free moorings to all yachts, I took exception to the charge. I demanded to see the manager. The desk clerk did better than that: she got me the owner, who had been having drinks with some hotel guests on the veranda. He was a very light-skinned islander, well dressed and rather corpulent, with a smooth shiny skin and a small black mustache. He looked as if he could be a pretty nice guy, but the look he turned on me as he approached was far from friendly.

"You wanted to speak with me?" he said coldly.

"I certainly do," I said. "I'm Gordon Stuermer, the owner and captain of the large American yacht which is currently attached to one of your moorings. My wife, my son, and another couple are aboard with me and we are on the first part of a world cruise. We picked up your mooring here because we were given one of your brochures advertising a free mooring for transient yachts for a reasonable period of time. I am now informed by the girl at your desk that I'm being charged five dollars per day for its use. I'd like an explanation."

He said quickly, "Well, you must understand that the moorings are free only to those yachts who make use of the hotel facilities."

"I understand no such thing," I answered. "Your brochure does not stipulate any provision on the use of a mooring. Furthermore, as far as that goes, we have made use of your bar, expensive as it is!"

"Well, we can't just let any yacht pick our mooring and then just use the hotel lobby as a transient point for island hopping."

I was beginning to see what had bugged this guy, but I decided to stay on the attack.

"I don't see why I can't do exactly that," I said. "I repeat, your brochure invites any transient yacht to pick up a free mooring. Most hotels are damned glad to have a few attractive yachts anchored in the bay beneath their guest quarters because in general they add a lot of interest to the scenery. Is that not so?"

"Well, yes," he said, "and you have a very nice ship. But you are not really making use of the hotel facilities. We are, after all, in business to make money. We do have island tours leaving the hotel every day and we generally arrange these tours for our guests through the hotel."

Ah, now it comes out! I said, "Do you mean to tell me that this sudden charge for the mooring is due to the fact that we took a tour of the island without arranging it through your hotel?"

"Well," he said, "it is customary—after all, we have a large investment here. It is a commercial venture we have worked hard to build up and we must protect our interests."

"Well, I'll tell you that we must protect our interests too, and when we find we can take a tour for one-half the cost which your hotel advertises, believe me, we'll take it. However, I do not believe that the tour cost is the primary bone of contention. I say once again that you have advertised free moorings for transient yachts, and your advertisement does not state any provisions. This constitutes false advertising, does it not?"

His eyes started wandering from point to point around the outdoor lobby. His voice was quite conciliatory now, and he said, "Well, Mr. Stuermer, I'll tell you what we'll do. We won't charge you for the mooring. How's that?"

"That's just fine," I said, "but to ease your mind, I've decided just now that we'll move the ship in the morning. We don't want to stay where we're not wanted."

"Oh, that's not necessary," he said. "Please make use of the mooring as long as you wish."

"Thank you, it's very kind of you, I'm sure, but we'll move on at first light tomorrow morning. I would, however, like to make one suggestion to you. You should send out new brochures as soon as you can, stating the provisions by which yachts can use your 'free' moorings. Then there will be less chance of misunderstandings in the future. It may also help you to know that, in general, cruising yachtsmen are generally a fairly frugal bunch. We can't afford expensive meals, expensive drinks and expensive tours. And one of the primary advantages of owning our own yacht is the independence it gives us. So, thank you for your hospitality, and good-by."

He held out his hand and said, "Good-by, please come again."

"Sure, next time around." We went back to the boat, all of us angry. Keren was very upset, but the confrontation became more amusing as we thought about it, and by sunset we'd rolled the incident from our backs. Dominica was still a beautiful island and we'd had a good time. Also, we had planned on leaving at first light anyway.

By 0700 we were on a beam reach and roaring across the channel separating Dominica from Martinique.

We dropped the anchor at 1600 hours at Anchorage des Flamands in

Baie de Fort-de-France. Kind of interesting getting in there—not at all spooky like some of the places we'd dumped the hook. For one thing, the anchorage is so big there is never any worry about going aground. As we closed with the anchorage we saw a real collection of boats there, about 40 in all, and we happily motored among them looking at the different rigs. We kept an eye out for a spot with enough swinging room to make us feel comfortable and found one fairly far out with about 35 feet of water on top of it. The big Herreshoff went down again with 35 fathoms of chain following along behind.

Everyone helped get the launch over the side in the traditional manner—with a drink in one hand. And I went ashore to clear the ship into our second French port, a procedure which was absolutely painless here. I checked with the nearest boat and was directed to a low brown building with a light green roof right on the waterfront, sporting a big sign which read "Martinique Charter Service."

The immigration officer was a slim, dapper gent who spoke good English and had a fine sense of humor. He had me fill out the declaration in triplicate and sign it, and that was that. No fee and no ominous warnings—very refreshing!

"Keep me informed of your whereabouts if you move the ship, monsieur—and do not kidnap any girls from the island. At least not the pretty ones. Au revoir."

Ah, Martinique! The first of the Windward Islands.

6

Through the Windwards and Make a Right Turn

The morning was hot and the harbor was glassy under the mid-December sun. At 0900 a small breeze worked its way down the mountain and through the town, began ruffling the water of the harbor, and caused the entire population of Martinique to lift its arms from its sides and say, "Ahhhh."

Having cleared, I walked back out on the dock carrying the ship's papers in their waterproof zip-folder and stood a moment delighting in the sound of French being spoken by the many people coming and going.

I shoved the launch clear of its many brethren floating in a big scramble of bow painters on the lee side of the dock, pulled on the starting cord, and carved a circle around the dock, dodging mooring buoys for the first 100 yards. I got a fix on the square yard, which I could pick out easily from the many masts outlined against the western sky, and headed for home to report progress.

We all went ashore. The launch was left tied to the end of what is called the dinghy dock. The gendarmes had assured me it would be quite safe there and it was, probably because there was nearly always a gendarme standing on the dock keeping an eye on the group of young pirates which gathered there to prey on the tourists as they disembarked from the cruise ship shore boats.

Our schoolbook French managed to get us cold beer at a pleasantly cool and dark bar on the Rue de la Liberté, after which we explored the town.

The Martinique people were quite helpful to us and very patient, in an amused way, with our poor French. Several went out of their way to direct us here and there; to the bank, the post office, the market.

We motored back to *Starbound* well after dark, tired and happy, discussing plans for the next day.

In the morning Nina stuffed her fishnet shopping bag into her purse and announced her intention to find lettuce, milk, bread, and meat. Don and Keren wanted to explore Martinique in depth and buy gifts for friends and family. Ernie and I decided to square the ship away, put on the sail covers, and then see if there was a sailmaker in town. The seams of the raffee were giving way and restitching seemed in order.

After taking the shoppers ashore, Ernie and I stopped by the small white sloop where I had acquired directions to the port authorities the previous afternoon and met her owner and captain, Horst Richter. Horst knew just where we could get our raffee stitched up: right on his boat. He was quite a competent sailmaker and owned a hand-cranked zigzag machine which kept him in eating money. We invited him over to *Starbound* for a tour and to look at our sail problem, and so got well acquainted. Horst worked in town and had been living in Fort-de-France aboard his boat for several months with his very attractive girlfriend. He planned to start cruising again as soon as his bank account looked healthy enough.

I studied the dinghy dock with the big ten-power binoculars and saw no sign of the shopping contingent, so I went ashore with Horst and Ernie to be introduced to the peculiarities of a French post office. It helped that Horst spoke a fair brand of French.

Our new "yankee" jib had not arrived. I had been certain that it would be here. Now what? I started thinking in terms of a wire to our Hong Kong sailmaker. Well, perhaps in a few more days . . .

Those few more days went by rapidly. We put Don and Keren and lots of packages in a taxi to the airport on the thirteenth of December, homeward bound. Bob and Edna Zahn arrived in the middle of the night two days later. They would go south to Grenada with us and then west on the 400-mile hop to Curaçao.

I'd been waiting up for them and finally heard a faint shout from the direction of the dinghy dock. I ran the outboard in and there they stood, with a few bits of hand luggage. The airlines had done it again. Bob and Edna's seabags were somewhere in Florida (the airline thought).

On the island of Saint Lucia, there is a harbor called Marigot Bay. It is reputed to be one of the most beautiful small bays in the entire world, and it had long been a dream of ours to be anchored there aboard our own ship. We decided it would be the perfect place to spend Christmas.

Three days later Bob and Edna's luggage turned up. Christmas was just one week away. We started to hustle. A phone call to Hong Kong got us the information that our sail had been air-freighted the day before via Los Angeles, New York, and Miami and probably wouldn't arrive for another week and maybe not then. I also found out that a five-minute conversation with a person halfway around the world costs $25. I arranged to have the sail forwarded to Curaçao.

Bob and I found a decrepit little outboard motor repair shop perched on the bank of the Rivière Levassor. Buried under a heap of moldering parts in the back corner of the shop we found an ancient, scratched, and greasy cowl which would fit my outboard motor, replacing the one we'd lost in Isles des Saintes. After much bargaining, which included animated arm waving, agonized screams, and simulated heart attacks, I bought it for $15 (they started at $50). I guess I was fortunate at that. The little shop suffered from that condition known as the Only Game in Town.

We made arrangements with the fuel dock located on the far side of the bay to pick up diesel fuel and water on Friday morning, so we spent Wednesday and Thursday filling out our stores lists. Nina found an American-type supermarket called Monoprix which had an extensive stock, reasonable prices, and a polite staff. I found a duty-free liquor store and bought Mount Gay Eclipse Rum by the case at a price which made me think that I could afford to drink after all.

Thursday afternoon, while striking our stores below, we looked up to see a big, beautiful schooner sail into the harbor, round up into the light breeze, and drop her hook not far away. It was *Shearwater*. We spent the evening talking with our good friend Captain Jim Shearston once again and traded tales of North Atlantic storms and Caribbean island hopping. Jim had just come north from Grenada with a charter party and would return in a few days with another one, so we worked up a radio contact schedule which would keep us in touch with each other as we wended our separate ways southward.

My pocket notebook was full of information about the Windward Islands—too full. There are so many "good" anchorages that the cruising sailor is overwhelmed with the possibilities. We were on a schedule, so since we couldn't visit all of the "good" anchorages we wanted to visit only a select number of the "best." Jim dragged out some charts and we used them for oversized drink coasters while he showed me where he thought the "best" places were.

Schedule! What a terrible word! At least the connotation is terrible. We had to be at a certain place by a certain time. We were becoming very aware of the disadvantages of carrying "passengers" while on an extensive cruise. Of course, none of our friends were passengers in the true sense. They were working crew who were kicking in enough dough to offset the cost of feeding them, plus a small amount for the boat. But they all had jobs at home to which they must return by such and such a time. And they all wanted to see and experience as much as they could during their relatively short time aboard. So a sense of urgency prevailed, and over no person so much as over the captain of our ship. I kept wanting to Jack London my way out of it. Perhaps every time someone pseudo-casually mentioned a date I should scream, "Monstrous and inconceivable!"

We made our run across the bay to the fuel dock next morning and topped off all of our tanks. It was then that the fuel people decided to tell me that I should have gotten a paper from the customs officials which would have allowed me to buy duty-free fuel. We were asked to pay the equivalent of 65 cents per gallon. Since acquiring the proper paper would take another day and another run across the bay, we paid it—but not before I told them what I thought of them for not telling me two days before.

We returned to our anchorage off Fort-de-France and I took the ship's papers once again to the customs and immigration office to clear *Starbound* for Saint Lucia. Once again my favorite official, M'sieu Breton, was fast, efficient, and amusing. "You are free to leave Martinique, M'sieu Stooair-mair, but not before eight in the morning. Please come again to beautiful Martinique. Adieu."

The anchor came aboard at 0800 next morning. It was Saturday, December 22. By 1600 we were putting the hook down in Vigie Cove near the town of Castries on the island of Saint Lucia.

Rhapsodies of prose have been written about each attractive anchorage in the West Indies. Suffice it to say that Vigie Cove is superior. That means it is pretty and protected, and it has good holding ground for any kind of anchor, and supplies are available close by, including fuel and water, and no charges are imposed.

We went Christmas shopping and parts shopping. Bob and I made some phone calls to track down an elusive resistor which might make the motor generator work properly. Then we took a wild taxi ride up a mountain with a driver who seemed to be in training for the Pike's Peak hill-climb race, to find the man who had the part we needed. After that we took an even wilder ride back down the mountain after I discovered that I'd cleverly left my wallet stashed in a booth at the telephone exchange.

Some splendid person had turned the wallet in to the clerk at the telegram counter and as I burst through the door of the exchange she waved at me and grinned widely, "Eet ees here, eet ees here!"

We found Nina and Edna at a crowded market buying a frozen turkey and the other holiday dinner trimmings for only about twice U.S. prices. Part of the American Christmas tradition seems to include a meal the size of which could keep an average Caribbean family going for a month.

Nina also discovered for sale huge 10-kilo blocks of New Zealand cheddar cheese. Cheese is a big favorite on *Starbound,* so she bought a block. I know cheese is a great source of protein, but all I could think of was "Where the hell are we going to keep it?"

We spent the next day, a quiet Sunday, decorating our little fake Christmas tree, which is designed to stand upright on the sideboard in the main saloon. It's green-fake, not pink-fake or blue-fake, and it looks very real. Our tree ornaments are traditional and some of them are quite old. Nina and I like the traditional stuff: Tiny Tim, cranberries, sugarplum fairies, the whole bit.

We sprayed a smitch of pine scent around the cabin from one of those pressurized cans and then tried to decide if it smelled like a Christmas tree or the men's room at a bus station. We all had a drink of Tanqueray on the rocks with just a shot or two of tonic water and a half a lime squeezed in and then decided it smelled like Christmas.

Marigot Bay was once used to conceal the whole British West Indies fleet from a numerically superior French navy during one of the battles for Saint Lucia. The British ships tied palm fronds to their masts to resemble the palm trees on the sand spit which hides the bay. We had heard this story and discredited it until we tried to spot Marigot Bay from one mile offshore. If we hadn't known it was there we wouldn't have tried to approach the coast, much less enter the bay.

It had taken us just over one hour to sail from Castries to Marigot and we were anchored inside the lagoon by noon. There were six other yachts anchored inside that fine little blown-out crater. The hills rise steeply on all sides with many houses showing bits and pieces of themselves through the tropical foliage coating the flanks of the old caldron. Marigot has been discovered.

We busied ourselves visiting a few other yachts and exploring the shoreline of the bay. Then we returned to *Starbound* and sat on the afterdeck and watched the sun set behind the palms scattered thickly on the sand spit. It was a beautiful sight—until a high-powered outboard motorboat came sweeping around the end of the spit towing a water skier. So much for paradise.

We had a merry Christmas, with good friends, good cheer, and good food. We gave each other small gifts and lots of well wishes, ran the launch around to all the other yachts, and wished everyone the merriest, then returned to *Starbound* and entertained some visitors in turn while dinner was in the oven. In the cool of the evening we ate hugely and returned to the afterdeck in a state of semiparalysis.

In the morning we retrieved our anchor from the mud bottom of the bay and got under way for Bequia (pronounced "Beck-wee"). Going directly from Saint Lucia to Bequia we bypassed the island of Saint Vincent, something we were very sorry to do, but that "schedule" was pushing us.

So we arrived in the Grenadines, that group of islands which are scattered in the Caribbean Sea over the 65 nautical miles between Saint Vincent and Grenada. Collectively they are low and dry with lots of cactus on them. The islands are surrounded by what may be the bluest, clearest water in the world.

Starbound sailed a broad reach down to Admiralty Bay and motored into the anchorage with some fierce wind bullets coming down the hills, over the town of Port Elizabeth, and banging her right on her broad bow. At least thirty boats were there, making a very crowded anchorage. We had some anxious moments finding a slot to fit into so that we could drop our hook and fall back on the chain into a relatively clear area. The strong and constant trades kept all the boats hanging the same way and the water was smooth in the lee of the island, so we felt secure, in spite of the fact that only 30 feet of water separated us from the boats off either beam.

Entry was simple. I took our passports and three copies of the crew list ashore and found the police station. The passports and one copy of the crew list were stamped and handed back to me and that was all. No charge this time. I could never tell whether or not I would be charged at each of these small places. There didn't seem to be any set rule. And the charge varied from island to island, anywhere from U.S. $1 to $3. We'd talked to other skippers who'd had the same problem. Some of them had been charged for entry at places which cost us nothing, and vice versa. We just played it by ear.

I went back for the crew and we repaired to the Whaleboner Inn, which is visited by every boat cruising the West Indies. The bar is fashioned from a whale's jawbone and the barstools are made from sections of vertebrae. The decor struck me as being a touch macabre, but the people running the place were very nice. A very small West Indian boy constructed excellent rum punches for us and his little sister served them with a proud flourish and a big smile.

We spent the next two days wandering around the countryside, buying fishing gear and cold beer at an establishment called Lulley's up the hill near the harbor, and trying to reach Martinique by telephone to find out if our sail had arrived yet.

The distance between Bequia and Fort-de-France is only about 80 miles, but guess how the telephone circuits are routed? Through Paris! That's right; all calls to and from Martinique go through Paris, France. How nationalistic can you get? One charming lady we met who'd lived on Bequia for some time, told us that she'd managed to get through to Martinique about three years ago, but not since.

I remembered a name Jim Shearston had given me. Ken Walker of

Antilles Yacht and Equipment Company. I found him with no trouble at all. Port Elizabeth is a very small town. Ken cranked up his big radio and called the yacht *Aquarius* which was anchored right off Fort-de-France. John Lawrence, who was Ken's business partner, answered and told us that he would check on the status of the sail and call us back at 1600. When the call came through, John told us that the sail had arrived in Martinique and was being forwarded to Curaçao that very day.

Radio is the only decent means of communication in the West Indies. Unfortunately, I didn't obtain the right crystals for our little rig before I left the United States, and when I found out what I needed it was too late. I was already in the West Indies and nobody had them to sell. The frequency that seems to be the most valuable is 2527 kHz. Everybody monitors that frequency twice each day, and if you're out of range anyone will relay your message.

There are over thirty good anchorages in the Grenadines. We passed about ten of them on the way from Bequia to Charlestown Bay on the island of Cannouan. We skipped Le Quatre Island and Baliceaux. And we let Mustique and Petit Mustique slide by our port beam. We ignored Savan Island and Petit Cannouan and so came to big Cannouan.

The books are correct. The Grenadines are dry isles. Oh, are they dry! Our anchorage was well protected and the anchor was set hard. The water was supremely blue and the fish were biting well enough so that Edna caught us a very tasty breakfast by merely hand-lining over the side. But the land above the shore was brown and sere and covered with a broadleaf prickly cactus plant.

An ancient Baltic trader named *Wernadia* came bonk-chonking into the anchorage not too long after *Starbound,* and after her huge rusty hook got settled into the bottom we went over to visit them. There were several young guys and girls aboard, all of them in their twenties, and one baby girl. The baby belonged to Skip and Roxanne Gordon, who came from the state of Washington. Skip was the skipper, naturally.

Wernadia was a working cargo vessel and she was engaged in hauling fruit and vegetables between Dominica, her home port, and the other islands, primarily Barbados. The way I figured it, without really asking, was that Skip and Roxanne owned the boat and the rest of the crew worked on shares. They were evidently making a nice buck out of it. Skip was talking about cashing in shortly and buying a cruising boat. He wanted to follow *Starbound*'s path.

There were a couple of interesting calico cats on board whose diet fascinated us. They subsisted entirely on cockroaches, with which the boat was overrun, and an occasional rat for Sunday dinner. It was an experience to watch one of them, seemingly asleep on the chart table, cock open one eye and then become a flashing streak of multicolored fur as he scooped up a hot grounder, then sit down, delicately eat his catch, and spit out the wings.

We spent the next morning swimming and lazing and in the afternoon weighed anchor and made a 6-mile run to Salt Whistle Bay on Mayereau Island. The bay has a long horseshoe-shaped beach lined with seagrape and coconut trees. It is reputed to be one of the prettiest anchorages in the Grenadines, pretty enough to justify spending an extra day there.

We spent most of that extra day ashore. Bob and Edna found a pathway through the seagrape across the narrow isthmus which separates the bay from the eastern shore. The trade winds blow right onto that east shore and the reef extends out several hundred yards from a white sand beach. We beachcombed for miles, dazzled by the colors of the water over the reef. We could look across the reef to the east and see the Tobago Cays just two miles away: tomorrow's goal.

None of us had done any "reef running" before. Sure, we'd read all about it—the sun behind you, and a man in the crosstrees, and a certain color of water means such and such—but we'd never really done it. The Tobago Cays were our first real introduction to the romantic-sounding procedure.

The problem with having a man in the crosstrees while running a reef is that the helmsman wishes he were up there too, or instead. Coming up to the Tobago reef Bob and Ernie were both aloft am I was at the wheel. All I could hear from them was, "Hey, look!" and "Wow, is that pretty!" and, "Look over there—see that?"

Finally I yelled, "Come on, you guys, am I headed O.K. or am I going to take the bottom out of her?"

We eased down the west side of Petit Rameau and then turned left between it and Petit Bateau, where most of the boats anchor. We shared the anchorage with eight other yachts, including *Shearwater.*

What a swimming pool! The very best anchorage in the Grenadines. We could see *Starbound*'s shadow on the bottom, and the anchor chain was visible all the way to the bottom, where it left squiggly snake tracks on the white sand. We had our masks, snorkels, and fins broken out in record time. I dove to the bottom in 15 feet of crystal water, followed our chain to the anchor, and held onto the upper fluke. I could see where the bottom curved up to meet the beach 50 yards on either side of me. Little striped fish swam around my head. Grinning broadly with a diving mask on makes it leak.

We spent three delightful days in that beautiful spot. The time seemed to flash by in an orgy of swimming, gin drinking, talking, eating, and boat hopping.

It was time to go. Our fresh water supply was getting low and Jim Shearston had advised us to pick some up at Union Island. There was a hotel and yacht club dock located on the eastern end of the island where water was available. So we did some more tricky maneuvers through the reefs, taking the south passage out of Tobago Cays, and made another short run of 5 nautical miles. You can always see your next anchorage in the Grenadines.

During the past seven years, whenever *Starbound* needed water we'd just motor her over to the nearest dock, hook up some hose, and fill up all four tanks. At Union Island it was a different story. There was a dock there all right, but not enough water depth for *Starbound* in front of it. We had to pick up a yellow mooring buoy which floated about 150 feet off the dock head, then carry a line from our stern to the dock and warp the stern over until the water hose would reach our tank openings. We didn't know it at the time but we were in training for the future.

We decided to spend the night in Clifton Harbor, so after our tanks were filled we let go our line to the buoy and motored over to a clear spot for swinging room.

We left for Grenada the next morning. It would be our point of departure for Curaçao.

Grenada had long wanted her independence from the British and finally got it. From then on, things got worse.

A few months before our arrival at that fair island, one political faction in opposition to the current government had expressed its displeasure by shooting up a conference with submachine guns, killing several people and wounding many others.

We had heard of these problems from other boats all the way down the chain of islands and we had seriously considered giving the island a miss in spite of its vaunted beauty. But we'd also conferred with Jim Shearston while we were anchored with *Shearwater* in the Tobago Cays, and Jim told us that everything was peaceful there for the time being.

We sailed into Saint George's Harbor, then slid through the well-marked entry channel into the yacht anchorage known as the Lagoon. We had expected to see a large charter fleet there, but the docks looked half empty and only a few yachts were anchored out. We anchored out too.

We only spent two days in the Lagoon. We walked around town and got stared at and glared at. And we made our pilgrimage to the famous Nutmeg Restaurant which overlooks the Carenage from the second floor of a waterfront building. The food and drinks were very good but the prices were quite high and the service from the black waitresses was superbly indifferent. So it goes.

We took a taxi out to Prickly Bay to visit *Shearwater* and Jim suggested that we get out of town with our boat and bring her around to the south end of the island and into that fine bay. A big yacht charter headquarters is located there and they have fuel, water, ice, laundry facilities, and marine supplies. We figured we might as well move *Starbound* over. Our decision was colored a bit by finding out that we should keep someone on our boat at all times in the Lagoon because of the very high incidence of thefts. A visiting yacht had been pretty well stripped just the week before.

We liked Prickly Bay. There were a few small supermarkets nearby and we finally got a taste of friendly Grenadan hospitality. We had started to think that it was gone forever.

Jim took us all out to dinner at the famous Red Crab Restaurant and we were not disappointed. Everything was superb. He also took us for a ride up to one of the most beautiful hotels we had seen in the islands. It was designed in a Spanish hacienda manner, perched on a seaside cliff overlooking a splendid view of the sea, and was very well appointed and almost empty.

We decided to go to the big supermarket in town the next day, pick up the remaining supplies we needed, and get under way for Curaçao.

Because of the political unrest on the island, most of the stores in town were closed. We couldn't figure out why, beyond some garbled explanations of a strike of some kind. The supermarket manager finally opened up the place for two hours on a limited-customer basis. That meant he'd only let five people into the store at a time. We waited in line for over an hour and then just Nina and Edna went in and picked up our stores. Nina was really happy to find eggs for sale. They were the first eggs we'd been able to buy since Martinique.

We taxied our goodies back out to Prickly Bay and ferried them out to *Starbound.* Then we raised our anchor, motored up near the fuel dock, and dropped it again. We pulled the stern over near the dock with almost practiced efficiency and managed to get the fuel hose aboard without dropping it into the water.

I left the fueling job to Ernie and Bob, gathered up the ship's papers again, and walked up to the Customs House. This was a different outfit from the one where we'd entered over in Saint George, but the attitudes were familiar.

I had been warned to enter and clear during working hours in Grenada, or to be prepared to pay stiff overtime charges. So here it was about 1545 hours, and quitting time for these people was 1600.

I sat there, waiting politely. They sat there, ignoring me. At 1555 I got to my feet, stretched, and said to them, "I wanted to clear for Curaçao this afternoon, but if you guys don't take care of my papers within the next five minutes I'm going back to my boat and wait till tomorrow, 'cause I'm damned if I pay you any overtime charges."

They looked at each other, startled. They looked at me. I stood there, still smiling. One of them reached out his hand and said, "All right, let's have 'em." Five minutes later I walked back to the boat. We were cleared for Curaçao.

For the benefit of those who might find the numbers game interesting:

On January 7 at 1645, Saline Point, the southernmost point on the island of Grenada, came abeam of *Starbound.* On January 10 at 1000 we were motoring up Saint Anna Bay, which cuts its way through the city of Willemstad on the Dutch-owned island of Curaçao. *Starbound* had maintained an average of 6 knots for sixty-six hours under square sail and raffee only. The wind had been a constant 15 to 18 knots from the east for the entire time. The waves stayed at about 5 to 6 feet from the east-northeast for the entire time. The barometer had never dropped below 30 inches.

We all made prayers to various gods that all of our passages should be so fast and uneventful.

7

To Panama via Curaçao and Cartagena

Starbound has been called a topsail ketch, a coasting ketch, a square sail ketch, and even "that there brigantine." I guess the term *square sail ketch* is the least confusing nomenclature for a cruising ketch which happens to carry a single sizable square yard on the mainmast. The yard is 40 feet long from tip to tapered tip, is 10 inches in diameter at its center, and weighs about 300 pounds. It's mounted on a chain and swivel arrangement in such a way that it can be braced 45 degrees to either side or cockbilled so that the ends of the yard can be tilted downward against the shrouds. The square sail (a purist would call it the main course) is a bit over 700 square feet in area. On top of the yard we set a sail called a raffee, which is a triangular sail and is set "flying" from three points; both ends of the yard and the truck of the main-topmast. The raffee is a little over 300 square feet. Since we usually carry both sails at the same time, our downwind rig gives us about 1,050 square feet of sail.

The trip from Grenada to Curaçao gave us our first chance to carry the square sail and raffee for a long enough period to really evaluate their performance at sea. It doesn't seem like all that much sail to push 35 tons of ketch through the water, but Bill Deed must have known what he was doing when he designed her. *Starbound* went 408 nautical miles in sixty-five hours, averaging a bit over 6 knots. The wind blew an unceasing 15 to 18 knots right on her stern. The following sea height was a constant 4 to 6 feet, and the barometer needle hardly wiggled either side of 30 inches the whole way. We varied in our course only once, a mere 10-degree change to give sea room to a few lonesome rocks called El Roque and Isla Aves.

On one star-filled night I was watching Nina at the helm and listening to the swish of water sliding past the hull and spinning off astern in swirls of phosphorescence. She exclaimed, "Gee, I wish all of our passages were like this—this is neat!" I had to agree. It was neat.

We were going to stop at Curaçao for several reasons: it was on the way, it was supposed to be a very good supply port with duty-free shops, our new yankee jib was waiting for us at the airport, and we had to switch crews.

Bob and Edna Zahn had to fly back to Washington, D.C., and our bachelor friend, Ray Kukulski, would join us for the Panama Canal trip and the big Pacific jump.

While sailing to Curaçao we scoured our library looking for more definitive information on the island than the Sailing Directions give. We didn't find much. Even a fairly recent book, *Beyond the West Horizon* by the famous Hiscocks, brushed the place off with a paragraph. Two phrases in that paragraph worried me: "... water was coated with oil," and "... most expensive place that we have ever visited."

Curaçao is a dry, fairly flat island about 40 miles long east and west and about 10 miles wide. It's the largest of the six islands composing the Netherlands Antilles and is located about 50 nautical miles northwest of Venezuela, where all of the crude oil comes from to get refined in the big plants near Willemstad.

The internal government is fully autonomous, although external affairs are administered by an appointee of the Dutch government. About 85 percent of the population of about 150,000 is black. However, they don't like being called "black," a term that seems to be popular only in those countries influenced by the "black power" movement. I guess you'd call them "Papiamenteros" since Papiamento is the unofficial principal language spoken there. It's a wild-sounding mixture of Dutch, Spanish, and English plus a little Caribbean gumbo tossed in.

Willemstad is the capital, the largest city, the primary harbor (the only one for big ships), and the port of entry.

Everyone makes mistakes, generally because of insufficient data. After all, one wouldn't step in a fresh pile of cow manure if one knew it was there, right? Wrong! We had been told and had read about the black oil that floats all over Saint Anna Bay in Willemstad. We simply refused to believe that there could be so much of it as to give us a problem.

We motored on and off the harbor entrance for about 30 minutes before the famous Queen Anna pontoon bridge opened up its 500-foot span and let us do a right-end sneak into the canal, a 3-mile cut leading to the big harbor where all the oil tankers go—but not the yachts. A gray police launch with big block letters on its side spelling DOUANE (Customs) told us where to tie up; right against the side of the huge canal. We looked at the monstrous sheet steel pilings and timber bulkheading dripping with black, sticky oil and shuddered. A constant chop stirred up by the tugs and police boats ensured a good splash effect. Now we could see patches of floating oil all over the water's surface.

The officials commanded us to tie up to the bulkheading, so we did. They boarded us and we proceeded to fill out many forms. They searched the boat—God knows what for. They claimed to be looking for weapons, but in the tea canister?

After the search was complete they were a bit more polite, but that didn't help the hull paint. It was enough to make you cry. It made Nina cry. *Starbound* had a complete coating of cruddy crude, or Bunker-C, or whatever the hell it's called, right up to the guard rail. I still had to check in with the port captain and Immigration and by the time I'd completed that and returned to the quayside, there was virtually no white paint left showing on the hull. The spring lines were dripping with the stuff from the backslop off the bulkheading. Very discouraging.

Well, the damage was done. We decided to check out the town, find where the supply points were located, and then see if we could locate a clean anchorage from which we could operate.

Furious action for the next two days resulted in the stores being ordered (400 dollars' worth), money wired for (vis Bank of America in downtown Willemstad), the laundry done (courtesy of the local brothel, whose girls were daylighting), the new jib picked up (at a shocking price for air freight and duty), and, best of all, a clean anchorage found.

Just west of oily Saint Anna Bay is a small indentation in the coastline called Pescadero Bay, on the eastern point of which is located the Curaçao Hilton hotel. There's a narrow but navigable slot at the back of the small bay which leads to a pretty little inland lake locally called "the lagoon."

We decided to move the next day but first we said our good-bys to Bob and Edna. We helped them stack their seabags in a taxi and kissed them good-by and off for the airport they drove, with all of us waving like tourists. Bob's last words as he looked at the oily topsides were, "Gordon, that's going to be one hell of a job."

We thought it would simplify matters if we watered up the boat in Saint Anna Bay before motoring around to the lagoon. So we made another mistake. We had to go to the big bunkering docks to get water, which in itself should have been a simple task, but it took the workmen at the dock four hours to locate and fetch the hoses and couplings to adapt their huge pipelines to our relatively small tank filler openings. It was late afternoon before we got out of the bay.

We anchored in the lagoon by the stern, with the bow pointing at the shore only 20 feet away and secured thereto by two lines attached to big iron posts set into the coral-lined shore. The scenery on the banks was sterile—crushed coral and mangrove—but the water was clear, clean, and blue with not a trace of oil in sight, except for the gluck on our hull.

We started to clean the topsides with a bucket of diesel oil and an old towel. Wipe, sponge, wring out, wipe again—for two days! Ernie did most of the really dirty work. After the heavy deposit of crud had been soaked loose, we commenced scrubbing off the residual brown stains with a highly concentrated liquid detergent called Teepol. We found if we mixed some powdered cleanser with that, the hull finally came white again with diligent application of elbow grease. Of course, the paint gloss was long gone, but at least the oil was gone with it.

Ray Kukulski arrived right in the middle of the whole sweaty operation and we put him to work as soon as he'd unpacked his seabag and found his raunchy shorts. He'd left a cold, wintery Washington, D.C., just a few hours earlier and there he was, crouched in a dinghy in 90-degree weather under a tropical sun, scrubbing down the side of a boat. I made him keep a shirt on so he wouldn't get broiled. He kept looking at me and shaking his head. I could hear him mumbling, "What is this? I'm supposed to be on a cruise!"

Nina had ordered our stores from a ship's chandlery called Henderson's. They gave her quick, courteous service and had a very extensive selection of groceries. Furthermore they wouldn't accept payment until all of the stores had been delivered to the boat, a refreshing change from the usual "cash in advance, take care of your own delivery" drill we'd gone through in Martinique and Grenada. Henderson's brought the stores right down to the waterfront, stacked them on the beach, and offered to help us ferry them out to the boat, but I let Nina pay the bill while Ernie, Ray, and I loaded boxes, bags, and bales into the launch, paddled the few feet out to *Starbound,* and stacked the stuff above and below. Then it was a full afternoon's job to get everything unpacked and stowed properly in bins, bilges, and lockers. Except for the eggs.

We had thirty dozen fresh, never-before-refrigerated eggs to grease. The reason we grease them is to make nature's nice little container even more airtight than it already is. An absolutely fresh egg will last easily over thirty days in an unrefrigerated condition and still taste fine. If a good coating of grease is rubbed into the shell, they'll last ninety days. We'd used vegetable shortening to grease the batch we brought from the United States, but it tends to get a little moldy after two months in a warm bilge, so this time we were using petroleum jelly.

Greasing eggs is a long messy job. I guess Ray figured we needed help, so he wandered over to the Hilton and captured three cute egg greasers.

That hotel was swarming with panting, humid, doe-eyed vacationing

New York working girls. Nina calls them "eye shadow junkies." I would like to see the brochures the travel agencies put out to lure all those little chicky-poos down to Curaçao. They must imply that droves of handsome single men are milling about just waiting to pounce and capture a nice American girl and carry her off into the rosy glow of American suburbia where she will have her very own three-bedroom, 2½-bath house with all-electric kitchen and raise fat bouncing babies and prepare delicious meals for her Paul Newman–type husband forever and ever, amen.

Ray gave three of them some memories. He brought them out to *Starbound* to "see a nice yacht" and we put them to work greasing eggs. They had names like Kathy and Sandy and Debbie.

Next day was Sunday and we spent it partying. It was another one of those good "just happened" parties. We'd seen a pretty white-hulled ketch named *Ilene Too* tied up stern-to at the Hilton dock and wondered whose it was, so we wandered over about noontime and met Ted and Ilene Waffa and their daughter Cindy from Huntington Beach, California.

One gin and tonic led to another and we transferred the party to *Starbound* so that Ted and Ilene could see our boat. A 36-foot power boat named *Eileen Ann* was moored next to *Starbound* with three personable young guys on board from Dania, Florida; Phil Chalker, Larry Howerton, and Martin Levy. So they came over too. Then Ray came back early, to my surprise—but he came back with a few more girls, so the party gained impetus with the addition of warm bodies.

Next morning I walked to the Hilton and rode the hotel bus into Willemstad. Then I blew the rest of the morning in the frustrating process of clearing the port. I trudged from customs to police to immigration to port captain's offices, all in widely separated locations.

I found a good marine hardware store hiding on a secondary street on the east side of town. I bought copper boat nails, and two eyebolts to go into the bow of the launch, and two half-inch single sheave blocks for spares, and two plastic squids for fishing. That exhausted my supply of "kroner," so I found the hotel bus stop and went back to *Starbound.*

That evening we used the moonlight to get our bow line off the stake on shore. Then we pulled the ship up to her stern anchor, which obligingly broke out of the sand without a tough fight. We motored out of the lagoon and past the hotel dock and called a soft good-by to *Ilene Too. Starbound* felt the surge of the Caribbean swell and she rolled gently until she was well clear of land and we could turn her downwind for Cartagena and set the square sail and raffee again.

Just west of Curaçao is the island of Aruba, and just west of Aruba is an unlighted group of islands called Islas Los Monjes (the Monks). The plan behind our nighttime departure from Curaçao was to clear those dangerous little islets during the daylight hours. At 1600 next afternoon we watched them slide by our port beam and disappear into the gathering blue dusk off our quarter.

We set our course to make a wide circle around the Guajira Peninsula. Well-founded rumors were floating around the cruising boats in the Caribbean that coastal pirates were on the make along the northern Colombian coast. Several yachts had indeed disappeared from that area over the last few years. Oddly enough, we took a sort of perverse pleasure in these rumors.

We made a wide sweep to the north such that by morning the coastline was out of sight in the haze, and then kept well out from the coast all the way down past the city of Barranquilla. The Sailing Directions mention that the big Magdalena River, near the mouth of which the city is located, can put out some debris and possible rough seas off its mouth inside the 100-fathom curve, so we stayed well off that underwater bank as we slid by. And still *Starbound* sailed for miles through an ocean discolored to a yellow brown by the silt being washed down the river and spread like a dirty fan far out into the blue sea.

As darkness came on we could see the loom of Barranquilla's lights reflected from the haze above the city. It was our fourth and last night out and Cartagena was just around the corner. Too close, actually. *Starbound* was ripping up the water at 7 knots under just the square sail. We'd doused the raffee before sunset when the wind decided to pick up to 20 knots from the northeast.

At 0200 I decided we'd have to slow the ship down by brailing up the square sail. Otherwise we'd have to heave to until daylight. After the square sail was secured, we could put up the main-staysail. It was a tough job in the dark, even with the help of the powerful spreader lights. Twenty knots of wind and 25-knot gusts kept pulling the fabric out of our hands as we tried to get it rolled tight enough to secure it with the shock cord which is semi-permanently attached to the yard. Eight-foot swells coming up astern kept trying to slew the ship around against the helmsman's pressure on the wheel. It took a good solid hour of grunting, straining, and cursing to make that sail change. We'd never tried it in those conditions before. But it's like building a barn. My grandpa used to say, "By the time you get it done, you know how." It would only take half an hour next time.

By 0800 we had turned the northwest corner of South America. The wind had dropped to a gentle 5-knot zephyr, the sea was smooth in the land's lee, and Isla Tierra Bomba was just ahead.

We urged *Starbound* through the Bocachica entrance to Cartagena Bay flanked by the impressive Castle of San Fernando to port and the equally impressive Fort San José to starboard. We were in Bahía de Cartagena. Now we had to turn *Starbound* back north for several miles to get her up to the city, which we could see skylined and gleaming in the morning sun, way up ahead of us. The wind should have been right in our faces but we were lucky. It was flat calm as it is so often on an early tropic morning and we motored along on a glassy bay with all binoculars working.

The Spanish discovery of Peru during the sixteenth century was the most likely factor leading to the founding and consolidation of Cartagena. They needed a Caribbean port as a jumping-off place for Spain to get the gold home which they had so gently removed from the Indians. Then, of course, they had to do something with those pesky natives who insisted they were taking a royal screwing, so by the middle of the seventeenth century Cartagena became the principal South American slave port, which contributed heavily to its economic prosperity.

The city reached its height of Spanish glory in the seventeenth and again in the eighteenth century, between being attacked and looted several times by pirates and foreign navies. In fact, the complaint was that you could hardly tell one from the other. Both Sir Frances Drake and the Baron de Pointis managed to take the city and sack it. As a defense against such unwelcome incursions, Cartagena built an impressive belt of walls and a series of strategically placed forts or castles. These defenses stand today in their full glory. They're not ruins. If the manpower were available and someone could whip up some old cannons, the city could be defended today just as in the past. Those fortifications make Cartagena so much more than just another city. The sense of history is overpowering. It takes very little imagination, while walking along those walls at night, to envision the shadows of Spanish sentries still patrolling the battlements.

We could see Bocagrande to our left as we approached the inner bay. Bocagrande means "big mouth," and Bocachica means "little mouth." It looks as if Bocagrande would be a good entrance to the city, certainly a lot closer than is Bocachica. But back in the old days the defenders of the city only wanted one entrance to the bay, and that as far away from the city as possible. So they closed off Bocagrande by building an underwater reef across the entrance. I guess natural coral formation took over from there. I keep wondering how many slaves died while constructing that underwater reef.

Past Castillogrande went *Starbound,* past the Base Naval, and into Bahía de las Animas right up under the city walls. There to starboard lies Fort San Sebastian del Pastelillo, the home of the Club de Pesca. Club is pronounced "cloob." That's where the yachts tie up. It's the only place where yachts tie up—that is, if said yacht doesn't want to get ripped off by every passing canoe. The Indians are trying to get some of their own back and they all carry screwdrivers and wrenches to help them do it.

What a bunch of classy yachts are there, all with their sterns turned to the big solid dock, and all with two anchors out off their bows. We put *Starbound* into a nice wide space near the dock's end, then carried out our second anchor with the launch. As our stern approached the dock, two dozen pairs of hands took our lines—mostly American hands.

With everybody talking at once we told them who we were and where we came from and where we were going. We got the same information back. Someone shoved a big cold bottle of Cartagena beer in my hand. What a welcome! What a place! The view of the city across the water of the bay looked like that Turner oil of Venice with its cathedral spires and domes. We were impressed.

The dockmaster, Señor Luis Calderón, walked down to the boat after the initial excitement had eased up and gave us an official but warm welcome to the club. He had called the port officials, who would be over sometime after midday to arrange our entry. It was expected that we pay their taxi fare, a customary custom (for customs?).

Water and electric power (115 volts 60 cycle) are laid on at the dock: lots of pure, drinkable water, and limited electricity but enough for battery charging. Fresh-water showers are available too. But best of all, all the cruising boats are there—a whole mess of 'em.

The Club de Pesca isn't free. Nor is it cheap. There's no charge for the first three days but after that it costs 10 cents U.S. per day per foot of overall length. So 50 feet of boat gets nailed for five bucks a day—payable weekly—in advance. We thought it was worth it, even though it was that old friend called The Only Game in Town. Of course, if a yacht is planning on making an extensive visit, I understand that some financial arrangement might be worked out with the club management. I personally found Señor Calderón to be *muy simpático*.

The fun started. Conservatively speaking, there were at least thirty yachts tied up to that big concrete dock. Just down the dock from *Starbound* was her little sister, the "Oxford" *Spray*, built by R. D. Culler in Oxford, Maryland, back in 1929. She was now owned by Ty and Doug Campbell, brothers from San Francisco. They bought her in the West Indies, I think, and were having a lot of work done to her there in Cartagena, where the labor rates are nice and low. She's supposed to be an exact replica of old Josh Slocum's *Spray*, being 41 feet overall. Ty and Doug were fascinated by *Starbound*, her being an enlarged version of *Spray*. We spent a lot of time crawling around in each other's boat and drinking beer and talking about square sails and self-steering and cruising.

We just couldn't bring ourselves to get all bothered about the required "whip-out." Not when beer cost 2 pesos (8 cents) per bottle. Not when diesel fuel costs 9 cents per gallon. Not when the four of us could go to town and get a good meal with beer for $1 each.

It's about a half-mile stroll into downtown Cartagena from Club de Pesca, and the scenery along the way is marvelous. The yachties usually walk into town and taxi back after their bags and baskets are full. Crossing the bridge from the Manga district, where the club is located to the Getsamany and Centro districts gives the pedestrian a spectacular view of the city wall-fortresses along the Laguna San Lazaro. It's difficult to view that stonework from a distance and keep any sense of scale. It's so huge, so massive, that one's sense of proportion goes haywire.

Once into the city the public square seems to be the target for everyone, the main meeting place. "Tell you what, John—I'll meet you in the square right there where the old lady sells the leather sandals, O.K.?" It's that kind of place. The mercado (market) is too busy to be a good meeting place. It's unbelievably crowded. But you can buy anything there. While walking around, Nina and I received within ten minutes offers to change money (at varying black market rates), to buy booze of all kinds (at an average price of $1 per bottle), to buy emeralds, to buy poor-quality hashish and cocaine and good-quality marijuana, to buy tickets to the bullfights, to go on a tour of the city, and finally, to sell any guns we might have. What a place! We picked up bread, milk, fresh vegetables, some excellent Fundador brandy, and a few other supplies, and headed back to the club.

The black market in Cartagena seems to operate on a wide-open basis. At least it did while we were there. From the club we could easily watch the daylight smuggling going on. Canoes would sail by one after the other with their huge dirt-brown flour sack sails pulling away, and their water lines right up to the gunwales, loaded with bags and crates and bundles of all shapes and sizes going directly to market. I guess "beat the tax man" is a worldwide game.

Nina and Ray spent one day taking a guided bus tour of the city. I didn't go because I had a local man and his two sons sanding and painting *Starbound*'s hull while I supervised and did topside maintenance. I heard great things about the tour when Nina and Ray returned that evening, mostly concerning the glories of Spanish history and architecture, but I felt that I was getting enough of that by osmosis while just wandering around town looking for things for the boat.

Ray was bitten by the emerald bug. Colombia has the world's prime emerald diggings and Cartagena is world-renowned as a fine place in which to buy them. So I went with Ray one day to one of the foremost emerald dealers in the city, who gave us a very interesting talk and demonstration on the difference between good and bad emeralds, and an indication of their prices. Ray told him he'd think about it for a while and come back.

One night we decided to go to a movie. Someone on the dock had mentioned that the Paul Newman picture about Judge Roy Bean was playing downtown, so a bunch of us hired a cab, argued the driver down to a decent price to carry us all, and went bonkety-queek off to the theater. What the "teatro" was, was an old bullfight ring—an arena which had been condemned for the bullfights because the ancient circular, wooden structure wasn't strong enough to carry big crowds anymore. Evidently the powers that be thought it was strong enough to carry a smaller movie crowd.

We sat in the presidential box, listening to the manic ravings of "Bad Bob" in English, reading the Spanish subtitles, and feeling the entire structure we were sitting on shift to our left each time a gust of wind struck its peeling painted sides. However, the place didn't collapse and we'd brought our own beer with us so we had a good time.

We hated to leave Cartagena but the time had come. We'd wanted to arrive at Panama by the end of January but here it was the first part of February and we still had quite a lot of salt water to cross.

I told the dockmaster that we wanted to leave on Tuesday, so bright and early Monday morning the port captain himself showed up and, with Luis acting as interpreter, introduced us to a young man about twenty-five years old named Jorge Selarón, a Chilean painter.

It turned out that young Jorge wanted to get to Panama to do some painting there. He'd about painted himself out in Colombia and wanted to see some fresh territory. Evidently Jorge's family is very influential in South America because the Colombian port captain was sponsoring Jorge to the hilt, telling us what a fine young man he is and urging us to take him with us.

So we said O.K. If he paid for his chow and stood watches with the rest of us, we'd take him to Panama—provided his passport and visa were in order. We only agreed after we'd talked with Jorge for a while. He didn't have much English but we managed to communicate. We thought it would be handy to have our very own interpreter aboard while cruising through the San Blas islands, which we planned to do for a few days on the way to Panama. Perhaps our Spanish and his English would both improve.

Jorge showed up with his gear that afternoon and we found out why he was reluctant to take a plane to Panama, which had been puzzling us. He had at least 500 pounds of paintings and paint supplies with him! All that gear would have cost him a fortune in overweight charges on any airline.

Tuesday morning we were cleared with politeness and dispatch. No list of charges was presented, even for taxi fare. And our dockmaster gave us a bill for dockage which we viewed with a good deal of surprise and pleasure. Evidently it helps to do favors for the local power structure.

We let go our stern lines and weighed our anchors while calling farewells to everyone on the dock. Then we motored over to the fuel depot and loaded up with nice clean diesel oil at that fantastic price of 9 cents per gallon. We also filled up the six big plastic containers we'd bought in town, which allowed us to carry another 100 gallons on deck. We strapped three containers to the bulwarks on each side deck.

Staysail and mizzen were set on the way down the bay, and then *Starbound* drove out of Bocachica on a broad reach to the west.

We slammed and bumped along for three days with the wind hooting at 18 to 20 knots from the east-northeast, pushing us across a lumpy sea. Then, as the sea moderated and the wind eased, *Starbound* came to the San Blas islands, a paradise on Earth—one of the few remaining.

The San Blas islands extend along about 200 miles of Panama's Caribbean coastline. The territory known as San Blas reaches from the seaward continental shelf to the top of the jungle-clad continental divide. Within this territory the Cuna Indians live and govern themselves in a virtually autonomous society. They make their homes on the hundreds of tiny palm-fringed islands which are scattered along the coast, almost at stepping distance to the mainland shore.

Every day most of the Indians commute from their island villages to the mainland in their dugout canoes (cayucos) to farm their crops, to wash their clothes in the rivers, to fish, and to trade. Some work the coconut crop on the outer islands. The coconut is still king, the crop their basic livelihood.

The Cunas are short, stocky people and are generally very friendly and charming. But I'd hate to get them mad at me. They have a reputation for being very able to take care of themselves. Whenever some wealthy American tries to start a tourist resort among their beautiful little cays, they chase him right back to Miami—and not too politely, either.

The Cuna women are amazing. Their everyday dress is the full regalia of embroidered mola-blouse, full long maxiskirt, gold nose ring and ear rings, beaded ornaments at neck, arms, waist, and ankles, and sometimes the white lace mantilla covering their short, black hair, which is always cut in bangs in a line traveling right across the eyebrows. The men, on the other hand, wear very undistinguished shirts and trousers. We were never able to find out if the men ever had a "traditional" dress before the "white man" came.

It's a matriarchal society in that the girls are allowed to choose their mates. Once the poor bloke has been pointed at, the final decision rests with him. That could be a tough decision, remembering that hell hath no fury, et cetera. Of course, as soon as he marries he is automatically part of her family, and works for her father—who is ruled by her mother. The women have the best of it for a change.

No yacht should sail near or among the San Blas islands at night. We had many charts and traded for a few more in Cartagena but still we were told, "Use 'em for guidance, not gospel."

We'd decided to visit a San Blas group called the Holandes Cays but we sighted Puyadas Island first, and since it was getting on in the afternoon we decided to find a place to anchor for the night. Puyadas was gorgeous, as are all of the cays, but it looked like an uneasy anchorage, so we ran downwind a few more miles to Farewell Island and anchored in its lee on a handy patch of sand between adjoining reefs.

Running *Starbound* right up to the beach to find water shallow enough for a good scope to the chain is a hairy proposition out there. The depth sounder isn't worth a damn because the transducer head is located well aft on the hull and the water is so clear that the helmsman's perspective goes to hell. We crept in dead slow, Ernie on the bow with a lead line, sounding constantly. The tidal rise and fall is small, so when Ernie called out 8 feet I backed the ship down and told him to trip the hook. It was a nice quiet anchorage and we all got a full night's sleep.

In the morning we had a quiet three-hour sail to the Holandes group and dropped anchor off Caobas Cay. The actual process of anchoring, with the bowsprit overhanging the white sand beach while the hook plummeted down, was anticlimactic after running the pass into the small lagoon. The channel through the coral involves running parallel with the beach and about 25 yards off it, then slipping through a notch in the reef just a little wider than *Starbound* is broad. Ernie and Ray were in the crosstress saying things like "You're fine. Just like that, now. Keep on that course, right for that big clump of palms. No! A little to the left—now, meet her! Good. You've got plenty of room—about 4 feet on each side! O.K., we're in the lagoon. Head for the beach right where that big palm log is washed up on the sand. We're coming down."

We spent two idyllic days there and wished it could be a month. Just a quiet, peaceful, beautiful tropical island with not a single object in sight that wasn't there 1,000 years ago, except for us. We swam, fished, ate, drank, and explored beaches of snow-white sand bordered on one side by coconut palms and on the other by a blue and emerald sea.

There was a small copra village located on the next cay to the east. We couldn't see it but we located it on the chart. So on the third day in paradise we took *Starbound* to another pretty anchorage about a half-mile from the village and motored over in the launch to say hello.

There were nine pandanus-thatched houses, with dirt floors. Everyone sleeps in hammocks suspended from interior posts. The kitchens are outside under a lean-to shed roof. All cooking is done over open fires, and smoke racks adjacent to the fires contained several kinds of fish and sometimes an iguana, being preserved in the only way possible in those islands.

Here's where Jorge really paid for his passage. With him as interpreter we had a fine time talking with the Indians and finding out something about how they lived.

It's a pretty spartan existence, even though they seem to have quite a lot of spare time. We figured out that each man spent about two hours each day gathering copra, and the rest of his time getting enough for his family to eat. Well, most of his time. A lot of time must have been spent in making babies. There were more children than adults.

Nina established an immediate rapport, as she always does, by talking with the women and playing nurse to the kids. Many of the children had small facial infections, mostly on their ears, probably due to a diet deficiency. So Nina sent me right back to *Starbound* for some medicines and dressing. Also for sugar, flour, and coffee, and candy for the chidren. Come and get your ear fixed and get a piece of candy. They really liked her.

I noticed a peculiar object lying beside one of the houses. It was an aluminum mast about 50 feet long, obviously out of a sailboat. I asked about it and Jorge finally pieced together the story. A fiberglass Colombian yacht had hit the windward reef one night a few months ago and had sunk. The people got off O.K. with a few minor injuries, but the yacht was a total loss except for the personal gear the owner managed to salvage before the yacht broke up and sank. The bow section was still visible, sticking forlornly up from the edge of the reef.

The Indians dove on the wreck for weeks, salvaging every piece of anything they might be able to use. The Indian who was telling us the story invited us to look at his store of salvaged goodies. He had done most of the diving on the wreck. I found coils of stainless wire rigging, bent turnbuckles, corroded light switches, and a galley sink pump. And then, under a crudely built bench in a dimly lit corner, I found a lovely winch with "Barient 20" stamped into its top. "My, my," I thought, "bet that'll work just fine for the yankee jib halyard." I said aloud to Jorge, "Tell him I might be able to use this. Ask him if he'd like to sell it."

Some Spanish dialogue flew back and forth. "He says all right," Jorge answered. "He says five dollars U.S."

A large blast of Spanish came from the Indian's wife, the one Nina had been talking with all morning with the aid of a Spanish-English dictionary, and a lot of rapport. The man listened to his wife a moment, then talked to Jorge some more. Jorge turned to me and said, "Gordon, he says your wife is very *simpático* with the children, so for you it is only three dollars." I gave the man his three dollars.

Ernie thought that the transaction was very amusing. He laughed. "That's great, Dad, but there's no winch handle. Do you realize that a Barient handle—just the handle, mind you—costs about thirty bucks?"

Next morning we raised anchor and headed for Panama, just one day away. We found it hard to believe that this out-of-the-way cruising paradise was only a day's sail from a major modern city. Of course, it's a hard beat against wind and current all the way from the Canal Zone. Maybe that's why it's still so beautiful.

8

The Panama Canal— A Piece of Cake

No one slept during the overnight trip from Holandes Cays to Cristóbal. We talked the night through, our primary topic being that the first leg of our world trip was nearly completed and that once we were through the Panama Canal the entire Pacific Ocean would be waiting for us— Galapagos, Marquesas, Tahiti, Bora Bora, Fiji, New Zealand—names with which to dream if we ever decided to climb into our bunks.

We didn't really know what to expect at Panama. None of our "cruising" books gave us enough particulars.

At 0600 we sailed *Starbound* between the arms of the gigantic breakwater at the Cristóbal side of Panama and found ourselves in the Canal Zone. A large pilot boat met us within five minutes of our entrance through the breakwater. We didn't call for it—such boats meet every ship and boat, large or small. An official-looking man handed us a sheaf of papers from the bow of the boat and told us, "Welcome to the Canal Zone. Please follow us to the small craft anchorage and drop your anchor there. Then fill out these forms. We'll return to pick them up shortly."

So we did, and what a bunch of forms; a cargo declaration about 3 feet long with printing on both sides, a ship's information and quarantine declaration in sextuplicate, and a crew list for incoming vessels in quadruplicate—and that's just the entering procedure; it has nothing to do with the canal transit.

We anchored as far into the anchorage as we could to cut down our distance to shore. We were still left with a quarter-mile of oily water to negotiate in order to land the launch and get ashore. Outboard motors cannot be used; yachtsmen must row. A Canal Zone license is required to operate any outboard and they are not issued to transiting yachts.

Of course, our next move, as soon as entry formalities were completed, was to see the port captain and initiate the paperwork necessary to get *Starbound* on the canal schedule for transit. We learned that we would be at the anchorage for three to five days because we must be "measured," *Starbound* never having been through the canal before.

As soon as the port captain had his say, I was faced with the problem of setting free our extra crew member, Jorge Selarón, the Chilean *pintor*. It's a very good thing that Jorge was allowed to go with me to the Panamanian immigration officials. Their English was on a par with my Spanish and alone I would have been incommunicado. But Jorge is smart and personable, so he put it all on the firing line and after much arm waving and paper signing he was free to wield his artist's brushes in Panama. We returned to *Starbound,* wrestled his gear into the launch, and rowed to the dock. I helped him find a taxi. He gave me a very South American *abrazo,* jumped into the cab, and waved good-by as the cab clattered off.

That evening we rowed into the Cristóbal Yacht Club and tried to get a berth, but the club docks were jam-packed with yachts, and anchoring just off the docks is not allowed. We had to stay outside in the main anchorage area and develop our rowing muscles.

The "no outboards" law is strictly enforced. One yacht was fined for breaking it. We heard that the law's inception was due to a constantly increasing number of serious motorboat accidents, mostly among the local Panamanians, who seemed to think that they could drink themselves into oblivion and then handle a high-powered outboard.

At the Cristóbal Yacht Club we learned that we must put in a reservation for a mooring at the Balboa Yacht Club as soon as possible or we might have no place to stay when we arrived on the Pacific side of the canal. We telephoned immediately and managed to secure a mooring.

Since we had two days to wait before being measured, we decided to take the little passenger train from Cristóbal to Balboa and back, a two-hour ride each way on the Panama Railroad, employing a narrow-gauge, old-fashioned choo-choo. The tracks roughly parallel the canal, so we got our first close look at the locks, lakes, and cuts from the passenger platform of a clackety railway car.

From the Atlantic entrance to the Pacific entrance the canal runs from northwest to southeast. A look at an atlas shows a dog-leg bend in the Panama isthmus which accounts for the surprising orientation. The airline distance between the two entrances is 43 miles. It's a little further by ship because there are a few bends here and there.

A ship going from the Atlantic to the Pacific gets raised 85 feet above sea level in three steps at the Gatun Locks and then is let out onto man-made Gatun Lake. This is a very big lake covering about 163 square miles. Ships have to stay in the channel while crossing the lake or they'll go aground. After following the meandering channel across the lake, the ship enters the Chagres River and runs that channel for 5 or 6 miles before coming to Gaillard Cut. The Cut, as it is called, is an enormous man-made ditch about 8 miles long. A lot of it was chopped through solid rock. With Gaillard Cut behind, the ship enters Pedro Miguel Locks for its first step down to the Pacific. It comes out onto Miraflores Lake, a small man-made lake about 1 mile wide. On the other side of the lake, the ship enters Miraflores Locks, which drop in two more steps down to sea level (Pacific version), with tides. Then there is about a 3-mile channel leading to Panama Bay where the open Pacific awaits. Balboa lies just to port as the ship comes out of the channel. The average transit takes about eight hours and yachts are not supposed to sail.

Our train took us to Balboa, where we booked our afternoon rail passage back before taking a taxi to the Balboa Yacht Club. The club is located within Fort Amador, just south of the Bridge of the Americas. Army soldiers guard the gate to the fort and may ask your business, but just waved us in. The club is small but nice, its primary feature of interest to us being a good bar with a balcony overlooking the bay, hot showers, and the first washing machine we'd seen since Bermuda. A long jetty runs out to a floating fuel dock and all of the boats are spaced out over a large area on both sides and in front of the jetty, each boat on a heavy mooring. The tidal rise and fall is about 15 feet and the current can run at 3 knots. Anchoring is not allowed.

We had an American hot dog and a cold beer, confirmed our reservation for a mooring, collected our mail, and took a taxi to the train station. We arrived back on *Starbound* before dark.

Next morning in the Cristóbal anchorage, a man came out to *Starbound* on a pilot boat. He carried a briefcase from which he extracted many papers and a long tape measure. He proceeded to measure *Starbound* with us holding one end of the tape, and by some complicated formula came up with the data by which the Panama Canal Authority would now and forevermore know and charge us for transiting the big ditch. It didn't take long—an hour or so.

Next day we went ashore and paid our charges for the Panama Canal. The total bill was some $70, $30 of which would be refunded at a later date. So it would only cost $40 or so to take *Starbound* through the canal—very reasonable. Especially so since a pilot was assigned to us for the entire trip. His daily salary alone was much more than $40. *Starbound* was given her Panama Canal Admeasurement Document (No. 168815)—which she and she alone would own for all of her life. The document, sealed in plastic, is displayed on the bulkhead in the "radio room," which on *Starbound* means above the chart table.

We were scheduled to begin our canal transit at 0900 next morning. Our two auxiliary crew members came aboard at 0700 and we gave them breakfast. They were Per Jangen and Tage Nilsson, both from yacht *Keewaydin,* a big 70-foot ketch full of Swedish kids on a world trip.

We needed these two extra men. Every yacht going through the canal must have four line handlers in addition to the helmsman. No exceptions are made. Also four dock lines, each 150 feet long. So I had the helm, and Ray, Ernie, Tage, and Per would handle lines. Nina was assigned the position of official photographer and beer bringer.

Our pilot came aboard promptly at 0900, with a briefcase and a portable walkie-talkie radio, introduced himself as Bill Boyland, and asked us to weigh anchor and get under way immediately. Ten minutes later we were motoring up the channel for Gatun Locks a few miles ahead.

Bill Boyland was my kind of pilot. On the way up the channel he explained what we were going to do and how we'd do it. He was a pleasantly calm, unexcitable guy. And he left the helm to me, merely telling me where the boat needed to go.

We were worried about "locking up." We'd read some cruising stories containing horror sequences about damage suffered in the Panama Canal while being raised. The maelstrom of water pouring into the locks causes a yacht to dance madly about, even one as heavy as *Starbound.* Our bowsprit and stern davits seemed especially vulnerable. I confessed our fears to Bill— we were immediately on a first-name basis—and he told me there'd be no sweat. He'd set it up for us to be tied outboard of a big tug which would take us through the Gatun Locks. He mentioned that he'd arranged this because we'd be locking up right behind a super-tanker. I didn't quite understand but held my peace.

The super-tanker entered the locks ahead of us. She was the *Nefeli* and her port of registry was Monrovia. What a monster she was. Her sides seemed to almost touch both walls of the lock.

The Canal tug *Morrow* entered the lock behind *Nefeli* and secured her starboard side to the lock wall. The big tug's skipper told our pilot to bring *Starbound* in. I put our ship alongside and we secured to the tug with two breast lines and two springs. Then the tug's crew put on four more breast lines and two more springs and hauled us very tightly against the huge rope fenders. We were glued to the *Morrow* like a leech! I raised a questioning eyebrow at Bill Boyland but he waved a placating hand and said, "You'll see why."

The huge gates closed ponderously behind us and we found ourselves in a huge well, 30 feet deep. Almost immediately the water came flooding in from the immense ports in the floor of the lock. Even hugged to the big tug I could feel *Starbound* try to pitch and yaw in the wild currents generated by the incoming water. We rose quickly up in the lock and were soon ready for the second set of gates. I thought we'd have to wait for a while, but they opened almost immediately.

Bill said, "Hold on now. This is why I asked for the tug." A boiling turbulence bubbled up from below the stern of the super-tanker and *Starbound* bucked hard. I watched our lines stretch and bounce back as she tried to tear herself loose from the tug. A flicker on the control panel caught my eye; the speed log was reading 9 knots!

"What the hell?" I asked Bill.

He explained, "The super-tankers are too big for the mules—the little railway locomotives which pull them through the locks. The mules can't overcome all that inertia so the ships kick their propellers over a few turns to get themselves started. Then the mules can handle them."

As suddenly as it had started, the turbulence died. *Nefeli* was moving into the next set of locks. The *Morrow* cast loose her lines and followed the tanker, taking *Starbound* with her still tied alongside. She made fast to the lock wall again and the gates closed behind us. We repeated the procedure twice more, and as the third lock opened its gates the *Morrow* moved us out onto Gatun Lake and its crew began to unweave the web of lines which held us to her.

We were grateful for the *Morrow*'s help. Her skipper, Joseph Beale, was very hospitable. Nina had deserted *Starbound* during part of the locking process and was given a tour of the tug. She was impressed.

"Gordon, you should go see that tug. She's two-thirds gorgeous engine and the rest of her is beautiful teak and mahogany paneling and polished brass—with carpeting in the pilot's house."

I've seen some very nice tugs before, but I'll remember the *Morrow* with regard. She made the scary locking-up process quite simple for *Starbound*.

Bill said, "O.K., Gordon, now all you have to do is beat that tanker and the freighter just ahead of it to Gaillard Cut. If you can't do it we might be held up for two hours. This is because you must enter the locks going down ahead of the ships. We'll take the route we call the 'Banana Boat Channel.' It cuts a few miles off the ship's route. It's well buoyed and I'll show you just where to go. Give her all the speed you can."

"Can we motor-sail?" I asked.

"Sure, if it'll give you more speed."

We put up the big yankee jib and the mizzen and I pushed the engine RPM's up to 2,000. We started making a little better than 7 knots.

In the excitement of the chase we still had time to admire Gatun Lake.

Very tropical and very beautiful islets were stationed on both sides of our route. Birds of all colors flew in profusion. We spotted several snakes swimming in the water and learned from Bill that they were deadly poisonous. Some small animals scuttled off into the brush at our noisy approach. It would have been more fun to just sail very silently through that green and glittering panorama and observe a real tropical jungle in the raw. But we had some ships to catch.

Nina had planned a beautiful lunch and to the delight of our two auxiliary crewmen, who ate mostly Swiss Army rations aboard their boat, she served a sumptious lunch of bread, cheese, ham, caviar with thin onion slices, crispy crackers, a tomato and lettuce salad, and, of course, beer and red and white wine.

Bill said, "Good God, do you always eat like this aboard?"

We caught the first ship just as we came out of our side route back into the "big ship" channel. At Bill's direction we made a left end run on the second ship, a medium-sized freighter, and slipped past her bow just as we entered the Gaillard Cut. Eight miles later we entered the Pedro Miguel Locks to make our first drop down to the Pacific Ocean sea level.

Now we put our line handlers to work for the first time. So far they had spent most of their time up in the crosstrees with camera paraphernalia strung around their necks. I stationed Ray and Ernie forward, each with 150 feet of heavy line reeved through the forward hawses and flaked down ready to run. Per and Tage came aft, one port and one starboard, each also with 150 feet of line ready to go over.

Bill told me, "O.K., Gordon, take your ship right down to the lock gates. I'll tell you when to stop her. The Panamanian line handlers will put four heaving lines aboard, two on each side. Have your men bend the heaving lines to the bights on your lines. The dock men will haul your lines to the dock sides and put the bights over the big bollards spaced along the lock walls there, and your boys will then take up the slack and keep us centered in the lock. As the water level drops, they must pay out line at a rate to keep us nicely centered."

We were approaching the gates at the far end of the lock at a good pace. I was worried about the Panamanians on the lock walls. What if one of them missed with a heaving line? I stopped *Starbound* where Bill told me, with her bowsprit about 10 feet from the lock gates, and Bill called to the line handlers on the dock. With a curious figure-eight wave of their arms ending with an overhand whipping motion, the four heaving lines arced gracefully through the air and four monkey's fists bounced simultaneously at the feet of *Starbound*'s line handlers. I quit worrying about Panamanian accuracy. Our crew threw a bowline on the bight of each of our lines and raised an arm, and our lines snaked through the hawses and over to the lock walls where they were dropped on the nearest bollard. Bill called to our crew to take in the slack—and there we were, secure in the center of the lock. The entire operation had taken about thirty seconds. Bill approved our technique.

The freighter behind us was pulled into the lock by the mules and stopped quite close to our stern. In a very short time the water level in the lock began to drop rapidly and we started slacking our lines. It seemed that the lock gates in front of us opened as soon as we quit dropping. I started *Starbound's* engine. Bill signaled the lock wall again and our lines were cast off quickly. Even more quickly, *Starbound's* crew hauled in our lines, and as the bights were captured, I put the gear lever forward and we motored out of the lock onto Miraflores Lake.

"O.K.," Bill said. "Now we'll go through the same drill. Head for the next locks at a good clip so we don't hang up the ships behind us." He spoke briefly into his portable radio, informing his brother pilots on the ships of our intentions.

The two sets of Miraflores Locks were a repeat sequence of the last locks except for one thing. Entering the last lock took some timing. Because of a peculiarity of the water flow into the last lock, *Starbound* had to beat a little riptide to the last gate and be secured to the walls before it hit our stern. The pilots call it the "lace curtain."

We roared out of the lock gates before they were fully opened and sprinted down the length of the last lock. Bill was yelling at the line handlers to run down to the end. I put *Starbound* in hard reverse just short of the gates and once again the heaving lines hit our deck with unerring accuracy.

I had time to look aft and see the foaming turbulence of the "lace curtain" coming rapidly from astern. It was traveling at about 3 knots. It hit us just as the boys secured our lines. *Starbound* yawed and pitched for a minute or so, then quieted. Bill smiled. "If we hadn't been secured you might have ended up with that long bowsprit into the gates." I swallowed hard.

An hour later we passed under the Bridge of the Americas and saw the moorings of the Balboa Yacht Club to port. Ahead of us lay the shining expanse of the Pacific Ocean reflecting the light of the dropping sun.

It was 1700 and a pilot boat was standing by to take Bill ashore. He'd be home in time for dinner. A good man, Bill Boyland.

The yacht club sent out a boat to show us to our mooring. We picked it up and hung with the current, which was easily able to overcome the sea breeze.

We took the shore boat over to the jetty and went up to the club on the bluff to celebrate our passage with beer and hot dogs. Our initial impulse was to walk into the veranda bar crowded with yachtsmen and say, "Hi, everybody. Know what? We just took our boat through the Panama Canal! How about that!"

Of course, everybody there had just come through, so we cooled it and waited for someone to say, "Hi! You off *Starbound?*"

"Yeah, just got here. No problems. Eight-hour transit. Great pilot. How about you?"

"Took us ten hours. We were hung up at Miraflores waiting for a ship."

"Too bad. Have a beer. What's your boat?"

And so on into the evening.

Per and Tage left for Cristóbal next morning to bring *Keewaydin* through. They were now experts. We offered to help but they had many crew so didn't need us. Nina and I went to the bank just down the road from the gates of Fort Amador and wired for money. We were getting short.

Something more about funds. Panama is where we learned some hard facts. Every yacht seems to work the money thing in a different way. Assuming that a cruising yachtsman has a stash of loot in his bank at home (at least I hope he does), he needs to have it readily available to him at different parts of the world. Wiring for money takes ten days to two weeks anywhere we've been. This isn't what I'd call readily available. Of course, the most available funds are those carried aboard. For us a heavy bunch of American dollars in a safe place on board would be the handiest. But in case of robbery or shipwreck or some other catastrophe, we'd be up the proverbial creek—our "cushion" would be lost and in most parts of the world this would mean real trouble. So the best thing for anyone to do is to keep the heavy stash in his home bank.

We found Bank of America and Barclays to be the two banks most ready to help us in the places we'd been so far. But since our bank is Riggs National of Washington, D.C., with branches only within D.C., we still had to put up with a time delay to wire for money. It was in Panama that we finally got smart and sent a request to our bank to move the majority of our funds from our savings account to our checking account. Then we could write personal checks for fairly large amounts and with our passports for identification we could usually get them cashed at Barclays or Bank of America. Also, an American Express card is a very nice card to own. We could buy American Express traveler's checks with our personal check, then cash them as we required money. Of course, the traveler's checks cost one percent, so we always tried to cash a personal check first. We found out that a BankAmeriCard and a BarclayCard are two other pieces of plastic which are handy to have. Maybe there's a way for a cruising yachtsman to acquire all three. We haven't tried yet.

Our second major Panama drill was to obtain a *permiso* from Ecuador to visit the Galapagos Islands. This was a long-time dream of ours.

We talked to other yachtsmen and found that we must submit a *solicitud* to the Ecuadorian Navy through their consulate—in Spanish, and in triplicate! We obtained a carbon copy from a friend who had applied and Nina typed up a beautiful document, complete as to times and places, and I signed it.

Next day I wandered around the city of Panama and finally found the Ecuadorian consulate. The most important person I could reach was an undersecretary. Tall, handsome, mustachioed, and very well dressed, he handled our beautiful *solicitud* with two fingers on one corner as if it were a dead rat. He informed me that it should have been submitted six months in advance of our visit, and implied that we had the chance of a virgin in Tahiti of getting a *permiso*. I offered to pay costs of a telegram to Guayaquil or Quito and he merely sneered, but politely, and told me it would do no good. I asked him to please expedite it and made my departure. I have a hunch our *solicitud* was carefully deposited in the circular file. We didn't hear another word from the consulate, and repeated phone calls over the next two weeks were carefully fielded and shunted into a limbo of stupid secretaries and insincere regrets from consulate officers.

We had to leave. February was rolling to a close and we wanted all the time among the Pacific islands we could get before late October, when the cyclones start in the warm equatorial currents above Fiji.

The captain made his decision. "All right, I've had it with Ecuador. Screw the Galapagos! It's too damn bad that we have to miss 'em, but we're out of time. Let's buy our stores and go."

The flurry of last-minute parties was fun, but now that we'd made the decision to get going, impatience grew in us with each passing day.

We split up the work. Ernie checked out our rigging from top to bottom, then busied himself with a stack of Pacific charts to make sure we had everything we needed. He checked out the RDF and R/T and made sure that Grumpy didn't have a bellyache; we'd have a lot of use for that auto-pilot crossing the Pacific.

Nina spent a lot of time and money on provisions, and Ray and I spent as much of both on spare parts. And, finally, I spent a lot of patience on officialdom.

One morning we were ready. We dropped our mooring and moved to the fuel dock to top off our tanks. Then when a clear spot between the ship traffic presented itself, we motored into the channel and started west again, waving to friends on moored boats.

It was good to be under way.

PART II

Galapagos to Tonga

The Eastern Pacific

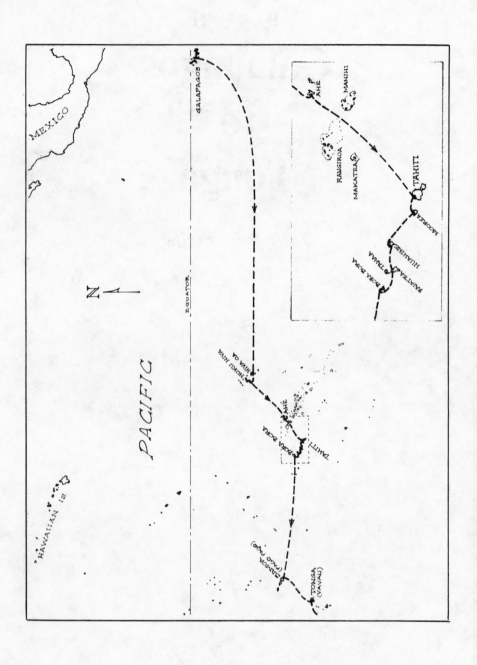

9

A Taste of the Pacific—Galapagos to the Marquesas

We left Panama with what seemed to be a ship full of semi-hysterical relief—always the same feeling after spending over ten days in any South American port. Our particular irritation factor grew in direct proportion to the number of times we came into contact with bureaucratic government officials, which during our Panama stay was heightened by uncooperative Ecuadorian consular people.

We had an errand to run, so we stopped by Taboga on the way to the open sea. Taboga is a small island about 10 miles south of the Pacific canal entrance. It doesn't have much to offer except an honest-to-God anchorage, of which there are none in Balboa. Take a mooring and pay for it or go to Taboga; the trouble being, of course, that there are no facilities in Taboga for boats except an anchorage, a place to buy beer, and a nice little beach. That can be enough if your ship is loaded with fuel, water, and supplies. If not, you must hoist the anchor and motor to Balboa—almost dead to windward—take on fuel and water, then sail back to Taboga. For supplies, the ship's storekeeper must take the daily ferry into Balboa and wrestle cartons in and out of taxis, boats, and carts.

Our errand to Taboga came about in this fashion; the day before we left Balboa, two young men wearing big black beards and gray T-shirts dropped by *Starbound* and asked us to ferry some gasoline over to their ship, which was anchored in Taboga. It seems no fuel can be transported on

115

the twice-daily ferry. The ship's name, *Topaz,* was emblazoned in green on
the front of their shirts with the outline of what looked like a big Baltic
trader under sail. They were very pleasant to talk with and they admired
Starbound, so we said O.K. Within a few hours they returned with four big
blue 15-gallon plastic *jugos* for delivery. We were told, "You can't miss her;
she's a ninety-footer with a green hull!"

They were right—we couldn't miss her. She must be one of the finest
examples of a large work-type sailing vessel converted to pleasure use we
had yet seen, and we'd seen several. She's a thirty-seven-year-old Baltic
trader owned jointly by the several people on board, who numbered
thirteen—four couples and five single men. All of the conversion work was
done by them in Grenada, and a beautiful job it was. Staying away from
the whole lot of available paneling, plywood, formica, and various
hardboards, the crew had made good advantage of the fully ceilinged hull
and massive structure of deck beams and deck house uprights which they
simply scraped down and varnished. New interior bulkheads were solidly
constructed of tongue and groove pine, also varnished. The main saloon
table is a huge 'tween-decks hatch cover—a real one—scraped smooth and
varnished with several coats. Saloon chairs are half barrels cut in such
fashion that one barrel makes two chairs. Each of the eight sleeping cabin's
interiors was designed and built by the persons who were to occupy it. Their
individual tastes lent a unique charm to the whole interior layout.

The remainder of the vessel was not neglected in the least. Her gear,
rigging, and sails were virtually new and in good repair, and her engine was
a modern, slow-speed diesel which will probably still be running when her
present crew are ready to join the shuffleboard set in Florida.

We spied *Topaz* as soon as we closed on the small harbor at Taboga, and
with shouts back and forth, which included the offer of cold alcoholic
beverages, we tied alongside rather than pass those heavy jugs down into
their dinghy. We don't usually raft *Starbound* up to another boat for fear
we'll do damage to delicate topsides but in this case we had no fear. One
hundred tons of ship with 4-inch planking hung with old truck tires makes a
comfortably secure floating dock. It's one of the few times we felt *Starbound*
to look a bit dainty.

One drink leading to another, we damn near didn't get away to sea that
day. As it was, we "waited for the land breeze" until about 1700 hours, then
regretfully departed, waving a slightly hazy farewell to the crew.

There we were with 4,000 nautical miles of ocean between us and the
Marquesas. We were not happy about having to miss the Galapagos, the
"Enchanted Isles," but we had exhausted all our resources in that direction
back in Panama. We tried to forget our disappointment.

We set the square sail and raffee and let Grumpy do the steering. The northeast trades were strong, and *Starbound* flew out of Panamanian waters, dodging ships the first few nights. The traffic going and coming from the canal makes a sharp lookout mandatory.

For four days we flew—and then we flopped. If there is anything more irritating than a sailing ship becalmed, with her top side gear banging back and forth with the roll, I can't name it. Good humor departs the ship almost instantly and the crew spends hours looking for a ripple on the water which might portend a breeze of sufficient magnitude to still the slop of the heavy rig.

Having owned *Starbound* long enough to know her characteristics, we also knew enough not to fool around looking for a magic breeze—not in the doldrums. We cranked up the main diesel, strapped in the fore and aft rig, and proceeded on our course. With the engine turning over at an easy 1,500 RPM and the sails drafting well, our roll was dampened considerably, and we made 5 knots with an economical consumption of fuel. This motoring was one of the reasons we'd topped up our main fuel tanks in Panama and then added 100 more gallons in the six big white *jugos* we had bought in Cartagena and carried topside lashed to the bulwarks amidships. As the hours went by we kept congratulating ourselves on having the foresight to put all that diesel oil on board. With the exception of a few sailing tries with random breezes that found us, we kept the engine working for three days.

We drove *Starbound* southwest and approached the Galapagos, intending to leave them to starboard and continue on to 10 degrees south latitude before turning due west. The faces of all aboard got more morose and wistful-looking. Curses at Ecuadorian officialdom grew more frequent. Finally, we had a general conference over the dinner table. It was the strong feeling of all four of us that to pass by the Galapagos without even trying for a look-see was something we would regret forever. We just might not ever come this way again.

Nina summed it all up when she said, "Dammit, let's take a shot at it—all they can do is throw us out!"

"Yes," I said, "and possibly slap us with a heavy fine. Let's think about it for another day."

Everyone grumbled, but my "Bligh Syndrome" prevailed. Frankly, I just couldn't make up my mind. In Panama we'd heard some scary rumors about boats going into the Galapagos without permission; rumors with words in them like "heavy fine" and "confiscation of property."

At 0230 the next morning, the third day of March, we turned from pollywogs to shellbacks. We crossed the "line." I stayed up for the occasion and Ray was on watch. Nina and Ernie were asleep below. When the taffrail log read the correct number of miles past our evening fix, I drew a bucket of water from the sea. I sloshed a hand in it, went below to the master stateroom, and then sprinkled it in the face of my sleeping wife.

She sat up in bed with a gasp and cried, "You rat! What in hell are you doing?"

"Congratulations, love," I said, "you are now a shellback. We've just crossed the equator."

Drying her face off with my pillow, she said, "That's nice. Now go away and let me sleep."

I trudged back to the companionway ladder and looked at Ernie asleep in the quarter berth. I shrugged, dried my hand on my shorts and went topside. Ray and I congratulated each other and admired the tropical night. I relieved him at 0300.

On Sunday we continued to motor. Our morning star shots didn't work out at all well but we had had such a good fix the evening before that I ignored them and continued on course. We blamed it on the rather cloudy conditions.

That evening I made the decision to try to go into the Galapagos and the crew cheered. The sky was still cloudy but promised to clear the next morning. A course laid from our deduced reckoning position showed us that we should steer 250 degrees by the compass. On Monday our sun lines seemed to confirm our course.

At 1800 hours on Monday evening, we had perfect conditions for celestial navigation. Ray and I unlocked our sextants from their cushioned boxes and went topside. Sextant lanyards around our necks, sextants gripped in right hands, our heads tipped back and our eyes searched for the first star to appear.

"O.K., there's Sirius."

"I see it, about sixty-five degrees—pretty high."

Next in order came Canopus, Capella, and Achernar.

"Very good, I'm happy with what we've got. I'll go below and work 'em out."

So I worked them out and we found ourselves way up north from where we should be—nearly back on the equator!

"Ray," I called, "check these, will you? Something's screwed up!"

So Ray checked—no mistakes in math. Then I checked again and everything looked fine. It had to be something basic that was wrong. Wait a minute! The azimuth in our calculations of Capella showed the star to be south and I knew Capella lay nearly due north at 1800. Good God! The equator! We crossed it and didn't change our rules for azimuths. The position we had plotted was a mirror image of our true position. Quickly we recalculated the azimuths, replotted our position, and found ourselves 80 miles southeast of San Cristóbal instead of 40 miles northeast.

Ray and I look at each other in amused chagrin. We had made the classic mistake in navigation. Well, at least we knew where we were. We changed course to 345 degrees, locked Grumpy onto the new bearing, and recalculated our ETA at Wreck Bay, the port of entry in "Las Islas Encantadas."

On March 5, seven days out of Panama, we dropped the anchor at 1900 hours.

The big three-masted charter boat *Eolus* was anchored a few hundred yards away. I saw her shore boat coming by and gave them a hail. They had arrived from Panama the day before and were leaving in the morning. They also had no permission to enter but informed me that there was a new commandant in charge and that he was a nice guy and had allowed them three days in port before they must leave.

This was good news, and bad. We knew now that we wouldn't be fined, but three days wasn't much time to see the Galapagos. Also, from what we could see of San Cristóbal, it looked a rather dreary place and we were told that Academy Bay was much nicer—but only three days?

The sunlight next morning didn't exactly improve the aspect of the island. The water of the bay was clear and beautiful—also cold. The hills of San Cristóbal are dry and cactus-strewn. Rather desolate-looking wooden buildings lined the waterfront—dirt roads gave rise to dust from the occasional vehicle. One rather large building at the foot of the major pier was pointed out as the office of the port commandant.

I dressed neatly while Ernie and Ray put the launch over the side, and with all of our documents and some trepidation I went to call on the officials. I tied the launch up to the stone stairs at the end of the pier and marched toward the building with what I hoped was a friendly, love-the-world smile on my face.

Out of the building to meet me came a slim, smiling man in uniform. With my few words of Spanish and his fairly understandable English we managed to convey our meanings to each other. This was none other than "El Comandante" himself, Lieutenant Fernando Toledo. I kept my surprise hidden as I realized that here was a very nice man who was really trying to be helpful. First he wanted to visit the boat. I took him out in the launch, introduced him to Nina, Ernie, and Ray, and put a cold beer in his hand. This was a good move—the Galapagos had been out of beer for a month.

When Señor Toledo found we had no *permiso,* he said, "Oh, that is very bad! How long did you want to stay and where do you want to go from here?"

"Oh," we said, putting another cold beer in his hand, "we'd like to stay here about three days and then we'd like to visit Academy Bay on Santa Cruz awhile; and then possibly stop by one or two other islands just for a day or two to see the flora and fauna. Is this possible?"

"Yes," he said, smiling. "It is possible. When you are ready to leave here, come to my office and I will fix the paper to allow you to do these things."

"Fantastico!" We were really delighted. "But Señor Toledo, do we not need to go to the tourist office and buy the tourist card for each of us, which we understand is six dollars apiece?"

"Now, how can you do that?" he replied. "You must present your *permiso* to buy the card and you have no *permiso!* When you are ready to leave just come to see me and I will prepare the paper to allow you to go to Santa Cruz. Is this O.K.?"

"Oh," we exclaimed, "this is very much O.K.! Have another cold beer—please."

We spent two days on San Cristóbal, mostly strolling the streets, doing some laundry, buying postcards at the local grocery store, and practicing our Spanish with the dozens of kids who swarmed around Nina whenever she went ashore. Nina loves children—perhaps too much. She insisted on taking a boatload of them out to *Starbound* to show them how we live. She gave all of them soft drinks aboard. But when they left the boat we had to unload the loot from each one as he climbed in the dinghy. Our fishing gear, our fruit, assortments of tools, nuts, screws, pens, and pencils all came to light and were left on the cabin top. One girl, old enough to know better, had to be divested of a pocketful of Ernie's coin collection. They didn't seem offended or embarrassed at our removal of the gear they'd picked up, and we didn't get angry—but we unloaded them. The problem is obvious; they have very little, so when they see all that we have, they consider us fair game. I told Nina no more kids aboard. She agreed.

On Friday I went to the office of Señor Toledo and received our permission to go to Santa Cruz. I had to pay port charges of $19, which would have been a shock if we hadn't been forewarned by other boats. We knew it would be another $19 when we cleared Santa Cruz, too.

By 1000 we were on our way. The compass course was due west and we had a nice 10-knot southerly breeze. Porpoises leaped and played at our bow the whole day. By 1715 our anchor dropped through 15 feet of the most beautiful turquoise water we'd seen since the San Blas Islands; Academy Bay. It was all we had expected. A place where the iguanas swim around your vessel and sun themselves on the beaches. The little penguins pop their heads out of the water and look you over as if to say, "Hi, I'm a penguin, what are you?" The porpoises and seals are almost tame enough to pet, and the blue-footed boobies look as if they'd been wading in sky-blue paint.

What really surprised us was the number of yachts in the harbor. There were seventeen boats anchored at one time in Academy Bay during our ten-day stay there. Their overall lengths ran from 26 feet to 50 feet. Two trimarans and a catamaran represented the multihulls.

We first heard the word "yachtie" at Academy Bay. It can be a derogatory term depending on who uses it; that is, a landsman will say,

San Blas native boat carries goods for the settlement
on shore.

Typical of the San Blas Islands is this small cay.

Sailing west from Panama
with squaresail set.

Starbound making knots,
viewed from aloft.

Welcome to the Galapagos from an escort of porpoises.

Karl Angermeyer and friends at Academy Bay in
the Galapagos.

A resident of Galapagos inspects the crew of *Starbound*.

A friendly seal was a neighbor at the Galapagos
anchorage.

Snake mackerel brought aboard during the Pacific
crossing exhibits an impressive set of teeth.

Over-navigated. The Skipper and two crewmen take
sunsights enroute from the Galapagos to the Marquesas.

Louise and Teato become friends at Ahé in the
Tuamotus.

Leaving Ahé in the Tuamotus gives some idea of the
low-lying islands and their passes.

First view of Hiva Oa on the Stuermers' wedding anniversary.

The landing place at Hiva Oa.

Outrigger racing canoes compete during the fete in
celebration of Bastille Day, Papeete, Tahiti.

Crowds line the harbor for the 24-hour festivities
during the fete days at Papeete.

"Goddamn yachties are buying up all the available supplies and clogging up the harbor." Or, a new arrival will walk into a bar and someone will call, "Hey, another yachtie—come over and have a drink."

We realized that there are a lot of people cruising the world, not just us "affluent Americans." There were English, French, German, Swiss, Australian, New Zealand, and Canadian flags flying in Academy Bay, as well as our own stars and stripes.

Why are they all out there on the oceans of the world? Name a reason; we heard them all. Some of the less erudite say, "Why—to see the world."

Others add, ". . . before it goes even further to hell."

A few reticently mumble, ". . . last frontier . . . solitude . . . independence . . . simple life."

Economics aren't usually given as a reason. We also were learning that the old chestnut about yachting being the most expensive way in the world to travel third class is true. But being able to pick our company, destination, and schedule—what an advantage!

We met the famous Angermeyer brothers, Gus, Karl, and John. They've been Galapagos residents from back in the thirties when they emigrated from Germany in search of a peaceful life style—which surely couldn't be found in Germany at that time. They found peace, but those early days must have been hard. All of the drinking water in the Galapagos comes from rainwater in catchment basins and the sole source of meat for many years was goat and turtle—and all the fish you could eat.

Karl was out on a fishing trip when we arrived but Gus rowed out to *Starbound* to give us a welcome and invite us to his birthday party. We never did learn if it was his sixty-second or sixty-third—he looks in his early forties. He's about five feet ten, my height, with a 50-inch chest and big muscular arms. He's got all his hair, which he wears fairly long around a craggy German face. He also has a real yen for female companionship. He had an arm around Nina within one minute of coming aboard.

We went to Gus's birthday party in La Cueva—"The Cave." The other brothers had built themselves more or less conventional houses on the bluff overlooking the bay, but Gus had built himself a cave of sorts from the lava rock which forms the islands. About 14 feet high, the parabolic-shaped mound is entered by a semi-tunnel. The inside walls are lined with Galapagos artifacts. Every available inch has its complement of bones, skeletons, tortoise shells, and sea shells. The floors are covered with goat skins sewn together. At one end there is a handsome raised hearth fireplace for warmth against the chilly nights. The log fire and at least fifty candles provided the light for the party. Behind a partition at the opposite end of the cave from the fireplace, Gus has constructed a complete kitchen. Hidden speakers play taped music. What a place for a party—and what a party! Gus was the life of it. He danced the feet off every female there.

While recovering, which took a few days, we set up the ship to leave Academy Bay. The Marquesas were waiting. Ernie checked out the rigging. I cleaned fuel filters and changed engine oil. Nina bought fresh meat and vegetables, although supplies were limited. Ray chased girls and helped Nina.

One morning we sailed to Post Office Bay on the island of Floreana. We found the famous barrel on shore adorned with the signatures of ships and yachts. That evening we used a soldering iron to burn the name of our ship and crew into a piece of broken sail batten and next morning attached the batten to the barrel with bronze screws, "mailed" our post cards in the barrel, and used up another roll of film.

We spent an afternoon swimming with the very friendly seals in a natural swimming pool about a half-mile down the beach from the barrel. The pool was formed by the collapse of a lava "bubble" long ago. The sea waves had eroded a narrow entrance through the basin's edge and washed in white sand to line its bottom. It is almost uniformly 4 feet deep and 300 feet in diameter. The black lava rim forms a low wall all around with natural steps on which a great number of seals lay sunning themselves. An occasional pup was nursing at its mother, and courting couples twined around each other as they swam through the crystal water. Altogether a very beautiful place. We petted seal pups and swam for several hours, then returned to *Starbound* for dinner. We slept well that night, tired from the day in the sun and water, full of Galapagos beef and French wine. I couldn't even work up a little trepidation about the 3,200 miles of ocean between us and the Marquesas. Next morning we raised our anchors and set sail.

The most desirable course to the Marquesas Islands lays along the line of 10 degrees south latitude. We took a southwesterly course from the equatorial Galapagos hoping to pick up the southeast trade winds within a few days. We were lucky; after four days of light and variable breezes with a few rain squalls each day, we met the trades. We braced the square sail hard to starboard and ran our southing down with the wind just abaft the port beam. The weather was a sailor's dream: puffy little cumulous clouds, a steady 12-knot breeze, a gentle swell and starlit nights.

Within two days, our sextants told us that we could square away to the west—we were on the 10 degree parallel.

Now started the kind of sailing which every sailor loves—running with the trades to a tropical island.

Each day was much the same as the day just past, and we knew the following day would be much the same as today. But not boring—never boring.

The Pacific Ocean is pure blue—not the cold black-green of the northern waters or the gray-green of the North Atlantic, nor even the azure blue of the Caribbean. It is that perfect penetrating blue which the late Eugene

Burdick called "the blue of Capricorn." Above this vast expanse of perfect blue float puffy little trade wind clouds, rows of flat-bottomed cotton balls which march in never-ending procession across a clean sky.

The nights are brilliant. Even without a moon the starshine illuminates the horizon. And with a moon we made star shots at midnight using a silver horizon.

We worked out a watch bill that worked well for *Starbound*. With Grumpy doing all the steering, the duties of the human crew were light. We decided that since there was always one or more of us up-and-about during daylight hours, no formal watches would be necessary from sunrise to sunset. The hours of dark were divided into four three-hour watches: 1900 to 2200, 2200 to 0100, 0100 to 0400, and 0400 to 0700.

Cooking can be fun aboard—now and then. If one person has to do all the cooking, it can be damned tedious. So we played "Peggy for a day." Whoever was Peggy stood the 0400 to 0700 watch, then had the day's duty to produce breakfast, lunch, and dinner and clean up the mess. On the night following the galley duties Peggy didn't have to stand a watch. This allowed the watch-standers to have a different watch each night. It worked fine. Peggy's duties also included sweeping, dusting, and cleaning the head. If someone's gear was found adrift, that person was likely to find said gear stuffed in his pillow, or draped unceremoniously over his head.

Everyone had extra duties. Ernie worked on the topside gear. Ray was the odd-job king and fixed "things"—the refrigerator latch, the spreader lights, the switch over the chart table, the securing device on the engine room door. I put in much of my time in the engine room—changing oil, renewing fuel filters and oil filters, fixing pumps, checking spares, and rebuilding relatively ancient equipment. I made sure the batteries stayed high by charging one and one-half hours each day. Nina was permanent storekeeper and cooking instructor.

We were, if anything, overnavigated. Ray had brought his sextant and the air tables with him. Ernie and I used our two sextants and the marine tables. We shot everything in sight: sun, moon, stars, and planets. We even focused on a satellite one evening before we realized how fast it was moving.

Let me describe just one watch, my favorite, the morning watch—in spite of the fact that that watch made me Peggy for the day.

Ernie reaches across our double bunk and gives my leg a shake. "Time," he says.

"O.K.," I mutter, "I'm aware and alert." I hunch myself down and slide off the end of the bunk, being careful not to wake Nina. I push my legs into a pair of raggedy dungaree shorts, grab a light nylon jacket, and stumble into the head. Ernie is in the galley putting the kettle on for coffee. While waiting for it to boil I give my face, teeth, and hair a quick slosh and come full awake. Then I make a cup of coffee and carry it through the main saloon and up the companionway ladder. Ernie is standing at the starboard taffrail arcing a stream over the lee side. After a perfunctory look around at the night I join him.

"What's up? Any problems?"

"Nope. Everything's fine—still on course and Grumpy's steering well. The square sail's full. Saw a ship's lights way off to port about an hour ago. Nice night."

"Yeah. Well, hit the sack. See you for breakfast."

"O.K. What are you going to fix?"

"I don't know. I'll think about it."

We finish our business at the taffrail and Ernie climbs into the big South American hammock he'd rigged between the main boom sheet bale and the forward mizzen shroud, turns over once, and is asleep.

Alone with my ship, my eyes adjust to the dark. I can see the big square sail and smaller raffee outlined against the stars, still a lighter patch than the surrounding sky. They pull well and are trimmed to the southeast trade wind flowing over the port quarter. *Starbound* lifts her stern to the following swell and surges forward a few yards, then drops her stern as the bow lifts to the same swell. Her bow makes a busy bustling noise with each surge which carries aft to my ears. I slide into my watch jacket—it can get cool at night on the tropic sea—and sip on my tin cup of coffee with the big "G" printed on it. No ships can be seen inside our little 8-mile diameter horizon-bowl. I go below and read for a while, popping my head up every 15 minutes for a scan of horizon, compass, wind pennant, and rig.

Then during one of the topside checks I realize that I can see the wave tops, silvery gray things moving up from aft. To the east the sky shows a subtle lightening. Then quite quickly, the tropic dawn flowers and all parts of the ship become visible, a light gray color with a barely noticeable shading of salmon pink as the sun, still well below the horizon, advertises its arrival.

All of the trade wind powder-puff clouds turn pink, almost all at once. The stars fade from sight except for Venus, still burning brightly, and the sea and the sky begin borrowing blue from each other. Then I see the flying fish, breaking water on either side of us, flutter away at our approach, afraid of being eaten (they *do* flap their wings).

A golden ray, then two and three, lance upward from the eastern horizon, followed almost immediately by a brilliant shining crescent—the sun. No wonder so many ancient peoples worshiped it as a god.

I can't imagine any sailor ever getting tired of watching the sun rise. What is it—a symbolic *something*, surely? New beginning? Life washed clean of the night shadows—a new start? From now on everything'll get better? Don't see how it could get much better, but the new sun always looks good.

The watch ends at 0700, but I don't wake anybody up. I am Peggy for the day. So I read the taffrail log and the barometer and fill in the deck log with those bits of information which sailors want to know: wind speed and direction, wave height and direction, appearance of the sky, compass heading, barometric pressure. Then I pour another cup of coffee and ponder breakfast. Omelet? Hot cakes? French toast? Maybe oatmeal, canned fruit, and toast?

On the morning of the tenth day of April, Nina's and my wedding anniversary, we sighted the island of Hiva Oa dead ahead. The Marquesas! Hiva Oa of the high, sharp-edged green mountains and the deep, dark green valleys and the sparkling rivers and the black sand beaches. We stood on the fore deck and held each other and laughed, and gave each other Hiva Oa for an anniversary present.

10

Polynesian Paradise

Hiva Oa kept rising from the sea and the afternoon waned. Despite a brisk trade wind *Starbound* didn't seem to be sailing very fast. The night caught up with our stern as the eastern point of the island came abeam. We could see Motane Island off to port.

Nina asked, "Are we going to go into Hiva Oa in the dark?"

"Yeah, unless we want to heave to right now—and I don't fancy that because the tide will take us right past the island."

We checked the nautical almanac and saw that a half-moon would rise about 2130. We *needed* that moon. There's a small islet right in the entrance of the twin bays of Atuona and Taa Huku and the only so-called navigational light was supposed to be high on a rocky point separating the bays. We never did spot that light.

The moon came shining over the cloud banks on the eastern horizon and illuminated the breakers at the base of the islet to port and Flat Point to starboard. The entrance of Taa Huku finally opened up off the starboard bow and we could see the lights of a small ship in the bay. We wanted to go in but it looked as if the ship were laying right across the bay entrance. So we decided to anchor in Atuona Bay for the night. The sailing directions said "good holding ground."

We could see a few lights showing from Atuona Village. They looked like pressurized kerosene lanterns. We idled into the bay, very slowly, with Ernie and Ray on the bow straining their eyes forward. No good listening for surf—the roar, of it was all around us. Then Ernie yelled, "Breakers dead ahead."

I wheeled *Starbound* in a tight circle and pointed her bowsprit into the swell. "How far?" I called. I was looking over the stern now at the village lights but couldn't see the beach. There was a clattering noise mixed with the surf roar, which confused our ears. We couldn't imagine what it was.

Ernie came aft with his good night vision and stared astern. "I can just see the surf, Dad. Why don't you take her out about 100 more yards and we'll drop the big hook. It's all set up."

We let out 50 fathoms of chain as *Starbound* fell off the wind toward the beach, then watched the chain surge as the winch brake took hold and the hook set in hard. I let the engine idle while we took stock of our position.

We'd just done two things which we normally avoid under almost any circumstances: first, we'd entered a strange, unlighted bay at night. Second, we'd anchored on a lee shore. Well, tired as we were, there would be an anchor watch tonight.

A brief morning shower swept across the anchorage. We four stood under the afterdeck awning and gazed at the sharp green peaks soaring above the bay. Little waterfalls cascaded down the slopes to the coral shelf lining the western shore. We turned our eyes to the black sand beach where coconut palms leaned out over the breaking surf. I saw the source of the clattering noise we'd heard in the night. Black lava rocks, worn round and smooth by the surf, tumbled over each other on the beach with each wave, then tumbled back again as the back wash fed the new incoming wave. A few girls in colorful pareus waved to us from the shore. How utterly beautiful!

It was obvious that we couldn't go ashore from Atuona Bay. We might have been able to surf the launch up to the beach but our landing would have been disastrous, and getting the boat back out through the surf well nigh impossible.

I started the engine and Ernie and Ray raised the anchor, then fished one fluke and pulled it forward, free of the cutwater. We powered around the point into Taa Huku Bay.

Now we could see the small ship which we thought had the bay blocked off the night before. It was one of the interisland "schooners." *Kekanui* was her name and Papeete her home port. The days of the sailing schooners are over and these little diesel coasting-type freighters have taken their place. She had two anchors out ahead and stern lines were carried ashore so that she hung perpendicular to a large concrete platform and ramp on the beach. Her stern lay about 100 feet off. Big brown Polynesian men were wrestling barrels and crates into a husky launch alongside. They waved as we eased *Starbound* past her bow.

Two other yachts were anchored in the bay. The catamaran *Illusion* from San Francisco and a big ferro-cement ketch called *Brenda Lynn,* also from California. They were anchored quite a distance out, so we took *Starbound* around them and sounded our way closer to the little beach at the innermost bight of the bay, where we'd have to land the launch.

When the anchor was solid in the bottom we put the launch in the water and went visiting. *Illusion* seemed to be sleeping late but *Brenda Lynn* showed signs of activity, and so we met Paul and Brenda, their two small daughters, and crew member Charlie.

Paul told us what the entering procedure was, so Nina and I gathered up our papers and took the launch into the pretty little beach. We hauled the boat up above the row of high water debris and started walking. It was 2 kilometers to Atuona Village following a small dirt road cut into the edge of the point separating the two bays. The view is worth the walk.

On the way we passed the navigational aid we'd been looking for the night before. It was a little white cupola affair perched just above the road with a small glass window, behind which was placed a kerosene lantern. Some NavAid!

We followed the meandering road through the village. Flowering trees and coconut palms were on every side. Hibiscus bushes lent their colors to the scene and the scent of frangipani was everywhere. The villagers strolled about their business, never hurrying, and all greeted us with their soft "Ia ora na." A literal translation of this delightful-sounding phrase means "May you live," and it is spoken in one flowing, "eeahrahnaa," with no accent on any syllable.

We found the office of the local gendarme. He was a tall, handsome man of about forty-five, graying along the temples. His English was hard to understand, but much better than our French. The entering procedure was quite simple. Within ten minutes we were following his directions to the nearest local trading store.

The proprietor of the store was another Frenchman, but this one had a comfortable stomach and a Polynesian wife. His English was very good. We picked up some beer, wine, and bread and asked in vain for fresh milk. All milk is condensed and canned or powdered. All of it is imported and expensive.

Aboard *Starbound,* Ernie and Ray had napped the morning away, and now it was our turn while they scrambled into the launch and headed for the beach.

Next morning we all went ashore on a shopping expedition. There were three stores in the village and we visited them all. Nina kept loading us down with supplies and when we had all we could carry we started back up the road. Just outside the village a Land Rover driven by a Marquesan gave us a lift, so we climbed into the back with small boys, dogs, and teenage girls who giggled all the way to Taa Huku Bay while Nina practiced her fractured French on them. I think the girls were more interested in Ray and Ernie.

Starbound needed diesel fuel. Ray and I took the launch over to the schooner *Kekanui* and tried to work out an arrangement to pick up some diesel from them but they'd off-loaded it all onto the dock. It comes to the island in 55-gallon drums. The captain told us that it would be cheaper if we waited for the next schooner, which would arrive in two days, and buy directly from it. We decided to do that, then spent the rest of the afternoon filling our big plastic water jug at the stand pipe on the beach and ferrying the water out to *Starbound.* Five trips were enough to put 75 gallons on board.

Easter Sunday was nearly upon us. Saturday morning Ray and I made the walk to town again to find some bananas and limes. We also wanted to find out if an Easter service would be held at the church. On the road in we met Marcel (Max) Pons, a thirty-two-year-old Frenchman ("No, no—I am a citizen of the world!") who had been living in French Polynesia for over a year. Max turned out to be a very good friend indeed. Beneath his cosmopolitan exterior there is a Polynesian soul. He planned to take the schooner back to Papeete to have one ear drum examined. He'd burst it while diving on the reef, and although the local dispensary could stuff it with medicine and cotton, he thought he'd have a specialist check it out. That meant a trip to Papeete where the "big" hospital is located.

Max walked with us into the village and we were like three schoolboys on vacation. First we bought some Hinano beer at the trading store. Then Ray wanted a can of Amstel beer, which he promptly knocked off the counter with a careless hand. It hit the concrete deck in a welter of foam. He bought another one under the quizzical gaze of Max and me and the proprietor. Next he wandered over to a wall hung with hardware. Reaching up to touch a machete, he brushed a rake handle, which obliged him by falling down, carrying two more rakes and a shovel with it. The tools landed with a resounding prolonged clash of noise.

The trader looked at Max and me. I shrugged, "You must understand, he's Polish."

Questioning eyebrows shot skyward. Max explained in French.

The trader's face cleared. "Ahh, oui! Il est polonais!"

Ray buried his face in his hands and cried out, "No, no—not Polack jokes! Not in Hiva Oa!"

We followed the trader's directions and went down the road looking for the described "big lime tree." A Polynesian man with gray hair and a build like those old Charles Atlas ads called to us. Max talked with him awhile then introduced Einaa Putatoutaki, who in turn presented his wife, Marcelle.

She was a lovely, smiling Marquesan woman with satin-brown skin and long gray hair which was loosely pinned up on her head, and she was wearing the flowered pareu favored by Polynesian women. She invited us to have the midday meal with them.

It's a very Polynesian thing, an invitation to eat. If they just say, "Haere mai tamaa!" (Come and eat), it's merely a polite greeting. Then you must reply, "Aita, paia roa!" (No, my stomach is full). But in this case the invitation was explicit and delivered in French.

Einaa told us where the lime tree was and suggested we collect a bunch of the fruit while Marcelle prepared lunch. We asked him if we could bring some beer for everyone and he raised his eyebrows in a peculiar fashion which Max told us means yes.

We gathered our limes, then picked up several big bottles of Hinano beer and strolled back to Einaa's house. Marcelle sat us at the large trestle table in the big semi-open "living" room of their house and heaped the table with plates of food. There was barbecued goat meat, and *poisson cru* (raw fish à la Tahitienne). There was a poe-poe, or pudding, made from the small rimarima bananas mixed with taro flour. Large, loosely formed doughnuts called fili-fili adorned two platters. They're eaten plain or with meat. French bread and carafes of red wine were on the table along with the bottles of beer we'd brought. When the meal was over, all we could do was sit back, rub our stomachs, and say, "Aue! Paia roa!" (Wow, my stomach is full!)

We found out that "midnight" Easter services would be held at 2130 that evening. Max laughed and explained that this is because no Polynesian could stay awake for very long past midnight. So the Catholic Church bends accordingly and has the services early.

Einaa and Marcelle asked us to bring the whole family along and attend services with them. Then, after services, come back to their house for food and wine.

We returned to *Starbound* and dug out our churchgoing clothes. Nina baked her famous apple chip cake and we carried it into the village at dusk.

All the small houses were alight with kerosene lamps and we could hear bursts of French and Polynesian from all sides as everyone made ready for the big event. Max told us that the entire village would be deserted during services.

With Marcelle leading the way we walked up the narrow streets to the pretty church on the hill. Outside the church a large crowd of villagers were laughing and talking together. Many of them carried lanterns or flashlights. I was glad we had taken pains to dress nicely. Every person was decked out in the best clothes he possessed. The priest stood in the large open doorway of the church and blessed us one and all, even we Protestants, and I imagine a few heathen (Ernie claims to be a Druid).

The entire service was in the Polynesian language—what a soft, mellifluous sound. The priest sang the mass and the entire congregation backed him up with great enthusiasm, the marvelous singing filling the space under the huge wooden beams which soared overhead. Dogs wandered up and down the center aisle, and small, fat brown children played with them until recaptured by their mothers. The scent of the tropic night wafted across the church, whose sides were open from the wainscot to the eaves. Pretty Polynesian girls kept turning in their seats to inspect the popaa tanes from the yacht.

After Holy Communion and the baptism of all the new babies, the congregation spilled out onto the front lawn and the priest blessed us all again, scattering holy water far and wide. We must have had a few drops fall on us for we felt particularly blessed to be at such a place at such a time.

The party at the house of Einaa and Marcelle was just plain family fun. We ate and drank everything in sight. I'm glad we had the forethought to bring along a big jug of the vin ordinaire sold at the trader's store. Max was translating at top speed and from the laughter some of his comments evoked from the islanders, I think he was adding a few fillips from his own store and knowledge of Polynesian humor. It was late when we got back to the ship.

Easter Sunday was a quiet day devoted to recovery from the night's party. In spite of that, Nina was determined that a little cleanliness was in order after twenty-six days at sea and debarked for shore with all our dirty laundry, intending to wash it in the small fresh-water river which fed into the foot of Taa Huku bay. As she sat on the bank singing and washing clothes she was suddenly joined in song by one, then two, then several Polynesian girls. They were fascinated by her old-fashioned washboard, which to them seemed quite a modern invention. She soon had at least twenty girls helping her with the laundry, each one determined to learn to speak English. Her solution was to teach them the Do Re Me song from "The Sound of Music," then every other song she could think of. After about three hours she reluctantly said good-by and returned to *Starbound*.

We discussed our departure time and decided to spend the next two days working on the ship, and then, perhaps, leave on Wednesday morning for Nuku Hiva.

As if in accord with our plans, another schooner came in on Monday morning. Max was visiting with us and told us that this was the one he planned to catch to Papeete.

"Hey, Max," I asked, "how long will it take that rust-bucket to make Papeete? Straight-through trip?"

"Oh, no! It will take, I think, nearly three weeks. The boat will stop many places to drop supplies and pick up copra."

Nina and I looked at each other. "Hell, why don't you come with us? We'll be there in three weeks too. You can have your passage free and we'll have a handy-dandy interpreter."

"But that is magnificent! Are you serious?"

"Sure!"

So Ray and I and our new crew member went to the schooner and talked to the huge Polynesian captain. "Certainement, M'sieu—just bring your fuel containers over and we will fill them aboard here and then deliver them back to the yacht with our launch."

The schooners have supply stores in them. People can go aboard and buy directly over the counter. When Nina found this out, nothing would do but that she see that store. Her sight of it cost us another $50 on top of the fifty I'd just paid for two barrels, 110 gallons, of fuel. However, the schooner left next morning, so we had some cash left for Papeete.

After the schooner had cleared the bay we upped anchor and reset it just off the concrete quay. Ray rowed ashore and caught a heaving line by which we payed out a long stern line to the quay. Then he threw the monkey's fist back to us. We bent it onto our water hose and Ray pulled the end over to the shore and connected it onto the stand pipe the schooners use for water. We filled our tanks and hosed the decks and took fresh-water baths topside. Then we disconnected hose and lines and went back to our last anchorage. We were ready to leave.

That afternoon we had a delightful visit from Einaa and Marcelle, along with other friends we'd met, Umo and his grandchildren, Marie Ange and Alfredo. We brought them out to *Starbound* and fed them lunch: spaghetti and meatballs, salad, cake and candy! We were all in hysterics while trying to teach Polynesians how to eat spaghetti Italian style.

It was time to say farewell. Ray and Max walked back to the village with our guests and finally returned after dark, laden down with flower leis. Nina was not well, and after repeated trips to the rail finally went to bed.

We decided to shove off at 0200 with a bright moon to show us the way through Haava pass. Our plan was to head west, then north around the island of Ua Pou, anchor on its northwest coast for the night, and proceed next day to Nuku Hiva.

"The best-laid plans" and all that! Despite a fresh trade wind, *Starbound* seemed to poke along. By 1800 the sun was dunking itself in the western sea, and we were just rounding the southwestern tip of Ua Pou. We weren't going to enter any more unlighted harbors in the dark. The chart showed a small harbor about one mile up the coast and we thought we'd check it out before full dark; maybe it'd offer us refuge for the night. We coasted into the tiny bay, just a cleft in the cliffs really, and didn't find soundings until we were nearly on the beach. We dropped the big anchor and backed off the beach. The anchor held, but the wind coming down off the precipitous rock walls of the bay started to push us toward the southern cliff. We dropped the launch over the side quickly and carried our small Danforth anchor out astern attached to a 4-fathom chain lead and 300 feet of anchor rode. I would guess it touched bottom about 70 feet down. At my signal from the launch Ernie took a strain on the rode from *Starbound*'s stern. A moment more, then he yelled, "It's not holding, Dad—I can feel it bouncing over rock!"

I raced the launch back to *Starbound* and went aboard. All of us began hauling on the rode. It helped swing the ship away from the cliff but it wasn't really holding. Vibrations bounced up the line to our hands as the anchor flukes seemed to hook onto rocks, then overturn them.

Ernie said, "Dad, let's get the hell out of here while we can still see. This is dangerous!"

Ernie and I have arguments at times, but this wasn't one of them. The engine hadn't been shut off. We hauled in the stern anchor as fast as we could and when it cleared the water we left it for Ray to untangle while I took the helm and Ernie raced forward to start the anchor winch. We wound ourselves back up close to the beach and when Ernie called "Aweigh!" I went into hard reverse gear and backed around in a circle away from the cliff. *Starbound* spun around and we powered out of that death trap. We secured our anchors and then turned north for Nuku Hiva, sailing a slow reach with just jib and mizzen.

We arrived off the south coast of Nuku Hiva by 0200. The moon had set and it was quite dark but we could see the loom of the high peaks against the stars. We sailed off the shore until dawn, trying to keep our easting so we wouldn't be too far west of Taiohae Bay.

The sun rose in a blaze of glory and illuminated the dark green mountains and slopes of one of the most beautiful islands in the world. We worked our way between the two conspicuous peaks guarding the bay—"Sentinel of the East" and "Sentinel of the West"—and stood into Taiohae Bay.

A few yachts were at anchor off the beach. We ran down near them and dropped our hook. Halloos came across the water. *Keewaydin* was there with her load of young Scandinavians. We saw yacht *Vega*, a pretty white sloop with a family aboard, and there was a very nice 50-foot ketch at anchor called *Morning Star*. We found a nice clear spot with plenty of swinging room, and anchored. The bay was very calm despite the fresh trade wind blowing just outside the entrance.

We had thought that Hiva Oa must wear the crown of "Queen of Islands," and now here was another one as lovely. These are very "new" islands when looked at from a geological time scale. They are purely volcanic, thrown up by eruptions from the sea bed during a relatively recent age, and have not had time to sink and then rise again to form a coral reef around themselves as Tahiti has done. They are called the "high" islands as distinguished from the "low" island or coral atoll. We would see the low islands when we passed through the Tuamotus on our way to Tahiti, which lay some 800 nautical miles to the west-southwest.

We went ashore and entered at the Gendarmerie once again. They kept our passports and would return them when we left the island. We were becoming acquainted with the new look of the French government in Polynesia. The French were conducting their atomic tests in the Marquesas and the rules were becoming stringent regarding the movement of yachts. They wanted to know where all foreign nationals were at all times.

The town was laid out in a very orderly fashion which lacked the haphazard charm of Atuona. The esplanade along the waterfront was immaculately clean and the road was flat and well cared for. We found the store of trader Maurice and picked up a few items for our food lockers—expensive items. We found some of *Keewaydin's* crew strolling the streets and renewed old acquaintances. They had on their back packs and were preparing to hike across the high mountain ridge which separates Taiohae Bay from Taipi Vai, the famous bay and valley of Melville's *Typee*. We had already decided to take *Starbound* into that bay before leaving Nuku Hiva.

Nina and I spent the rest of the day strolling up the beautiful valley road winding away from the bay. We found the wood carver's house the *Keewaydin* crew had told us about, and Nina bartered for a small carved Tiki for the boat. Then she went overboard and bought a beautifully carved ukulele, called a "banjo" by the Polynesians. On the way back down to the bay we were given mangoes and breadfruit by the people living in the houses by the road. The mangoes were huge, and so delicious—something like a firm, tart peach which has had just a touch of turpentine added to it.

We met Ray Triplett from *Morning Star* on the esplanade and he told us that his fuel pump was broken and unfixable. The French Navy ship *Oueregon* had come into harbor that morning and the navy engineers had dismantled it and found that the main cam shaft in it was fractured. Ray was disgusted. "To hell with it, Gordon. We sailed the boat here from Papeete and I guess we can make it back to Honolulu without an engine. When are you people leaving for Taipi Vai?"

"Oh, next week sometime; maybe Wednesday or Thursday."

"How would you feel about towing *Morning Star* out of here, say, about a quarter-mile off the island, so I can pick up the trades?"

"Sure, Ray—be glad to. But why don't you take that little plane that lands here to Papeete and pick up a new pump? You could have one air-freighted in from the States."

"Ah, hell!" he exclaimed, "It'd take weeks, and I've been to Tahiti. I don't want to go back now. We can sail her home O.K."

If it had been me, I'd have wired for the part, but when a man has made up his mind . . . "All right, Ray, when we're ready to go out I'll come over and we can discuss how to pick up the tow."

Saturday night in Taiohae is really an event, especially when the French Navy is in town. Beside the esplanade was a large plot of grassy land on which was built a beautiful open-sided pavilion with carved wooden columns supporting a thatched roof. A raised stage at one end was used to support a movie projector or a band of musicians.

First we saw the movie—a French detective thriller, Mike Hammer type. Everyone brought a mat and sat on the concrete floor: moms, dads, kids, sailors, and yachties. The kids screamed and yelled at the sight of their screen hero being bashed about by the incredibly villainous foes of "good." It was a ridiculous grade Z movie, but somehow enjoyable because of the atmosphere of the "theater." Hinano beer tops kept popping during the entire film. When it was over, everyone got to his feet and moved mats, kids, and beer out to the lawn surrounding the pavilion.

I noticed what had been missing. Where were all the pretty young women? Then they started drifting in by ones and twos, dressed to the hilt in their Polynesian pareus, some with their long, glossy black hair done up in ornate twists and curls, others with it hanging in glorious waves down to their hips. The Polynesian men, the Navy men, and the yachting men all moved together. Each girl was greeted by a large group of admirers. A paper cup of Hinano was offered and accepted. Laughter hung like a silver cloud over the assembly. Down with the lights! Action!

The Polynesian musicians gathered on the stand. Nina cried, "Oh, no! The Beatles themselves! Look at all those amplifiers."

They fooled us, though. They started off with a mild, popular two-step, then graduated to a wild tamure, then fell back to some fairly good rock. The Polynesians could dance to anything.

The glorious Marquesan girls flung themselves into the tamure with the abandon prevalent during Captain Cook's time. Nina and I tried it with some success, our bashfulness being overcome by a goodly amount of beer. The vahines would drift over near us and smile, then nudge Nina and indicate to her to watch them. Then they would pull their pareus tight across their hips, drop the back of one hand delicately on their waist, arm slightly akimbo. Then they'd slow their incredibly sexy hip action down to a half-beat so that Nina and I could see how they did it. And I studied very, very hard! The man's dance is different, of course; lots of aggressive thrusting action, knees flapping in and out symmetrically as the feet are raised alternately from the floor with each beat. I became relatively proficient. A beautiful girl called Fleurette taught me a few things—on the dance floor, of course. She was willing to teach me a lot more, but Nina was keeping a weather eye out while she danced with the French Navy.

I was puzzled by the periodic disappearance and reappearance of first one, then another of the Marquesan girls. Finally I noticed that their pareus were different on their reappearance at the dance. They'd gone home, taken a bath, changed clothes, and redone their hair. I asked Max about it and found out that the girls will do this sometimes three times during a dance. They are purely delectable females.

The next day was Sunday. We slept late and slowly recuperated. About noontime a big navy launch came alongside *Starbound*. It was full of chief petty officers from the *Oueregon*. They were feeling very good indeed, having suppressed their hangovers from the dance with good French wine. They asked if they could fix anything on *Starbound*. I gave them the anchor winch brake band which needed brazing across one end. Then we decided to have some wine with them. We drank everything on board! There was Jacques (Josef) Chevrier, Yves Tregoat, Maurice Larroque, and Roger, a Polynesian who was in the French Navy and who played a guitar with an expertness seldom matched by anyone I'd heard.

When the wine was gone, Yves and Josef decided to go back to *Oueregon* to get more. Roger had to go on duty so he reluctantly went with them. At the last minute Ray decided to see the *Oueregon* and supervise the movement of alcoholic stores from the French ship to the American ship. He fancied himself to be more sober than the rest. Nina and I told them to go and return quickly and we'd light off the the charcoal broiler and get Max to make a salad. Maurice stayed with us to talk about yachts.

I heard the entire story from Ray when they returned from *Oueregon* two hours later. One of the petty officers on board had just made chief, a very meaningful promotion. So he had a "wetting down" party on the ship and Ray, Yves, and Josef walked right into the middle of a big drunk-up. They finally escaped. When I saw them coming across the bay in the launch, I just laughed. The wake was like a snake. They climbed aboard with the overly careful step and owlish expressions of those who have put down a lot of booze and know it.

"Hey, man, you'll never guess what happened." And on and on into the soft tropic night. They'd brought back several bottles of very good French wine as well as two bottles of twelve-year-old Rhum Clément.

About 0200 we lowered Maurice headfirst into the launch. Josef and Yves could still navigate. Ray was snoring on the cabin top, so I motored the Navy back to *Oueregon* and landed the men alongside their liberty launch which was secured outboard of the rope ladder leading up 30 feet to the main deck. A good thing, too. Yves and Josef just left Maurice in the launch for the night because they couldn't get him up the ladder.

Next day seemed a bit dim till about noontime. Then Nina and I went to town for bread. The trick in Polynesia is to find the Chinese bakery. We just followed that fascinating scent of fresh loaves.

Back on *Starbound* we held a planning party. Everyone wanted to visit Taipi Vai. We decided to leave on Thursday morning, return Friday evening, and leave for the Tuamotus on Saturday.

Nina's foot was giving her some trouble, probably from all the dancing. She had managed to achieve a magnificent blister from a new pair of sandals while in Hiva Oa, and by the time we got to Nuku Hiva it was badly infected. The hospital in Taiohae was small but efficient. One of the female doctors had made a snip-snip and removed Nina's toenail, cleaned the infection and dressed it. Now it was sore again. I walked with her back to the hospital where the big Polynesian nurse looked at it, smiled up at Nina, and said, "You dance?"

Nina replied, "Yes, I danced with many men last night."

The nurse inspected her toe, redressed it, and said, "You should not dance for one week, O.K.?"

Nina said, "O.K."

Back on *Starbound,* I decided to check the bottom to see if it was clean. It'd been ten months since our last haul-out. I broke out the scuba gear and went over the side. A yacht next door yelled to me, "Get out of the water!"

That urgent tone startled me. I climbed back up our rope ladder and shaded my eyes toward the voice. It was the owner of a small William Garden cutter, called *Puffin.* She had just come in that day and I hadn't met the people yet. I yelled back, "What's the matter?"

He pointed out at the bay. I could see two shark fins cutting through the evening water. I hit the quick-release catch and shrugged the scuba pack off my shoulders. Then I jumped in the launch and steamed a fast arc over to the little cutter, tied the launch to the stern, and went aboard to meet Jerry and Ev Taylor from San Diego.

"Hey, man, thanks for the warning."

"It's O.K.," Jerry said. "I hate the sight of blood. It'd ruin my dinner. Have a glass of California wine. We just got it cold." He told me that the sharks in these waters will come into the bays in the morning and evening to feed. "Swim at high noon," he said. "There won't be any around. But I'd have someone keep a lookout in any case."

Next day at noontime, Ray and I both went over the side, Ray using a snorkel and me with the scuba. Nina and Ernie kept lookout for those ominous black fins.

I was shocked at the sight of our hull. Goose barnacles were everywhere, growing up to 3 inches long on the bottom of the keel. No wonder we hadn't been making any speed through the water lately. I called to Ray, "You scrape the water line and as far under as you can reach with the snorkel. I'll take the rest of it!" Ernie handed us each a broad-bladed scraper.

Two hours and two bottles of compressed air later we were back on board. *Starbound's* copper sheathing was clean, although a bit bare of paint in spots.

Ray wandered ashore in the afternoon and came back with a funny story. He and Max had been over on the main quay talking to the skipper of the interisland schooner *Kaoha Nui*. They'd been telling him how much we'd enjoyed Hiva Oa, his home island, and how Ray had managed to fix two portable radios for people there. The big Polynesian immediately broke out his portable. "Maybe you fix dis bugger!"

Ray looked at it and said, "Maybe!" He had it working in half an hour. Then he asked the captain, "Maybe tomorrow we can come alongside your ship and take on some fresh water?"

"Sure ting! You bring da yacht 'longside. We gonna fix you up!"

We cranked in our chain and anchor next morning and loaded up with fresh water. Our only mishap occurred when I backed over my own spring line and cut it into two breast lines with the propeller. Thank God it didn't wind onto the prop. We went back onto our anchor and checked out the boat for an early morning departure. I went over to *Morning Star* and arranged with Ray Triplett to tow them out next morning.

It was slow going to Taipi Vai—dead against wind, wave and current. By 0830 we were anchored just off the beach at the foot of the bay and we all went ashore to explore up the river, looking for the village.

Then, instead of following the river, we decided to set off across the river delta and ended up coated with mud to our knees.

Nina and I wandered through the village together and had the great privilege of meeting Madame Clark, a French and Polynesian woman, about seventy years old, who had been married to one of the famous sea captains and settlers of the Marquesas. She told us that if we'd come back next morning, she'd take us up through the woods to see a very sacred Marae, a famous Tiki place. We made a date.

Nina and I found Ray, Ernie, and Max sitting in a pleasant local restaurant drinking beer. We joined them and met the roly-poly French-Chinese man who ran the place. He was leading a life that many men must envy: married to a charming Polynesian woman, raising a half-score of beautiful children, and working when he felt like it.

We went into the village next morning at 0830, this time taking the launch clear up the river at high tide, and met Madame Clark at her house, an old island-type home which her husband had built fifty years earlier. It had two stories and huge deep verandas running all around. Madame Clark was a slim woman with sparse gray hair pulled tight back behind her ears and pinned into a bun. She had a great sense of humor and joked with us in her scanty English. She gave us nuts and fruit to eat, then led off at a fast walk for the Marae. Her two dogs trotted along with us. She told us that we would have to hike about 3 kilometers up the mountain. I wondered if she would make it—an old lady like that!

One hour later I wondered if *I* would make it! Madame Clark was still

going strong. She stopped three-quarters of the way up and showed us how
to collect green drinking nuts from the trees. We shinnied our way up one
of the lower coconut palms and twisted off the nuts she wanted. Ernie
hacked off the ends with the machete he was carrying and we drank the
cool, delicious coconut water, then ate the young jellylike flesh from inside
the nuts.

The Marae was a place of foreboding which still contained tupapau,
spirits of the dead. The full-blooded Polynesians wouldn't come near the
Maraes, especially this one, which was inhabited by "live" Tikis.

The squat, gross, incredibly ancient Tikis were carved out of solid lava in
some bygone age, and were situated at each corner of the Marae. The
Marae itself was 200 feet on each side, a vast square built of carved lava
blocks fitted together with a beautiful precision.

Madame Clark warned us not to touch the Tikis. "Something very bad
happen if you touch Tiki!" We didn't touch them. Then she sat on the edge
of the upper platform of the Marae and pointed to where the sacrificial
victims were killed to appease the ancient Polynesian gods. I was really
getting into her story, looking at the carved holes where the victims' bodies
were thrown. The dense foliage of the trees nearly met overhead, and we
were standing in the greenish half light of a tropical jungle. The tupapau
were there, I knew.

Suddenly a horrible screaming squeal rang out along with a crashing of
brush and barking dogs. Madame Clark added to the clamor, yelling and
throwing rocks. Finally she turned to me and said, "Goddamn jungle pigs!
Stupid dogs! What you gonna do with 'em?"

We got back to the village about noontime. We were whipped, but
Madame Clark looked fresh as a springtime morning. We thanked her, as
well as we could, for an unforgettable experience.

Back in the village again, we followed Max to the house of a man who
had organized some fruit for us. We loaded the launch with two immense
bunches of bananas, about a hundred limes and a dozen "pamplemousse,"
those huge, sweet grapefruit which make the United States version look like
lemons.

We worked the launch down to the river mouth, then had to haul the
launch over the shallows. The tide was out.

We got Starbound under way and had a very fast sail back to Taiohae.
We were anchored in our old spot by 1430 and went ashore to pick up the
last supplies we needed: fresh meat, fresh bread, fresh lettuce, and red
wine.

Getting wine at the little trading stores is interesting. We'd take in our
own containers. Then we'd sample the wine out of one of the huge wicker-
covered jugs they sell it from. Some of it is vinegar! When we found a jug
with something in it that tasted like a decent vin ordinaire, we'd tell the

proprietor and he would drop a wine-stained old rubber hose into the mouth of the jug. We'd put our containers on the floor. Then he'd suck away at the end of the tube until he had a syphon flow started, which he would interrupt by placing a large dirty thumb on the end of the tube. Then he'd fill our containers one after the other, always with the thumb handy to stop the flow when he wanted. Nina would always whisper to me, "What if he has syphilis or something?"

I'd whisper back, "Don't worry, babe—that wine'll kill anything that lives!"

A French frigate came into the bay and another dance was organized for the evening. All the yachties went to this one and it was a fine way to say good-by to all our friends, yachtsmen and Polynesian.

Next morning at 1000 hours we sailed out from under the almost perpetual cloud cover of Taiohae Bay and broke into the brilliant sunshine of the pass. The sea air felt clean and dry and our spirits felt the same.

We turned *Starbound* west for the Tuamotus.

11

The Tuamotus and Tahiti

"The Tuamotus? Goddamn, lousy, dangerous bunch of reef-infested islands—I wouldn't give you a nickel for the whole bunch of 'em!" Thus spake the paid captain of a very fancy 90-foot schooner.

"You're going through the Tuamotus? Man, what for? That's a hairy passage, boy! Didn't you hear about that Frenchman, what's his name? The single-hander, round-the-world type? He stacked that pretty fiberglass yacht of his right up on the southern tip of Rangiroa." So proclaimed the skipper of a cruising yacht in Panama.

But I could still hear our Scandinavian friend Rene Concord, talking to us in Annapolis one snowy evening three years earlier. "Listen, Gordon. Let me tell you about the Tuamotus. The only reason cruising skippers knock 'em is that they don't want a big mess of boats screwing up their favorite cruising ground. Yeah, the currents are fast and unpredictable, and the passes are a bad dream, and you shouldn't sail at night.

"But you can see from one island to the next! And once into the lagoons—beautiful—they are the perfect coral atolls! The people are wonderful, and unspoiled by tourism because there isn't any! You must stop there, for a while at least. Actually, next time I go back, I will spend at least six months just cruising the Tuamotus."

So here we were. We had decided to visit the island of Ahe because it was right on the way to Tahiti and was supposed to have a navigable pass into the lagoon. Rangiroa and Manihi also fit that description, but Rangiroa had an airstrip and therefore was bound to be infested with tourists from Tahiti,

143

and we had heard that the French were planning on putting in a small airstrip on Manihi, and that it might already be there.

We had a beautiful sail to Ahe. Five days of light trade winds put us about 10 miles off the island at dawn on a Thursday, just when and where we had planned to be. Ray and I shot nine morning stars for a pinpoint fix, and when we had our position plotted I said, "Bet I can see it from the crosstrees!" I ran up the ratlines, grabbed the futtock shrouds, and threw a leg over the square yard. Sitting astraddle the big spar, I looked ahead and there it was—Ahe! About a point off the starboard bow I could see Manihi, too. Even the shape of the islands was apparent. I climbed down to the deck again and then looked. Nothing! I blessed our ratlines again.

A cruising boat has to have an easy way of going aloft, on both masts if she has two. Solid ratlines are best. *Starbound* has solid white-oak ratlines which are seized to the marline-served shrouds with copper wire. A smaller boat might want something a bit more delicate in appearance; then "Lord Nelsons" are useful. They're made by splicing a small eye in either end of a short piece of line, then whipping the eyes onto the shrouds so that the line acts as a ladder rung. We use them up aloft on *Starbound*'s topmast where ratlines would look clumsy as well as creating additional windage. *Starbound* has more windage than most yachts despite our years of ownership, during which we've done a lot of work to reduce our tophamper windage to a safe minimum. But we keep our ratlines and Lord Nelsons.

I finally caught a glimpse of Ahe from the cabin top by using the binoculars. The tops of the palm trees just showing above the horizon looked exactly like the fish traps which are scattered throughout the shallow water areas of the Chesapeake bay. "Ray, take a look and tell me what you see." I handed him the binoculars.

He steadied himself against the main boom and focused on the horizon. "Hey! Chesapeake Bay fish traps!"

Slowly the atoll rose from the sea. This was no "high" island with its crown of clouds and mysterious dark green valleys and shadowy bays. This was a real coral atoll encircling a huge lagoon nearly 7 miles across. The combination of blinding white sand beach separating green palms and incredibly blue water actually hurt our eyes. It was too vivid.

We found the pass by counting the number of small islets, or motus, of the atoll down from its northeast corner. I said, "My God! Is that it? The pass?"

Ernie replied, "Must be, but it sure looks narrow. Hey, there's a motor boat coming out." There was indeed. A 14-foot open launch using a big outboard motor swept out of the pass and came about in a big circle. Two Polynesian men were in it along with some fishing gear.

We dropped our jib and mizzen—the main had come down earlier—and motored *Starbound* within hailing distance of the launch. "Ask 'em if this is the pass, Max."

They informed us that it was indeed.

"Ask 'em if the tide's right to go in."

The answer came again in French: right now would be a good time to go in, and we shouldn't wait because when the tide turned, which would be very soon, it would ebb out through the pass at several knots.

Then, surprisingly, the huge fat man sitting aft in the launch pulled on the starting cord of his outboard motor and brought the launch right under *Starbound*'s quarter, matching her slow forward way. The other man, a handsome brown guy with black curly hair and a big grin showing a few missing teeth, picked up a sizable fish from the bottom of the launch and stepped up to our rubrail, then onto the afterdeck. He presented the fish to Nina. "Pour madame." Then he turned to Max and said in French, "Please tell the captain that I, Teato, will steer his ship through the pass for him."

I received the translation with mixed emotions, indignation not being the least. "Not on your life!" I said. Then quickly, "Don't tell him that, Max. Ask him if he's taken other boats through the pass."

The reply came back with a somewhat hurt expression, "But yes! I take all the big boats through the pass. Why, just the other day I took the very large ketch *Keewaydin* through. She is anchored off my village right now."

I thought again. If this guy could take *Keewaydin* in through that narrow slot, he could surely take *Starbound* in. I made up my mind. "O.K., Max. Tell him to take her through. But also tell him that I will stay by the controls to give the engine more power if it is needed. Ask him to turn the boat in a full circle before starting through so that he can get an idea of her response to the wheel, and tell him that there are six turns to the wheel, lock to lock. Make sure he understands."

Teato listened to Max, nodded with the big smile again, took the wheel, ran *Starbound* in a big circle, feeling her out, then straightened her onto a course for the pass. I turned to Ray and Ernie. "You guys scramble up to the main crosstrees and tell us where the coral is. This is going to be a bit hairy!"

We started in. Teato signaled to me for more power and I upped the engine RPM's to 1,800. Ray called down, "We're on the left side of the pass but we're heading just right! There's a solid coral bank on the far left where that pole is sticking out of the water, and right in the middle of the opening is a bunch of coral heads! He's taking us through the clear area between 'em!"

Max translated that into French for Teato, who grinned and made a forward cut with his hand indicating we'd go straight in now. I looked ahead and choked up. We were passing the coral bank about 10 feet from our port side. I looked to starboard and could see all too clearly the underwater coral heads an equal distance away. I grinned what must have been a sickly grin and pointed them out to Teato. He smiled happily and nodded. What the hell, I thought, he can smile—it's not his boat!

Ernie yelled down from aloft, "Hey, Dad, you ought to see this pass from up here!"

"No thanks! It's spooky enough from the deck!" I could see overfalls in front of us now: a series of violent small breaking waves sweeping directly across the opening of the pass into the lagoon. Oh, boy, I thought. "Max, ask Teato about those rips up ahead."

More French. Max replied, "He says the tide is starting to run out, but it is not yet strong. We will go right through the overfalls, then turn to the right to miss another big coral head." I swallowed hard and nodded. Teato grinned and nodded.

Nina scowled and nodded, then said, "I'm gonna fix a drink. I think I need one."

"Fix us all one, honey. Ten in the morning doesn't seem too early today."

Suddenly we were through the pass and into the lagoon. Riffled by the trade winds, the calm expanse of blue water lay placidly under the tropic sun. It was much bigger than we'd envisioned. We could see the encircling green motus which formed the atoll all the way around the lagoon's perimeter, each motu with its crown of coconut palms. How very beautiful it was.

Then Ray called, "Hey, down there! There's coral heads everywhere in this lagoon. Does that guy know where he's going?" Teato assured us that he did. He said that he would steer us right across the lagoon and into the village anchorage.

It was 7 miles across the lagoon. As we approached the village we could see other yachts at anchor and identified *Keewaydin* by her towering masts. We made the last turn around a protecting reef and motored past the sterns of the anchored boats. *Keewaydin*'s crew tumbled out of the cabin to greet us.

I asked Teato if it would be possible to put us where we could set our anchor in sand rather than coral. He put *Starbound*'s bow within 100 feet of the beach and signaled that the anchor should drop. Ernie spilled it over the side and *Starbound* fell back between two large coral heads. Another three-way conversation assured us that there was no danger; the trade winds would hold her from swinging.

We put the launch over to take Teato ashore and told him to bring his wife back with him for lunch. He was still all smiles as he accepted.

A delegation from *Keewaydin* came aboard and we renewed acquaintances. They told us that they were planning on leaving that evening. The captain was in a hurry to get to Papeete. They were going to anchor just outside the pass for the night, then spend the next morning spearfishing and shelling, and they would be on their way by the following evening. We couldn't convince them to stay another day. The skipper was in a real hurry to get around the world this first time, then pick up another paying crew and do it all over again.

We went ashore, landing the launch at the concrete quay jutting out from the beach. The village was very open and sunny with lots of space between the houses. Coconut palms and frangipani trees were everywhere, and the brilliant sunlight filtered through their foliage. The trade winds blew gently from the southeast. No steep mountains and hidden valleys here. A very different atmosphere from the Marquesas, a buoyant atmosphere that seemed to be reflected by the people. Children were everywhere, running and laughing, busy with their games. Men and women smiled at us and called softly, "Ia ora na." At one house we passed, a pretty young woman stepped down from the raised platform which formed the floor and approached us. She dropped a beautiful shell necklace over Nina's head and kissed her on both cheeks, then did the same to me.

We finally returned to the quay in an ambulatory mental haze. For years we had dreamed about a place like this—and we were here! Nina kept letting a tear leak down her cheek.

"Why are you crying?"

"I'm just so happy."

"So laugh, don't cry!"

Next morning the chief of the village and his secretary paddled an outrigger canoe to *Starbound*'s side and came aboard to enter the ship officially and to greet us. The chief's name was Tauratoa Tarana but he told us to call him Toa. He looked like the chief of a Tuamotuan village should look: a big brown man in his fifties, with gray wavy hair and a substantial stomach. Twinkling brown eyes with laugh crinkles at the corners looked out benignly over a large flat nose at his small, sunny world.

The secretary, named Piu Pere, was another type altogether. He was of a slenderness rare in Polynesians. His one-sided, thin-lipped smile never quite reached his eyes and his hatchet blade nose twitched first to one side, then the other. I found myself wondering who was chief in fact.

They told us the rules and regulations of Ahe. The two important ones were: don't throw garbage in the lagoon and don't give the islanders any booze because they're mostly Mormons.

In the afternoon, after another stroll through the village, we got pulled into a volley ball game with a bunch of very active young islanders and other yachties. The court is located between the church and the school and is surrounded by coconut palms and flowering trees.

Volley ball is played everywhere in French Polynesia. Since it is played with great exuberance, the Polynesians rapidly adopted it as their own. The game suits their spirits: much running and yelling with a lot of opportunities for comical errors which set everyone howling with laughter.

That evening will be one to remember when I am a very old man, no longer able to sweat up a halyard. We had finished dinner aboard, and the sun was well under the horizon. Nina, Ernie, Ray, and I were sprawled on the afterdeck transom seats, resting from our volley ball aches, and just soaking up the tropical twilight—the feel of the warm breeze, the sound of the sea pounding onto the reef on the far side of the atoll, the smell of frangipani drifting across the lagoon from the shore, the sight of the last pink remnant of sunset giving way to the first star sparkle. Then we heard it—a guitar and ukulele playing in perfect accord with one another, a Polynesian melody augmented by two male voices singing in harmony. They were on the quay!

We piled into the launch and with a few strokes of the oars—no noisy outboard here—glided up to the landing steps. We were late. Three dinghies from the other boats were already there. Everyone had a mat or pad to sit on. I grabbed the seats from the launch to keep our backsides off the concrete. Ernie had brought his guitar, which was immediately appropriated by the islanders. All the young single people from the village were strolling down. Most of the yachties were there, and later on I noticed a few older Polynesians walking toward us, carrying woven mats with them. The guitars and banjos passed from hand to hand for nearly two hours. Then, slowly, people started to melt away, the villagers to their homes, the yachties to their boats. Time to sleep.

The crews of *Starbound* and another yacht, *Dulciana,* were invited to the house of chief Toa for dinner next evening at 1900. It seems that the crew of every yacht that comes to Ahe goes one night to the chief's house, and it was our turn.

Dulciana is a pretty little 32-foot cutter owned by Pete and Jan Kurst and their son, Nick. Nick and Ernie were about the same age. They both had blond hair worn shoulder-length, part of their uniform, so they hit it off well together.

Dinner was superb, although I felt a tinge of disappointment when we were served the delightful island food in Western style. The chief's wife, Fana, was very proud of her white china and stainless ware, all laid out on a white tablecloth covering a big table, with chairs surrounding. Fana was the perfect female counterpart of Toa, fat and brown with wavy gray hair. Her smiles reached to her brown eyes as she kept up a running commentary in French and Polynesian with a few English expressions tossed in for spice. She served us chicken and noodles Tuamotuan style, the ever-present rice, Maori poi made from breadfruit, and my favorite dish, *poisson cru.* Green drinking coconuts were sitting at each plate to quench our thirst. Max said, "Magnifique!"

Next morning we met three young French people who had been living on Ahe for several weeks: Claude Marco, Michel Tanner, and Michele Dassonville. Chief Toa had given them a vacant house to use and the three of them had each assumed a place in the island's economy according to their individual abilities. Claude, an expert spear fisherman, went out with some of the men each day and brought back fish for the community. Michel often fished too, but more often went with a group to the other motus and helped with the gathering of copra. Michele helped the women of the village with their sewing and homemaking chores, and also helped teach the children. Quite an existence—but I think they all three had had a sufficient amount of paradise to last them for a while. They were planning on leaving shortly for Papeete and then back to France.

Claude, an extremely handsome young man with curly black hair and a build like Michelangelo's Apollo, was particularly delighted to meet us when he discovered that Nina owned a pair of thin rubber gloves. One of his hands had been severely bitten by a moray eel during his last foray on the reef and he couldn't get the wound wet. Nina helped him put the glove on his bandaged hand and taped the gauntlet to his arm to make it waterproof. Claude ran to his house to get his spear, mask, and fins. I've never seen anyone so eager to dive. Michel told us that he would spend hours in the water every day, playing tag with the reef sharks. He returned in record time with his gear and went with Max and Ray in the launch out to the pass to get some fish for our dinner.

Nina and Ernie and I went ashore for another game of volley ball. When we returned to the boat in the late afternoon we could see the launch returning from across the lagoon, just a speck at first, growing larger.

What a bunch of fish! The bottom of the launch was full of them. We all grabbed knives and started to clean them. We saved out a big green parrot fish for *poisson cru* and a grouper-type fish called "losh," brown with blue spots, which Nina wanted to bake. Claude distributed the rest of the fish in the village and on his way back picked up a few ripe coconuts.

The preparation and eating of raw fish is not restricted to, or peculiar to, French Polynesia. In South American countries it is prepared in a slightly different way and is called *cerviche*. In the Hawaiian Islands I've heard it called *lomi-lomi*. The Japanese fix it several ways and one of those ways is called *sashimi*. But in French Polynesia, it is *poisson cru*.

We cleaned and filleted the big green parrot fish and made a huge bowlful of the lovely stuff. The baked losh was superb, the *poisson cru* stupendous!

I was determined to get under way for Tahiti the next afternoon at the stand of the high tide, about 1700 hours. I discussed it with Nina but not quietly. She wanted to stay for at least another week. My arguments finally prevailed; the ship comes first and we were growing another nice collection of goose barnacles on our hull—and we were short of water because we'd been careless with it, and our food supplies were running low.

The next morning was the same old thing: a beautiful, sunny day with a steady southeast trade wind. We had a farewell lunch with Teato and his wife, Louise, at their little house on the waterfront. Nina cried all the way back to the boat.

We waved good-by to the village at 1500 and were at the pass at 1645. The tide was still coming in, but weakly, so we powered through the overfalls and found our way through the coral, our own pilots this time.

Just outside the pass a beautiful yawl, *Sabrina,* lay hove to. We'd last seen her in the Galapagos. We spoke her and gave all the information we could about the pass which they were about to enter. We told them we'd see them in Papeete and waved good-by.

We brought *Starbound* into the wind and made all fore and aft sail. Our course lay between Rangiroa atoll and Arutua atoll to the south. We wanted to sight the pass just at daylight. The northerly current worried us. It was reported to be strong. We laid our course to just shave Arutua, the southern boundary of the 19-mile-wide pass.

At first light I was in the crosstrees gazing at the southern reef of Rangiroa. We would pass just one mile south of it. We had been set 18 miles to the north in just twelve hours. The reports about current were correct.

Rangiroa is a very big atoll, almost 80 miles long by 20 miles wide. We didn't see the last of it off our stern until late afternoon.

We set our course for Tahiti. 210 degrees magnetic would allow us about 10 degrees leeway—that current again.

Tahiti—the dream island of all sailors.

On a beautiful sunny May afternoon just two days from Ahe, Ray lowered the binoculars and with a startled expression said, "Hey, Gordon, those aren't clouds; that's an island! I can see mountains!"

"Well, hell, Ray, how fast have we been going? It looks like we'll get in tonight and that's much too early! I want to sail past Venus Point in the morning with the sun well up."

Ray said, "I don't know, but that's got to be Tahiti. There's no other big island between it and the Tuamotus!"

The right thought occurred to us and we swung below for the Bowditch. Page 1254 gave us our answer. Mount Orohena, the principal mountain on Tahiti, is 7,339 feet high and, according to Table 8, is visible for about 100 nautical miles—if we assumed perfect visibility in optimal atmospheric conditions. Well, we had good though not perfect conditions and the taffrail log stated that we were about 70 miles away from Venus Point.

We whiled away the afternoon watching the mountain grow through the clouds. Our conversations were speckled with observations like "Wow, look at that!" and "Hey, I think I can see Moorea off to the right!" and "Is that Huahine way off to starboard there?"

In the late afternoon, the southeast trade wind started doing the right thing and piped up to a fresh breeze. *Starbound* went romping along at 7 knots and a quick calculation told us to slow her down if we didn't want an 0300 arrival. We dropped the mainsail and main-staysail and let her go along at 4 knots with just the yankee jib and mizzen pulling. New calculations predicted a 1000 hours arrival off the harbor entrance.

Of course, the gods of the sea curled a lip at our calculations and the wind continued to increase gradually all through the night. Except for catnaps we all stayed on deck and watched the lights increase in number and brightness as Tahiti rose from the sea. The whole scene was beautifully illuminated by a full moon. By 2000 hours the wind was blowing at 20 knots and on a nice fat reach had *Starbound* back up to 6 knots with just her shortened rig. We slapped the sails with an open palm and they bonged like a West Indian drum.

A French Navy destroyer off Venus Point silhouetted herself against a lightening sky as we flew toward the Papeete Harbor entrance buoys. The sun rose from the sea off the port quarter and illuminated the dramatically green mountains of Tahiti. We had the reef about a half-mile to port. Inside the reef the shape of buildings grew more clear and masts of moored boats were discernible. Four pairs of binoculars were in constant use. We were all excited and pointing and exclaiming, mostly telling each other of our immediate plans on arrival.

Ernie said, "Man, I'm gonna take my bike ashore and ride all over those mountains; man—lookit that!"

Nina said, "The first thing I'd like is a huge, tossed green salad with fresh tomatoes, and about a quart of fresh, cold milk."

Ray said, "I think I'll get laid—and the sooner the better!" Ah, Ray, my friend—so simple, so basic.

Max smiled and said, "For me, some *pan*, *paté* and *vin* in a quiet little place on the waterfront, while I watch the oh-so-lovely Tahitian vahines walk by and smile at me, as of course you know they all will—because they all fall in love with me."

As for myself, I thought, I'll sit on the afterdeck, responsibilities over for a time, mind in neutral, a tall, icy gin and tonic in one hand. I will examine the waterfront with its varied people and many boats, and the storefronts with their French, Tahitian, Chinese, and English signs. And I will wonder how fast I can slip Ray, Max, and Ernie ashore so that Nina and I can have some longed-for privacy.

Leaving jib and mizzen drawing, and taking advantage of the cape effect Tahiti was imparting to the wind direction, we sailed swiftly to the harbor entrance with started sheets. The very visible red and white striped range markers started to close up and we came to port almost 90 degrees, strapping in the sails as we turned. We had the engine ticking over, ready for instant use. We proceeded a few hundred more yards and turned left onto the second range with the wind heading us. I engaged the engine's clutch, Ernie and Ray dropped the jib, and Nina and I let the mizzen come rattling down.

The smell of vanilla and copra wafted across the harbor. What a wonderfully tropic smell—especially when mixed with the perfume of flowers and the always present underriding scent of damp tropical earth.

A cruising friend in Nuku Hiva had told us to tie our stern into the park area rather than the quay. We could see the difference between the two areas. They were essentially separated by a reddish-colored monument, a tall piece of abstract art dedicated to De Gaulle. A clear spot between two of the dozens of sailing yachts presented itself just west of the monument. With only an occasional curse we made *Starbound* secure with two anchors out ahead and two stern lines crossed to heavy black iron bollards which were projecting up from the grass of the park at intervals of 50 feet. We stationed *Starbound*'s stern about 30 feet from the stacked boulders which line the water's edge. Green trees shaded the little park. Just past the grass, cars and motorbikes of all description whizzed by.

We were here! In Tahiti! But first—les gendarmes. We must enter. So I dressed in a relatively sedate fashion for Papeete: Dacron slacks, a sport shirt, and boat shoes. Max and I headed for the port captain's office on the waterfront. Max went along in case I needed an interpreter and I'm glad he did. We had to satisfy three individuals, the port captain, the immigration officer, and the customs officer. Only the port captain had any English and that rudimentary. But personable Max made it easy for me. We filled out papers for nearly an hour and then were allowed to leave with more forms in our hands, and a promise to return next day with our guns and ammunition and a complete list of canned stores and liquor on board. That'll make Nina happy, I thought—two hours of checking stores against our check-off lists. So now we were free to go ashore. That's where we went.

The procedure we followed during our first few days in Papeete is our procedure in all big ports. First we checked the post office for mail. Then we scouted the local banks and found the one which seemed to really want to help us. The biggest banks seem to be the best. It's been our experience that the small banks just don't want to bother with any out-of-the-ordinary requests, like wiring to your bank in the States for money. La Banque d'Indo-Chine in Papeete was excellent for our purposes. They had a handy form we filled out to wire for money, and they did it for no service charge. The cost of the wire was absorbed by my bank in the U.S. and charged to my account. Of course, it takes about ten days for the money to arrive. Since we needed money immediately, they were kind enough to cash a check for me. Not a personal check, although I found that would be possible too, but a state tax return check for a substantial amount. We had just picked up that check at the American Express agency with the rest of our mail. The bank gave us the highest rate of exchange for our check in Polynesian francs: 87.70 francs per U.S. dollar. If we had had cash, the exchange rate would have been 85.50 francs per dollar (remember that these were the rates in May 1974).

Higher exchange rates for checks seem to reflect the ability of the bank to retain the checks until the rate is more favorable. I'm not sure of this, but I do know that there was approximately a two-franc difference between changing cash and changing checks, including American Express checks.

So now we could operate—we had local money. We went to Donald's of Tahiti, a big store on the waterfront that sells everything including groceries. We soon found out that in general it is also the most expensive store in Tahiti. Everything, including groceries, seemed to be a little more expensive than anywhere else. But what the hell, it was our first day. So we bought a fifth of gin at 420f ($4.90) and some bottles of tonic water at 33f (38¢) per very small bottle and milk at 41f (48¢) per liter and Hinano beer at 82f (96¢) per .65 liter bottle. The beer bottles are returnable at 40f per bottle, so the beer is actually only 42f (49.2¢) per .65 liter. For beer drinkers, the price for the equivalent of a six-pack of beer worked out to about U.S. $1.60. One never sees beer bottles littering the parks and roadways in Tahiti—a cleanliness ensured by the heavy deposit on bottles.

Then we bought tomatoes, celery, lettuce, cheese—all for prices comparable to the United States. There was an occasional shopping shock; beef, for example, is very high in Papeete. It's all imported from New Zealand, and hamburger is 360f per kilo. A kilo is 2.205 pounds, which means that hamburger is about $1.92 per pound. It's very good hamburger; in fact, it's ground round, but that's still pretty expensive stuff. We bought some anyway. This was our initial splurge.

Back on *Starbound,* sitting on the afterdeck transom seats with tall drinks in our hands, we discussed the situation, that is, how to live in Papeete without going broke. We'd already stopped by several boats and talked with friends we'd seen in the Marquesas and with newer friends just met.

We took their advice to heart and worked out a modus operandi.

First rule: we must stay out of bars and restaurants. They are truly very expensive and the food and drinks aboard *Starbound* are generally better.

Second rule: we must shop for each item we needed in lieu of buying everything in one big supermarket. It would take longer, but Papeete is a small town and the necessary ground can be covered quickly. If we shopped early—the big open-air vegetable market starts business about 0530—the produce is freshest then and also cheaper. By the time we finished that, the other markets would be open.

In the afternoon we could go back to the vegetable market to buy fresh fish just taken from the fishing boats.

The small markets away from the waterfront are substantially more inexpensive. Even better, they are all owned by Chinese, and at least one person in every Chinese store in Papeete speaks good English.

Third rule: We carry bicycles on board for running around town. Ernie owns a fairly exotic racing machine, but Nina's is a plain, old, one-speed bike—now rusty, but serviceable. We can pedal all over Papeete to do our shopping and be back to the boat in an hour. Taxis are very expensive and completely unnecessary unless there is an emergency at night. When traveling any distance we could take "les trucks," but they stop running at 1800 hours. A trip out to the airport and back by taxi would cost 800f ($9.35). Round trips on le truck were 60f apiece. We learned quickly.

We had been worriedly counting our dollars and computing expenditures against the three-month period we planned to spend in the Tahiti area. We had read again the articles pulled out of magazines over the past year and had winced at the words of one particular article published in a leading U.S. boating magazine. It stated that a hamburger purchased at a "decent hotel" in Papeete would cost the equivalent of $4 American, and that fish and fruit are more or less in line with the rest of Tahiti's prices, which are "staggering." That sort of shotgun survey seems irresponsible. In the first place, no yachtsman I know goes to a hotel to get a hamburger. If a cruising yachtsman were in Miami, it is doubtful he would go to the Fontainebleu for a quick bite. If he did, he'd be lucky to get one for only four bucks.

Just one block up from the waterfront we found—guess what? A hamburger stand! We could buy a good hamburger there for the equivalent of 50 cents.

We had a lot of boat work to do in Tahiti. Lists were taped up and fluttering all over the bulkhead above the chart table. We had to haul Starbound and put fresh antifouling paint on her bottom. The topsides needed painting again. The square sail and raffee seams needed restitch-ing—we were lucky they'd held together this long. New stainless wire halyards for the yankee and mizzen had to be fitted and rove. New parrel wires were needed for the mainsail. Standard maintenance on the engines was due again; new fuel filters and lube-oil filters had to be installed, and the oil needed changing. We had to find light bulbs and wire and transistors and batteries and tools and paint and outboard motor parts, and dozens of other items. Nina had to find and buy ship's stores at a decent price—a tough job where there are no cut-rate supermarkets.

Nina's sister, Betty, made the big decision to fly to Tahiti from Los Angeles and spend two weeks aboard. We wanted to finish most of the ship's work before she arrived.

Officially, Bastille Day is July 14, but in Tahiti the festivities of "Tiurai" (July) go on from July 5 to August 5. Very few Polynesians know or care about the significance of the celebration, which marks the anniversary of the capture of the Bastille, but they are very happy to take advantage of the holiday to unrestrainedly whoop it up for one solid month. We'd carefully planned to be here for most of the fun. Of course, we wanted to see something of Tahiti besides Papeete. And we wanted to sail to beautiful Moorea, just a few miles away, for a few days, then come back. Also, we had a lot of visiting to do with other yachties; there were over sixty yachts stern tied into the quay and park when we arrived, and more were on the way.

Max found a job and an apartment within a week of our arrival, and Ray started an individual whirlwind tour of sightseeing before he had to fly back to his job in the States. Nina, Ernie, and I started work on *Starbound.* We put in our daylight hours on the boat and spent the evenings entertaining or being entertained. It made for long days and a few mornings that weren't worth thinking about.

Our first Saturday night in Papeete was one to remember. By common consent passed by word of mouth, all the yachties decided to have a party in the little park near the De Gaulle monument. "Bring your own chow and booze and a charcoal grill if you wanna cook out." What a bash! Including the Tahitians who joined us, there must have been 250 people there. Most were on the thick grass, drinking, smoking, eating, playing guitars, and telling lies to attractive strangers. Another group was dancing the tamure with the Tahitians with a bottle of scorpion juice in one hand, an uninhibited dance style was obligatory for good form. I remember sampling from a bottle offered me by a pretty brunette with short curly hair and green eyes. The bottle was a white porcelain decanter with a fancy stopper which contained ice cold vodka into which peppercorns had been placed and allowed to steep for a few days. A few swigs of that had me howling a mating cry, but Nina was keeping a weather eye on me so I sat back down in the grass. Then, to pour a little more gasoline on my inner fires, a very lovely girl in white short-shorts with wavy blonde hair hanging to her waist sat down beside me, draped herself half across my chest, and in French-accented English offered me a drink from her private stock—another decanter. This one contained a quantity of very good old rum which had a vanilla bean steeping in it. Both the drink and the blonde were warm and smooth.

"Listen," Nina said to the blonde. "Let me introduce you to our friend Ray. He's a bachelor. Gordon, why don't you go find Ray!"

"Oh, Hell, do I gotta?"

"Yeah, you gotta!"

I untangled myself from long blonde hair, tanned legs, and rum bottle and walked the few steps to the beach where Ray was about to get into the dinghy. "Where you goin', man?"

"Out to the boat. That girl I had a date with didn't show," Ray grumbled.

"Well, come on back here right now, boy. I think I'm gonna make your evening." I gave him a quick rundown. He didn't believe me. Then he believed me. I took him back and introduced him to Anne. I couldn't stand the grin on his face, so I went looking for a cold beer. That's what I said— right on top of the rum and vodka.

We didn't see much of Ray during the next several days. He was spending his nights ashore and some of his days too. He appeared at odd hours to pick up some of his gear, looking progressively weaker, and became the butt of certain sly jests.

I'm always boasting that I never get sick. I take my vitamins, and eat pleny of protein, and exercise every day—usually boat work exercise. Then I got sick. We thought it was flu. After three days of misery I snapped out of it, just in time to accept a luncheon invitation from the French Navy.

The *Oueregon* had arrived in port while I was on my back. Jacques, Yves, Josef, and Maurice came marching down the quay arm in arm, singing La Marseillaise, and delivered the invitation which requested the presence of the crew of *Starbound* aboard *Oueregon* at 1200 hours next day.

Ernie had a bike tour going with some buddies, but Nina, Max, Ray and I showed up at the appointed hour and were escorted to the chief's quarters for a pre-lunch *pastis*.

With the French, a *pastis* means a nice little aperitif. In this case it was Pernod, an innocent-tasting anise-flavored liqueur with about the same potential as nitroglycerin. It is mixed about 1 to 3 with water and a few ice cubes are added. It goes down easy. We drank a lot of it.

Lunch was superb! We ate in the chief's mess on tables laid with snowy linen, good china, and nice silverware. The food was beautifully served by enlisted men on mess duty—and what food!

We started with a paté served with freshly baked, thinly sliced French bread, then progressed to a salad containing tiny pink shrimp. The *plat de résistance* was a lovely steak fillet served with French fried potatoes. This was followed by a tossed green salad.

Dessert consisted of a choice of delicious French pastries. We opted for the rum cake. Of course, the meal was served with wines, the French Navy most decidedly not being "dry," and very good wines they were. The levels in our glasses never dropped under an inch below the rim before they were refilled.

Near the end of the meal I could see the alcohol getting to Nina. We're not used to that much wine in the middle of the day. Then they broke out some more of that twelve-year-old Rhum Clément. "But you must have rum with rum cake!"

The rum finished Nina. She didn't quite disgrace us but I had to help her down the companionway to the dock. Maurice was delighted. He finally regained the "face" he'd lost by getting snockered aboard *Starbound* back in the harbor at Nuku Hiva.

Two days later I was flat on my back with another bug. I couldn't figure it out. It couldn't be influenza again so soon. I snapped out of it long enough to see Ray off at Faaa (pronounced "Fah-ah-ah") airport, while Nina stayed aboard, taking her turn at being ill.

The farewell party at the airport was short, but intense. Ray nearly missed his plane. Anne and a bunch of her friends were there. The French Navy appeared in mufti, and Nina, Max, and I helped with the noise. An airline official finally found us at our table on the balcony overlooking the strip and told Ray that they were holding the plane for him. He staggered out to the customs counter with the whole group cheering him on. He had shell leis around his neck stacked up to his ears. There had to be pounds of them. His wide-brimmed planter's hat was pulled down firmly and squarely on his head. A pipe was clenched between his teeth. He walked with great concentration. We all helped him with his carry-aboard luggage and dumped it on the customs counter located in the open air at the edge of the strip. Palm trees waved their fronds over our heads as we yelled good-by. We were very noisy. Anne leaned across the customs gate and gave him a last kiss, then a last belt of straight scotch out of the bottle in her hand. We cheered him across the tarmac, up the roll-away stairs, and into the plane. We had bets going whether he would make it under his own steam. He did.

Nina's sister flew in from Los Angeles two days later, just in time to help us with the haul job on *Starbound*. After three days of slavery in the hot sun, Betty looked up with a paint-spattered face and snarled, "For this I came to Tahiti?"

Moorea is considered by many to be the most beautiful island in the world. It's only 11 nautical miles from Papeete. There are two lovely deep bays on its north side.

The day after *Starbound* slid back into the water we checked out with the Papeete port authorities and sailed to Moorea. It is indeed a beautiful island, but it has caught a not-so-rare tropical disease which is visibly spreading. There exist, as of this writing, six tourist hotels and a village of the Club Méditerranée on Moorea.

We anchored in Cook's Bay near the Aimeo Hotel. All good anchorages in Moorea are near one hotel or another.

Betty enjoyed it. We invaded the hotel bar that evening and listened to some good island music. Late in the evening the local girls unpinned their hair and the island dancing started.

We slept the morning away, then took the launch over to the hotel dock to go for a walk ashore.

A small red-hulled sloop called *St. George* was secured to the dock and her owner, Jean Louis Bideaud, was trying to fix his forestay which had carried away on his way over from Papeete. We'd met Jean Louis the night before. I asked him how it was going and he said, "Merde!" So I offered him a ride to Papeete if he needed parts. He took me up on it.

We had a quiet night and were under way for Papeete at 0700. Using both motor and sail against a lumpy sea, we made it in four hours, and anchored off the park. The wind was blowing 25 knots in the harbor and we decided to wait for it to drop off before snuggling in between other boats.

At 0500 next morning we worked her in quietly and secured her stern to the park again between *Vela* and *Ella,* both from Honolulu.

Betty flew back to Los Angeles next day and Nina, Ernie, and I had the ship to ourselves again. Then Ernie disappeared with some friends and Nina and I were left alone. We refused to answer hails from the park.

We had been in Tahiti for over a month now. Most of the major work items were completed. The fête—Bastille Day—was before us, and the town was gearing up for the month-long party. And I came close to losing my life.

On a Friday evening, the 28th of June, my nose started to bleed and wouldn't stop. I have never been subject to bleeding from my nose except when struck smartly on it by a hard object, like, say, a fist. I tried lying down and I bled down my throat. I tried plugging my nostrils and bled out my mouth. I was scared. Nina was too. Luckily Max had been visiting with us that evening. He took the dinghy ashore and found a taxi, running for four blocks to do it. Ten minutes later I was in the Clinique Cardella with two doctors and a nurse working on me. Both doctors specialized in tropical medicine. Seven hyperdermics and a packed sinus later, the bleeding stopped. I had lost nearly a quart of blood. I felt rather poorly. Blood tests were negative, but after reviewing the history of my several "flu" bouts over the last few months, the medical opinion was that my sinus blow-out was the aftermath of dengue fever, which I had probably contracted in the Marquesas. It's carried by mosquitoes, like malaria. It weakens the structure of the mucous membrane tissues in one's system, and nasal hemorhaging can be one of the results.

I was back on *Starbound* again after three days and sixty more hypodermics. I had a box of iron and vitamin K capsules to take, but I felt fine. I'd even lost some weight.

Now the boats started to pour into the harbor from sea. *Topaz* came in—

we'd last seen her in Panama—another party! The Transpac racing boats began to arrive. The whole town came down to the dock to cheer them and help them tie up.

Little *Puffin* came into port. *Junk* arrived, a fascinating boat built and sailed by Tom and Terry Kurth. She is a 60-foot, ferro-cement junk—full battened lug rig, high poop aft complete with chicken coop, painted eyes on the bows, the works. All major cooking is done on the afterdeck over charcoal, although there was a small galley in the joss house. Also a radio/navigation center with very fancy electronics. Also a double bed. The main saloon is entered from the joss house by swinging under the double bed and sliding down a slide. And what a main saloon! During one of the several parties aboard I heard one muttered description: "This compartment looks like a cross between a Persian whorehouse and a Chinese opium den." The thick shag carpet was carried right up the bulkheads and stopped at the huge slabs of tropical hardwood which concealed lockers both port and starboard. Gigantic pillows were strewn around to sit on. An air plant about 6 feet high was suspended in one corner. The lighting was soft and indirect; some of it came from big sea shells mounted on the end bulkheads, some of it came from the two thick, tempered glass ports set into her bilge, which allowed the sunlight to bounce off the white sand bottom and give an eerie light below.

She had a forward engine room and a hydraulic drive, and she was three-compartmented with watertight doors fitted with six dogs between compartments.

I have never been much of a "junk" fan, speaking as a naval architect and a cruising sailor. And my heart just doesn't go out to ferro-cement as a boat-building material. But I liked *Junk*. So did Nina.

The fête was upon us. For days people had been pouring into Papeete—natives from the countryside and from other islands, tourists from the airport, yachties from more yachts, the French Navy from warships. The town was stuffed like a child's Christmas stocking.

The quaysides of Papeete were covered with small wooden huts decked with palm fronds and flowers. A carousel and ferris wheel made their somehow not incongruous appearance. Small Polynesian musical groups vied with recorded rock amid the general hubbub.

Racing paddlers sent their one-, three-, and seven-man canoes crisscrossing the harbor, smoothing their strokes into powerful harmony, training for their races.

Dancing and singing competitions are held at night and draw tremendous crowds. Tickets are expensive, seats are reserved, and must be reserved early because not even standing room is left by the time actual competition begins.

We spent a few days watching the canoe races from *Starbound*. The crosstrees were the best two seats in the house. The flag halyard was rigged to bring up a cold beer now and then. Two days of hydroplane races added a touch of noisy modernity to the scene. But the fête is getting too commercial in Papeete. We had heard that each of the islands has its own competitions and old Tahiti hands advised us to sail to Huahine or Bora Bora. "It's more like the old way there," they said, "not so damn many tourists."

In the early evenings we strolled through town amid throngs of people, all dressed in their best, and sporting flower leis and head bands. The intoxicating scent of that special flower, the Tiare Tahiti, was everywhere. We wandered among the quayside huts, soaked up their carnival atmosphere, and bought raffle tickets and beer and good things to eat. We threw rings at the necks of wine bottles and, winning, drank the wine.

The evenings hummed along in an atmosphere of alcohol and flowers. We struggled to our seats for the dancing and singing competitions and were enthralled by the torchlit spectacle. The torches were for atmosphere. Some very modern stage lighting was hidden among the palm fronds. We returned to *Starbound* tired and happy, shouting goodnights to friends.

We endured two weeks of the fête then decided to leave before dissipation dissolved us. Also, we were getting bored with Tahiti—at least with Papeete. To see the old Tahiti we wanted to see, we had to drive to the other side of the island, a long way from our floating home. We thought of sailing *Starbound* around and anchoring in one of the smaller bays. Then Nina said, "To hell with it. I'm tired of this tourist trap. I mean, it's fun, but we didn't sail all this way just to slop up drinks with a bunch of turistas! Let's go to Huahine."

12

Iles Sous le Vent

Iles sous le vent; Islands under the wind. A sailing ship which follows the trades from Tahiti will come to that delightful group of islands, green tropical gems strung one after the other on a string of coral in the azure sea; Huahine, Raiatea, Tahaa, Bora Bora, Maupiti . . .

Huahine is just one day's sail from Tahiti. We took two days. We wanted to visit Moorea again and see beautiful Papetoai Bay. We'd missed it on our first visit.

We sailed all the way into the deep bay and found Robinson's Cove. We took a stern line ashore and tied it to a palm tree. We could nearly jump to knee-deep water from the stern. We sounded the water depth under the bow—30 feet. The anchor chain disappeared in a catenary downward. What a beautiful, quiet place—especially after the frenzy of our Papeete party time.

We did a very important thing that evening. We simply sat together on the afterdeck transom seats, soaked up the peace and beauty of the surroundings and talked quietly. Just Nina, Ernie and I.

One other boat came in at about sunset. A fiberglass rowing boat decked over on both ends. She was owned and rowed by Andy Svedlund. We asked him aboard. Andy had built the boat and had *rowed* across most of the world's oceans. After hearing him tell of some of his adventures, our seafaring accomplishments in our big, comfortable yacht seemed fairly tame.

We were off for Huahine by 0930 next morning and had a fair wind all day and night.

Passing the east end of the island at first light, we slipped through the eastern pass of the harbor and suddenly were back in old Polynesia. A pint-sized town lined the waterfront with its ancient wooden buildings scattered along two dirt streets. Kids and dogs played on the small quay. Trees and flowering bushes were everywhere, hanging over the water, shading the streets and quay, and softening the appearance of the somewhat dilapidated buildings into a rare kind of beauty. A Maugham scene! A Stevenson vignette!

Topaz, *Brenda Lynn*, and *Orca* had preceded us from Papeete and were situated side by side about 500 yards east of town, anchors out ahead, sterns tied to coconut palms on shore. There was a big space between *Topaz* and *Orca*. The harbor was so quiet we were able to back *Starbound* into place as if she had wheels.

Lazy days of sun, salt water, and reef crawling. We worked on *Starbound* in the cool of the mornings, snorkled on the unspoiled reefs in the afternoons, and socialized in the evenings.

More boats came in. *Junk, Puffin, Dove, Scaldis, Dulciana, Spirit*, and three French boats, two of them local charters based in Papeete. The exodus from the city had started and even this paradise was getting crowded.

One early afternoon Nina called from the afterdeck. I was at my desk in the master stateroom. "Gordon! Ernie! Come and look at this."

"I'm busy."

"Me too!"

"O.K., if you two don't want to see a beautiful girl undressing on the beach . . ."

"Where, where? If it's required, we'll look!"

A pretty Polynesian girl was just removing the last of her clothes as we hit the afterdeck running. We watched Pete Lenker from *Topaz* rowing to the beach to take her out to the big Baltic trader. Of course, while rowing, his back was toward her. When the dinghy grounded on the sand and he turned around, the expression on his face was something like a man who'd just discovered one hell of a tax loophole. She handed him her small bundle of clothes and said, "Please take them out to the ship for me, Peter, and I will swim."

"Uh, yeah, that's cool."

She dived into the water and beat Peter to the boarding ladder. He was really churning up foam with those oars.

Ernie appeared beside me. We watched the sunlight glisten on a sleek golden back plastered with long black hair. Rounded buttocks flexed as she climbed the ladder to *Topaz*'s deck. Ernie said casually, "Say, Dad, I just remembered—*Topaz* asked me over for lunch." He beat Peter to the ladder in our launch.

Her name was Bebe, he told us later, and while the *Topaz* crew ate lunch,

Bebe sat nude on their companionway ladder and carried on a conversation with them. The guys didn't mind, but the *Topaz* girls weren't too enthralled.

After Ernie left, Nina kept telling me, "You've already had lunch. Just relax."

I visited the Gendarmerie next morning, cleared for Raiatea, and retrieved our passports. As I left the building I could hear the administrator talking on the radio to Papeete, reporting our movement. The French really keep track of the yachts during these days of atomic testing.

The trades were blowing about 20 knots. We entered the pass between the twin islands of Raiatea and Tahaa just four hours after leaving Huahine.

We laid *Starbound* to the quay at Raiatea right behind *Orca*. The wind was blowing harder and we doubled our spring lines. Fresh water was available so we topped up our tanks, washed clothes, and took showers. We explored the town. It was five times the size of the village on Huahine with one-tenth its charm.

We spent the night tied to the quay. The wind honked all night and I got up several times to check our lines and fenders. In the morning it was still fresh. I checked with Bill and Ginny from *Orca*. The port captain had told Bill that both yachts must clear the dock by 1200. A copra boat was coming in to load its cargo. That was fine with us. Our main reason for stopping had been for water.

Raiatea and Tahaa are surrounded by a single reef. On the chart the twin island complex looks like a gigantic dumbbell. But Tahaa is very unusual in that its reef allows an inside passage all the way around the island. We decided to circumnavigate.

Bill was missing a critical chart, so he asked to follow *Starbound* through the tricky passage across the "bar" of the dumbbell to Tahaa. The water was chopped up by the wind and made reef spotting difficult. The passage was buoyed but the buoys were hard to see. The current was strong in places. No place to be without a good engine.

Orca waved their thanks and split off to the left for a leeward anchorage on Tahaa. *Starbound* headed to the right for Baie Haamene. The bay was on the windward side but inside the protecting reef and nearly 3 miles deep. The wind was down to about 10 knots at the head of the bay so we anchored for the night.

Next morning we started around the island. It's a very beautiful island, almost a perfect circle, and the reef is splendid. There are little bays and settlements all the way around—and not a decent anchorage in any of them! We had been warned about that but wanted to see the island anyway. The problem is, each small bay is 80 feet deep right up to the coral at the edge of the shore. The local fishing boats are pulled out of the water every time they come home.

We sailed north, then west, then south down the leeward side of Tahaa, and finally came to Baie Tapuamu, one of the bigger ones. There floated *Orca* and *Dulciana*—at anchor. I checked the chart. It was another deep one. Maybe they'd found a shoal spot. We motored near them and hailed.

"Welcome," they called.

"Can I anchor?"

"Sure, right there."

"What's the depth?"

"Ninety feet."

"Nineteen?"

"Ninety! Nine Oh."

"Wow!"

We let out 450 feet of chain. Ernie and I remembered when we'd lugged that chain up to Baltimore to be regalvanized, and what it weighed. We were very glad to have a big power windlass to get it in again.

We went ashore for a walk along the almost deserted beach road. Jan from *Dulciana* came with us. We spotted a big lime tree loaded with fruit. It was in a coconut grove behind a fence with "Keep Out" signs in French, English, and Tahitian. A man rode up on a bicycle and saw us leaning on the fence, contemplating the tree. He was fat and brown and smiling.

"You want citron?" he asked. "Please, help yourself. Is plenty."

We indicated the signs. He waved a hand deprecatingly. "No, no, is for coconut. Land belong my brudda. Is O.K.—take all da citron you want." We loaded Jan's knapsack to the brim. Limes keep a long time and they transform cheap vodka into a drinkable drink. In Papeete they wanted 10 francs apiece for them.

Next morning we weighed anchor and were running out Passe Papai under square rig by 1000. The craggy green spires and turrets of the mountains of Bora Bora showed plainly against the blue morning sky.

Starbound flew; 15 knots dead on the stern make a fast boat out of her. We came around the western shore of Bora Bora and braced the yard hard over for the reach down the extensive reef protecting the harbor. The waves creamed green against the underwater coral. It was pretty as poisoned candy.

Bora Bora is so beautiful an island, so dramatic in appearance. The magnificent peaks of Pahia and Temanu, the loveliest lagoon in all Polynesia, reefs swarming with fish, motus capped with coconut palms, the best dancers, the friendliest girls.

We dropped the raffee, and clewed and bunted the square sail to the yard. Then, sticking *Starbound*'s nose into the wind, we powered into Passe Teavanui. We could see many masts. It was obvious that most of the yachts had bypassed Raiatea and Tahaa.

The Oa Oa Hotel has a small dock and a dozen boats were clustered around it. Another was moored to a defunct sea plane buoy. We could see several masts at an anchorage about a mile to the west. *Topaz* was tied up across the entire end of the town's main and only quay.

Topaz invited us to raft up alongside, so once again *Starbound* looked like a small white duck against the green topsides of the big Baltic trader.

The town spread out in all directions from the foot of the quay. Bora Bora was still *a fête,* but in a desultory way. A group of local drugstore cowboys sat around on the grass in front of the plaited-frond-fronted huts and sucked up cold Hinano beer. They called friendly greetings as we headed for the Gendarmerie. Once again our passports were held pending departure.

A moderate-sized Chinese supermarket supplied Nina with eggs, bread, lettuce, and tomatoes at prices only slightly higher than in Papeete. And I found LP gas for the stove. We couldn't get any in Papeete before we left; they were sold out until the next "gaz" ship arrived. I laid out a 2,000-franc deposit for the big bottle and packed it down to the quay. Ernie moved the empty gas bottles from *Starbound* to the quay and dug up the Rube Goldberg manifold we'd made up. We hooked up the big bottle to one of ours and opened the main valves, then the bleeder valve on ours. We decanted until liquid propane rose to the bleeder valve and started spraying a smelly white mist into the air. Then we closed all the valves and disconnected the lines. We did it again on our second bottle. I returned the empty to the store and got my 2,000 francs back. A very cautious Chinaman; 2,000 francs equals about U.S. $25.

A good-sized swell occasionally sets into the harbor of Bora Bora. *Topaz* started thumping her hull against the quay, and *Starbound* started thumping against *Topaz*. We moved to the Oa Oa hotel anchorage, one anchor out ahead and our stern to a buoy just off the dock. About a dozen boats radiated out from that buoy. We held each other in position.

Bora Bora would be our last stop in French Polynesia. We were pushing mid-August already, and the big hop from Fiji to New Zealand was scheduled for the first part of October. The western South Pacific weather becomes unsettled in November and cyclonic in December. If we wanted to visit Samoa, Tonga, and Fiji, we'd have to "get cracking," as a British yachtie put it, over beers in the Oa Oa bar.

After the pilot charts, sailing directions, and other assorted piles of paper have been perused, a yachtie's best source of cruising information comes from other yachties. It was not that way ten years ago because there just were not that many cruising yachts around. But in the last decade their numbers on the world's oceans have increased almost geometrically, year by year. Today, wherever there's a good harbor and a good sailing season, there will be an international assortment of yachts present. Their owners will often be in the nearest bar if they're not aboard their boats. Within hours, if not minutes, after securing an anchorage, mooring, or dock space in said harbor, a yachtie will know something about all the other yachts present. When two yachties get together, it's brain picking time. And when a yachtie arrives who has been where another yachtie is going, his mind will be scraped clean of every tidbit of information on the point of interest that he possesses. Of course, it's all automatic anyway. Most yachties are garrulous as hell, and they generally like to talk about things that interest them most—which are yachts, cruising, and the appurtenances thereto.

A big group of us were sitting topside on *Topaz* one evening soaking up Hinano beer, a sovereign remedy for the grismals, and playing that famous game, "When we do it again, here's the way we'll play it . . ."

For what it's worth, we're going to include the French Polynesia game plan right here. We say for what it's worth because the paradise of today might be the tourist trap of tomorrow and the paradisiacal elements of every place we've been seem to be in inverse ratio to the number of tourists imposed on the place—a number which increases tenfold with the installation of an airstrip.

I can hear somebody say, "He keeps talkin' about yachties and tourists. Ain't a damn yachtie a tourist?"

My answer is an unequivocal NO! A yachtie spends several years dreaming, planning, and laboring to get where he is with his boat. He didn't just go out and buy an airplane ticket. Consequently his entire philosophy and attitude is very different from the tourist's. A yachtie doesn't have a plane to catch, a plane which in a few hours' time projects him back into "his world." He is living *now* in his world. Grandma isn't baby-sitting the kids back in Des Moines. The kids are with him, playing on the beach with the local gang. The deep tans they acquire make it hard to tell the yachtie kids from the locals, except for the occasional blond head. And there's a few blond heads among the locals, too. A yachtie isn't thinking about his job and who's playing office politics while he's away. He doesn't have a job anymore, and he'll worry about another one only when this particular cruise is completed. The next job might be in New Zealand, or France, or Samoa.

We were playing a game, this particular game concerning French Polynesia.

"Hand me another beer. Tell you one thing; next time we're going to spend a lot more time in the Marquesas. Two weeks wasn't enough."

"Two weeks? Hell, we were cruising there for two months. Did you go to Fatu Hiva?"

"Naw. Only Hiva Oa and Nuku Hiva. Hiva Oa was great!"

"Yeah, but Fatu Hiva, man, it's like a hundred years ago. We were only the second yacht there all year. The village had a pig roast and tamure for us. You should have seen this beautiful island girl trying to get young Eric off into the bushes. He's just thirteen."

"Did he go?"

"Well . . . he disappeared for a few hours and was unbearably smug the next day."

"You know, next time we're gonna spend two months or so in the Tuamotus. Say, cruise down the string, staying a week each at about eight different islands, then jump off for Tahiti."

"Yeah! Well, you can keep Tahiti. Too many boats, too many tourists, and too expensive."

"O.K., it's expensive. But where else can you supply? The little trading stores and the schooners cost that much more. They all get their stuff from Papeete. We got so low on basic chow that we finally had to run for it. And we needed line and stainless wire and some other hardware. And we had to get hauled. The bottom was loaded with goodies. We dove and scraped 'em off but the paint would go too. Then we had no worm protection."

"Yeah. I guess Papeete's a necessity. But next time I'm restricting my stay to three weeks—say from July 1. Put in two weeks' work on the ship, one week partying after the opening of the fête on the 14th, then I'm off to Huahine and Bora Bora to see the dancing and spear throwing the way it used to be. It really bothered us to pay eight bucks a seat to see the dancing!"

"I'm with you! Someone said that Maupiti really has an old-time fête too."

"Yeah, but the channel into the harbor is a bitch. Long, narrow, and twisting. Good idea to have local knowledge to get in there."

"I've heard it's worth it."

"Hell, they're all worth it. These islands—the whole French Polynesian group—are the most fascinating and beautiful places we've seen."

"So far. But Samoa, Tonga, and Fiji come next for us."

"How about another beer?"

A young, plump Chinese man owned a bicycle rental stand about a half-mile up the road from the main quay. We walked down and pedaled back on new French machines. No fancy gears—just basic bikes.

We set out around the perimeter road of Bora Bora, stopping every 200 yards, the first mile to adjust seats and handlebars using the adjustable wrench I'd brought along. We had a container of water apiece and a knapsack full of cheese, bread, and beer. Twenty-five miles later we had seen a lot of beautiful island, had met many friendly islanders, and had discovered that the Hotel Bora Bora sits on the prettiest stretch of beach on the island and serves very good, and very expensive, drinks. We were convinced that the seats on French bicycles were made for iron bottoms. My bike seat had worn its way through my tail bone and was lodged somewhere in my kidneys.

The weather was good. The wind was fair. It was time to go. We cleared for Samoa on August 15, retrieving our passports from the gendarme. Back on *Starbound* we rove a running stern line through the ring on the communal buoy, then brought the launch aboard and lashed it down.

We slipped the stern line as the anchor chain came clanking in over the freshly painted wildcat, messing up the red enamel put on it three days before.

Square sail and raffee were set even before we nosed out the pass. American Samoa—it would be good to be in an American port again—we thought.

13

Cruisers, Tenders, Anchors—and Samoa

The time has come to get very heavy about three subjects: "best" cruising boats, dinghies or tenders, and ground tackle. Because, by the time we were on our way to Samoa, we had formed some strong opinions.

I'm iconoclastic when it comes to cruising boats. It amounts to this: Any well-found boat, no matter how small or how large, is a good cruising boat if her owner likes her and is aware of her strengths and weaknesses as far as performance is concerned.

Ketches, sloops, yawls, cutters, schooners—we've seen successful cruises being made in them all.

For the kind of trade wind cruising that we do, I think that the downwind capability of a cruising sailboat is of paramount importance. Over 90 percent of our cruising has been off the wind. Maybe 9 percent has been beam reaching, and 1 percent or less has been on the wind.

So a good downwind rig is mandatory: twin genoas with whisker poles, or a square sail and maybe a raffee, even a small spinnaker if there's enough crew aboard to handle it.

Windward ability is useful. It comes in handy now and then. But for those long passages with the trades, it sure is nice to set some carefree sail up forward and then forget it for days on end.

Self-steering gear—a must. We use an auto-pilot because our overhanging mizzen boom and large rudder make a wind vane impracticable. The A-P works fine but we have to keep our batteries charged. Most cruising boats

169

use wind vanes, and the terrible truth seems to be that the more expensive they are, the better they work.

How big should a cruising boat be? For deep-water cruising over long distances, we've found that 30 feet on deck is as small as anybody wants to go. My own chop-off point would be 36 feet and I'd prefer 40 as a personal minimum. Why? More room, more versatility in sail patterns, more stores, water, and fuel—and much more comfort in port, where every cruising vessel spends at least two-thirds of her time.

If there's plenty of money in the till and if extra crew doesn't offend one's sense of privacy, then 60 feet of boat is just fine. But operating costs go up with size geometrically rather than arithmetically. It takes a pretty healthy bank account to cruise 60 feet of yacht.

Getting down to what most people want to know—and what we couldn't find out from anyone or anywhere while we were planning this cruise—the cost of cruising *Starbound* on a world voyage works out to about $400 per month, based on a 1974 economy. And that's for just the three of us: me, Nina, and Ernie. One more person can add quite a lot because meals get considerably more formal. That cost is also predicated on no outside labor costs—all maintenance being done by us—and no restaurant or bar bills.

We do all of our eating and drinking on *Starbound,* except for an occasional cold beer in the middle of a shopping or sightseeing expedition.

So there's a cost base: about $5,000 a year if you're careful. We know a couple on a 30-footer who do it on $2,000 a year, but many amenities of life are lacking. On *Starbound* we live in fairly plush circumstances compared to most cruising families we've met.

Cruising sailors place a lot of importance on yacht tenders because in nearly all parts of the world that are worth cruising, a good tender is, and will remain, the only way to get the crew and nearly everything else in to shore and out to the boat—and in many places fuel and water have to be ferried too.

Another reason why sailors have strong feelings about tenders: many times a second anchor has got to be set out, and I've yet to have that happen under happy circumstances. It's always blowing like hell, otherwise a second hook wouldn't be needed. And naturally, the bow of the ship is pitching up and down while you're trying to maneuver the dinghy to a point where the second anchor can be put into it. All this usually happens on a rainy night as black as the inside of a cow. We've carried several anchors out for yachties who mistakenly tried to get their little 8-foot piece of plywood to windward through a steep chop using a pair of oars while sitting on a pile of anchor lead chain and rode.

My favorite yacht tender for cruising is a 13-foot Boston Whaler with a 20- to 30-horsepower outboard on it. I don't have one, and I'm not about to ever have one, for these reasons: I can't afford the initial cost, the boat is too heavy to get aboard without some really big davits, and I don't have enough topside space to stow it properly.

When we bought *Starbound* she had a light 9-foot fiberglass rowing dinghy hanging on stern davits, quite high above the water and safe from following seas. It's still there. We call it the captain's gig because I use it to escape the boat whenever the rest of the crew has taken the "big" launch and left me stranded on board.

The "big" launch came right out of the Sears Roebuck catalog. It's an 11-foot Ted Williams Super Gamefisher constructed out of foam core sandwiched fiberglass. We stow it upside down on the house top and cross-lash it in place to four husky bronze eyebolts. The fuel tanks, oars, and seat tops store under it. We drive it with our ancient but dependable 5.5 HP Evinrude.

The launch does a good job for us, and our next tender will be another one just like it. Nina and I can horse it aboard by hand after the engine and tank are removed, and we can pull it up above the tide line on a beach. It's a bit tender-skinned and we've punched a few holes in it on various reefs, but a little plastic putty and fiberglass make a satisfactory repair. It doesn't row very well, but better than a Whaler. It'll carry five adults and keep them dry.

The only other tenders that I think are worth a damn are the good-quality inflatables; Avon or Zodiac being the most popular. Avon is British-made, Zodiac is French. Avon has better oarlocks and hangers. Zodiac seems to withstand chafe better. Since I've owned neither, I'm parroting the words of other yachties. All inflatables are expensive—for us, anyway. We choked when we heard the price of the big ones. Rowing them against a stiff breeze can break your heart, so a good outboard is necessary. I've seen a lot of Seagull motors on them. I still prefer OMC outboards. Maybe when I'm rich I'll buy a nice Mercury. Owners of Seagulls swear by them. But they're noisy little bastards—the Seagulls, not necessarily the owners.

For a boat like *Starbound*, we're happy with the tender we've got. If we were cruising a smaller craft, we'd get a medium-sized inflatable and use an American outboard. If we had a very large yacht with a bank account to match, we'd buy a Whaler or large inflatable, use a husky American outboard, and maybe add a good sailing dinghy for fun.

When gunkholing around home waters on a nice weekend with a good weather forecast, one anchor might be O.K.—for somebody else, not for *Starbound*. We always carry two anchors at least. And they're stowed on deck, not below under a pile of other gear.

Earlier, we wrote about that squally weekend in Cape May, New Jersey, when we rigged and put that second anchor over the side in less than one minute, thereby stopping *Starbound* from going aground stern first onto a very inhospitable shore. The main engine was partly disassembled and our first anchor was pulling right through a loose mud bottom no matter how much chain we let out. The good weather report had made no mention of the 30 knots of wind in those squalls, or of the squalls for that matter.

A cruising boat needs at least two good hooks. *Starbound* carries three, the third a lighter anchor than the first two and handy for stopping the stern from swinging in a tide or for holding it away from a too friendly mud bank or coral head. Our third anchor is carried topside too, but aft.

Seven to one, length of rode put out to water depth, is a proper scope and anyone anchoring with less scope needs a reason far better than any I've ever found—save for that time we anchored in 90 feet of water and only had 450 feet of chain to use.

The strength of any "chain" is only as good as its weakest link. So if an anchor has a horizontal holding power of, say, 10,000 pounds and the chain lead is tested to 15,000 pounds, there isn't much sense in using a nylon rode which is good for only 5,000 pounds, and even less in using a bronze shackle with a breaking strength of 2,500 pounds.

"Horizontal" holding power is the maximum holding power of the anchor, which can only be developed when the shank of the anchor is flat on, or horizontal to, the bottom. That is why chain and lots of scope are used.

Coral heads will cut through a nylon rode in a very short time. So when the boat is anchored in a beautiful South Seas lagoon and the tide is running back and forth, it is a very good idea to have the hook out on an all-chain rode. We know three yachties who lost their anchors by using nylon rodes in coral; one nearly lost his boat.

Even a light displacement multihull should have one all-chain rode, in spite of the extra forward weight. It doesn't have to be a very long rode for a shoal draft boat if the anchor can be set in relatively shallow water; 100 feet of chain is enough for most situations. More is better.

Heavy anchors are better than light anchors of the same type. How heavy? As heavy as can be managed with the available crew and equipment.

A good anchor winch is a real necessity. We've come across a few, a very few, cruising boats without winches and they have a tough time of it. Also, they tend to put out less rode than is safe because they know it'll all have to be pulled in by hand.

Types of anchors—well, I'd better cite my sources of information. The first source is experience, some of it bitterly gained. The second source is a good friend of ours, George Prentice, another naval architect for the U.S. Navy. George has put in a lot of years studying and developing ground tackle and anchoring techniques for our navy's ships.

Danforth-type anchors are good in sand or firm mud. The fluke angle is fixed for sand. Some of the bigger Danforths have fluke angles that can be adjusted for varying bottom conditions, but that's generally a "big ship" thing and doesn't apply to the Danforth a yachtsman might buy in his local marine hardware store. A yachtie's Danforth will generally slide over grass, skip over rock, and pull through soft mud. But it's great in sand.

A plow-type anchor is good in sand and firm mud. It's fair in grass. Sometimes it'll hold in rock if it can be wedged in, but I'd hate to try to sleep with a plow anchor in rock, knowing that the tide might swing the boat around. A very heavy plow anchor is fair in soft mud. It'll keep burying down until it grabs something firm. Then it's tough to break out.

A yachtsman's anchor is something I'd better explain. That's the anchor shown on all of the U.S. Navy's insignia, the anchor which is always and incongruously shown fouled, with a line wrapped around the shank and stock. If you ask someone to draw a picture of an anchor, that's the one he'll probably draw. Our English friends call it an "Admiralty" anchor. Nat Herreshoff improved on the old design by moving the stock way up to the end of the shank making it harder to foul. He also increased the fluke area to give it greater resistance to horizontal pull and tapered the "arrow" heads of the flukes so that a fouling line might slide off it more readily. Some yachties call this type a "Herreshoff." They're better in rock, coral, or grass than a plow or Danforth type. With the increased fluke area, they're good in sand and firm mud and if they're heavy enough they're not so bad in soft mud. In general, they should be much heavier than the other two types to achieve an equivalent horizontal holding force. That is their disadvantage.

Starbound carries a 130-pound Herreshoff on 450 feet of half-inch chain as her primary anchor (chain size is measured as the diameter of the link material, the dimension being taken at the point where the links intersect each other). Our second anchor, ready at one minute's notice, is a 70-pound high-tensile Danforth with 20 feet of half-inch chain behind it, shackled to 300 feet of one-inch-diameter eight-strand plaited nylon line. Plaited line can't rotate and unlay itself like three-strand standard laid line, so swivels are not required. Our third anchor, generally used to stop *Starbound* from swinging her tail into an embarrasing situation, is a 35-pound high-tensile Danforth we picked up at a garage sale for $15. When we can afford it, we'll sell the 35-pounder, buy a 105-pound plow as a second anchor, and relegate the 70-pound Danforth to stern anchor position. But the big, heavy Herreshoff remains our primary ground tackle.

Now, readers, before ganging together and coming down the dock with flaming torches, shouldering pitchforks and scythes, remember that I'm talking about ground tackle for long-distance cruising, and anchoring in every conceivable bottom condition. If you're forever weekending in a nice sandy-bottomed bay, keep that light, handy Danforth. It's easy to bring aboard and stow.

Before closing on the subject of dinghies and anchors—every dinghy needs an anchor. We carry a small stockless anchor for general use. We also have a "reef-pick," something like a grapnel, to secure the launch when we're diving over coral. They are valuable and much-used pieces of equipment.

Our money was running low. We planned to work in New Zealand, but New Zealand was still a long way away. We considered sailing to Pago Pago and from there straight to Kiwi land, missing Tonga and Fiji, but the thought wasn't very palatable.

A letter from my parents, received just before we left Bora Bora, heartened us considerably. They wanted to meet *Starbound* in Suva and sail with us to New Zealand. Their offer to pay the tab from Suva to Auckland lifted some of the worry from us. *Starbound* was going to need another injection of cash to refurbish gear and replenish stores when we got to Suva. We'd been hoping to pick up some sorely needed parts in American Samoa, but we figured now to shorten our stay there, make a quick run through Tonga, and be on our way to Fiji.

Excerpts from ship's log.

15 August, Thursday: We clear for Pago Pago at 0900. Picked up six cans of beer—money very low—mailed post cards. We square the ship away and slip the buoy at 1100. Out of the pass at 1200 under square sail and raffee. Set taffrail log. Wind 12 knots off starboard quarter, sunny, barometer 30.10 inches. Watches set for the night; 3 on, 6 off. Tuna sandwiches for lunch. Will leave Maupiti to port and pass between Scilly and Bellingshausen.

16 August, Friday: 106 miles noon to noon—ran engine four hours last evening to clear Maupiti. Winds light this afternoon.

17 August, Saturday: Very light trades this day. 60 miles made good noon to noon. Showers from astern bring winds of short duration. Average speed about 2.5 knots. Ran engine one hour in A.M.

18 August, Sunday: Some wind in the night but very light again by morning. 65 miles noon to noon—our slowest sailing of the whole trip these last two days. Evening star sights put us 8 miles north of the rhumb line. Wind up by dark and averaging 4 knots. Beautiful evening.

19 August, Monday: Very light winds again at sunrise. We crank up the main diesel for two hours. A southerly swell setting in. Light breeze from SSE by 1000. 70 miles noon to noon. Breeze up to 8 knots in P.M.—Yay!

20 August, Tuesday: Good breeze all night—95 miles noon to noon. Sunny, pleasant day. Breeze falls off at nightfall and we barely maintain steerageway. Too much rolling. We start engine at 0330 when ship won't answer helm. Glassy sea—no wind!

21 August, Wednesday: Engine at 1100 RPM all day. Only 50 miles noon to noon. Very light breeze veering to southwest by sunset. We drop raffee, brail up square sail, and set yankee and mizzen. Motor-sail till 0200. Breeze picks up about midnight from SSW. Cloudy to the south. Maybe some weather by morning.

22 August, Thursday: Secured engine at 0200 with fresh breeze from SE. Morning brings 10/10 cloud cover and rain but a fair wind. We secure fore and aft sail and set square sail and raffee. Wind fair all this day. Average speed 4.5 knots. Blows up at sunset 16–18 knots. Making 6–7 knots. More rain coming up astern with 10/10 nimbo-stratus. 108 miles to noon today.

23 August, Friday: Lost raffee sheet at 0100—chafed through at block—doused raffee. Weather clears with dawn, and wind drops to 12–14 knots, still fair. Made 120 miles to noon. Noon running fix puts us 10 miles north of rhumb line, so correct course to pass 20 miles south of Rose Island. ETA at Pago Pago Tuesday forenoon.

24 August, Saturday: Clouds astern in the morning blew off to the north. Jibe mizzen at 0900 and all aback. Drop mizzen and correct the situation with the engine. Put on the raffee. Made 115 miles to noon. Wind drops after dark. Down to 3 knots by 2400.

25 August, Sunday: Wind gone by 0600, so we start engine and motor-sail all day. Sight yacht 3 miles to the south at sunset. Might be *Brenda Lynn*. We up engine to 1500 RPM and start making 5 knots. Brail square sail and drop raffee at 2100. Put on yankee and mizzen and strap them in for the night.

26 August, Monday: Glassy sea, flat, very hot! Rose Island abeam at 0800 19 miles to the north—not visible in haze. Motor all day; good thing we have plenty of fuel. Paint-code the anchor chain—old paint was almost gone. Forward water tanks go dry, so open up aft tanks. One propane tank is out—switch to second tank. Catch a beautiful 18-pound wahoo on the trolling line, fights like hell—used red plastic squid on 100-pound test. Not sporting but damn effective. Wahoo steaks for dinner—very white meat—delicious! We raise Tau Island in early P.M., abeam by 2100. Still under power this night. Half moon, glassy sea, great amounts of phosphorescence—wake is a sheet of cold fire! Should make harbor by 1300 tomorrow.

27 August, Tuesday: We motor all the way in and drop anchor in Pago Pago harbor at 1230 hours.

A few thousand millenniums ago, Pago Pago harbor was the smoking, burbling, fiery pit of a volcano. One day the pressure got too high way down in its stomach, and with an extra violent belch it blew out one of its sides into the sea. I wonder if some early ancestor of man was around to watch as the lava blew out and the sea rolled in. That must have been a smash spectacular. Eventually the sea won, and now the old volcano walls rise in dark green splendor around what has been called the most beautiful harbor in the world. I guess it would be, if all the man-made crud could be scraped off the shoreline.

The entrance is easy for a yacht, and well buoyed. Just make a straight shot down the middle and turn left, then continue past the docks to port and the tuna canneries to starboard, and anchor with the other yachts in about 50 feet of water. Try not to smell the odor of the canneries, and ignore the green-brown clouds of gluck being discharged directly into the harbor from them. Good old American knowhow has fixed it so that they are permitted eighty times the pollution level permissible in the States. Hooray for "progress"!

We flew our Q flag all the way in, then waited two hours on board for someone to come out and grant us pratique. Finally I took our papers and buzzed the launch over to the main wharf where the customs house is. The very officious Samoan officials told me to go back to the boat and wait some more. Then they came out in their launch—along with their girlfriends and "go-fors." Eight people. Two had any business aboard. It was a strain, but we remained polite. I made the mistake of offering a drink and thereby prolonged the visit. It was a bit too much of a storm trooper routine, and their attitude explained why several yachties had told us that American Samoa wasn't worth visiting anymore.

Actually, we had a pretty fine time in Pago Pago. Burns Philips, the famous South Pacific trading company, provided nearly all the food stores we needed. What we couldn't find there, Nina found at a nice little warehouse operation called TOKO.

Parts for *Starbound* were something else again. I couldn't find Onan generator parts. I did manage to con the parts department of the big boat-building yard next to the canneries complex out of a few maintenance items: paint, sandpaper, a wire brush, assorted paintbrushes, and some small fuel line hose for the outboard. And they had copper tubing and fittings, and exhaust hose. I found through-hull fittings and some other stuff too that I didn't need. I didn't find several items that I did need, like certain sizes of water hoses and alternator belts to fill out my spare-parts locker.

A big bundle of mail was waiting for us at the post office, including a letter from my parents. They said to wait for them; they were flying to Samoa to join us because it was much cheaper to fly there than into Fiji—something to do with taxation on airline tickets. They also said that there was $500 waiting for us at the bank in Pago Pago. A boy's best friends are his parents!

We moved *Starbound* over to a new jetty being built and dropped our anchors again, then pulled the stern in close to shore, securing to the heavy, iron bollards sunk into the concrete retaining walls. This move stopped us from swinging back and forth on the harbor tide and also laid us broadside to the prevailing wind. It was fairly comfortable below with the windward leaves of the doghouses cranked up.

Topaz came in the morning after we moved and the crew laid the big Baltic trader right beside us, and secured her the same way. Party time again.

We did a few tourist things while waiting for my parents. There is a cable car which goes across the harbor. It goes from Solo Hill all the way to the top of Mount Alava on the ridge of an ancient volcano, 1,610 feet above the harbor. It's quite a ride and well worth the $2.50 for the round trip. On top of Mount Alava there is the American Samoa educational television station which broadcasts all over Samoa. The view of the harbor is worth it, too. If one looks almost straight down, one can even see the canneries with Japanese and Taiwanese fishing vessels stacked twenty deep outside their wharves, and admire the colorful streams of the tuna sewage slowly overcoming that ugly old blue color of clean salt water. One can even buy a laufala mat or some tortoise-shell jewelry on the mountain—if one wants some tortoise-shell jewelry.

We needed diesel fuel and cooking gas and water. In spite of being an American port, Samoa is not very well set up for yachts. We had to buy a 100-pound tank of propane from the gas company and transfer it to our tanks using the lash-up manifold we'd put together in Bora Bora. Then we got together with *Topaz* and ordered 500 gallons of diesel fuel, which was delivered to the quay by truck. *Topaz* managed to haul her big stern within 5 feet of the rocky corner of the quay and took 400 gallons aboard from the truck's hose. We couldn't get *Starbound* close enough without swapping places with *Topaz*—a big operation—so Ernie and I took our six big plastic jugs ashore, filled them with the 100 gallons left in the truck, and horsed them back aboard with the launch. We killed the whole afternoon just getting fuel. Then we were told we'd have to go to the main shipping wharf for fresh water, no facilities being available on the quay. That could wait until we left.

We could not understand what the Samoans were trying to do with their waterfront. The "development" we saw seemed to make the shoreline more ugly without providing any real facilities. We were tied stern onto the newly constructed quay, which had no water, no fuel dock, nothing—and no plans for anything as far as we could find out. The port captain's office didn't seem to know either. The outfit controlling the bay and the rest of the island appears to be the American Samoan Development Corporation. Their plans include opening up beach land to sell to wealthy retired people. We wonder how that's supposed to benefit the Samoans. It is reminiscent of what is happening up and down the American coastlines. A few are making a bundle by taking public land, making it private, and calling it progress.

Pago Pago is a pretty good supply port and not too expensive. Maybe in a few years they'll get that beautiful harbor back in some kind of shape. Of course, they'll have to start by cleaning up the cannery operation.

Mom and Dad flew into the airport at Tafuna on the fifth day of September. We got them and their gear safely ensconced in the forecastle and made ready to leave. It was as complicated a procedure for clearing as it was for entering, the only advantage being that no one came aboard the boat. *Topaz* was also on the way to Tonga, so her crew worked her over to the main wharf and laid her alongside a big barge. We put *Starbound* outside of her. We hooked up all of the water hoses from both ships and strung them across the barge and filled our nice, clean tanks with the rust-colored, brackish water which the port captain's office called "fresh." I filed a "float plan" with the port captain and found myself nearly running back to the ship in order to leave sooner. *Topaz* was right behind us.

A beautiful southeast breeze off the harbor mouth put both ships on a broad reach for Tonga. The water was blue again, the foam sparkled white, the sun shone, and we flew along a few boat lengths from *Topaz*, taking dozens of photographs of her while her crew reciprocated. My dad had the helm and Mom sat on the transom seat with her back in the curve of the taffrail. She smiled and smiled. Another of her dreams was coming true. She was sailing to a South Sea kingdom.

PART III
Fiji
to
Cocos

The Western Pacific

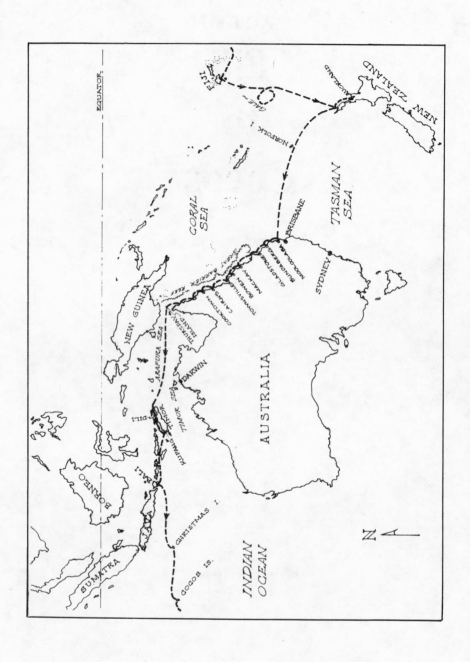

14

Tonga and Fiji

The ocean road from Samoa to the Vavau group of Tonga lies fair and straight three days to the southwest. On the way down I taught my parents a bit of celestial navigation. The questions which the lessons engendered caused the thought to occur to me, and the same thought occurs to me now: there has been a very large amount of confusing material written about celestial navigation. Perhaps I can clarify the process and get rid of the bogeyman for whoever is interested.

When I say "celestial navigation" I'm talking about locating oneself at sea, using a sextant, an almanac, and the appropriate tables. That's all we have on *Starbound* except for an old but workable radio direction finder which is handy when there are reliable radio beacons around. Loran and Omega would be very nice to have, and one day we'd like to install an electronics navigation system aboard *Starbound*, but they are currently beyond our financial grasp. Also, for a world cruising yacht they have drawbacks. They are electrical, so they occasionally break down and have to be fixed—and there is no electronics shop around the corner. So if the skipper can't fix them himself, he'd better break out his sextant and know how to use it.

With a sextant, the navigator can shoot the sun, the moon, certain navigational stars, and four of the planets. The sun is easiest because there's no mistaking it, the horizon is obvious, and the calculation is simple. Stars are almost as easy, but the timing has to be right. In either the morning or evening it has to be dark enough to see the primary stars and light enough to have a clearly discernible horizon. The same applies to planets, except for Venus, which is so bright that it can often be seen in broad daylight. The moon is, I think, the most difficult heavenly body to use for navigation. Being closest to the earth, it moves fast. Also, the calculations involve some corrections which are confusing to the beginner.

The best procedure for the beginner is to learn to shoot the sun, calculate a line of position, and place it on the chart. When the point is reached where you're asking yourself, "Is this all there is to it?" then it's time to start shooting stars and planets.

One question I keep getting asked is "How do you know which star to shoot out of all that glittering stuff up there?" I have to say it's easier at sea. There's a horizon all around and the atmosphere is generally free of dust and smoke. I myself hadn't realized there were so many stars above till I went deep-water sailing. The answer is, use a "starfinder" and study the constellations—a perfect way to while away the night watches. I'll simplify it further: the nautical almanac lists fifty-seven stars. There are only twenty of them which I consider to be bright enough to shoot at any time, and on a given evening, or morning, only four to six of those twenty will be available to shoot. The others will be too low, too high, or below the horizon. So it isn't that tough. During the day there is the sun, and sometimes the moon. In the evening there are four to six stars and a planet or two. In the morning the same.

A single shot of a single body, be it sun, moon, star, or planet, will give the navigator one "line of position" (LOP) and the navigator will know he is on that line. If it's daylight, only a sun LOP is possible. Sometimes that LOP can be crossed with a moon LOP, if the moon is visible, and give the navigator a two-body "fix," but more commonly the sun will be shot again a few hours after the first shot and the first sun LOP will be advanced however many miles the ship has sailed to the point when the second sun shot was taken, and a "running fix" is thusly obtained—accurate enough when the ship is far from land.

When approaching islands or a coastline, position accuracy is mandatory. We've been in places where the wind has been blowing like blazes with the ship on a beam reach and we were approaching a harbor on a long, inhospitable coastline. We knew that if we raised the coast downwind of our harbor we would play veritable hell motoring back against sea and wind. We shot evening stars and got an accurate fix. Then we adjusted the ship's speed so we would raise the coastline about 0900 next morning. In the morning we shot more stars plus a planet and adjusted our course accordingly. We hit the harbor buoys perfectly and ran in to safety with no trouble and much relief. Two other yachts were not so careful and spent a rotten day and lots of fuel trying to get back up the coast.

Most books on navigation list all the tables available and then try to show how each is used. Cutting through all that confusion, I will hereby state that there are two sets worth considering: the Nautical Almanac used with Sight

Reduction Tables for Marine Navigation, H.O. publication 229; and the Air Almanac used with Sight Reduction Tables for Air Navigation, H.O. 249. Taking it one step further, most cruising yachtsmen prefer H.O. 229, the "marine" tables, because the almanac is good for the entire year and the tables are good forever. The "air" tables allow a method of calculation which is slightly faster, but they come out quarterly and if the yacht is on a long cruise the navigator is liable to find himself with the latest tables unobtainable. Also, the short-cut method used with the air tables is not quite as accurate as with the marine tables. On the way to the Marquesas from the Galapagos, our friend Ray Kukulski used the air material and Ernie and I used the marine. Ray consistently finished his calculations one to two minutes faster than Ernie or I. He was also consistently up to 5 miles away from our position. We had three sextants on board and switched them around with the same result.

So we use the current nautical almanac and H.O. 229. H.O. 229 comes in six volumes, each one covering 15 degrees of latitude, up to 90 degrees. If the navigator doesn't plan on sailing north or south of 60 degrees of latitude (God knows we don't), he can get by with four volumes of the set: O–15 degrees, 15–30 degrees, 30–45 degrees, and 45–60 degrees. The current year's nautical almanac can be obtained in most seaboard cities in the world. The American version has an orange cardboard cover. The British version has a blue cloth cover. The contents are identical in every respect.

The only other equipment necessary is a set of parallel rules (a draftsman's triangle is handy), charting or drafting dividers, a sharp pencil for plotting, a dull pencil (we use a ball point pen) for calculations, some means of identifying stars (we have a Star Identifier No. 2101-D put out by Weems and Plath, and a Bowditch), a chronometer and shortwave radio receiver, and a sextant.

A few words about sextants: we use an old Mark 2 navy sextant with a micrometer-type read-out on it, and it works fine. We also have an ancient instrument of World War I vintage with a vernier read-out which also works fine. We have met several yachtsmen who navigate with a "cheapie" plastic sextant—not as accurate as ours, but they found the same islands as we did. We would like to have a new Plath sextant with its huge mirrors and that fabulous star scope and astigmatizer on it (or the Japanese copy of it), but that instrument costs a lot of money. We bought our surplus Mark 2 for $50.

When a beginning navigator obtains a sextant he should carefully study the instructions before ever opening the box (which also should not be dropped, thumped, banged, or in any way treated roughly). If it's a used sextant he should study Bowditch's chapter on the subject before fooling around with the instrument. We allow nobody to handle our sextants unless we know that they know what they're doing. One careless rap and the least you've got is a lengthy readjustment job (Bowditch tells how to do that, too). If a used sextant is obtained from an instrument firm, make sure it has been checked out. If it is obtained from a private individual, take it to a reputable precision instrument shop and have it checked out before purchase—it could be beyond adjustment, in which case it'll make an interesting conversation piece for the den or bar.

A long paragraph ago, I mentioned a chronometer and shortwave radio receiver. These are used to obtain accurate time—to the second. Four seconds of time equal one nautical mile of distance; that is how fast the earth turns. A stopwatch is also handy so that one doesn't have to gallop from topside to below to read the time. Many navigators employ a very good chronometer-rated wrist watch, such as a Bulova Accuquartz or a Rolex Seamaster. We'd rather have a bulkhead mounted chronometer belowdecks. Ernie and I are hard on wrist watches, so we wear inexpensive ones. The shortwave receiver is used to get a time tick so the rate of the chronometer can be checked from time to time. We check ours every day and keep track of the rate in the nautical almanac. We just write in how fast or slow it is opposite the (Greenwich) day and hour.

To expand the explanation on time, it is this simple; all navigational time is based on Greenwich Mean Time (GMT), which is now called Coordinated Universal Time. Don't ask why the change—I don't even know how the universe got in there. All the yachties still call it GMT. It is the time at the zero-degree meridian, the meridian which passes north and south through Greenwich, England. We have never failed to get a time tick on our short wave receiver anywhere we've gone so far. I can hear somebody ask, "So why a chronometer?" Easy answer: when somebody drops the radio! I won't go into all the ways to get a time tick around the world. We usually get ours from WWV, Colorado, and WWVH, Hawaii, on 2.5, 5, 10, 15, and 20 mHz. At night, 2.5 and 5 mHz are good; during the day, 15 and 20 mHz are good; and 10 mHz works almost all the time.

Now that all the tools are present the navigator can take his sun shot. A nice time for a morning sun line is 0930 (local time)—or any time when the sun's altitude is between 30 and 60 degrees above the horizon. So he takes his shot and punches his stopwatch. I'm not going to explain the shot-taking procedure—it's all in Bowditch anyway, and taking accurate shots from the rolling deck of a yacht is a matter of practice. Someone has said that after two thousand shots a navigator becomes proficient. I think it depends on the person. Ernie became capable in one day and expert in two weeks.

The navigator goes below, looks at his chronometer, and punches the stopwatch again when the second hand passes a handy mark. Then he writes down the chronometer time, the stopwatch time, and the sextant reading—all this without letting go of the sextant, which he is holding carefully. He never lays the sextant on a bunk or chart table. He puts the

Contrasting faces in the crowd watching the festivities
at the Papeete Bastille Day celebrations.

Offshore, a traditional outrigger takes part in a canoe
race during the fete days, Papeete.

Starbound at anchor in Robinson's Cove, Moorea.

Starbound anchored at Huahine.

Sailing in the Trades. Skipper Gordon on watch.

Watching from *Starbound* as water piles up against the
breakwater at the tail end of a typhoon at the Bay of
Islands, New Zealand.

View of the Bay of Islands during calmer days.

At the Voss shipyard in New Zealand, *Starbound* gets her bottom scraped and painted.

Starbound in port at Mooloolaba Yacht Club, Australia,
with her bowsprit projecting over the seawall.

Starbound anchored at Nara Inlet near the Barrier Reef.

An Aussie "ringer" (cowboy) with the Australian
national beverage at Cooktown.

A starfish found at Vavau, Tonga.

Before the coup d'etat at Dili, cockfighting was the
favorite entertainment.

On the quay at Dili, a truck roars past during the
coup d'etat.

sextant away in its box and the box away in its safe and permanent storage spot. Now he can calculate his sun line and plot the line of position on the sailing chart.

The answer the navigator is looking for is similar to the following: "blank" nautical miles toward (or away from) the sun at a true azimuth of "blank" degrees. Actually he'll scribble something like: "6 miles T @ 106°." How the navigator gets to this point is the process which snows most beginners right under. My suggestion is: forget the theory! "Cookbook" the problem and learn the theory after the sun line is on the chart. Ernie learned in this way. He knew how to find his position at sea long before he fully understood the theory behind it. Then when he started to study the theory there was no mental fumbling at all.

An experienced navigator can shoot the sight, make the calculation, and plot the LOP on a chart in less than five minutes. The first time I did it, it took me over an hour. The second time, half an hour. The third time, twenty minutes. Now, both Ernie and I can work a sight in five minutes. It takes practice.

A few last remarks on navigation: printed forms can be purchased which may help the beginner with the calculation for each shot. Most yachties don't bother with them. If we shoot five stars in the morning, a 1000 sun line, a noon latitude shot, a 1500 sun line, and five evening stars, we would use 13 forms each day, probably more. Instead, we employ inexpensive thick bound notebooks with $8\frac{1}{2} \times 11$ lined paper and work our shots in them. We can calculate three shots on a page.

I've mentioned that we shoot five stars (one or two might be planets) in the morning or evening when we want an accurate fix. Actually, a fix can be obtained by just shooting two bodies if they're at near right angles to each other. But if a mistake is made on one of them, the fix could be off a good distance. If we shoot three bodies and the final plot gives us a small triangle, which it usually does, we know we're somewhere in the triangle. But if we screw up one shot, say because of a bad horizon or a misreading of the sextant, we might end up with a very large triangle. Then we're in the quandary of not knowing which shot was faulty. So we shoot five bodies. One of them might be off, but the others will give us a good fix. We can work a five-body fix in about thirty minutes, just dawdling along.

Let's see now; we were on our way to Tonga from Samoa. We were shooting many shots with the two sextants because the trip is short and we wanted to be spot-on when we raised Vava'u.

Starbound nosed across the International Date Line on the night of September 8, a Sunday, and when the sun came up it was Tuesday morning on the 10th. We sighted Vava'u from the crosstrees at 1230 just as the southeast wind deserted us. We sheeted in everything and drove *Starbound* forward over a smooth sea, creating our own breeze.

The northern coast of Vava'u is steep-to with no reasonable spot to drop an anchor. Darkness was falling like a curtain as we rounded the northwest tip of the island. We didn't want to lie off all night, so we headed for a small cove shown on the chart as Port Refuge. Well named, it was. The anchor went down as the last of the daylight fled. It was a very dark night and we could hear the reef chortling to itself on three sides of our ship. It is a very tight little bay. We were worried about swinging into trouble, so we set up anchor watches for the night. We could have relaxed. Morning found us sitting safely in the center of the small anchorage. Tropical foliage cascaded down the steep bluffs of the cul-de-sac to a small beach at its head. A fisherman was using a circular throw net at the edge of the reef. I took exquisite pleasure in calling to Nina and my mother to wake up and come topside to look at a real tropical paradise. It was an idyllic scene which few people get to experience. We felt very fortunate.

The port and center of government of Vava'u, Neiafu, was just a few miles around the corner, down near the end of one of the most beautiful channels in the world. Smaller side channels led here and there, and islands were everywhere, their sides very steep-to and undercut by the sea.

Topaz had laid off at sea for the night and came in at first light. She had secured to a huge mooring buoy just off the main dock of Neiafu. They invited us to tie alongside while we went through the official entering procedure. A government boat came alongside. The officials came aboard and granted pratique to both yachts but informed us that all weapons must be turned over at the local police station during our stay. We detected a faint note of hostility among the officials and couldn't figure out the cause. After some friendly questioning on our part we finally got the story: three or four American Peace Corps kids had just been arrested for growing pot on the local farms, while they were showing the Tongans how to grow better crops. Yes, they had been doing a good job on the legitimate stuff, but the Tongans really frowned on the extracurricular agriculture, even though the kids were growing the grass for their own use. The youths would go on trial the following week. In the meantime they were incarcerated in the local jug and were doing hard labor under armed guard during the day. We made suitable exclamations of dismay and chagrin, and the officials' strict attitude relaxed to a point where they accepted several alcoholic drinks each.

In the afternoon we picked up a few supplies in Neiafu—primarily fresh bread—then explored the small town. Children were everywhere! One-third of the population of 80,000 Tongans is under the age of ten! The government has finally started a birth control program but it's the same old problem: too little, too late. Tongans stay in Tonga. It's an independent kingdom and there is no outlet for surplus population and no incentive for outside investment other than tourist hotels. They're trying that in a small way, but Tonga is a long way from any of the wealthy tourist-producing countries.

The ills of overpopulation are showing too. Neiafu is crowded and relatively scroungy compared to photographs we had seen from five years before. Also, a flotilla of canoes full of men and children besieged our boats. They wanted to sell or trade for almost anything. They had shells and baskets and mats and coconuts and bananas. They wanted clothes and tinned food and empty containers and money. We traded for some coconuts and bananas and finally got everybody back in their canoes. We had been told that thievery was not a problem, but someone in Tonga has got some nice fishing tackle and a hell of a good boat knife.

We decided to leave Neiafu next morning and go to some of the other anchorages in the group. *Topaz* went with us. There are at least twenty good anchorages within an eight-hour sail of Neiafu. One of the most delightful spots is the beautiful bay on the north side of Vakaeitu. Eleven people live on the island. Kaho is the leader of the family. His daughter, Lucy, is married to a transplanted New Zealander named Ian McReady, who acted as translator for us. The crews of *Starbound* and *Topaz* were invited to a feast on Sunday, two days hence. Kaho gifted us with coconuts and fruit, so we gifted him back with some 410 shotgun shells, which Ian explained were needed to kill the chickens which ran loose in the woods. Kaho had an ancient Enfield that had been rechambered to accept the 410 shells. We arranged to borrow the old gun to go pig hunting next day. I had some 410 gauge rifled slugs which we thought might bring down a pig if we hit it right.

Next morning Ernie and I set off with two of *Topaz*'s crew to do our pig hunting. We got a great deal of sweaty exercise but no pig. A few shots were banged off but nothing was downed. Those jungle pigs must be a cross between a jackrabbit and a ghost. They're hard to see and fast as a cockroach. We finally headed back for the bay, pigless but happy.

The feast on Sunday was a splendid occasion. A Tongan minister and two other church officials came over from another island to officiate at the feast. The food was all spread out on a long table. We were seated all around it on benches covered with beautifully figured tapa cloth. Kaho reigned at one end, the minister at the other. The crews of *Topaz* and *Starbound* lined either side interspersed with the two lesser church officials and Ian. Altogether there were twenty-three people at that table. The Tongan women served the meal and were to eat after the men were through. The women from the yachts were allowed to eat with the men.

There were two suckling pigs on the table and one 150-pounder that had been cooked in the underground oven, called an *umu* in Tongan. There was squid, and raw fish in lime juice and coconut cream, and taro leaves which had been cooked and folded into squares with coconut cream between the folds. There was taro poi and banana poi. And there were speeches—and prayers, long ones—both before and after the feast, all in Tongan. The minister was particularly long-winded. He also got the prime cuts of the pig. They take their religion seriously in Tonga.

During the concluding speech, I turned to Ian. "What's he saying this time?"

Ian smiled. "He's making a speech of thanks for you."

"I was all set to make my own speech thanking everyone."

"That's not the way it's done here. If you can't speak Tongan, someone is supposed to do it for you. Speech making is a very big part of life for Tongan males. He's really enjoying himself."

"Oh, yeah? What's he saying now?"

"Oh, he's telling them for you how grateful you all are for the wonderful food because you hardly ever eat that well from where you come from."

"He's not far wrong."

At the feast's conclusion, we were given wrapped packages of more pig and taro. We returned to the boats and Larry Cross, the captain of *Topaz*, and myself dug through our belongings to come up with three packages of pipe tobacco for Kaho. Nina found some nice pieces of pareu cloth and a mosquito net for the women and I ferreted out another box of 410 shells. We gave the gifts to Kaho and his family that evening and said good-by.

Early next morning both boats set out for "Mariners Cave," a remarkable sea-sculptured cavern located on the north coast of Nua Papu Island. The cave has an underwater entrance. We left one person at the helm on each boat because we couldn't anchor. The water just off the cliff is over 200 feet deep. The rest of the two crews went over the side with masks and fins and swam directly into a black hole located 6 feet down. After about 10 feet of tunnel the cavern opened up and we could rise to the surface to be greeted by semidarkness, an eerie blue light coming from the sun reflected from the white sand at the bottom of the entrance perhaps 50 feet down. Our voices bounced back and forth when we called to each other. There were rocky ledges to sit on while our eyes slowly adjusted and allowed us to see more and more of the craggy domed interior. The surge of the sea pressing into the cave with each wave caused our ears to pop as the pressure rhythmically increased, then decreased. Even more fascinating was the magical fog which appeared and disappeared to the same rhythm. When we finally swam out into the sunlight we were astonished to learn that we'd been in the cave for over an hour.

It was time to leave Tonga. *Starbound* and *Topaz* ran back up the channel to Neiafu for supplies. *Topaz* hooked back on to the big mooring buoy, but we took *Starbound* in close to the beach just off the big, but almost empty, tourist hotel. It's a quiet anchorage and much prettier than off the town.

Next morning Nina went with Mom and Dad into town for supplies while Ernie and I arranged with the hotel to take water on board. We took a stern line ashore and secured it to a palm tree, then winched *Starbound*'s stern to within 100 feet of the beach. All our hoses together just made the distance from the water tap on shore to the forward tanks. We filled the four water tanks and let each overflow for a while. The water was sweet and clear—a far cry from the slop we'd put aboard in Pago Pago. The hotel charged us 40 cents, very reasonable for 300 gallons of water.

Dove, Puffin, and *Jaga* had come in while *Topaz* and our crew had been sailing around and eating pig. We had met Dave and Sue Alpson of *Dove* in Tahiti, and of course Jerry and Ev Taylor of *Puffin* were our friends from as far back as the Marquesas. Now we met *Jaga*, crewed by Dave and his beautiful wife, Virginia. Visits between boats went on well into the night.

I went ashore early next morning, Thursday, and cleared for Suva. Back on *Starbound* by 1000, we found amusement in watching something happen which we had seen before and had experienced ourselves. It could be called the "What Am I Waiting For?" syndrome. It happens whenever one yacht watches another shoving off for the next port. The first thought is, "I ought to get the hook up and get out of here too."

We were pulling our sail covers off when *Dove* came motoring by. I called to Dave and Sue, "Where you goin'? Thought you were gonna stay awhile."

"Naw—we've seen it. Went in and cleared."

"Swell! Let's get together on the radio at 0900 and 1500."

A call across the water came from *Puffin*, "Hey, you guys leaving?"

"Yeah, we're off for Suva."

"Hey, I'm going too—I've got to clear. Any strain ashore?"

"No. Go ahead. We'll wait for you!"

Starbound weighed anchor at 1100 and started for the harbor entrance, *Dove* and *Puffin* ahead of us by 500 yards. As we went by *Topaz* and *Jaga*, heads popped out of hatches. "Hey! We'll be behind you in half an hour. 2182 kHz at 0900 and 1500?" Evidently *Dove* and *Puffin* had given them the word. And so five boats rolled out of Tonga leaving an empty harbor behind.

It was a passage made for fun! We always had one or two yachts within sight and radio communications were very good. We eased *Starbound* south to clear Nukusonge reef, finally sighting it off the starboard bow by 0700 on Saturday, just as planned. The dangerous passages must be made by daylight.

At 1000 we changed course to the northwest for the passage between Matuku and Totoya Islands. We cleared the islands before dark and before the wind dropped off. By 0100 Sunday morning we were gliding over a glass-smooth sea, the sails furled and the big diesel ticking along at 1200 revs. Grumpy steered a very accurate course and we stood our watches in the deck hammock, gazing up at the stars.

Some clouds appeared with the first light but we managed to shoot Sirius and Canopus. Ernie and I worked with both sextants and our separate fixes were within one mile of each other, so we were satisfied.

A light breeze was blowing abaft the port beam by 0900. The sea was still silky smooth. We started to put on sail: first the square sail, then the raffee. We braced the yard over. We put up the main, the mizzen and yankee jib, then, just for the hell of it, the main-topsail. We had to leave the staysail furled because it would foul the square sail. We were flying over 2,600 square feet of sail, the absolute maximum that could be set, and Ernie said, "Gee, Pop, if we take that old roller furling jib and set it upside down as a mizzen staysail ... ?" Even with the light breeze *Starbound* was logging 6 knots. What a beautiful day! At 1900 the wind started to haul aft and we could see lightning far ahead, so we dropped the fore and aft sail and continued at a slower pace under the square rig.

The squall failed to live up to its advance billing and Monday morning dawned fair. *Dove* was abeam about 3 miles off. Jerry on *Puffin* came on the air right at 0900. I answered before the other boats and said, "Good morning, Jerry—can you say something intelligent this early?"

He replied "E equals mc squared."

We sighted Suva from the crosstrees at 1000 and cranked up the diesel to avoid standing off all night.

Another small digression is in order here. As long as we've been sailing we've heard the words, "Don't go in strange harbors at night." We have broken the rule a few times when our favorite girlfriend, Prudence, advised us that it was going to be very hairy outside indeed, and that we'd better find shelter. But those situations are rare and unusual. The more we sail the more we learn, and one of the more important things we've learned is to make our own luck. Good planning is nearly everything, and the smartest plan of all is to be in the right part of whatever ocean you are sailing at the correct time of year for fine weather and fair winds. To further increase the benevolence of Lady Luck, it is not only a very wise thing, but also a very interesting thing, to canvas all the other yachties at whatever port you are in, to find out what lies ahead. Independence be damned! You just might find some sailor, as we have several times, who knows a lot about the problems of the next port.

We were told to enter Suva in the daylight because the reef is extensive (it is) and the lights at night are confusing (they are). We were also told to drop anchor in the quarantine anchorage and await further developments.

We did as we had been advised. *Dove* came in right after us and we invited Dave and Sue to tie alongside *Starbound* since we already had our big anchor down.

We were having a cup of coffee on the afterdeck and wondering if we two skippers should go ashore. The owner of *Tsuru*, a big, beautiful, very expensive ketch out of Los Angeles, ran out to the quarantine anchorage in his launch and told us to stay on board until the doctor showed up. Officialdom here was evidently very touchy. *Tsuru*'s owner, another Dave, let his launch float just off our quarter and related to us the story of an unfortunate yachtie who, a week ago, had anchored off the Suva Yacht Club and gone ashore in search of customs and immigrations people—the common procedure for yachties the world over. When he found them he was summarily ordered to go back to his boat and re-anchor in the quarantine anchorage until cleared by the port doctor. They let him sit there for three days before granting him pratique! There is an ancient nautical term for this kind of practice, but it's unprintable. However, it's their country, not ours.

There was no doctor by dark, so we all turned in for a quiet night.

Puffin came in at 0800 and tied up to our starboard side. At 0900 the doctor turned up, declared us healthy, granted pratique to all three yachts, and told us to haul down our Q flags. In the meantime *Topaz* and *Jaga* came in and circled around until the doctor finished with us. We were told to proceed to the main ship's wharf to clear customs and immigration. I laid *Starbound* in first. Then *Dove, Puffin,* and *Jaga,* in that order tied outboard of us. *Topaz* went in behind *Starbound.*

We all cleared at once in a flurry of paperwork. All guns and ammunition from all yachts had to be declared. The weapons were removed to the local armory and we were given receipts. *Jaga, Topaz,* and *Dove* had to sign a bond of 500 Fiji dollars each for their cats and dogs. Animals are a problem.

Water had to be obtained at the same wharf we were on, so we arranged for it on the spot, then went back to the yachts to fill our tanks and make ready to move to the yacht club anchorage. We couldn't stay at the main wharf. That is only for ships. Yachts must anchor off the club.

The Suva Yacht Club is a very famous and very active club. It has hot showers available, two movies each week, and a weekly barbecue. The yachtie gets charged $2 per head per week. It has the best bar in town, and its hospitality is unexcelled. At least it was while we were there. We have heard since that overseas yachts can no longer anchor off the club or use its facilities. I hope that rumor is wrong. If true, it will make Suva a much less attractive place for the cruising yachts.

The regular members of the yacht club made us very welcome. A real bunch of sailors, that group, and passionately interested in details of our voyage. However, the chunky Indian manager was quite a bit less than friendly. He seemed to tolerate us, barely, as a group. He was always quite friendly to Nina and me, and my parents, perhaps because we dressed with discretion when we went ashore. But Ernie's long hair and mod jeans seemed to infuriate him, and *Topaz*'s crew turned him livid with rage. I had quite a discussion with him one day, explaining to him that what he termed "long-haired, bearded hippies" were in fact a very well-educated and level-headed group of young Americans, most of them college graduates, the women married to their husbands, and all of them quite far from being destitute. After that he tolerated them but still didn't quite approve, in spite of the fact that the young set of regular members were often present in more bizarre garb than the yachties. A very curious world, this!

Yacht club or no yacht club, Suva is a fine supply port. My advice to cruising yachts is to stop there. Enter with care and discretion, then go to where the other yachts are. They're the main source of fun anyway. And there are several fine anchorages in Suva harbor.

Fiji is an independent state within the Commonwealth of Nations. Suva is a delight. It's a city of about 60,000, the capital and chief port of Fiji. It's located on the south coast of Viti Levu. Coconut oil, sugar, and soap are still among the chief products. The important thing to remember is that as far as the economy goes, the Indians control Fiji and Suva. There are more Indians than Fijians. Conversely, there are more Christians than Hindus, meaning that many Indians are Christian (mostly Methodist). We found the Indians in general to be friendly, polite, hard-working people with too-large families. Overpopulation there is as big a problem as in most other places in this world.

Suva is a "free" port. It has to be the best place to buy electronics gear we have yet seen, but you must know how to comparison shop and how to bargain. Since the Indian deals a hundred times each day and you deal once, remember who's got the edge.

My mom wasn't feeling too well when we got to Suva. We'd called up the American Consul, who'd recommended a good doctor to us. The doctor diagnosed her problem as a basic "plumbing" infection. Antibiotics were finally getting it under control, so Mom and Dad started getting around town more. They really loved the Indian markets. So did Nina and I. They're the kind of places you can walk through for hours and spend three bucks. Nina looked at goodies and I looked at people.

We were going to try to get away for New Zealand during the second week in October, so Nina started looking for all the places where basic stores could be bought inexpensively, and I continued my search for small parts I needed for the boat. Nina had more luck than I. Nearly all machinery in Suva is metric, and the shore power is 240 volt, 50 cycle. However, 12-volt direct current gear seems to be universal, especially for cars and boats. I managed to get "bits and pieces" for the auto-pilot, the radio-telephone, and the main engine electrical system. But there wasn't a 32-volt light bulb to be had in town. I hoped New Zealand had some; there were only a few spares left in the locker.

I'm afraid that 32-volt systems are getting to be a thing of the past. Maybe I'll have to switch *Starbound*'s "ship's service" to 12 volts before I try a second trip around the world. Too bad—those old 32-volt motors put out good power to *Starbound*'s various pumps, compressors, and winches.

While we were in Suva, a fellow we had met in Tahiti stacked his lovely cutter, *Vega,* up on the Suva reef. I won't go into detail on how he did it, but I will say that the skipper shouldn't be asleep below leaving his twelve-year-old daughter on watch, and the boat on wind vane steering, while the vessel is within even 100 miles of any reef. And once again I'll say: don't approach unfamiliar shores at night. Luckily, no one was hurt. Lately we heard that they'd finally managed to salvage *Vega* but that she was badly damaged. It was a hell of a way to end a lovely cruise.

As the days went by I watched the weather more and more closely. New Zealand lay some 1,100 miles south, and just a tad west, from Suva. It was important to get well south of Fiji before an early typhoon decided to come down from the north and stomp us raggedy. At this time of year, big, well-developed cold fronts sweep across that southern section of Pacific Ocean, the systems moving on a general course from southwest to northeast. They swing like a gigantic scythe, one chop per week. The trick is for the yachtie to leave right after one goes through Suva, then move out fast, get hit with the next one where there's plenty of sea room to run off with it if necessary, then move on to New Zealand before getting socked with the next one.

We checked with the meteorological office and studied the synoptic charts every day. By the 10th of October, my forty-fourth birthday, we knew we'd leave on Saturday the 12th. We arranged to clear. We had to give forty-eight hours' notice to retrieve our guns. They're hardly worth carrying, for the trouble they cause.

We said good-by to everyone at the club and waved to our friends on boats. Many of them were leaving on the same day. We took *Starbound* back over to the main wharf, where we had entered. Once again we topped off her water tanks, and bought fuel which had to be delivered by truck, an archaic procedure for what is supposed to be a modern city. Finally the officials brought down our guns, a rusty old 410-gauge and a little pea-popper of a .32 hand gun. They said good-by and they meant it; as soon as the weapons were aboard we were required to cast off our lines and leave the harbor. Nor could we stop anywhere else in Fiji.

I was impatient to get to New Zealand. I felt a real need to go to work and make some money. The strongbox was far from healthy.

Out through the reef-lined passage we flew and headed down the rhumb line at 185 degrees by the compass. Six knots she was making under all fore and aft sail. The deep blue of the sea looked good after the muddy green-brown of the inner harbor.

15

New Zealand, Aotearoa

Aotearoa, the Maori name for New Zealand, means the Land of the Long White Cloud. It lay 1,100 miles to the south of us. We had hoped to make it in ten days. It took twelve.

For four days we sailed peacefully, with an easterly wind blowing at 8 to 10 knots. Then the frontal system we'd been expecting came through, just about on schedule, and the wind veered to the southeast. As the wind increased, we dropped everything but the yankee jib and hanked the storm jib onto the mainstay, ready to go up. Three hours later we doused the yankee, rolled it tightly, and tied it down to the bow basket. The storm jib went up and we turned the ship, running off before 25 knots of wind. The seas continued to build and by midnight were evil, towering black genies with white hair, occasionally 20 feet high. At its strongest the wind was over 30 knots, gusting to 40.

By noon next day we were out of it, which means the front had passed over us on its way east. The wind had veered to southwest and *Starbound* had made nearly a full clockwise circle. A few clear spots allowed us to shoot the sun. We put a small cross on the chart 100 miles northeast of our position twenty-four hours earlier. We started to work our way south again.

Every boat is an individual in the way she performs in heavy weather. Perhaps the stomping we had gotten on the way to Bermuda during the first few days of our voyage was a camouflaged benediction. We'd learned a lot during that storm, our first real trial at sea. We'd found out what *Starbound* would do and, as important, we'd learned what our own limitations were.

During this latest tussle with an adverse weather system I found myself able to do two things: to watch carefully how *Starbound* performed in heavy seas and a strong wind, and to examine my own feelings—to evaluate my own performance as master of the ship—under the same conditions.

Looking at myself first, I will say that I made a good start; I put the ship into the optimum position to withstand inevitable bad weather. We had sea room all around and we knew what to expect. When the front started coming through we reduced sail in time and battened down properly. All loose gear was stowed and double lashed. The bilges were pumped dry and kept that way.

Was I frightened? No. Apprehensive? Most decidedly! I feel a rather perverse, amused contempt for skippers of small craft who are overly casual, after the fact, about bad weather at sea. I know damn well that they sweat it out just like I do. Scared isn't the right word—I think "apprehensive" fits nicely into my psychic top drawer. But apprehension shouldn't affect a skipper's decisions on how the ship should be handled. I found that I made the right decisions with logic and speed. I am very careful not to communicate any sense of my own apprehension to the crew—they're busy enough with their own. It seemed O.K., though, to own up to the fact that it was a big sea and a lot of wind, but that the ship was doing fine. She was.

Starbound likes to run. She runs better than any other yacht we've seen. She reaches well too, but running is her strong suit. This ability is primarily due to her hull lines, and secondarily her rig. She's what the old Maine boys call "cod headed and mackerel sterned." Her maximum beam of 17 feet is well forward of amidships, actually just abaft the mainmast. Her broad bow gives her tremendous "lift" forward. It also gives her a very commodious forecastle and chain locker. From her point of maximum beam she gets progressively more narrow aft and at the transom measures 13 feet "out to out" of the hull planking. That is a wide stern, with a lot of buoyancy where it's needed. *Starbound* has never been pooped, and she doesn't tend to "surf" down the front of a big wave. When running before heavy seas she'll lift her broad·butt up and up, and as the wave travels forward her buoyancy will continually increase forward because of the steadily increasing beam that the wave "sees." Then she'll level out quickly and her bows will lift as the wave passes under her. She finishes her act with a surge forward on the *back* of the wave, the surge created by the suction of the water on her rounded bows. It's a relatively comfortable ride, and she never feels as if she's getting away from the helmsman.

So when the going gets really heavy and we have sea room, we run. If we're running in a direction contrary to our preferred course, we take all sail off—even the storm jib—and run the engine at slow speed; about 1,000 RPM gives her a fast rudder action and keeps her moving at about 4 knots. The windage from our mainmast rigging forward helps to keep the bow pointed downwind.

If there is danger to leeward and the wind and sea won't let us reach away from it, we heave to. To "heave to" means to lay a vessel where she takes the seas most comfortably while riding out the "storm," rather than to make progress on the voyage. In general, the less onward motion a vessel has, the safer she rides. A sailing vessel is generally laid on the wind (her nose mostly into it), with the helm to leeward (tending always to turn her up into the wind), and with the sails so trimmed that she will come to and fall off, but always head up out of the trough of the waves. The sail trim depends on the hull and rig of the boat. Most cruising vessels use a backed storm jib forward (a very small, tough sail set with the clew pulled over to windward) and a storm trysail on the main or mizzen, sheeted in hard. The way it works is that the storm trysail will try to make the boat point up and sail, but the backed jib prevents her from doing so. So she'll sit there, with her bow about 45 to 60 degrees off the wind and waves, coming to and falling off, and at the same time will forereach very slowly. If there is danger to leeward, this forereaching will often take her clear of it, if the skipper is smart enough to know on which tack to heave to. If he's unsure of his position relative to the danger, he can switch tacks every so often by starting the jib sheet and driving her over to the other tack under power. A more dangerous way to do it is to jibe her around. Some boats with good windward ability might be able to start the jib sheet and get on enough headway to sail her through to the other tack. I've never heard of a cruising boat that's done this, but I suppose there are a few. Most of us yachties use our engines.

Starbound heaves to in an interesting way. If it's not blowing too hard, say 30 knots, she heaves-to under just the mizzen alone—sometimes with a reef in it, sheeted in hard. She has so much windage forward with the big bowsprit and square yard and associated rigging that a storm jib is superfluous as hell. We've used the storm trysail in lieu of the mizzen too, but if the weather gets up bad enough to go to the storm trysail, we'll dump everything and run her off slowly, under power—if we have sea room.

Our front went grumbling on its way to bother some other poor sailor and *Starbound* continued south. We wanted to hustle now, to be into a safe harbor before the next system came along.

We were having a lot of fun with the radio-telephone again. We had a communications link running from yacht to yacht all the way from Fiji to New Zealand. Dave and Bev Taskett on *Fairwinds,* Mark and Leslie on *Lissa,* and Merle and Marge on *La Cosse* were all ahead of us. *Bendora* with Joan and Jean aboard and two other yachts, *Samarang* and *Windchimes,* were all behind us. Seven yachts, including *Starbound,* were strung out over 1,000 miles of ocean. We got on the air at 0800 and 1600 local time on 2738 kHz and passed on our location and weather situation up and down the line. It was very nice indeed to know that the weather ahead was nice. Also, it's a good feeling to have proof that you're not all alone in the big ocean.

Dave Taskett on *Fairwinds* was our weather mentor. He's an electronics expert and his boat is filled with marvelous communications gear including a ham rig. He can send and receive Morse as fast as anybody I've seen, so he'd receive all the coded stuff from New Zealand, then transmit it by voice up the line to us less talented sailors.

One morning in a flat calm the engine wouldn't start. It had been getting progressively more reluctant in spite of a fully charged battery. Ernie and I unbolted the starter from the big Ford diesel, an easy job because it is accessible, and tore it down. It was full of grease and guck. The stuff had probably worked its way in through the bottom drain holes from the soupy mess I'd allowed to slosh around in the copper catch pan under the engine last time I'd changed the oil and checked the salt water circulating pump. (That combination of jobs makes a real mess.) One of the two field coils was shorting to the starter case and the commutator brushes were partially frozen in their holders. We disassembled the whole mess, cleaned the grunge off with electrical equipment cleaner, and polished everything dry. We reinsulated the shorted field with black plastic tape, made sure the brushes were clean and working free, then reassembled the thing and bolted it back into place. We wire-brushed the electrical terminals until the copper shone, and hooked the tagged wiring back up. (We always tag our wiring with masking tape and a marking pen when we work on electrical stuff.) The revamped starter kicked the engine over like it was new. The whole job took five hours.

I make the point of this little repair to highlight a few things I think are important. Working on engine systems is usually a messy procedure. If we didn't have a big copper catch pan under the engine, the mess would have been in our bilge. If I'd cleaned out the engine pan right away, the stuff wouldn't have gotten into the starter motor. But since I didn't, and it did— kindly note that we had the tools, parts, and knowhow to fix the starter, without which we would have been in the soup since there ain't no other way to start a big six-cylinder diesel like ours. Well, that's not quite true. An air starter can be installed but retails for over $1,000 and takes up a lot of space on the front end of the engine, space which we don't have. An extra starter is a nice spare to acquire but it costs over $200 for the ones for a big diesel. We settled for an extra solenoid and spare brushes.

We motor-sailed the last four days to get into Bay of Islands, New Zealand. The wind was generally fluky out of the south, and cold. We sighted the loom of Cape Brett light at 0120 on October 24 while still 40 miles away from it. At sunup we ran up to the beautiful coast south of

Whangaroa and tacked, but the wind headed us so we dropped all sail and motored. Up the bay we went, past the pretty little town of Russell, right to the head of the bay. There, nestled in among the green hills, is the port of Opua. We tied up to the main dock behind two other yachts. The harbor master came down to tell us he'd already called for the officials to come up to enter us. They had to drive up from Whangarei, 30 miles further south.

The yacht entrance procedures for New Zealand are tough. We couldn't get off the boat until cleared by the agricultural inspector. He removed all fresh fruit and vegetables and egg shells—not the inside part, just the shells. Nina broke our last two dozen into a jar. He put the stuff into a plastic bag and sealed it. It would be incinerated. Then he checked the boat for animals. A $500 (N.Z.) bond must be posted for each animal. If the animal gets off the boat it is destroyed and incinerated, and your $500 bond is lost. Tough? You bet, but very nice, very polite, and very friendly. Happy to accept a whiskey (meaning Scotch), and tell you about New Zealand. But International Immunization cards get examined very closely. Next comes customs and immigration with lots of paperwork. All passports are checked including visa stamps. Customs declarations are filled out in detail. All hand guns must be deposited with the police constable at Russell. (Hand guns are a no-no!) Very nice guys, but they don't fool around. It was 1700 hours before they finished with us.

We filled our water tanks and moved *Starbound* to a pretty anchorage across from the main wharf. We'd move the boat to Russell tomorrow. It was lovely to sit on the afterdeck seats with a gin and tonic and watch the sun go down. The local radio predicted bad weather by tomorrow night. Somehow that made it even nicer.

It stopped being "nicer" the next night when it blew 40 knots from the southeast and rained hard. *Starbound* was secure in the lee of the land with two anchors down, but we were listening to radio Auckland talking to poor little *Puffin* with Jerry and Ev on board. The bobstay had carried away and they were laying ahull in very steep seas, 30 miles north of the upper tip of New Zealand, unable to set sail with the mast not stayed forward. They couldn't make any headway under power against the wind and sea. Even a big ship would have had a tough time doing that.

Most of the night was spent listening to the weather reports and worrying about *Puffin.* Next morning the weather was much improved and we heard through radio Auckland that *Puffin* was on her way in under power. What a relief!

We spent two weeks anchored near the town of Russell. I say near the town because in the town harbor proper the bottom is shingle, which makes poor holding ground in any kind of blow. All the yachties anchor in little Mautawhi Bay, get ashore by their dinghies, which are tied to a raunchy old dock, and then walk the half-mile over the saddle of a hill into Russell. The main hangout is the Duke of Marlborough Hotel, which has a lovely pub. In fact the only pub in Russell.

Our two weeks in Bay of Islands were spent loafing, reading, writing, shopping, sightseeing in the immediate area and drinking lots of New Zealand beer at the Duke of Marlborough.

Ernie found a job at a meat-packing plant located near the town of Kawakawa on the eastern side of the bay. There is a youth hostel nearby where a number of people in his age group were staying. I think his exact words were "I don't want to work in some big city like Auckland. I like it up here. Besides, I can live at the youth hostel for practically nothing if I pitch my tent, and then I can save some money and also live on my own for a while."

"O.K.," we said.

The trip to Auckland was a true pleasure. A nice 12-knot westerly wind gave us a broad reach for the whole 120 miles. Just a lovely overnight sail.

We arrived in Auckland to find the serpent in paradise. In all of that big lovely harbor, there is only one yacht basin to which a cruising yachtsman can go: Westhaven Marina, located just east of the Auckland Harbor Bridge on the City shore. We had been told that Westhaven was already jammed with cruising yachts and that we couldn't get in there. We'd made arrangements with Wayne Young, the owner of the Duke of Marlborough pub, to borrow his mooring in Okahu Bay, home of the Royal Akarana Yacht Club. Wayne told us we'd have to "find" his mooring, since the buoy had sunk, but we figured that since there was no room at the inn, a stable would do us.

We found the place his mooring had been, all right. It was an open spot in one of many long rows of moored boats, all of them much smaller than *Starbound.* We dropped our anchor so that we hung clear of the other yachts. We had to use a short scope of chain or *Starbound* would swing into the boats on either side when the tide or wind changed. Then Dad and I broke out the launch and the grappling iron and started to drag the bottom, hoping to pick up the sunken mooring chain. After about four hours of it we gave up. I speculated on using the scuba gear, but the water was solid murky brown and the current was strong. The tidal rise and fall was 12 feet. Our big Herreshoff anchor seemed to be holding well in the soft mud bottom, so we told ourselves we were O.K. for the time being.

Getting ashore was a problem too. The landing at the yacht club was a quarter-mile away across water which becomes very choppy when the wind blows up or down the harbor, which is nearly always. Every time we went ashore we got wet from wave slop and spray. And when we got to the landing we couldn't leave the boat there. It had to be taken to the launching ramp, put on a dolly, hauled up the ramp, and parked with the other dinghies. It was a thirty-minute job, either direction.

The problem was resolved on our third day in Okahu Bay, a Saturday. Hospitable New Zealand friends had invited Nina and me and Mom and Dad up to their house for lunch and laundry facilities. When we returned in the late afternoon we were aghast. A heavy west wind had made itself felt, and *Starbound* was 100 feet from where she should have been. She'd dragged her big anchor and that short scope of chain right between two smaller boats without touching them, thank God, and had stopped when her keel aft met the bottom mud. And the tide was beginning to fall.

We scrambled on board. Mom tended the launch and led it aft for towing. Nina and Dad went forward to raise the anchor, washing down the chain with the deck pump hose as it came in. I started the engine and kept the ship's nose into the strong wind. The pull from the anchor and the push from the propeller freed her keel from the mud just as the anchor popped loose. I cranked on the power and drove her into the wind and back through the narrow slot between boats, then turned left out of the mooring area and into the harbor. We headed for Westhaven Marina, 4 miles away. The sun was still above the horizon. Good-by, Okahu Bay!

It was still daylight when we pulled up to the fuel dock inside the breakwater at Westhaven. The rules are different in New Zealand; they wouldn't let us lay at the fuel dock overnight. We took on diesel and water and finagled a place for *Starbound*. It was an awkward makeshift berth, with her bowsprit almost touching the rocks of the breakwater and lines spun out to various pilings to keep her out of danger. The only dock designated for cruising yachts was filled, with boats laying two abreast. No hope of our getting a place at that dock!

We stayed where we were over Sunday. Monday morning we spent with the Westhaven dockmaster, a salty old gent named "Flap" Martiningo. He just didn't have any room for *Starbound*. We couldn't stay where we were, either. We had the access to three berths blocked off. Finally, after he'd had a long conversation with the Boats and Harbors office, Flap told me that they'd arranged for us to have a temporary berth at Marsden Wharf, right on Quay Street in downtown Auckland.

We weren't too overjoyed about going to a commercial wharf—not right then anyway. We visualized a dock area like the ones in big American cities, with drunks soiling our decks, muggers lurking behind stacks of cargo, and a 2-mile walk into town if we wanted to buy anything. We just didn't understand New Zealand yet. Marsden Wharf wasn't exactly lovely, but the New Zealanders were, and just across the street were shops and markets. We could walk a few blocks and see a movie, a seemingly mundane activity, but we were ready for the small diversion it provided.

We decided to stay at the wharf as long as we could.

We met Lou and Iris Fischer during our second day at Marsden. We didn't know it at the time but Lou is one of New Zealand's leading industrialists. We began to get a hint of this when he and Iris took Nina and me up to their home for an afternoon drink. They picked us up in a Bentley and drove us to their very beautiful home situated on 40 acres of landscaped hill overlooking the Tamaki River. A few race horses were strolling around the manicured lawns. It was a truly lovely place.

I mentioned to Lou that I needed a job and suddenly I had one, drafting shop drawings for one of his companies—and at a reasonably good rate of pay for New Zealand. The overall cost of living is lower than in the United States and paychecks reflect this fact. For instance, one friend of ours, the hired manager of an engineering firm in New Zealand, with eighty men under his supervision, earns about U.S. $15,000 per annum. In the United States a job carrying that amount of responsibility would probably pay $50,000.

So I had a job. Then Nina found one working in the office of a small prefabrication concern. We rode the city buses for a few days, then managed to buy a little club coupe made by Holden, an Australian motor car company. The car had 90,000 miles on the odometer and had seen better days. I managed to keep it running with baling wire, a few judicious kicks, and frequent addition of cheap engine oil.

We started to enjoy New Zealand. Our immediate problems were solved for the time being: *Starbound* was in a secure berth and the dollar flow was reversed for the first time in more than a year.

The days began to flow, one into the next, until we'd tend to lose our handle on the passage of time. We were once again becoming victims of the workaday world.

Starbound saved us from a prosaic fate. She kept breaking things: the refrigerator motor needed new brushes, the 32-volt charger blew a diode, and the washdown pump ate a bearing. Even some of the topside gear started giving problems: the anchor winch broke out with chronic rustitis, a swaged fitting on one mizzen shroud developed a stress crack, a few deck seams opened up in the dry weather and, when it finally rained, water dripped on our bunk. The propane tanks had to be taken to the New Zealand Industrial Gas Company and tested to New Zealand standards before they could be filled. We even had to buy a new hose fitting so we could fill our water tanks. American hose fittings are the wrong size.

Everything topside needed painting. Mom and Dad fixed that. Having lived on their own boat for years they really know how to swing a brush. They would sand and paint all day, then have a nice dinner ready when Nina and I came home.

I spent most of my evenings for two weeks head down in various pieces of gear. Finally the servo mechanisms started going click-buzz-chonk again, and then *Topaz* sailed in. The big Baltic trader had left Suva about one week after us. Her crew had taken her to Kandavu Island and spent an extra glorious week diving on some of the island's beautiful reefs with an occasional excursion ashore. Of course, on the way to New Zealand they were caught by a big nasty frontal system and were hove to till it blew across. Every yacht that made that passage caught a piece of the action.

We moved *Starbound* away from the concrete wall at the end of Marsden Wharf and tied her up temporarily to one of the piers. We helped warp *Topaz* into the spot we'd vacated. She took up the entire end with her extreme length of 120 feet. We brought *Starbound* back in and again nestled up to our big dark-green mother goose. *Topaz* made a fine floating dock for us; we didn't have to tend our dock lines to accommodate the 9-foot tidal range.

Two more peaceful weeks raced by. Then the port captain told us we'd have to move. "One month is all we can allow you at Marsden," he said, "and you've been here nearly six weeks. We have three more overseas yachts coming in and they have to have their turn, you see." Very polite chap.

I trudged up Quay Street to talk to the director of Boats and Harbors again to find out where we could go.

He told me, "There are so many cruising yachts now. It makes things very difficult for us here in Auckland. In the past there were only three to five yachts each year. We could roll out the red carpet for them and put them up free of charge at Westhaven. But now we have over thirty cruising yachts right here in Auckland, and God knows how many more in Whangarei and Bay of Islands. I hear that there are a dozen or so down in Wellington. We simply do not have any place to put them. Why, I've even written a letter and had it sent to all the yacht clubs on your West Coast, asking them to tell your yachtsmen not to come to Auckland because of this problem!"

I guess I shouldn't have laughed. But I could just picture the secretaries of those hundreds of yacht clubs dashing about the docks searching out the deep-sea cruising people, many of whom don't belong to yacht clubs, and saying, "Sorry, but you can't go to New Zealand. They don't have room for you."

We parted amicably. At his suggestion I drove out to Half Moon Bay, a private marina on the Tamaki River. It is a big marina by New Zealand standards and small by American standards. It is simply a bight in the coastline of the river across which they've thrown a breakwater. A small part of the breakwater is a stone embankment. The rest of it is a swash bulkhead: pilings driven close together, strengthened with diagonally driven concrete pilings, and capped with a concrete walkway which leads out to the fuel dock. The breakwater encloses perhaps 400 slips, all of them formed by floating docks and finger piers to accommodate the big tidal range of 11 feet.

The management was very courteous to me and thought they might allow us to lay *Starbound* up to the freestanding pilings spaced 10 feet apart and running parallel with the breakwater walkway. Eventually those pilings would form the inner edge of a new pier, but for now—there they were. One hitch, they told me—no one was allowed to live aboard by order of the Boats and Harbors Office. That office must personally give them the O.K. before we could bring *Starbound* in.

I made two more car trips back and forth to get everybody together. Finally, on a Saturday morning, we took our leave of Marsden Wharf and our friends on *Topaz* and sailed *Starbound* the 12 miles to Half Moon Bay. We'd found a home for the remainder of our stay in Auckland. It took seven weeks to do so.

In retrospect I think we should have taken the ship way up in the northeast corner of the bay and anchored out. It's very pretty up there and we could have found work on the north side of the bay. Also, if our yacht had been smaller, we might have been able to wangle a corner in Westhaven.

Many yachts stayed up north in the Bay of Islands, but it is tough to find work there and it is a long trip to Auckland to pick up hard-to-find parts for necessary repair jobs.

A very few smaller yachts managed to find a spot in Whangarei, halfway between Auckland and Bay of Islands. Whangarei is located about 15 miles up a shallow, winding, not particularly attractive river. Once there, there are very few spots to put a yacht. The transients usually raft up three abreast at the city dock. At low tide their keels are in the mud. We'd heard that jobs were almost nonexistent in Whangarei.

Next time we sail to New Zealand, Nina and I have already decided to sail right past Auckland and put into Tauranga, about 100 miles south of Auckland. *Topaz* went there for the duration of her stay. We nursed our old Holden car down to visit one weekend and were sorry we hadn't followed them down with *Starbound*. Tauranga is a beautiful little vacation port. It also has a thriving lumber industry. Best of all, there is some dockage available for "big" boats. *Topaz* was actually put in a slip—all 120 feet of her!

Nina and I are agreed that if we were a bit younger and had two or three children to raise, we would seriously consider emigrating to New Zealand. We met several Americans who did just that. Some of them retained their American citizenship.

The entire country is so clean, so sparkling with its smog-free blue skies, its unpolluted waters, its quiet agrarian atmosphere, that it reminded us of a gigantic national park, with all the charm that phrase implies.

Cruising sailors should learn as much as they can about their host country before they get there. Nina and I collected all the information we could find for every country we planned to visit. Some knowledge about the history, current government, and international political relations can be damn important. And it helps to find out something about the social and educational systems too. Potentially embarrassing situations might be sidestepped. Americans overseas tend to take for granted that everything is "just like home." Tourists do this more than yachties, but we've seen some yachties really goof up. It always pays to know what you're getting into.

Initially the most important things about New Zealand which a yachtsman should know are these: the harbors are good along the east coast, and not so hot on the western side. Also, the western side generally gives a yacht a lee shore. Tasman Sea weather can inject a lot of trouble into a cruise on the west coast.

Dockage facilities for transient yachts are almost nonexistent compared to the United States, but there are many fine places to drop the hook.

Work is available if earning a buck is necessary, but the "work permit" situation should be checked.

All materials and gear a yacht might need can be obtained in New Zealand except 115-volt, 60-cycle electrical equipment; Kiwis use 240-volt, 50-cycle power, so if power tools are needed make sure the motor generator is in good shape. Otherwise, power tools can be rented.

Haul-out facilities are available most places; lots of fishing and yachting goes on in New Zealand. But unlike the yards in the States, the general thing is for the crew to do its own work: scrubbing, sanding, painting—the works. Labor can be hired but we found mostly that the "rich" yachties hired the "poor" yachties. It works out fine for everyone.

Sailmakers and riggers are available but relatively expensive. It pays to do your own if possible. I bought Nina a hand-cranked Singer sewing machine for $30 in Auckland with which she repaired the square sail and made a new awning for the afterdeck.

Canned food in quantity can be bought from discount warehouses in the cities. We simply told the managers we were Americans on a cruising yacht and they gave us a full discount. New Zealand is a fine place to stock up on fresh meat if the yacht has a freezer on board.

One last general piece of information; New Zealanders are hospitable and do everything they can to help out. The sea is close all around them, so they're ocean-oriented. They like yachties and they like Americans. Stop any Kiwi on a downtown street and tell him your troubles and odds are he'll escort you to his car, drive you wherever you need to go, and help you unravel your problem, even if he has to take the day off to do it. When hitchhiking, which we had to do a few times, it was rare when the first car along didn't pick us up. Ernie hitchhiked all over New Zealand—long hair, backpack, and blue jeans—and had a wonderful time. His comment: "I've never met so many nice people in my life!"

We made friends with many New Zealanders during our nearly six-month stay. Two couples with whom we became very close friends are Colin and Pam Corbett and Bevin and Joy Stewart. Both couples would often drop down to *Starbound* and ask us what they could do to help us, and help us they did. They drove us all over Auckland for parts and all over the beautiful countryside on weekends to look at splendid scenery. Pam Corbett spent several of her days with my mom and dad taking them on tours of North Island. And Colin, who was building a steel-hulled boat of his own, was an expert at tracking down material I needed for this job and that.

Bevin Stewart is a real devotee of traditional sailing craft. He loved *Starbound*. He was putting together the plans and specs to build a Texas Bay Scow, a big one, with which to sail New Zealand waters. He'd already built several small wooden boats and was a most excellent craftsman. Bevin noticed that the gunwale of our small 9-foot fiberglass dinghy was broken and coming apart. He showed up one day towing his empty boat trailer behind his car. He carried our dinghy home and built an entirely new gunwale for her out of beautiful kauri wood, laminating each piece with loving care around the sharp curves. Then he refinished the whole dinghy and brought her back to *Starbound* in gleaming pristine glory.

Colin Corbett showed up one day to talk about boats. He said, "When you're quite ready to haul *Starbound* for her scrubdown and paint job, let me know and I'll give you a hand. If you're interested, I have access to a big water-jet machine. It operates at about 2,000 psi. Since *Starbound* is copper-sheathed, maybe we could use it to clean her bottom. It does a hell of a good job on ferro-cement and steel boats. Of course, on a planked bottom it would knock the caulking out of the seams, but since you're sheathed . . ."

We arranged to haul *Starbound* at Vos Shipyard in Auckland, located just east of Westhaven Marina. We set it up six weeks in advance to make sure of the schedule, because we wanted to be on our way sometime in the first half of April. The New Zealand fall would be nosing in by then and winter storms would start working their way up the Tasman Sea.

My cousin Tom Hoff wrote us a letter asking if he could join us for a while. We wrote him back and told him to be in Auckland by April Fool's Day so that he could have the dubious pleasure of helping us haul, scrub, and paint *Starbound.*

We wound up our jobs by the end of March. Mom and Dad left about the same time, flying back to San Diego via Honolulu. It was time to start moving, and we were getting excited about it. It's funny how easy it is to get stuck in a rut, though. The six months we'd spent in New Zealand had gone by as if they hadn't existed.

Tom flew into Auckland airport one day and the next day was helping Ernie hoist the mainsail for a short trip to Vos Shipyard. "Wow!" he exclaimed. "Just last week I was working my tail off in an office in Los Angeles, and here I am—sailing on a yacht in Auckland Harbor."

We hauled *Starbound* on Friday, April 4. I pulled the propeller as soon as it was clear of the water and gave it to the yard manager with instructions to put two more inches of pitch in it and balance it. Colin brought the big water-jet machine down and it worked fine. All the old paint came off with the marine growth and the copper sheathing was smooth and clean, ready for new antifouling paint.

That evening we received a telegram from our Pan Am stewardess friend, Alice (A.J.) Goodfellow, asking if she could fly out and join us for a few weeks. We wired her to come ahead. She might even have time to cross the Tasman to Australia with us. A.J. can sail on *Starbound* anytime. She is a fine sailor and is extremely attractive.

Saturday morning we rolled on the first coat of bottom paint. On Sunday the second coat went on, Tom and Ernie doing all the work while I ran into Auckland and picked up A.J. She was as pretty as ever, a petite girl with brown curly hair and one of the world's great figures. We had a minor celebration on the afterdeck that night, sitting high above the concrete, rails, and paint-splotched timbers of the marine railway.

The propeller arrived back early next morning, pitched, balanced, and burnished. I socked the lock nuts down tight on it one minute before the yard rolled *Starbound* back into her element. We moved *Starbound* over to Vos's holding dock and started to check off our lists to see what was left to get aboard. I checked the meteorological office. They told me a nice southwesterly would come in on Tuesday night. We decided to head north on Wednesday morning.

16

The Ship's Log: Across the Tasman Sea

Excerpts from the ship's log:

9 April, Wednesday: 1100 hours; the weather is fine and sunny with light winds from the southwest. The radio forecasts more of the same.

We depart Auckland, New Zealand, this A.M. (*Starbound* entered New Zealand 24 October 1974.) We should have enough money now to get us to South Africa. After that "the Lord will provide . . ."? We are under way this morning to Russell, Bay of Islands, via Kawau Island and Great Barrier Island, both in the Hauraki Gulf. Hope to clear N.Z. from Russell by 20 April. Our crew now includes my cousin Tom Hoff and Alice (A.J.) Goodfellow.

1700 hours; the anchor is down in Kawau Bay just off the Mansion House. In fact, the little bay we're in is called Mansion House Bay. It's a pretty little anchorage. We are made welcome by the New Zealand Navy who are here with a couple of survey boats; charts of the area are not completely accurate. They have a lot of Aussie beer on board which we are helping them with. I think A.J. is the big attraction.

10 April, Thursday: Our wedding anniversary! We celebrate by doing nothing constructive all day. We visit the Mansion House and have a few drinks at the bar.

11 April, Friday: 0900 hours; sky partly cloudy, wind southwest at 10.

Forecast is for 10 to 15 knots out of the southeast with occasional gusts to 20. We weigh anchor and head for Great Barrier Island on a course of 030 magnetic. We run the engine two hours to charge batteries, also to clear the cross-swells.

1200 hours; wind southeast 10 to 12, a moderate easterly swell, mostly sunny. We approach South Point of Little Barrier Island.

1600 hours; we enter South Pass to Port Fitzroy on Great Barrier Island, a well-protected place but very lonely. No one here except sloop *Shadow* from Vancouver and a few small local powerboats. This day closes with the wind piping up—forecast is for 30 knots southerly. We'll sleep light tonight.

12 April, Saturday: Woke up four times last night to check our position. Gusts are funneling down the pass at 40 knots.

1000 hours; we drag anchor! The big Herreshoff is down with 30 fathoms of chain out and we still drag—a shingle bottom? We weigh, motor clear, and re-anchor, this time with 50 fathoms of chain to the hawse. Ernie and I break out the launch and set the 70-pound Danforth out on 20 feet of chain and 250 feet of nylon rode. Now we'll stay put. We sure as hell aren't going anywhere today!

1518 hours; weather forecast says 30 knots southerly.

1800 hours; some forecast; wind is falling clear off. We'll put the dinghy aboard in the morning and get out of here at first light. Whangaruru is 50 miles up the coast, so we'll try to make that.

13 April, Sunday: 0645 hours; anchors are up in a flat calm. Under power till 1100. Wind southwest at 15 knots, so we put on all fore and aft sail. Poor Knights Rocks abeam at 1600. Whangaruru is too far, so we opt for Sandy Bay. We drop the hook in the southeast corner of the bay and are happy we came in. It's a very pretty place. Tuna for dinner—we caught a nice 8-pounder off Poor Knights Rocks.

14 April, Monday: 0630 hours; the anchor is up. Wind is still 10 to 15 knots southwest. We sail all the way to Cape Brett. We round the Cape at 1100 and get the wind right in our face. The sails come down and we bang into it for the 11 miles to Russell light. The pivot on the outboard motor is frozen up—again! Ernie fixes it on the way in. Isolated rain squalls catch us once in a while.

1700 hours; the anchor is down in Mautawhi Bay once again. *Puffin* is here! It's great to see Jerry and Ev again. Also *Stormstrutter* with John and Pat Sampson, *Bobolink* with Gil Rodin and family, *Sea Foam* with Herb and Nancy Payson on board, and *White Horse of Kent* with Colin Usmar making a round-the-world trip on a fiberglass boat with no engine. We hauled Colin off a coral bank in Tahiti with our launch and have been good friends ever since. We all repair to the Duke of Marlborough Pub for beer.

15 April, Tuesday: A lazy day with a little boat work.

16 April, Wednesday: The same as yesterday.

17 April, Thursday: We go to the bank at Paihia across the bay and change our New Zealand money to U.S., except for a little for last-minute things. We visit the Treaty House at Waitangi where the Maoris signed the treaty of peace with the British in 1849, then back to Russell on the ferry and call customs. There is no chance to clear before next Wednesday, the 23rd, which means A.J. won't have time to go with us across the Tasman. Too bad. Also find out that we can't buy duty-free booze in Russell. The last port for that is Whangarei. Disgusting! We should have loaded up in Auckland.

18 April, Friday: We work on the boat all day, change the engine oil, and do some touch-up paint jobs.

19 April, Saturday: Again we work on the boat all day and go to the pub in the evening. Fish and chips for dinner. (Love the stuff!)

20 April, Sunday: We motor to Otahei Bay in the morning just to break the routine. It's a very pretty bay; looks like a small tourist resort is gaining a foothold there. Re-anchor in Mautawhi Bay about 1700 and spend a quiet evening aboard.

21 April, Monday: A stiff northeaster is blowing. We pick up more supplies in town. Our tentative departure date is Wednesday, but it doesn't look too good as far as weather is concerned. We must wait for a nice stable high-pressure system in the Tasman to feed in the southerlies for a long enough period to get us well north of New Zealand.

22 April, Tuesday: Well, we're stuck for awhile. Meteorology says there is a very complex low-pressure system in the Tasman with another low sitting on top of Lord Howe Island. I call customs in Whangarei to cancel our clearing date for tomorrow. We spend the evening in the pub with all the other yachties and bitch about the weather.

23 April, Wednesday: It is pissing down rain. We pick up some of our supplies in town and leave the rest in the store for later. More pool games and beer in the pub is the order of the day.

24 April, Thursday: More rain today but Saturday looks good. A big high coming up from southern Australia will be shoving this poor weather out of here by then. Trouble is, customs and immigration won't come up to Russell on Friday because it's ANZAC Day. The word is that they won't clear any yachts until Monday. With that big high forming over Tasmania, we want to get out of here and take advantage of it.

The damn reefer breaks down; water shorts out the control switch and it's a corroded mess! I hitch a ride to Opua with Gil Rodin and take the car ferry across. I buy a new switch for $4.60, catch the same ferry back, and hitch back to Russell. I install the new switch and it works fine. Glad it failed here instead of out in the Tasman. In the meantime Nina takes our meat to the Russell Butchery and has Duncan put it in his freezer for us. We'll pick it up Saturday with the other stuff we've ordered from him, which includes some nice smoked pork. We go to Herb and Nancy's *Sea Foam* for dinner. Dee-licious!

25 April, Friday: ANZAC Day is a national holiday in New Zealand, and Australia too. The initials stand for Australian/New Zealand Army Corps (from World War I). The holiday is taken very seriously by the Kiwis. The town is decorated and there are parades and other patriotic doings. The pub at the Duke is closed until 1300 but the stores are open. Skies are clearing but the wind is still northwest at 15 to 20 knots. I try to call customs, but no luck.

1600 hours; I find out from Warrick Bain on *Archiv* that we can clear on Saturday at 1000 hours. Hooray! We will go to Opua for water in the early A.M. We go to the pub for a last evening but it is so crowded and noisy we go home early.

26 April, Saturday: We are up at first light and on the way to Opua at 0700. We take our last hot fresh-water showers for a while as the tanks are filling. Just before heading back to Russell the customs officer hails us from the dock and presents us with our clearance papers so that we can fill them out on the way back to Russell. He won't clear us at Opua—says it has to be from Russell. We can't figure that one out. He had seen us from his car while waiting for the little ferry which carried everyone over to the Russell peninsula. Two other boats are waiting to clear, *Archiv* and *Rodion,* and he asks us to inform them, when we get to Russell, that they will have to lay their boats up to the Russell town dock so that he can board them. But since he had boarded us at Opua all we have to do is bring our filled-out forms in to him at the dock.

We motor back to Russell and anchor about 200 feet off the main dock-head. Warrick Bain from *Archiv* comes over in his dinghy and we pass on the word from customs. He swears and takes off to *Rodion* to let them know. As we go ashore to turn over our papers, the westerly wind starts really howling. We keep a nervous eye on *Starbound.* Nina goes for the rest of our groceries and meat, while I run down to the constable's office to pick up the small pistol I'd left with him six months earlier. When we get back to the dock, we find that Ernie has gone out to *Starbound* and we can see why. The wind has piped up to 30 knots and is gusting to 40. Ernie waves to us from the afterdeck. We can see that he's started the engine and probably has it engaged in forward gear to take some of the strain off the ground tackle.

The wind eases momentarily and Ernie races into the lee of the dock with the launch and picks up me and the chow. We zip back to *Starbound* and climb aboard just as another heavy gust blasts out of the west. We are soaked with spray. We keep the engine running with the forward gear engaged and watch the frantic action on the other anchored boats.

White Horse of Kent starts to drag her anchor and we can see Colin standing on the dock, watching helplessly. His peapod of a dinghy just isn't suited to get out to his boat through that wind and chop. Warwick Bain tries to row out to the ketch with his dinghy and ends up half swamped. So I take our big launch in, running the outboard at full blast to stay up to the speed of the waves. As I come alongside the dock landing and put the bow of the launch into the wind, Colin makes a mighty leap and ends up in a pile in the bottom of the launch. We get very wet but make it out to *White Horse of Kent.* I hold onto the gunwale of the ketch while Colin scrambles aboard and forward to break out another anchor. It takes a while. The extra anchor, chain lead, and rode are all buried in the forepeak. Finally, just as he has it all hooked up and is about to lower the anchor into the launch for me to carry out, I hear a voice over my shoulder, "Hey, you guys! Just let her keep draggin'. She's goin' to dock herself!" She was indeed! She had dragged the ground tackle right up to the dock, and now I and the launch are in danger of getting pinched between the dock and the ketch. I crank up the outboard and get the hell out of there. I race around to the lee of the dock, tie the launch so she rides free of the pilings, and run back across the dock just in time to help dozens of people who are helping Colin fend *White Horse of Kent* off the pilings.

The wave action is terrible. Nina is in there with the rest of them and I am afraid that she is going to get hurt. Finally she scrambles away from the mess and runs across the dock. I can see her in agitated conversation with the skipper of one of the small ferry boats which are tied up on the lee side of the dock. Those boats are highly maneuverable twin-screw jobs with a lot of guts in the engine compartment. Nina talks the skipper into bringing his boat around the dock and giving *White Horse of Kent* a tow back out to the anchorage area. It takes the skipper three tries in that really terrible chop to get his boat's stern positioned right so that a line can be passed to the ketch, but he finally makes it. Those Kiwis can really handle boats. Slowly, *White Horse of Kent* is peeled away from her trap and pulled out into the clear. We all stand on the dock with the wind whipping around our ears and pray that the towline doesn't snap. Three yachties had climbed on board with Colin to give him a hand, and they are frantically getting the big anchor ready to go over the side, flaking down the rode along her side deck. Finally the anchor rode which they are dragging, the one attached to the first anchor which is still on the bottom, comes up taut. The skipper of the ferry boat puts more and more power into the screws and the towline is humming, but now the offending anchor won't drag at all. We see Colin make his decision as he picks up the big hook and casts it as far forward as he can. The towline slacks as the ferry boat skipper shuts his engines down, and *White Horse of Kent* falls back on her new anchor line. Colin finally snubs her and her bow snaps around into the wind. She is safe.

I take Tom out to *Starbound,* then come back for Nina. When we are all aboard we talk it over and decide to get the hell off this lee shore. Otherwise there'd be no sleep for anyone tonight. We say good-by to everyone, we are cleared, and the engine is running. Ernie and Tom start to take in anchor chain as I run *Starbound* forward. Ernie shouts as the anchor stock clears the water but it doesn't make any difference—I have the engine revs up to 2,000 already and we are making about one knot against the wind and waves. But we are making it.

Mission accomplished! We are anchored under the lee of the hills of Opua and it is flat calm in here although we can hear the wind howling high up on the hill and the trees up there are lashing back and forth like buggy whips. *Archiv* and *Rodion* followed us out of Russell Bay and are anchored nearby. Nina has just invited their crews over for stormy-weather soup and a belt of antifreeze.

Much better! We talk it over and listen to the last weather report. The wind is supposed to die off tonight, so we decide to leave in the very early A.M. So to bed in a safe and peaceful anchorage on the eve of departure.

Excerpts from ship's log:

27 April, Sunday: We are up at 0300 in time to watch *Archiv* ghost around the corner and up the bay under full sail. *Rodion* has already left. We have *Starbound* underway by 0415 and we motor up the bay in a flat calm. What a change from the previous afternoon! It is a beautiful clear night with a whole sky full of stars. Finally a light southwest wind springs up and we put on all fore and aft sail. We catch *Archiv* off Russell light and exchange good-bys, then keep *Starbound* motor-sailing until Ninepin Rocks are abeam. We put the engine to sleep and stream the taffrail log. The southwest breeze increases to 15 knots and *Starbound* starts making 5 knots through the water. We hold the course to 325 magnetic to stay well clear of North Cape. A fine day!

28 April, Monday: Dawns fine. Wind SSW 10–15 knots, barometer 30.24 inches. We have squalls at 1100 hours with the wind backing. We change course to 285 degrees and at noon we are 100 nautical miles north of North Cape and making good time—about 6 knots. Evening comes with fine weather. Swells are out of the south and wind is the same but getting a bit fluky between isolated showers. We finally started the engine at 2015 to keep way on as the wind drops to 5 knots and less. We must get north far enough and fast enough to pick up the easterlies. We motor-sail all night.

29 April, Tuesday: Another beautiful morning with the wind 8–10 southwest. Barometer is still high at 30.20 inches. We change course at 0500 to 275 magnetic to pass well south of Norfolk Island. Long swells have been rolling in from the southwest all morning. We add the topsail to the main as the wind lightens. It helps stop the main boom from slopping around. The sea is very calm all afternoon with the same long swells. The periodicity of

the swells is still about nine seconds, so we're not worried about anything unusual. Besides, it's well past the hurricane season ("typhoon" season down here). The sky is clear except for some cumulus to the east which seems to be increasing. Our hope is that the Tasman high will spread north and give us a tailwind from the east. The day ends with the wind still light and heading us. We fall off on a course of 295 magnetic to keep the sails quiet. Motor-sailing again!

30 April, Wednesday: Once again the day dawns clear and fine. Even though we are motor-sailing we think we are blessed; a flat Tasman Sea is a rarity. Middle part of the day is still fine. We are on a course of 300 degrees magnetic now, which should put us within sight of Norfolk Island tomorrow morning. The day ends with clouds to the south and southeast. We are still motor-sailing at 1,200 RPM. A check of fuel consumption shows that we are using about one gallon per hour. Very good! At least for a 380 cubic-incher.

1 May, Thursday: The night was good and the morning is another beauty. Moon, sun, and RDF shots put us about 30 miles SE of Norfolk Island. We sight land at 0800 so I guess we haven't forgotten how to navigate. All day the island rises from the sea. By mid-afternoon we are within a few miles of the southern coast and we can see the famous Norfolk pines which form the island's green crown. We can also see the tremendous break of the swell on the rugged shoreline. There is no harbor on Norfolk. If a yacht can raise them on the radio, they will come out and get you in a whaleboat; that is, if the swell is not running too big. Well, we try to call them, with no luck at all. Not even a whisper. We look at the white foam spewing upward as the truly huge swell humps its back and batters headlong into the island's coast. It didn't seem that big out at sea. In any case, there is no way anybody is going to come out through that break. The wind is absolutely flat.

We drop all sail and wait. We want to see if we can raise anybody at all. Then, clear as a bell, Auckland radio comes on the air with that fabulous Kiwi accent. They are talking to some ship too far away for us to hear the reply, but we can hear Auckland perfectly. We give them a try on our little 75-watt set and to our surprise they answer us. Since we are 540 miles away from Auckland at this point, all we can figure out is that we must be getting a helluva fortunate bounce off the Heaviside layer. We ask them to report our position to Whangarei, and then we request the weather situation for our area. We arrange with them for us to transmit on 2738 kHz and receive on 2207 kHz via our Panasonic. It works fine! They come back in about fifteen minutes and give us a complete synoptic report. The forecast is for 5 knots out of the southeast for the evening, becoming 10 to 15 and backing to the east later on tonight and continuing easterly with winds to 20 knots at times for the next few days. Beautiful! It just can't be better for us. We thank them very much, sign off, set the square sail and raffee, and head due west for Australia.

Excerpts from the ship's log:

2 May, Friday: Doing 5 knots at daybreak plus a little. Wind is east at 15. The day is slightly overcast but the barometer is steady at 30.04 inches. Overcast increases by noon and winds are gusty but still off the stern. At 2100 the wind drops to zero! Can't figure what the hell's going on. We start the engine to keep moving. The batteries need charging anyway. So ends this day.

3 May, Saturday: The wind comes back strong at 0300 and increases to 20 knots by daybreak. A few light rain showers come with the wind. Good sailing until 0800 when the square sail port clew cringle lets go. It takes Ernie, Tom, and me two and a half hours to secure the sail, which we finally manage to do by blanketing it with the scandalized raffee. Should have tried that in the first place. At least we learn how it should be done. Split one seam open in the square sail with all the flogging around. We are all exhausted by the time it is brailed, but grit our teeth and set the big yankee jib along with the raffee. Looks a bit strange but the combination seems to work well. By 0930 the wind is up to 25 knots with gusts to 30. We get the raffee off and ease her a bit. Good thing we brailed the square sail securely! Rough, short following seas for the rest of the day and night. The wind eases to about 20 by 2400 hours.

4 May, Sunday: We run all day with the yankee jib and raffee pushed with 10 to 15 knots of east wind. Seas smooth out by nightfall. Run the main engine quite a while today to ease the roll, so the dropping seas are welcome. We are getting tired of engine noise. Put the mizzen on at 1700—it helps to steady her and increases our speed almost a full knot. And so through the night.

5 May, Monday: 350 miles to go! We decide to drive for Mooloolaba, a small port about 80 miles north of Brisbane. Reasons: the port of Brisbane is 15 miles up a river full of sandbars, and we've been told the anchorage isn't very good. Also, we can enter Australia at Mooloolaba, there is fuel and water there, and one of our Aussie friends in New Zealand told us there's a nice little yacht club with a good bar. It's within bus distance of Brisbane, so we can catch a ride down and check our mail. Sounds fine. We roll along well; 130 miles noon to noon.

6 May, Tuesday: Another beautiful sailing day. Starts with a real cloud mix and scattered showers. Clears to trade wind conditions by 1000. A noon latitude shot puts us 20 miles north of our rhumb line. Evening star shots confirm our position. We should be in by Thursday forenoon if the wind holds.

7 May, Wednesday: The day starts with early morning showers. The

wind veers to southwest, then back to southeast by noon. Morning sun lines put us north of our course again, but a noon latitude shows us to be right on the line. Either the taffrail log is overreading or my sun lines are sloppy. Used chart N.O. 74003 to get a better scale for our approach to the coast with 130 miles between us and the Mooloolaba jetties. We decide to motor-sail to buy ourselves some time. We sure don't want to come in to that small port in the dark.

Damn! We discover traces of salt water in the transmission and the fluid level is low. We must have a leak in the heat exchanger. A good thing that the pressure differential causes the fluid to leak into the salt water circuit rather than vice versa. We add hydraulic fluid and will check every few hours to keep it full. We keep on motor-sailing through the night.

8 May, Thursday: We sight land by 0900 hours! Rain squalls and rainbows all morning, a beautiful sight. Full double bows arcing across the sky. Our course takes us right under them. A sign of good fortune, perhaps. A good thing we're nearly in. The wind is falling light and veering to the southwest, probably because we're on the coast of a major continent.

We find the Mooloolaba jetties with no trouble at all. Hit the coast right where we want and pick up the jetties with the binoculars right at 1200 hours. Makes us navigators feel good to do that! We even have the flood with us as we run down between the rock walls, doing about 7 knots. Make a hard right turn at the end of the jetties in order to stay in the channel, find the small public dock, and spin *Starbound* around and dock her, playing the tide for all we are worth. We are visited at once by a harbor pilot who calls customs for us. Find out that they won't clear us until tomorrow. Australians are very, very friendly people. They tell us to go have a few drinks at the yacht club! We walk the 200 yards to the club and meet the secretary, Doug Fortune, who extends club privileges to us. He shows us a big berth right in front of the club and tells us to bring *Starbound* into it as soon as customs and immigration are through with us. We spend the evening in the bar drinking "Four-X" beer with our hosts and looking out over the calm waters of the pretty little harbor. Australia is a very nice place indeed!

17

Inside the Great Barrier Reef

We waited aboard all morning for the customs and immigration officers, who finally showed up at noon. The procedure was a little bit simpler than it was in New Zealand except for one thing: the new law in Australia requires visas for even a short stay. They entered us anyway pending a ruling from Brisbane.

We moved *Starbound* over to the yacht club berth. The bowsprit extended right up to the front lawn. We tied our bow lines to big iron rings sunk into the concrete retaining wall and the stern was held between pilings; a very snug berth. At low tide we could walk out on the bowsprit, climb down onto the martingale shrouds, and jump down to the beach.

It was too late in the day to think about going to Brisbane for mail. We entertained visitors for the rest of the day and let them entertain us too. There was lots of action on the lawn for us to watch. The South Pacific Laser sailing championships were being held and the Mooloolaba Yacht Club was the host. I found out that some very good-looking women sail Lasers.

It looked as if we'd better wait until after the weekend to go to Brisbane, so we spent the next few days working on the ship and gathering information about the availability of things in Durban. We had to get a new transmission cooler and I really wanted to find a good sailmaker. Our square sail needed some professional attention. On Sunday we met John and Connie Frew, Peter and Livvy Sachs, and Ray Hope. Suddenly our transportation problems were resolved. John was driving to Brisbane early the next morning and offered us a lift, sailbag and all.

We whizzed through some fascinating countryside next morning in John's big Jaguar sedan and got into Brisbane just as things were getting moving for the day. John was a great help. We used the conference room of his offices as our headquarters for the day. Then John ran us all over town. We found a new heat exchanger at Clae Engine Company down in the industrial area. It cost $65 Australian, but it was a very good cooler with a nice big zinc pencil fitted into it. Back in town again, John drove us down a few narrow streets to the establishment of Les Allwood and Sons, Sailmakers. We dropped off the square sail. Mr. Allwood told me he'd have it finished by the end of the day. I hadn't heard a sailmaker say that for many years. Then John drove Nina to his doctor so she could get her shoulder looked at. She'd been having a lot of pain in it. I told her it was just old age, but she didn't think that was a damn bit funny. We left her there and I went to the post office to see if we had some mail. We did and I went back up to John's lovely suite of offices to answer a few of the more urgent items. We were supposed to catch a bus for Mooloolaba at 1630, so I kept an eye on the clock. Finally Nina called and said the doctor wanted her to stay overnight. She had a nice case of bursitis and he was going to have to give her a painful shot in her shoulder. I didn't want to leave her but she said to go ahead, so we found her a hotel room.

Nina came home the next night with her arm in a sling, even though she said it felt better. Between the doctor and shopping she had managed to go through another $100. I was starting to get worried about money. At that rate it would be gone before we got to Bali.

We planned to leave on Thursday for Wide Bay, just an overnight run to the north. It was time to get going. We started to pick the brains of our hosts. The club was loaded with good sailors and many of them had sailed the reef all their lives. The first thing they all recommended was that we should obtain a copy of a paperback book called *Cruising the Coral Coast* by Alan Lucas, an Aussie who's been up and down the coast many times. Luckily, we already had a copy of the book. I say luckily because no copies were available in the bookstores. Ours had been given to us by a Kiwi friend in Auckland who'd recently returned from a cruising vacation on the reef.

We'd always wanted to cruise the Barrier Reef. There are other ways to get up to the top of Australia; most yachts in fact go from New Zealand to New Caledonia, then to New Guinea and run through the Torres Straits from there. Well, maybe next time we'll do it that way, but first—the Great Barrier Reef.

We were cautioned to make day hops only after we entered the actual reef passages, which wouldn't be until we reached the town of Gladstone. Then we would start up what is known as the Coral Coast, that part of the coast of the state of Queensland which is protected from the Coral Sea by the Great Barrier Reef. The Coral Coast is 1,200 miles long, extending from 60 miles off Gladstone in the south to the Torres Straits in the north. Actually, the term *barrier* is misleading. The reef is not one unbroken piece of coral wall but is made up of thousands of individual reefs. The eastern and western borders of the reef are well charted. That is to say, the inner and outer reefs are, but in between these two borders is a no man's land, except where a passage through the reef to the open sea exists and has been charted. There are a lot of these, some better than others. The navigable inner route, between the inner reef and the mainland, is well charted. The southern part of the inner passage is fairly easy, and yachts can sail overnight if they're very careful with their navigation. But further north the reefs close ranks, and by the time Cooktown is reached, the passages between the reefs, islets, and mainland are only half a mile to 3 miles wide.

We decided to leave Mooloolaba Thursday evening and arrive in Wide Bay Friday morning. We checked on fuel and found we could take on diesel at Markwell's wharf, just down the harbor where the fishing trawlers lay. We squared *Starbound* away. Ernie and Tom put the square sail back on the yard and I worked in the engine room, cleaning the filters, changing oil and transmission fluid, and putting on the new heat exchanger. Nina picked up meat and other fresh stores in town. We had another good evening at the yacht club Wednesday night and slept in late Thursday morning.

On Thursday we picked up the last of our "bits and pieces," as the Aussies say, and said good-by to our extremely hospitable hosts at the Mooloolaba Yacht Club: John McFarland, commodore; Mike Keeley, vice-commodore; Peter Webb, manager; Doug Fortune, secretary; and Eric Lewis, PR man for the club.

We moved out at 1500 and went into the fuel dock. We took 190 gallons of diesel on board, then found out to our dismay that we were supposed to have a diesel certificate or else pay the road tax, which doubled the price of the fuel! We talked fast, and the manager, recognizing that we were a bunch of "bloody amatchoors," checked with the captain of one of the fishing trawlers nearby and got permission to apply the amount of fuel we'd bought onto his permit. We promised to send a letter to Brisbane from Bundaberg, requesting a diesel certificate. We waved to all our friends and backed into the stream. The kids fishing from the jetties called good-bys to us as we motored out into the small bay, and *Starbound* once again felt the open sea and started her slow roll on the gentle swells which were colored orange by the sunset.

Double Island was abeam by 0500. We puttered offshore until daylight and then put into the Wide Bay anchorage for a few hours and had breakfast. We could see the anchor and chain laying on the white sand bottom. Seven fathoms of water were under us. After breakfast we took the flood tide across the Wide Bay bar and anchored in a tiny cove just around Inskip Point. There was a heavy current and lots of sand bars. On the way across the bar we saw an amazing sight. A porpoise was giving birth, just floating on the surface, turning once in a while. She was very busy having her calf and just ignored us. Nina said, "Poor momma porpoise! If I were having a baby, I'd ignore us too."

We were anchored in the southern entrance to the Great Sandy Strait. This strait is a large waterway separating Fraser Island from the mainland, and we were going to run the strait rather than go around the island. Fraser Island was really in the news. The Dillingham Corporation was trying to get permission from the Australian government to mine the ore-laden sand of which the island was entirely composed. Of course, the Aussie public was dead set against it. They wanted the island to be declared a national park so everybody could enjoy its natural beauty rather than have a few people get rich from it by essentially destroying it. We were on the side of the Aussie public, but having seen that sort of thing happen so often in the United States we were afraid they were fighting a losing battle.

We took the launch over to Inskip Point and walked around just kicking sand. Ernie and Tom set the gill net which we had found on the reef in Tahiti and caught some slender silvery fish. We cooked them for dinner but it was a mistake. They had millions of hairlike bones in them, although the teaspoon of meat we were able to get from each fish was delicious.

We started up Sandy Strait next morning at 0900. It was low tide before flood, which is when a yacht has to start. The trick is to run the flood all the way to Moonboom Island, arriving at high tide, and then carry the ebb tide all the rest of the strait. We really rolled along. There was a 2-knot flood with us. I made one mistake: I read a channel marker wrong and stuck *Starbound* on a mud bank. Not too hard, fortunately. We carried the little 35-pound Danforth out abeam and winched the bow around with the capstan head on the anchor winch. The ship popped loose from the suction of the gluey mud and we were back under way within twenty minutes. We arrived at Moonboom Island exactly at high tide. Since the strait floods from either end, now we were all set to take advantage of the ebb to carry us the rest of the way. It's a very nifty system that Mother Nature set up for us.

By 1700 we were anchored under the southern tip of Woody Island. We had just enough time before dark to set the gill net, then explore the shoreline and look at the fascinating rock formations. We took seven nice trevally out of the gill net for dinner, cooked and ate them, and went to bed early.

Under way at first light, we ran up the channel on the east side of Woody Island, then headed northwest for the resort town of Urangan, located on the mainland. We tied up to the end of the huge jetty and got permission from the port captain to stay there until evening. We strolled into town and had a cold beer at a little pub just across from a lovely beach. We picked up a few supplies from one of the markets and caught a ride back to *Starbound* with some people who saw us walking along the road. We let our lines go and were off for an overnight trip to Bundaberg by 1600 hours. We put on the square sail and raffee for the trip with the wind coming nice and steady over the starboard quarter.

At 0300 we raised the lighthouse off Burnett River and brailed up the square sail to slow the boat down. By first light we were moving into the river mouth. It was low tide, just as we wanted. We had 7 miles to go and we wanted to carry the flood all the way. The river was a beautiful winding waterway which reminded us of the rivers on the eastern shore of Maryland. The smell of burning sugar cane and molasses was heavy on the air.

We anchored off the town of Bundaberg at 1130, right in the middle of the river. It was a soupy mud bottom and for some reason we decided to put down the Danforth instead of the heavier Herreshoff anchor.

We went into town, a center for the sugar cane industry. The Bundaberg refinery and distillery are just down the river from where we were anchored and we decided that the distillery might be worth a visit. We were hoping to pick up a case of Bundaberg rum for a decent price. We arranged with the sugar company offices to take a tour next morning. Then we picked up some lovely big prawns down at the wharf where the trawlers dock, found a place that sold cold beer to go, and went back to *Starbound* for a nice dinner. Australian prawns are big, tasty, and reasonably priced. We ate every one.

We caught up on our sleep next morning. Our tour of the distillery was scheduled for 1500, so we just relaxed all morning long, studying our charts and making plans for the next hop northward.

The tour was very interesting and we enjoyed it, but were really disappointed to find that we couldn't buy any rum direct from the distillery. Australian law forbids it as being unfair to the distributors. So a bottle of Bundaberg rum costs $5.60 Australian, anyplace in town. We decided we could do without it.

We had wanted to see a movie that evening at a new theater in town. We had reserved our tickets right after our tour and found out from the theater manager that there was going to be a special event before the show—a wine and cheese tasting party! Hooray! It was going to be a fairly fancy event for Bundaberg, with all the notables in town coming, so we decided to head back for the boat and change to our "nice" clothes. When we got back to the landing dock we could see that *Starbound* had dragged her anchor quite a distance. She was 200 yards further up river than where we had left her. We ran out to her in the launch. Another boat came over with an Aussie sailor running the outboard. He told us that she started dragging on the flood tide with the wind blowing hard up river. He'd gone aboard and let out about another 100 feet of chain and she'd held her position, so he'd kept an eye on her for us for the rest of the afternoon. We gave him a drink and thanked him a million times, then started questioning him on where we could put her to find some good holding ground. He told us there wasn't any such thing in the Bundaberg River but that we could pick up a mooring over near his yacht which would be able to hold her O.K. since the mooring was held by a huge concrete block sunk into the jelly mud bottom. Evidently lots of weight was the only thing which would work. We got our anchor and moved *Starbound* onto the mooring. Then we cleaned up and went to the movie.

The wine and cheese party was delightful. The mayor of the town was there with his charming wife, along with many others of the community's social elite. A newspaper reporter discovered us and we gave him an abbreviated story of our cruise while we availed ourselves of the excellent wines and cheeses. There were three different types of wines offered: the still wines, the sherries, and the white bubbly. We worked on all of them with great enjoyment. The Yalumba wines seemed especially good. After two hours of sipping wine, the debris was cleared away and the movie started.

We dropped our mooring at 1030 next morning, high tide, and zipped down the river running the ranges, or "leads," as the Aussies call them, all the way to the river mouth, dodging trawlers as we went. Popping out of the channel into Hervey Bay, we set a course for Gladstone, situated on the shore of Port Curtis.

This was to be one of our last overnight runs on the Coral Coast and we were happy to have a bright full moon to light our way. Bustard Head light came abeam at 0100 and we tried to beat the moonset into small Hobb Bay, bypassing Pancake Creek where we had thought we might stop. The hook went down at 0300 in 6 fathoms of water. It was a rolly anchorage. Finally, at 0600 we got up and changed anchorages, motoring into a much smoother spot right under the lee of the headland to our east. We slept the morning away, finally getting underway for Gladstone at 1200. *Starbound* carried the square sail right up the channel into Port Curtis. Then we were presented with a long run to the city, past the alumina refinery and into Auckland Creek. We tied up to O'Connell's Wharf at about 1600 and found out the charge would be $2 per day for dockage—not too bad, considering that the option was to anchor in the mud about a mile upstream. It was a very handy dock; the pub was only a short block away.

The *Illawarra Range,* a big steel trawler, was tied up right behind us. Her owners, brothers named Tim and Chris, came over to make us welcome and we had a fine time. The Aussies were particularly interested in the Chesapeake Bay and how the oysters and clams were dredged. They invited us aboard their ship and showed us all around. She was extremely well equipped. The pilot house reminded me of the bridge on a Navy ship, with electronics gear lined up in rows. The refrigerated hold was full of scallops in the shell, caught the night before. Tim and Chris gave us a big boxful of them to take back to *Starbound.* What a dinner we had that evening! It was the first time in my life that I had all the scallops I could eat.

Gladstone is a good supply town for yachts. The shops are within easy walking distance of the dock, and fresh water is available without any hassle; the hoses are coiled up right next to the boats. We topped up the refrigerator with meat, milk, eggs, bread, and beer. Also some Yalumba rosé wine to which we had taken a shine. We had decided to leave in the morning for Cape Capricorn and anchor in the lee of the Cape.

We motored out of the creek and into the harbor next morning. It looked like a fine day. Ernie had the helm and I went into the engine room to check out the main engine, just to see if everything was O.K. It wasn't! Water was dribbling out of the main heat exchanger overflow pipe. I tasted it. It was salty! There is only one way for salt water to get into the fresh water tank of the heat exchanger: through the tube bundle in the exchanger itself. I went topside and told Ernie and Nina what the problem was while I turned *Starbound* around and headed back. We were able to lay up to the dock in our old spot.

Joseph Engineering, a big marine concern, is located just a few hundred yards away. I found John Joseph and his brother Norman in the shop. They told me that there were no heat exchangers available in Gladstone. They could get me one, probably from Brisbane, but it would be a big job to set it up properly, and would cost us about $800 Australian. On the other hand, they thought that they could fix mine for a reasonable amount. Of course, next day was Sunday and everything was closed, so I spent the rest of Saturday pulling the exchanger apart and checking the damage. Electrolysis had set in and three of the tubes in the bundle were leaking. It was late Monday afternoon before we had the damage repaired. I did a lot of the work myself using their equipment, so the bill was only $36. We sent a special delivery letter to the Osco Corporation in Pennsylvania and asked them to air-freight a new exchanger to us right away, and told them to be sure that the new one included a cathodic zinc anode in it to protect against electrolysis. The original exchanger did not have one damn zinc pencil in it—not one!

The Joseph brothers were fascinated by a marine heat exchanger sans cathodic protection. "How in bloody hell did you get this far, mate?" they asked. Actually the whole problem was my own fault. I had assumed that the engine company would have set up a proper cathodic protection system for me when I bought the engine from them. I shouldn't have assumed anything.

We headed out again on Tuesday morning. I hung over the engine for half an hour watching the water level in the heat exchanger. It seemed to be holding. I hoped the repair job would hang together until we got to Cairns, the last good-sized town we would visit on our way north and the destination of the new exchanger.

Now we were finally inside the Great Barrier Reef. It was going to be a day-sailing kind of cruise. We knew that it was possible to sail at night with local knowledge, but we didn't have any.

We sailed north with fresh trades coming over the starboard quarter. Alan Lucas's book *Cruising the Coral Coast* was kept on the chart table, perpetually open to the proper pages. The current chart was laid out and our courses were plotted with great care and followed minutely. We took many bearings each day and knew exactly where we were at any time.

In three successive days we anchored at Cape Capricorn, Great Keppel Island, and Island Head Creek. This last anchorage was a real adventure. The wind continued fresh and the entrance to Island Head Creek is hairy in the best of circumstances, which we didn't have. We had to buck *Starbound* into the creek against a 3-knot current while just skirting a long row of mean-looking rocks sticking out of the water on the north side of the entrance. We finally pushed through the treacherous entrance, then turned up the creek for 2 miles until we couldn't go any further, and anchored under a 1,000-foot mountain.

A steel ketch named *Djabalo* was anchored just ahead of us. There wasn't another trace of civilization anywhere. Between towns, the Coral Coast is a wild place. And so we met the crew of *Djabalo,* Wilhelm (Bill) and Julia Sellentin. Julia is English, a real knockout with dark auburn hair and a gorgeous figure. Bill is from Germany originally and met Julia in Hamburg. Now they were both citizens of Australia. They'd built their boat themselves and were using their vacation time to shake her down. Eventually they wanted to cruise to Europe.

We stayed in the creek for three days and let the strong trade winds blow themselves out a bit. Then both *Djabalo* and *Starbound* left for Marble Island in the Duke group of islands. The wind had eased from 30 knots to 20. The square sail and raffee had us moving at 8 knots most of the day but the southeast swell was rough.

We arrived at Marble Island at 1500 but the recommended anchorage looked very uncomfortable. The swell was leaking around the corner of the island. We finally ducked through the narrow pass leading to the west side of Hunter Island and found a small cove which gave us a nice lee. We put both anchors down and *Djabalo* followed suit. We spent the rest of the afternoon enjoying a beautiful beach which was loaded with small shells and bits of red coral.

The wind picked up again during the night but we got under way in the morning for Digby Island. This time we had to put up with a rolly anchorage. There just wasn't anyplace else to go. It was getting to be a very normal thing to put down two anchors. There was no way in the world that we would have been able to sleep with just one hook down in those gusty, rolly places. But now we were approaching our next "big" town: Mackay (pronounced "Muh-kye"). We were ready for a respite from the lonesome wild places.

We were up at 0530 next morning and got under way very quickly. It was a fast square sail run all the way to Mackay. We ducked into the harbor between the two huge stone jetties and headed for the big wharves to port, which were usually occupied by the Roylen Cruise boats. Peter Webb, the manager of the Mooloolaba Yacht Club, had told us that we could get alongside the wharves during the weekdays when the cruise boats were out. He was right, but as soon as we were secured I took the launch across the harbor and reported our arrival to the piermaster. That is what a cruising boat should do in any Australian harbor, because the authorities can get a bit upset if they're ignored.

The piermaster told us we were O.K. until Friday evening when the cruise boats would start coming in, so we relaxed for the evening and had fun answering hundreds of questions put to us by dozens of Aussie visitors.

The shopping area of Mackay is 4 miles away, so it isn't the best supply town on the Coral Coast. And when the wind is blowing hard, as it was for the entire time we were there, a nice little swell leaks around the jetties and into the harbor. We were on the leeward side of one of the big wharves, so the wind kept us off the pilings.

We decided to stay until Friday morning because Nina wanted to pick up a few supplies in town. So on Thursday we were driven around by Jack and Joan Stayt, another splendidly helpful Aussie couple, and we got all our shopping done quickly. Then we saw the sights. Mackay is not a very pretty town, but it's loaded with money. The sugar and coal business is growing by giant leaps and all other associated businesses are following suit—a real boom town. We were impressed with the action-filled atmosphere of the area.

Next morning we were awakened by a howling wind and we knew that we weren't going anywhere for a while. The radio told us that a gigantic high-pressure system had moved into the Australian Bight. The barometric pressure of the system was measured at 1,033 millibars. That equals 30.50 inches, and it was pumping a strong southeast wind right up to us. It was blowing 30 knots and we were very happy to remain inside that nice harbor, swell or no swell.

Our problems started in the afternoon when the first of the Roylen Cruise boats came crashing through the waves breaking across the bar at the harbor entrance. We knew others would be close behind.

I checked with the piermaster and was told to move *Starbound* across the harbor and tie her up to a big steel barge which was laying alongside the main shipping wharf. It looked O.K. to us and we counted ourselves lucky—until that night. The harbor swell increased and *Starbound* started to pound against the barge. We already had four old car tires between our heavy rub strake and the barge but we could feel the impact right through them. The night watchman on the wharf found two more tires for us and we doubled up the cushion. It seemed to work out all right, so we went to bed.

A hard bump woke us up. The sky was just getting some early morning color to it and the wind was still blowing a half gale. I checked our "fenders" and found two tires gone completely, two others cut nearly through by the sawing action between *Starbound* and the barge, and, worst of all, a one-foot section of our bronze rub strip bent and broken. We started the engine, cast off the lines, and got away from the barge. It's what we should have done the night before, but by the time we'd realized we had a problem, it was too dark to find a place to go.

The day before, two yachts had anchored over by the jetty, close to and in its lee. We could see now that it was a good place to be. They were rising and falling with the swell, but they weren't rolling and in spite of the wind whipping high in their rigging, the water in the immediate lee of the huge jetty was very smooth. We went over and joined them, then went back to bed.

Three days later, days of reading, writing, and maintenance work, the wind eased back to a mere 20 knots. It was Tuesday morning. About 1000 a harbor tug hailed us and told us that the piermaster wanted us to move on the other side of the two neighboring yachts so the tug would have enough room to bring in a big freighter and swing her into the main wharf. We started the engine and began to winch in the anchor chain. As the anchor broke free from the bottom and *Starbound*'s bow started to swing around with the wind, I discovered that we had no steering; the damn wheel spun right around with no effect on the rudder! I yelled to Ernie and Tom to dump the anchor again. It bit into the bottom and we let out enough chain to get a good set. Now we were really in the way! The big tug eased back up to us and asked what the matter was. By then Ernie was into the lazarette and called up to me that our starboard steering cable had parted. I didn't have time to wonder at the accident. I simply told the tug that we'd lost our steering and asked them to give us a tow to where we'd be out of the way. They checked with the piermaster by radio, then eased up to our bows and took a line as we raised our anchor once again. They were experts. Five minutes later we were anchored securely and well out of the channel.

I spent the rest of the morning rounding up some new steering cable. Stainless steel wire was not to be found. "Not north of Brisbane," I was told. I finally located some galvanized steel wire of the proper size: seven-sixteenths, 6 by 19, hemp-core wire, extremely flexible, and made just for steering cable. We had lucked out again! I bought enough for two full sets of cables.

While I was running around town I had plenty of time to contemplate the failure of that steering cable—and the remembrance that I had checked it just about one month ago—and the things that I had read about stress fatigue in stainless steel wire rope—and what would have happened if that cable had failed while I was steering *Starbound* across the bar at the entrance with 20 knots of wind pushing her toward the rocks. Why hadn't it failed a few days ago while we were getting off that damn barge? Lucky us!

Ernie, Tom, and I spent the afternoon reworking the steering gear. We were finished by 1500 and rewarded ourselves with a cold beer. The wind was definitely slackening. We would leave in the morning for Brampton Island.

We were outside the breakwater and on our way by 0800 next morning, and had the anchor down again at Brampton Island by 1230, a fast run.

Brampton is a pretty place, a resort area which seems to swing well even at half capacity. They had an attractive bar with a very tropical motif, and Cairns beer on tap. *Altair* came in about 1430, so we ran the launch out to her and picked up Noel and Beryl Mottershead, a nice British couple. We had met them for the first time in Suva, again in Bundeberg, and now in Mackay. We returned with them to the pub and celebrated their arrival, then made it home somehow by 1930 and found our bunks.

We upped anchor at 0730, ignoring the slight throb behind our eyes, and got under way for another resort called Happy Bay located on the north end of Long Island. It was beautiful square sail sailing all the way with a soft, warm, 12-to-15-knot breeze. We ran between the mainland and the island up Long Island Sound and dropped our anchor in the notch of the V between two coral reefs. When we took the launch in to say hello to the club manager, he told us that we were anchored right on top of two "bommies," which is Australian talk for coral heads. We looked at each other, had a fast beer, and went back out to the boat. From the crosstrees we could see the two bommies about 50 feet off our bow. The anchor chain ran along the bottom right beside them. A good thing it was high tide when we came in. The water was roiled up with a lot of sand particles in suspension and from the deck we couldn't even see the obstructions. And they weren't shown on the charts—not our American charts! The American charts of this section of the world just weren't that accurate.

We decided to stay put and up anchor at high tide next day. And so began our comedy of errors in this beautiful place. The resort had a quartet playing music that night and we all went in to listen, dance, and drink. We didn't take the launch's small anchor with us. It was low tide on the very gradually sloping beach, so we hauled the boat up the wet sand for a distance of 200 feet from the water and decided to check it in half an hour to see how fast the tide was making up the beach. Half an hour later I walked down to the beach and found the tide well up and the launch gone. What a panic! We borrowed the club launch and searched the dark water to leeward for over three hours before we gave up for the night. The club boys dropped us off on *Starbound* and we went to bed feeling terrible. Wherever would we get another launch? And how could we afford it?

I was up at first light and in the crosstrees with the binoculars, searching every inch of whatever shoreline I could see. No launch.

I decided I would rent the club launch and go looking. There was one big and obvious problem. The nearest chunk of land to leeward onto which the launch might have drifted was 7 miles away. If I really covered every place it might be, even allowing for the fact that the trade winds were very constant from one direction, I could search for a week. I was going to have to depend on luck.

I rowed the small dinghy ashore, again glad that we had it aboard, and found the club manager. When I explained what I wanted to do, he smiled and said, "Why don't you rent one of the planes? It'd be a bloody sight cheaper than renting the boat. You'd be out there for days covering that much water. Talk to Kevin over there. He's the head pilot for Air Whitsundays."

So I explained my problem again, this time to Kevin. I also told him that I was worried about cost. Renting planes to search for yacht tenders seemed to be a bit extravagant. He told me, "Look, now, the plane rents for sixty dollars an hour, but we're not going to be up much over fifteen minutes. We can cover the whole bloody area in that time. Don't worry, we'll find it."

We found it—and in just fifteen minutes! Kevin had gotten on the air to the tour boats as soon as we were airborne and filled them in with a description of the launch and where it might have drifted. There were at least a dozen tour boats operating in the immediate area and all the skippers knew Kevin. One of them came on the air and said that he'd seen something on one of the small beaches on the south shore of South Molle Island. Kevin banked the Buccaneer and made a pass over the beach and there it was, our errant launch. For the first time in fourteen hours I felt good.

The launch was sitting high and dry on the beach. It was a small beach, only about 100 yards long. If the launch had come ashore on either side of the little cove, it would have been bashed up on the rocks and probably destroyed.

Kevin grinned at me and banked the Buccaneer to the right. Two minutes later, we were on the water beside *Starbound* and heading for the beach. I paid him his $15 and tried to thank him too much. "Glad we found it," he said. "Now you'd better get over there and pick it off that beach before the tide comes in."

I rowed back out to *Starbound*. We put the small dinghy back on the davits, then prepared to get under way. The bommies in front of the ship were clearly visible now. I steered right and drove the bow clear of them while Ernie and Tom took in chain with the winch. As the anchor broke free I backed her off until her bow cleared the coral heads, then let the wind blow her bow around to head out of the little bay. We cleared the bommies by 10 feet.

One hour later we were anchored off the little beach, looking at the launch through the binoculars. It looked fine. Ernie volunteered for sea duty. We were anchored close to the beach on a lee shore with some pretty good wave action bouncing us up and down. I kept the engine running, just in case.

Ernie rowed to the beach in the little dinghy, inspected the launch, then waved his arms in the prearranged fashion which meant that everything was O.K. He dragged the launch down into the water and tied the bow painter of the dinghy to a stern cleat. Finally both boats were in the water and Ernie was rowing at a furious rate against wind and waves. I wondered why he didn't start the outboard until I saw the shallow coral reef which protected the beach. He had to row across it first. Then we saw him drop the oars and scramble aft to start the outboard. It kicked right off and he was on his way back. Nina acted exactly like a mother during the entire operation, in spite of Ernie's 6-foot frame and nineteen years.

Both small craft were taken on board, a hectic job with the waves bouncing *Starbound* up and down, then made ready to get out of that dangerous place. Once again I took the helm and Ernie and Tom watched the anchor chain come in. We must have been anchored in about 40 feet of water. Finally the chain was straight up and down. Then *Starbound*'s bow dropped as a wave passed, the winch sped up and wound in the slackened chain, and as the bow bounced up on the next wave there was a terrific bang. The whole boat shuddered and I wondered if we'd hit a coral head. Ernie yelled, "She's free! Get us out of here!"

When we were in the clear, and the anchor was on board and lashed down, Ernie called me forward. Nina took the helm and I walked up on the foredeck to see what had happened. The shank of the anchor, made of steel with a 1 x 3-inch cross-section, had a 30 degree bend in it about one foot up from the crown. It must have been wedged under a coral ledge. It's a wonder the chain didn't break! Well, we'd gotten the launch back, anyway.

We headed for Hook Island, heading between South Molle and little Denman Island to get back out in the channel, pounding hard across the waves which were now being kicked up by a 30-knot wind out of the southeast. Hook Island was just 10 miles away, so we powered all the way.

Nara Inlet on Hook Island is one of the most popular anchorages on the Coral Coast. It's a minifjord cutting into Hook Island's south coast for over 2 miles and lined with steep rugged hills.

The water of Nara Inlet was smooth and lovely. Pine trees lining the shore made me think of Puget Sound. The best anchorage is all the way up the inlet opposite the "painted rocks," a famous signpost for cruising yachts. The rocks are big, smooth sheets of black lava rising at an angle of 45 degrees from the waters of the inlet. They're covered with yachts' names.

We have never been the type of people who have an insatiable desire to dash about defacing Mother Nature's handiwork with initials, names, and symbols. However, the defacing was already thoroughly done over the years by many, many boats. We recognized dozens of the hundreds of names. Australians had told us that it was a kind of tradition for cruising yachts to paint their ship's name on the rocks. O.K., we decided, vive la tradition; we would find a blank spot to paint a modest-sized "Starbound" up there tomorrow.

Two small sailboats were already anchored in the head of the inlet. We did an end run on them and anchored even further in. There was plenty of crystal blue water over a white sand bottom; just about as perfect an anchorage as we'd ever seen, and as isolated. The surrounding hills protect it from the heavy trades, so all we had was a light breeze ruffling the water and making it sparkle in the sunlight.

We put our launch into the water and went over to say hello to our neighbors, Ian and Keri Johnson on *Ventura,* a nice little "Vertue" sloop out of New Zealand, and Dick and Val Roberts on *Escapade,* from Brisbane. We invited them over to *Starbound* that evening, then went ashore to scramble over the rocks and stretch our legs.

Ian gave us a lot of information that evening. He'd sailed through Indonesia on someone else's boat. He advised us to pass Darwin by. The typhoon which had passed over the city the past Christmas had so destroyed the town that recovery was going to be a slow and painful process. He also suggested that we avoid Thursday Island because of its strong winds and currents, as well as its marginal anchorage. We listened to him without much comment. We'd never been to Thursday Island and it was one of the places we'd always wanted to see, bad currents or not. He told us a lot about Indonesia, giving us some advance insight as to what we might expect from the officials there. It sounded complicated.

We spent next day scrambling around on the rocks with a brush and a can of old paint looking for a good spot to leave our calling card. We finally found one and took turns painting the big letters. It took a surprising amount of paint. After that we joined the crews of *Ventura* and *Escapade* and took a hike up the rugged steep watercourse which fed a good-sized stream into the head of the inlet. At this time of the year just a trickle was running, but we could see that during the rainy season a thundering torrent must come hurtling over the rocks.

While we were all up on the bluff overlooking the inlet, we watched *Altair* come in and anchor not far from *Starbound.* The evening was predictable; the crews of all four boats lounged around on *Starbound* and talked cruising.

The anchor was up at 0900 next morning, and we were on our way to Townsville. We had thought our overnight sailing was done for the duration of our time on the reef, but now we found an opportunity to have one last go at it. We ran under square sail all day making 5 to 6 knots and put the raffee on at 1930 as the wind fell off. It was a really glorious night for sailing. The sky glittered with stars from horizon to horizon. At 0500, just as Scorpio plunged headfirst into the mountains of the mainland, we rounded Cape Bowling Green and went onto our final leg for Cape Cleveland, the loom of the lights of Townsville was ahead.

We went into the very crowded harbor at 1200. There was no place to anchor. We layed up to the Eveley Cruise wharf for just long enough to find out the lay of the land. We'd have to get off the wharf at 1500 because a cruise boat was coming in. We started looking for a place to go.

A lot of boats were on permanent moorings in the middle of the harbor. A big, beautiful, John Alden schooner named *Pavana* was one of them. Her owners, Mike and Georgie Green, invited us to tie up alongside of them until we could find a better spot. That's what I call hospitality! *Pavana* was 51 feet on deck, as is *Starbound,* so we matched up fairly well. We found out that we could move back onto the Eveley dock next day after the cruise boat had left with her passengers. So we just relaxed with Mike and Georgie for the evening and watched the passing parade from our vantage point.

Townsville is a big place with a population of about 75,000. It's an important sugar terminal and also a coastal outlet for various mine products. Also, the tourist industry is booming along the Coral Coast, and Townsville is a good centralized location, hence the crowded harbor. It has been predicted that a new state of North Queensland will be formed and that Townsville will be its capital.

We spent two days in Townsville. We did the laundry, bought stores, filled our water tanks, and engaged ourselves in the ever-present boat maintenance. We even went to the movies and saw *Godfather II.* What a strange movie to see in Australia. We hoped that other countries didn't really think that America was like that, but some of the comments we overheard made us wonder.

Away at 0900 on the 19th of June for the aboriginal reserve on Palm

Island, we anchored in the harbor at 1500 and I went ashore to check in with the manager, a Mr. Dillon. He gave us permission to land, so I returned to *Starbound* and brought the crew ashore.

We started north next morning and turned back within one hour. The weather report said we would get northeast winds at 25 to 30 knots and we didn't want to get caught out in that. We reanchored at 1000. The wind stayed west-northwest until 1200, then dropped flat. The afternoon forecast verified the northeast winds, but only for Gladstone and below, so we had wasted a day.

At 0900 we were under way with all the fore and aft sails flying. We had a good reach to Hitchinbrook Island and anchored off the north end near a very beautiful beach. Ernie found coconuts, Nina found sea shells, and Tom and I slowly retrieved our sense of humor, which we had lost at Palm Island. The anchorage was like a lake that night.

We made a short run to Dunk Island next day and anchored just off the resort there. The beach was pleasant. The pub was pleasant too, although expensive for cruising folk. We had a good time swimming for a change without fear of sharks. The sharks don't come in to Dunk Island for some reason, perhaps because the water is clear. They seem to like murky water.

Next day was hot, clear, and windless. We motored away from Dunk Island at 0900 and went looking for a breeze. We didn't find one. We kept the engine going all the way to Mourilyan Harbor on the mainland and dropped the hook in the middle of the small anchorage. There wasn't much there except the sugar wharf where the ships come in to load up, but it is a good overnight anchorage. There was a brilliant full moon that night.

Our next big town was Cairns, in fact the last big town on the north coast. We left Mourilyan Harbor at 0600 and planned to anchor off Fitzroy Island before dark and go into Cairns Harbor next day. A north wind came up in the afternoon and stopped that idea. North winds are rare at that time of year, but there it was. It made the anchorage at Fitzroy Island untenable. We kept plugging into the wind and finally rounded Cape Grafton. Then we put up the yankee jib and with the engine helping managed to get into Cairns just at full dark and found our way to the public wharf. Within minutes a night dockmaster showed up and told us we'd have to move to the main wharf—not in the morning but right away. We were already filling our water tanks, so he allowed us to finish that first. Then we moved to the big wharf, and it was really big! There were full-sized ships ahead of and behind us.

In the morning the piermaster assigned us a berth outboard of an old steam tug called the *Empire Peggy*. She was sitting without engines outboard of a huge dredge. I wasn't sure if I wanted to be the third ship out on that assembly, but when an Aussie piermaster says to go there, then you go there.

Captain Harry Siborowski and his wife, Lily, lived aboard the *Empire Peggy* with their two small children. Harry was born and raised in Poland and Lily came from England. We hit it off right away with them. Harry was requalifying for his captain's ticket for Queensland. In the meantime the government had assigned him to a caretaker position for several of the old ships which were owned by the state but were not being used. They were at anchor way up the inlet, just sitting and deteriorating. Harry also had to keep an eye on the two Formosan fishing boats which had been detained by the Australian Navy for illegal fishing in Aussie waters. The crew was still on board one of the boats, so Harry really had his hands full—especially since only one of the Formosan crew spoke English, and that not too well.

We decided that we liked our berth after all, especially after we saw that the yachts which were moored on the other side of the inlet had to ferry everything back and forth to the main dock.

My cousin Tom had to fly back home. He had really wanted to go on to Indonesia with us, but a letter from his company contained certain ominous phrases which convinced him that his job might be in jeopardy if he was gone from it much longer. With his education and ability he should never worry about a job, and I did my best to convince him of that, but to no avail. We saw him off at the airport in the early morning. Too bad. Tom is one of those easygoing guys who is a delight to have on a cruise. We would miss him.

We were notified by the post office that our main heat exchanger had arrived and could be picked up at Ansett Airways cargo office. I walked uptown and got it, after they had relieved me of $217 Australian for C.O.D. charges, freight, and insurance. That put a dent in the budget which really hurt. And there were dents in the exchanger to complete my happiness. There was no question about sending it back; I had to accept it as it was. At least a nice big zinc pencil had been fitted into it. I hoped our electrolysis worries were over.

We stayed in Cairns for two weeks, our longest stay anywhere in Australia. We would have moved out much sooner if Tom had still been with us, but with his departure went any reason for us to hustle. There was a lot of work to do on *Starbound* and Cairns was the last place we could be assured of getting parts we might need, for a long time to come.

We fixed a leak in the toilet mechanism in the main head. The anchor winch brake lining was worn out and we had to find the right kind of lining and rivet it back into place. We straightened the shank of the big anchor— almost. And oil and fuel filters were replaced on the main engine and motor generator. The temperature gauge wouldn't read properly and we traced it to the sender unit in the engine block. The 12-volt alternator wouldn't excite; we found a loose connection and fixed that.

There is a little train which takes people from Cairns up to the tablelands of Australia. It's only about a two-hour ride, and the tracks pass through some of the prettiest country in the whole world. Nina and I declared a day's holiday. We climbed on the train one morning and just sat back and relaxed. The train rolled through pastureland and farmland, then climbed and climbed, with switchbacks, trestles, and tunnels by the dozens. Waterfalls crashed down gorges on either side and the scenery became more green the higher we climbed. Finally we were on top of the plateau. We really weren't prepared to find a tropical paradise up there. We just hadn't associated that kind of thing with Australia. But there it was! Tree ferns and palm trees and that wonderful smell of damp jungle vegetation rotting away in dark green glades which never feel the sun through the heavy foliage overhead. We looked and sniffed and enjoyed until the tooting of the train whistle called us aboard for the return trip.

A young friend of ours, Jim Wegner, wanted to sail with us to Thursday Island. We'd met Jim at Suva, in the Fiji Islands, where he was sailing through with a few other young guys on a big trimaran named *Allegro*. He is American and was working in Cairns to put together the wherewithal for a boat of his own. A boat builder himself, and a real artist with a welding torch and steel, Jim was in the process of building a beautiful hull for Doctor Dick Turpin and his wife Kay. He had another contract for a similar hull after he was finished with Dick's boat. Jim hoped to realize enough profit from his work to be able to build a hull for himself. When Jim saw *Starbound* at the main wharf he hurried right down to say hello and let us know what he was doing in Cairns. We asked him if he'd like to cruise with us for a while and he jumped for the chance. His job on the boats was being held up until delivery of a new welding machine was made, so our offer was timely.

On the 8th of July we waved good-by to our friends in Cairns and motored into Trinity Bay. A light southeast wind kept our sails full all the way to Low Islets. They are tiny islands but very beautiful, and they made a fine anchorage for the night. By dark the wind had picked up again and heavy gusts were coming across the coral reefs, but we were so protected there wasn't any swell to make an uncomfortable night. The big lighthouse flashed its signal across our ports all night long and let us know that our anchor was still in the same spot. Trawlers came in and went out continuously.

Next morning we were under way at 0700 and already looking for an anchorage for the night. Hope Islands were touted as a nice place to stop but they were wide open to southeast winds, and that is what we had—about 20 knots of them.

We drove hard for Cooktown and *Starbound* was plugging up the channel by 1530. It's a very narrow channel with not much room to anchor a boat as big as *Starbound*. No matter that Captain Cook took *Endeavor* in there. The place must have silted up a lot since. We nudged the mud twice before we found a hole in the bottom wide enough to give us some swinging room.

Cooktown is like no other place we'd visited, even in Australia, which has its share of character-filled places. Of course, Captain Cook established the place, but the big boom came 100 years later when the Palmer River gold fields were discovered. Many thousands of people lived there during those wild days, but when the gold ran out, so did the people. Now Cooktown has barely 500 inhabitants, but is still a fascinating place, enriched by its history and loved by Australians. It has a small but steady tourist industry going for it.

I had wired to our bank in the United States for money while we were in Cairns and asked them to send it to the bank of New South Wales in Cooktown. So naturally we headed for the bank first. They hadn't received any money for us yet, but they did inform us that the yearly Cooktown race meet was going to take place next day and that we should go see it. The bank would be closed for the races, so if our money didn't arrive by wire before 1500, it looked as if we would be in Cooktown for the next three days, till Monday anyway.

The pubs, all three of them, were full of "ringers," Aussie cowboys. We were immediately adopted as honorary Aussies and naturally had to sit down and drink beer like an Aussie. Now that is a tough job! I was damn lucky to make it to the bank at all. Our money authorization was there. I drew cash on it and took the teller back to the pub with me. It's the Aussie way, mates!

Next day we went to the races. The entire town was there, as were the owners and hands from every station, as the ranches are called, in the area. There were a lot of Aussie tourists from other parts of Australia too. Everyone dresses nicely, especially the girls. There is a small grandstand over a flat concrete slab with benches where people can sit out of the sun. A lot of beer was sold, all Aussie brands, all very good. Children were running around all over the place. It was like an old-time county fair.

The big trophy race was being held next day but we decided to take advantage of the high tide at 1120 and get on our way. We lay *Starbound* alongside a small trawler which was tied to the little dock at the entrance of the river and filled our fresh water tanks. The trawler's skipper also gave us a whole bucket of fresh rock oysters.

We cleared the channel by 1215. The wind decided to blow from the east, so we put on fore and aft sail and made Cape Bedford by 1500. The anchorage in the lee of the cape looked good, but the tidal current was strong enough to hold *Starbound* across the wind. We rocked all night with gusts whistling through the rigging, keeping us up to check our position. We were glad to get under way in the morning.

The next two days were spent at Lizard Island in Watson's Bay. The land isn't very attractive: low, dry, and flat. But the water of the bay is the most beautiful we'd seen anywhere on the reef. It's clear blue-green over a very white sand bottom. We put two anchors down, almost on the beach, and hung very well with the bow pointing into the strong southeast wind coming across the saddle of the island. We hunted for shells and swam and just took it easy for the rest of our first day.

There is a small resort west of Watson's Bay, but we'd heard that they didn't welcome yachties, I think mainly because they claimed to be a very small, very exclusive outfit. In fact, we'd heard they were so exclusive they were going broke.

A young couple we'd met in Cooktown arrived by plane at the resort but chose to camp on the beach. This can be done on many of the islands of the Barrier Reef, but a permit is needed. Jan and Alistair set up their tent right in front of *Starbound*'s anchorage. Ernie and Jim brought them out to the ship for the afternoon and we all decided to eat on the beach that night, just for a change. At dusk we took in steaks, hamburgers, rock oysters, and salad. It was a grand dinner, made even grander by its being cooked over an open fire on a beach of the Great Barrier Reef.

We were rapidly approaching the top of Australia now. During the next four days we anchored at Howick Island, just off the northwest tip of Flinders Island, then at Hannah Island, and finally at Night Island.

Night Island scared us. The anchorage is located on the west side of the island, and to get to it a northbound yacht should go around the southern tip of it, being sure to give the coral reef extending off of that tip a wide berth. Well, that's what I did, but going west in the evening, naturally the sun is smack in the helmsman's eyes and there is no way to see that reef with the sun reflecting off the water. We hit the damn thing twice! Two big bumps before I could spin *Starbound* around and get her out of there. We checked the bilges and didn't find any sign of a leak, so we took a much wider sweep than was shown on the charts, nearly double the distance from the end of the island than we had first tried. We got by O.K., but when we looked back we could see that we hadn't cleared it by much even on the second try. The charts just aren't as accurate as they could be. Also, coral grows at a fast rate on the Great Barrier Reef.

We anchored and I went overboard to inspect the bottom. The water was clear but the rest of the crew kept a close watch for sharks anyhow. They generally feed in the morning and evening hours. I couldn't find even a scratch on our bottom copper. We must have hit a couple of coral heads directly with the shoe plate, which is three-quarter-inch-thick bronze, and just busted right through them. Lucky again! I lay awake quite awhile that night, thinking about the things that could have happened. There is no nice

Coast Guard out there to lend a hand. A lot of people have died on those reefs.

Excerpts from the ship's log:

19 July, Saturday: Both anchors are on board by 0815 and we set sail for Portland Roads with jib and mizzen up. Have to fall off at 1200 and change the rig to square sail. We sail by Restoration Rock at 1500, a pretty beach with a few campers on it which we are surprised to see, so far from anywhere. We are into Portland Roads and tied to the rickety dock by 1600. The dock planking is caved in and dangerous. There is a fresh-water tap on shore under the dock, so we all take baths. We meet Joseph, a German lad who has been here two years and says he is about ready to move on. We also meet Ross Pope, a retired lighthouse keeper who lives in one of the seven occupied houses here with his wife, mother, two sons, and one daughter. A rain catchment for water, a vegetable garden, chickens, pigs, and fish. City necessities are shipped in about once a month to the Abo settlement replenishment point about 20 miles south. A lonesome place, this!

20 July, Sunday: We drop the lines from the dock at 0830 and get under way through the reefs for Margaret Bay. Another good square sail run. We drop the hook at 1530. This is a very good anchorage with the wind southerly. The beach is beautiful, with a river mouth forking and splitting it into three pieces. Nina and I go ashore and pick up some very good shells for the collection. There are big sea trout in the river mouths, but we don't have the gill net with us and the tide is making very fast. We spend a quiet evening aboard and have a steak for dinner.

21 July, Monday: We get under way at 0515, in the dark! Margaret Bay is one of the few places from which that can be done, and a good thing it can be because we have 70 miles to make before dark today. We carry the square sail till noon, then brail it up and switch to the yankee and mizzen for the remainder of the day. Big waves have been building all day as the wind increases and the water depth decreases. We can see them breaking on the bar across Turtle Head Island entrance, the mouth of the Escape River. We've got to go in there. It's getting toward dusk and there is no other place to go.

We make it, but wow! It's the first time *Starbound* has ever surfed! It's a funny feeling to have over 35 tons on plane. Once into the creek the water is smooth even though it's still blowing like hell. We duck around the north corner of the river and anchor off the pearl rafts of the Japanese pearling industry which has been established here. We put out two hooks again. The wind is really howling outside. The gusts must be 35 to 40. It's too choppy to go ashore. If this doesn't let up we might have to stay through tomorrow.

22 July, Tuesday: 0600; wind is about 20 knots and the tide is coming up to low-water slack. It's now or never for today. We make it and we're out! What a rough bitch that entrance bar is! As soon as we get out in the channel and start running with the waves, it isn't so bad. Now we're across the shallow area and things settle down, but the wind is picking up again. We're at the top of Australia now and though it's been fun in places as well as exciting, we won't be sorry to see the reefs drop into our wake. Albany Passage is just ahead. We should be through it by 0930 and anchored off Thursday Island by 1400. Good-by, Australia!

18

Coup d'Etat in Dili

"You don't want to go to Kupang first, Gordon. That's not the way to go. That southwestern strait of Timor has some hairy currents running through it. What you should do is sail directly from Thursday Island to the eastern tip of Timor, run up through that strait, and then head right down the coast to Dili."

Ian took the chart dividers from my hand and walked them across the chart of the Arafura Sea. "See? It's just a thousand nautical miles; about eight days' sailing with the prevailing trades."

It was too warm below. I got up from the settee and edged my way around the varnished teak table spread with charts in *Starbound*'s main saloon. Grabbing the hatch coaming, I helped myself up the six steps of the companionway ladder and onto the wide afterdeck. My ankle still hurt me from the bang I'd given it that morning while scrambling up the boulders of a dry waterfall.

It was full night now and the stars were brilliant points of light overhead. One part of my mind concerned itself with sailing routes while another part identified navigational stars. Rigel Kent and Hadar were pointing their finger at the Southern Cross, and when I turned my head to the opposite side of the sky, Vega blazed brightly at about 40 degrees above the horizon and was rising. Another turn and I could see Arcturus, also about 40 degrees high but setting. It was a pretty night.

Starbound was anchored in Nara Inlet on Hook Island, part of the Whitsundays group, on the Great Barrier Reef of Australia. Ian and Keri's little Vertue sloop was anchored just in front of *Starbound*. Ian and Keri were headed for Indonesia too, but Ian had been there twice before, so we were inclined to listen to his advice—with reservations. After nearly two years of cruising on the world's oceans we had yet to find a place—a town, a

241

country, a coastline, an island—which matched the description given to us by someone who'd "been there before." Reason one: each person "sees" differently. Reason two: places "forgotten by time" are becoming increasingly rare.

We talked some more. We drank Australian beer. We laughed a lot. When I looked at my watch again, it was just past midnight and the calendar dial said that the new day was the fifteenth in a series for the month of June 1975.

Thirty-seven days later, with another 800 nautical miles of reef dodging behind us, *Starbound* popped out of Albany Passage like a cork from a champagne bottle. She was making 12 knots, the current accounting for five of them. We carried the flood for another 25 miles and rounded Horn Island with Thursday Island right ahead.

The southeast trade winds really whoop it up at the top of Australia. We were broad reaching across a 35-knot wind with the yankee jib and mizzen hard as plywood, and a 3-knot current carrying us down the reef-infested passage at a white-knuckle clip. We could see three or four yachts nestled under the lee of Horn Island. As we looked across the choppy water of Ellis Channel, the town of Port Kennedy on Thursday Island was clearly visible now, and its entire waterfront was a very uninviting lee shore.

We made a fast decision. We'd anchor under Horn Island, as recommended by the Sailing Directions. Ernie and Jim horsed the jib and mizzen down and put temporary gaskets on them. We turned to port into the anchorage and then watched with apprehension as the current continued to sweep us sideways at 3 knots toward the Horn Island jetty. When our position looked about right, we dropped the big Herreshoff anchor. Chain whirled out of the locker, over the wildcat, and through the hawse, making a little cloud of rust particles which the wind snatched away. Ernie finally spun the hand wheel of the winch brake and the wildcat slowed its clatter, then stopped. *Starbound* snubbed on the chain with the 30-fathom marker on the water, and her stern swung downstream with the current.

All hands furled sail. Nina and I tucked the mizzen into a tight roll while Ernie and Jim bundled the big jib into a neat package in the bow basket. After the foredeck was clear we let go the lashings to the launch and swung it over the side and into the water. Then Ernie and I lowered the 70-pound Danforth into the launch and took the anchor out from *Starbound*'s bow at an angle of 30 degrees, paying out the anchor rode as we went. When the chain lead started rattling its way over the gunwale of the launch, we spilled the Danforth over the side. Back on the foredeck Nina started the winch motor and wound in the rode on the windlass side of the anchor with the chain wildcat disengaged. When the chain of the first anchor and the rode of the second looked as if they were splitting the load between them, Nina secured the winch motor and then the anchor rode. We could sleep well with two anchors out.

Thursday Island is somewhat of a mess. It is administered by Australia, but for some years has suffered from a severe case of apathy. First the pearling industry failed; then the replacement industry, cultured pearl farming, followed suit. The islanders tried prawning with moderate success, but it wasn't the big boom that was needed. Now "good old T.I." is becoming the headquarters for several governmental departments such as the Lighthouse Department and OTC (Overseas Tele-Communications). The Torres Straits Pilots are firmly ensconced here too. And now tourism development is being talked up, so it would appear that T.I. is slated for increased development.

T.I. is a small island, only about 2 square miles in area. The larger islands around it protect it from the worst of the Torres Straits weather, but also funnel some very fast tides by it—often over 6 knots.

The island's primary interest to the cruising yachtsman is basic: supplies, water, and fuel are available. T.I. is the jumping-off spot for Darwin, if anyone has a desire to see that Northern Territory town. And it's the launching point for those "hurry up" yachts that want to head directly to the Indian Ocean via Christmas and Cocos islands. Also, it's the last supply point for those yachts fortunate enough to possess a cruising permit for Indonesia and are heading that way. We were in the latter group.

To sail Indonesian waters, a yacht must first obtain a "Cruising Permit and Security Clearance" document from the appropriate embassy in Djakarta. We had gone through the procedure while waiting out the typhoon season in New Zealand. It took us ten weeks to obtain the document from the American Embassy. After we received it, we had to find the nearest Indonesian Consulate who would 'issue visas on the crew's passports. We finally finished the procedure in Wellington, New Zealand. Nina took an overnight train ride from Auckland, had our passports stamped, then caught the next train back north. It cost her two days, but the trains are superb in New Zealand. She enjoyed the trip.

We had already decided not to include Darwin in our agenda. That city was still recovering from the effects of the devastating typhoon which had literally flattened it the previous Christmas. The word was out that fuel and supplies were available but very expensive. The fact that Darwin experiences 25-foot tidal ranges didn't attract us either.

We spent nine days at the Horn Island anchorage; me writing, Nina shopping, Ernie painting and boat hopping. A small ferry boat operates between the jetty there and the main dock at Port Kennedy on T.I., so all of our shopping was accomplished that way. We had fueled the ship at Cairns, the last big town on the Queensland coast for a northbound yacht, so we were O.K. for diesel. A good thing, too, since the price was twice as much on T.I.: 49 cents per Imperial gallon.

The strong winds finally gave us one morning of respite and we spent a hectic two hours getting in our anchors, running the dog-leg reef passage to the CALTEX dock on T.I., filling our tanks with water (for a 50 cent charge), running the passage back to Horn Island, and re-anchoring just as 25-knot wind gusts began slamming across Horn Island once again.

We used the morning of the last day of July to do our last-minute shopping and mailing. At 1030 the customs and immigration officials gave us a motor boat ride back to *Starbound* and left us with the necessary clearance papers for Dili, Portuguese Timor.

We were under way by 1100 and piloted our way west, past the reefs studding the water between Goods Island and Friday Island.

We sighted Booby Island with its 12-mile light by 1230. The lighthouse was abeam to port by 1400 and we streamed the taffrail log line on the starboard quarter and 100 meters of fishing line on the port quarter. Our square sail was pushing us along at 7 knots with a 20-knot breeze right behind us. We were in cruising trim and Grumpy was doing the steering. We were very happy to be out of the reefs and the strong currents.

Early in the morning on the eighth day of August, Liran light flashed its white "group" at us. The Arafura Sea lay in our wake; 1,000 miles of good weather, following seas, and an unfaltering trade wind. What more could a sailor want?

We could see the buildings of Dili in the early morning light, scattered along the gently curving Timor shoreline—almost an open roadstead, but protected by a small barrier reef.

The entrance buoys were hard to pick up. They were very small and well hidden against the varying shore colors. We entered cautiously with Ernie standing in the crosstrees pointing out the channel.

We moved in close to the main wharf at the beckoning of a white-clad figure who turned out to be a pilot, and took him on board. With a little broken English and some gestures he showed us where to anchor temporarily. It's a very small harbor and the several reefs and wrecks don't allow much swinging room.

The port captain, a big Portuguese man, came aboard from the harbor launch and inspected *Starbound,* but he didn't want to go through any entrance formalities on board—probably because we were out of cold beer. We'd drunk it all on the way.

I went ashore with the officials to the customs offices located on the wharf and started filling out forms. It took an hour to satisfy the somewhat complicated entrance procedure. And the immigration people were not happy about our lack of visas. We had Indonesian visas, but Portuguese Timor is not Indonesia. They retained our passports and told me I could pick them up the following day for a small fee for the visas.

Ernie answered my wave and came over to the main wharf in our launch and we returned to *Starbound.* We weighed anchor immediately and moved from the "safe spot" our erstwhile pilot had selected for us, since we were in imminent danger of swinging into a submerged wreck. We motored *Starbound* eastward along the quay until we came to a pretty spot marked by a small park with big trees shading a curve of the quay which at that point was notched with embrasures, each equipped with an ancient cannon pointing seaward.

We re-anchored, let our stern swing to within 100 feet of the quay, and carried two stern lines ashore, intending to secure them to the heavy concrete stanchions supporting the railing along the quay. The rail also served as a bench for our audience, consisting of four adults and about fifty children who were fascinated by our anchoring technique. Dozens of willing hands pulled on the stern lines while I shackled short sections of chain around the stanchions and secured the lines to the shackles. Then Ernie and I carried out our second anchor with the launch. When all of our lines were adjusted, *Starbound* lay stern to the quay, about 100 feet away. We were the only yacht in Dili.

Ernie stayed aboard watching the watchers watching us, and Nina and I went ashore to investigate the town. One of the officials at the customs office had mentioned that the Tropical Hotel might change some money for us, since the banks were closed. I'd asked what the official exchange rate might be and was told 34 escudos per Aussie dollar, but the rate was given me with a wink and the word "official" was stressed in such a manner that I thought it might be a good idea to find out where the black market exchange might be.

I was soon enlightened. We met a bewhiskered, sunglassed, and sandaled Aussie named Keith who got us "put straight soon enough." The barber shop was the answer. "Don't take a bloody escudo under forty-nine for the Aussie dollar," said Keith. "The Chinese here are doing all of the money changing and they're hard after Aussie dollars."

It was fun! The Chinese who owned the barber shop had hustlers all over town. Everywhere we heard, "Psst, Meester, you like change money? Plenty good rate!"

If I started by asking 60 escudos to the dollar and they started by offering 40, we'd eventually arrive at the "standard" black market rate: 49 escudos, and once when I was feeling hard-nosed, 50.

With escudos in our pockets, Nina and I walked another two blocks past the barber shop to the Tropical Hotel and found a table in a cool patio with a breeze rustling the leaves of the green foliage growing in profusion around the perimeter of the open space. They had Asahi beer. Yes, beeg bottle, very cold, 25 escudos, sir.

We went back to *Starbound* and went to bed very early to make up for our lack of sleep the previous night. The gentle swell leaking in past the reef rocked us to sleep.

The next day was August 9, Saturday—a good market day. We got to the mercado about 1100, which we found was five hours too late. We should have been there about 0600 to get a good selection. We bought a "hand" of bananas for 5 escudos but everything else looked pretty well picked over, so we wandered back to the waterfront, found a small shop on the way which sold roti (bread) in small rolls for 1 escudo each, and bought a dozen of them.

I stopped by the immigration office to pick up our newly stamped passports and found that I had to pay 900 escudos to get them out of hock. About U.S. $18—at the black market rate—for a thirty-day visa! And no bargaining! Just a jet-eyed gendarme covered with guns, ammo, and little bits of braid. How was I going to argue? Especially when he doesn't speak English and I don't speak Portuguese?

We wandered around town collecting kids and souvenir sellers like lint. The kids are taught basic English in school, but most of them restrict their conversation to "Hallo, Meester, Hallo, Meesus, where are you going?"

The phrase "Where are you going?" is evidently considered a polite form of greeting, and takes the place of our American "How are you?"

We answered the children, "We are going to our boat. Where are you going?"

They would say, "We are going to our house," or "school," or "the mercado," and smile widely at us. The little girls would giggle and hide their faces. After we had gone by we would always hear the child who had spoken say to the group, "See, I told you I could speak English!" They would say it in Indonesian, or sometimes Portuguese, but it was so obvious to us what they were saying by the inflections they used, and the fact that their last word was always "Ingles."

We picked up some excellent Singapore beer in town, returned to the shore, and whistled for Ernie to come get us in the launch. He had rigged the afterdeck awning and it was a very pleasant thing to sit in the shade with a nice breeze blowing, sip on a cold beer, and say to ourselves, "Well, here we are in Dili."

We heard a splash alongside and noticed two heads bobbing in the water beside *Starbound*. The head with the long curly hair spoke. "Good day," it said. But not exactly like that. Actually it said, "GuhDye," a pronunciation which immediately marked the speaker as an Australian. So we put the rope ladder over the side, asked them on board, and passed some beer around. Mick Finnerty was from Orange and Ray Benjamin from Buderim, both Australians, sure enough. They indicated two friends standing on the quay, and Ernie ran the launch up to the beach beside the quay and picked up Bob Rix, another Aussie, and Rolf Meier from Zurich, Switzerland.

Ernie was delighted, lots of guys about his age—long hair and beards, backpacks and fun!

Late in the afternoon they all went ashore, Ernie too.

Another yacht had come into harbor the previous evening. She'd anchored way over by the main wharf, so we'd decided to wait until she had cleared before going visiting. In some places a dim view is taken of anyone visiting a boat before it has officially entered. The yacht was a 36-foot sloop named *Noelani,* flying the New Guinea flag. We watched the customs launch visit her and then leave. Now she motored over and anchored next to *Starbound* and put out one stern line to the quay. We waved to the couple on board and when they got the sloop settled in they rowed over in their dinghy to make our acquaintance. And so we met Noela and Graham Byrnes from Port Moresby. We gammed the evening away.

Ernie returned about 2200, very enthusiastic about the "great little Chinese joint" where they'd filled up on a "kind of chow mein and rice." And of course we heard a glowing report about the "beach house" where about fourteen young world wanderers were staying.

We found out that the big market day was tomorrow, Sunday, so next morning we rolled out of our bunks at 0600 and went ashore to find some fresh vegetables.

The market was crowded and fascinating. A tourist, meaning any Anglo-Saxon, is besieged by cries from all directions, "Meester, Meesus! Look, look!" And naturally the prices always start at four times what they should be. Nina is a hard bargainer, though. She'd learned the routine in some rough schools: Martinique, Curaçao, Panama, Tonga, and Fiji. This place was child's play for her.

We came away with a nice selection of vegetables and fruit, and the information that the cockfights would start at 1500. We hustled back to the boat, put our goodies away, collected Noela and Graham, and headed for the cockfights. We'd never been to a cockfight before and were eager to see one.

On our way to the mercado area where the cockfights were being held, we gathered up another couple, Kerren and Wayne Crowhurst, who are both in the Australian Army and were in Dili on holiday. We saw them sitting in the patio of their hotel taking their ease over a couple of Cokes, so we asked them to come along with us.

Five escudos each was the price for the "primo" seats at the cockfight. The central ring was dirt-floored, about 20 feet in diameter and fenced with chicken wire. Around that was a cement walkway about 5 feet wide. Then there were the concrete benches where the spectators sat. Many of the handlers sat with the spectators, their fighting birds on the floor between their feet. Each bird had a braided cord tied to one of his legs with the other end of the cord under the foot of the handler. The birds could move around to a certain extent, so of course the spectators usually had a bird or two looking out from between their legs. Us, too.

Another group of bird handlers strolled in both directions around the ring on the concrete walk, stopping now and then to challenge other walkers or sometimes one of the handlers sitting among the audience. Everyone had a fighting bird with him, carrying it against his stomach with one arm, or rather casually slung on top of a shoulder, keeping it there with one hand.

Two men appeared in the ring with their birds. A tremendous flurry of noise and arm waving came from the surrounding crowd and we saw a lot of escudo notes being waved around. The two handlers in the ring were suddenly on their haunches, each with both hands on his bird. They cited the birds, thrusting them toward each other once, twice, then let them go. The birds flew at each other feet first, wings flapping and necks outstretched, the neckruff fluffed out to a diameter as large as their bodies. A quick flurry of feathers, a roar from the crowd, and both handlers leaped in simultaneously to capture their respective birds, grabbing them by the tail feathers.

One of the handlers started whooping with delight and ran in circles to show all who could see, particularly his opponent, that his bird's fighting spur had drawn blood.

Those spurs are cruel-looking things. About 2½ inches long, they are double-edged and razor-sharp. Each handler had his own little packet of varied-shaped blades. They looked like miniature swords. After a challenge had been given and accepted, each handler would select a blade from his packet. He would have someone else hold the bird and then, by a careful and lengthy wrapping process with a piece of yarn, would affix the blade to one foot of the bird so that it projected from the heel, simulating the bird's real spur.

The first several fights were all of the one-shot variety, and only one cock was actually killed, through a lucky stroke by the opposing bird. Then the fights to the death began. The handlers would cite the birds at one another time after time until one bird was killed in an explosive clash or until one of them refused to fight, which wasn't often.

The dead birds were dropped in a gruesome pile of feathers and blood over on one side of the ring's perimeter. We learned that one of the restaurant owners had bought all the dead birds for the day. They don't waste protein in Dili.

Starbound's "refugee" travellers from Dili.

Kupang, Timor from the harbor.

At Benoa, Bali, woodcarver Linggi came aboard to
carve panels for *Starbound's* main cabin.

View of a Balinesian anchorage from the landing.

Nina and a young businessman trade old coins in Bali.

Temple of the Goddess of the Waters, Bali.

Starbound enters Durban harbor.

Michel Santander came aboard to help crew from
Capetown to Martinique.

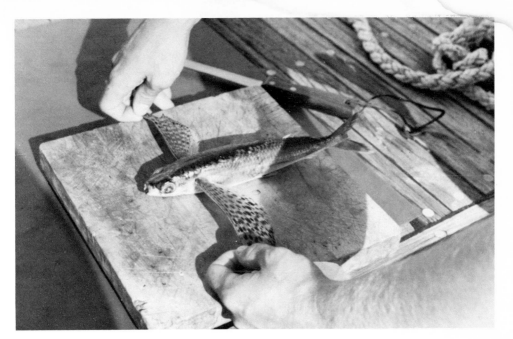

Flying fish for breakfast again.

Entering Mauritius harbor with Ernie on the bowsprit.

The harbor at Christmas Island. *(Starbound* is at center
left.) Cloud of pollution is from a freighter being loaded
with phosphate. Water depth under *Starbound*
is about 500 feet.

Diamond Rock in the Caribbean marked the crossing
point of the round-the-world voyage.

Almost home, June 1976. Gordon at the helm in the
Intracoastal Waterway.

After the tropics, *Starbound* faces the heaviest winter
in decades at her Annapolis dock.

One thing became very clear to us right at the beginning of the fights. The Chinese and the Timorese were at odds with one another. A rather intense rivalry was very evident, perhaps springing from the fact that every business in town seemed to be Chinese-owned. Each time a "Chinese" bird met defeat from a "Timorese" bird, the shouts of acclamation were deafening. And when a "Chinese" bird won, a generally disapproving silence fell over the crowd.

Our group didn't stay for the whole show. After two hours we were all rather tired of blood and feathers. We were also tired of the noise and heat and dust. I, personally, was tired of the hacking and spitting all the local people seemed to think was necessary. The entire floor area was covered with gobs of spittle, and here and there a red splotch identified a chewer of betel nut.

We had a quiet evening aboard *Starbound.* I don't allow any spitting on the teak decks, so we walked around barefoot, sipped on cold beer, and looked out over the reef to the blue sea beyond. A cool breeze kept us all comfortable. Ernie had rolled up his sleeping bag, announced his intention to spend the night ashore with his buddies from the beach house, and had me run him in to the shore.

Ernie and the gang must have eaten somewhere in town and then gotten restless. They stopped on the beach near *Starbound* and called that they were going over to the capital building where an anti-Communist rally was in progress in the public square. They don't seem to be very fond of Communists in Dili. We could hear the roar of the crowd from three blocks away.

Nina woke me up at 0630 next morning. It was August 11. She exclaimed, "Gordon, get up! I hear gunshots!"

"Ah, come on, Nina—it's just some car backfiring or something."

"It isn't! It's gunfire! I've heard it several times now. And Ernie is down at the beach house, and I've heard several shots from that direction."

I lay back in the big bunk, listening. Then I heard it; it sure sounded like rifle fire.

Graham called from *Noelani,* "Hey, Nina! Tune in your radio to Radio Australia. A coup d'état has taken place here. Those are gunshots we're hearing!"

Oh, boy! What a way to wake up. We peered out of the main hatch at the streets of the town. One of the main thoroughfares comes down through town and ends at the street just east of the government buildings. Our stern was directed at a point on the shore just a few feet east of this intersection, so we could see into the city for several blocks. The streets seemed deserted except for groups of armed guards at each intersection and an occasional truck which would tear by at high speed, its back filled with men in civilian clothes and carrying rifles. Another thing we noticed: a small locally owned freighter had moved from the wharf to an anchorage out in mid-channel of the harbor entrance. We wondered if the port was blockaded.

Graham and Noela rowed over at our invitation and Nina made coffee while I tuned into Radio Australia, Voice of America, and BBC. Radio Australia seemed to have the best information, so we stayed with their frequency and listened to what little they had to offer.

There were evidently four different factions at odds with one another in Portuguese Timor. First there were the Portuguese, whose colony this east end of the island of Timor had been for several centuries. The unofficial word we had heard was that Portugal had plans to let the colony go independent by 1978. Second there were the U.D.T. (the Union for a Democratic Timor), who advocated a gradual approach to independence and a continuing voluntary association with Portugal which would continue to administer their defense and external affairs. Third there were the Fretelin, who, unofficially again, we heard were riddled with *Communistas* and whose stronghold was in the hills above Dili. The Fretelin wanted complete independence now and no ties with anyone, including Indonesia, which controls the western half of Timor. Fourth there was a "mystery" group, who wanted union with Indonesia. While in town we had met U.D.T. fans, who gave us a V for victory salute, and we had met the Fretelin backers, whose salute was the raised arm with clenched fist. We never did meet anybody who claimed association with the "mystery" group, possibly because the mere display of an Indonesian flag had caused a riot several weeks earlier.

The morning advanced, occasional gunshots rang out from the city streets, and we commenced to worry more and more about Ernie. All we could do was keep our heads down in case a stray rifle bullet might find its way out to the boat.

Ernie and Mick Finnerty finally showed up about 1000 and proceeded to tell us about the "soldiers" they had talked with in the streets and about the wounded they had seen. We were appalled!

About 1030 three more of the beach-house boys appeared on the quay, again necessitating ferry service from shore.

By 1200 we had some fourteen English-speaking people on board *Starbound,* possibly drawn by our big American flag or by our slight isolation from shore. Since all but two were Australians, we were quickly dubbed the unofficial Australian Embassy in Dili.

As near as anyone could tell at that early date, the U.D.T. had begun the coup to prevent the "mystery" party from instigating their own coup. Now, having beaten them to the punch, the U.D.T., as well as the Portuguese, seemed to be worried about the Fretelin forces coming down from the hills and taking over everything, à la Castro. There also was a rumor that the

Fretelin had joined the U.D.T. forces, and together they were taking on the Portuguese. We saw nothing to confirm that. The Portuguese didn't seem to be shooting at anyone, but had put their military barracks, the radio station, and the wharf and naval base under heavy guard, and were evidently gathering their dependents into the military encampment to protect them from harm.

Now many trucks, jeeps, and autos began running back and forth on the waterfront street just 100 feet away from our stern. All of the vehicles were jammed with men, some in civilian clothes, some in uniform, but all of them armed with an assortment of weapons. We identified Mausers and sten guns and a variety of bayonets; I even saw a cutlass or two. The majority of the "soldiers" looked about sixteen years old, but from my age of forty-four all soldiers looked young. Trouble is, a rifle in the hands of a boy can kill you just as dead as one in the hands of a man. Also, I was worried about the amount of discretion a sixteen-year-old with a rifle in his hands might employ. (Hey, let's take a shot at the yacht just for fun.)

After noon things quieted down. We hadn't heard any shots for some time. The only change ashore we had most definitely noticed was that a truck had dropped a man off at the quay directly behind our boats. He was armed with a rifle and walked back and forth along the sidewalk. He didn't seem to be keeping a particular eye on us, but had several conversations with people in the "military" vehicles which stopped by. When he looked our way, we waved to him. He waved back. No harm in being friendly, right? Hi there!

Ernie wanted to go ashore with his friends. They wanted to get back to the beach house and make sure their gear was still intact. We let him go with some trepidation, and several injunctions to come back to *Starbound* if things got rough ashore.

Then we told the fellows that if we had to leave Dili, we would take any of them with us who had visas for Indonesia. They held a short conference. Several of them were in the process of obtaining Indonesian visas. Their passports were at the Indonesian Embassy and they wanted to pick them up. We didn't know if the embassy would be open or not, but it wasn't too far away from their beach house, so they voted to stroll up there in a circumspect manner to investigate the situation.

We discussed pulling out of Dili that evening, but even though the streets were fairly quiet, the radio had announced that the airport and harbor were closed. We were undecided.

Ernie said, "Tell you what. I'll go uptown with this bunch and we'll try to find out what's going on. If it looks like more trouble is going to break out I'll come back to the boat. But if things are quiet I'll go to the beach house with them and spend the evening. I can get back to *Starbound* by just walking down the beach. One thing, though; if we do decide that things are getting too hot here and we decide to scram, where are we going?" This led to a hasty consultation of our Indonesian charts, with the result that Kupang, the major town of Indonesian Timor and on the western end of the island, was chosen as the closest port with the most possible means of onward passage for our prospective refugees.

"O.K., why don't you guys see if you can get your Indonesian visas all squared away. Then go on down to the beach house and spend the evening. Ernie, if you want to spend the night there, it's all right. But if any heavy shooting starts again, come right back to *Starbound.*"

I took them to the beach in two trips. Before I had the second group ashore, the first group was carrying on an animated conversation with our young waterfront commando.

"He doesn't know anything," they reported. "He's with the U.D.T. and his orders are to stay at this intersection and stop any unauthorized vehicles." The group of young men trudged on down the beach, staying on the sand. I took the launch back to *Starbound.*

Graham returned to *Noelani,* grabbed his camera, and came back to *Starbound.* For the rest of the afternoon we sat on the afterdeck seats, watched cars and trucks full of men and weapons race by, and took an occasional picture when we were sure no one was looking our way. We heard a rifle shot now and then, but there were no active signs of fighting. The sunset was beautiful. Another small ship came in from sea and anchored in the channel. Her port of call was Singapore.

The 2000 news from Radio Australia finally confirmed that a coup had indeed taken place in Dili. Well, we pondered, at least the rest of the world now knows for sure that there is some kind of trouble here.

At 2200 the British Overseas Radio Service of the BBC came out with the amazing statement that Portugal had denied that a coup had taken place. Good old Portugal. I guess they were having enough troubles at home and in Angola without having to admit that another of their colonies was raising hell. We decided to try to get some sleep in case we had to pull out unexpectedly. I'd never tried to sleep before with rifle shots punctuating my dreams.

At 2345 Nina woke me by saying, "My God, we're being boarded!" A male voice called out, and at the same time, a thumping came from the stern.

I was already headed for the afterdeck. As I jumped up the companionway ladder onto the dark afterdeck, I could see a man clambering over the taffrail. Wet shoulder-length strands of hair were plastered across his face. I was reaching for one of our bronze belaying pins when he spoke. "It's me! Bob!"

He climbed onto the afterdeck, wet and shivering, wearing only his shorts.

"What the hell, Bob?"

"We didn't want to raise too big of a commotion to wake you up, so I swam out," he said. "Everyone else is there on the quay. Portuguese troops came into the beach house armed with machine guns, told us we had to go to the military barracks under guard, and gave us five minutes to get ready. Ernie told the guy with the gold braid that we were off the yacht, so this head dude with the artillery told us to go to the yacht immediately or they would take us to the barracks because there was going to be heavy fighting and our safety could not be guaranteed. Then they loaded us into a big truck and brought us down here."

"How many are on the quay?"

"Ernie and four more. One of them is Beverly, an Aussie girl who is traveling through Indonesia."

"O.K., go below and rinse off in the shower. Nina will get you a towel. I'll go in and pick 'em up."

When we had everyone on board, including Graham and Noela, who had come over to find out what was happening, we sat around drinking hot coffee while we worked out the complete story.

The story was essentially as Bob had told us, except that three of the young men at the beach house didn't have Indonesian visas and had been taken to the military barracks by the soldiers who were saying something about a refugee ship which would leave for Darwin in the morning. We were sorry now that we had restricted our offer of passage to those with visas for Indonesia. It would be damned unpleasant to spend a night under armed guard in a barracks which was likely to be attacked at any time.

Graham and Noela and Nina and I had a consultation. We decided to wait until morning; then Graham and I would take the launch over to the main wharf and check with the port captain to see if we could get clearance to leave Dili.

We took turns studying the dock area and naval base with binoculars, where much activity was taking place. Truck headlights kept sweeping over the dock area as trucks swung out onto the wharf, then parked here and there at both ends of the dock. Finally we were able to discern that there was a large group of people on the wharf—as many as 100, probably more— and we could make out piles of what seemed to be luggage. We wondered who they were, but our guess logically included Portuguese dependents, foreign nationals on interrupted holiday, and possibly some local Chinese. We decided that now we knew why the Chinese merchants wanted those Australian dollars badly enough to pay high black market rates for them.

I may have slept for two hours. At 0700, when it was light enough not to get shot at by nervous kids, Graham and I jumped into the launch and motored over to the main dock acting just like happy yachtsmen. We landed at the east end of the dock where we could climb up on the lowered ramp of a landing barge and tied the dinghy off to one of the big chains which stopped the ramp from dropping further than it should. When we were on the ramp we looked up at several smiling Timorese faces. They were all smiling over rifle barrels which were pointing at us!

"Hi there," I said brightly.

"Who you want?"

"The port captain. Is he here?"

"You come. Go that way." They pointed with their rifles, still smiling, those cheerful rascals.

We climbed up the wing tanks of the barge and looked down the dock. Our guesses had been almost right. Portuguese dependents, foreign nationals, but no Chinese. Lots of luggage. And those funny-shaped things that we had seen being thrown from the trucks last night had been mattresses. Some people were still asleep on them, mostly women and kids.

Interesting! U.D.T. men on one end of the dock, and on the other, refugees, surrounded and seemingly guarded by the Portuguese military. Big guys they were, in full battle dress and carrying some very fancy automatic weapons.

A handsome lieutenant detached himself from a group of matronly women who had been plying him with questions.

His English was pretty good. "May I help you?"

We explained who we were, which he seemed to know already, and asked him if we could speak to the port captain.

"You're too early," he said. "The Port Captain is on that ship out there and will be back here at 0800." He said it in military style, "oh eight hundred."

"Are they going to bring the ship into the dock?" we asked.

"Maybe. You must go now. Come back at oh eight hundred."

He didn't want conversation. We left the wharf, once again under the eyes and guns of the smiling rifle brigade at the east end, and returned to *Starbound.* We told everyone what we'd seen, but the binoculars had been busy, so they knew already.

Just before 0800 we saw the pilot launch leave the biggest of the two freighters and head for the wharf. Graham and I beat her there, ran the U.D.T. gauntlet again, and nailed the port captain before he could be swamped by the crowd of Portuguese ladies who were bearing down on him.

We went through our spiel.

"Go," he said. He had less English than the lieutenant.

"How about customs?" we asked. "Don't we have to clear?"

"Customs? No customs! Customs will not come. Just go!"

"Ah, yessir, we can see that there is trouble here in Dili, but we are going to Kupang in Indonesian Timor. Won't they want to see our clearance papers from this port?"

"Clearance papers? Hah! Just go! Tell them in Kupang you come from Dili. You will have no problem; they know what is happening here. It is good you have a yacht. I wish I had a yacht! All you need to do is go! It is very good! I wish I could go. Good-by, good luck." He shook our hands, then turned with a weary and patient smile to meet the fat ladies who were having a race to see who could grab him first.

I called to Graham above the noise of the outboard as we motored back to our boats, "Let's drop our stern lines and get out of here!"

"I'm with you, but I want to run up to the Indonesian Embassy first. Our visas need to be renewed. Also, Noela and I don't want to go to Kupang. We thought we'd head up around Alor Island and then coast-hop down the north side of all the islands, then stop in at Bali for a few weeks."

"O.K.," I said. "I'm going to head for Kupang first and drop these kids off. Then Nina, Ernie, and I will decide where we go from there. Tell you what; I'll go to the Indonesian Embassy with you. Maybe they'll give us some kind of clearance document."

We arrived back at the yachts and filled everyone in on the latest news from the wharf. Ernie took Graham and me in to the beach, and we walked the six blocks to the embassy.

It was a madhouse, full of people trying to get permission to enter Indonesia. The harassed clerk issued Graham and Noela visas without any problems, but when we asked him for some kind of clearance document, he smiled and said, "No got; no can give. Just go. Kupang O.K. for your boat. Tell customs there you come from Dili. Everything O.K. Good-by now."

I left Graham at the embassy filling out a few more forms, and started back to the quay. It was a hot day, about 90 degrees. My dry mouth yearned for a cold beer. I pulled a handful of crumpled bills out of my pocket and counted: 700 escudos and some change. Hell, that was more than enough for a case of Laurentina beer! I swung into a faster walk and moved one block deeper into town. On a small side street there was a hole-in-the-wall snack bar which was the only establishment in town open for business. I stepped around a bamboo screen and went to the small serving window. There were many cases of beer stacked in the back. I bought a case at the high price of 600 escudos. But there was no hope of exchanging escudos for dollars, and they use rupiahs in Kupang, so the escudos were essentially useless to me unless I could spend them here.

Ernie met me at the beach and exchanged the case of beer for an adjustable wrench.

I went over to the stanchions around which the chains were shackled, securing our stern lines to the quay. Our young patrol guard came over and watched me as I strained at the shackle pins to loosen them.

"You go now?"

"Yes, we go to Kupang."

"Ah, Kupang! Very good. Good-by."

"Good-by, and good luck!"

He cradled his ancient Mauser and watched with interest as I cast the lines off, slung the pieces of chain around my neck, stuck the wrench in the rear pocket of my shorts, and walked back to the beach where Ernie was holding the launch just off the surf's backwash. Nina had our "crew" hauling in the stern lines.

Back on *Starbound* again, I started the main diesel and flicked on the power to the anchor winch. Ernie went up on the foredeck and with the help of Mick and Keith started to take in the nylon line to our starboard anchor.

Nina sat on the afterdeck seat checking to make sure everyone had their passports and visas in order. We had on board Beverly Wayne, Bob Rix, and Michael (Mick) Finnerty from Australia, Keith Buckley from New Zealand, and Rolf Meier from Switzerland.

I checked the quay. There were three young men standing there, watching us. I asked Keith, "Aren't those three friends of yours?"

"Yeah, that's Ray Benjamin, Ashley Fletcher, and Douglas Bailey, all Australians. They stayed in the military barracks last night. They were going to try to pick up their visas this morning."

I held a quick conference with Nina, then turned to the shore and called, "Hey, you guys! Do you have your Indonesian visas?"

"Yes!" A cappella.

"Do you want to go to Kupang with us?"

"Yes!" Resounding a cappella.

"Hey, Ernie," I yelled forward. "Stop the winch. We've got three more passengers."

Another hail from the quay. "We've got to go pick up our gear!"

Mick, Bob, and Rolf came up to me.

"Listen, Gordon. We've got a lot of escudos between us and we're not going to be able to change them back to dollars either here or in Indonesia. How about we go in town with those guys and on the way back we'll buy a few more cases of beer so we have plenty on the way to Kupang? There're going to be eleven on board!"

"Great! Here's the last of my escudos. Anyone else?

Everyone unloaded their Portuguese money, and Mick stuffed his pockets.

Mick called to the three on the quay. "Wait for us, we'll be right there."

We spent an hour waiting, watching the quay. We also watched the activity on the main wharf. One of the freighters had moved into the wharf and the refugees were lined up waiting to get aboard. There must have been over 250 people standing in the sun with their baggage.

Ernie and I broke out the Danforth anchor, washed it down with the deck pump, and secured it. We flaked out the 3-inch line on the foredeck to dry. Then we shortened the scope on the chain rode leading down to our remaining anchor.

A hail from the quay signaled the return of the group on "shore leave," and Rolf made three trips with the launch to get beer, backpacks, and people on board. While Nina supervised the stowage of backpacks and miscellaneous bundles below, we secured the launch and were ready to go.

I started the main engine again and Ernie hove us short on our remaining anchor, then broke it out of the muddy bottom. We started to wend our way through the reefs toward the channel.

As we passed the main wharf we could see the refugees being herded aboard the freighter there. People were spilling over the gunwales, and the main hatches amidships swarmed with humanity. There was still a long line of people waiting to board.

I heard an Australian voice behind me. "God, I'm glad I'm not on that tub. They don't have any cabins below—I guess everyone's going deck passage. Can't you just imagine all those women and kids barfing all the way to Darwin? I'll bet it takes 'em three days to get there!" We waved to the freighter and several arms waved back.

We motored out the channel into the Ombai Passage leading to the Savu Sea, turned west, and headed for Kupang. We set the square sail and raffee and secured the main engine. I popped the top from a cold bottle of beer, sat on the teak taffrail, propped a foot against a spoke of the varnished wheel, put an arm around Nina's waist, and said, "Thank God we're out of there!"

"Amen!" was her reply.

Next morning, as we were approaching Kupang, the radio announced that the waterfront area of Dili was being bombarded with mortar shells.

19

Bali: Temples and Rice Paddies

American Embassy
Consular Section
Jakarta, Indonesia

Dear Sirs,

My wife and I and our son are sailing around the world aboard our yacht *Starbound* and are at present in New Zealand awaiting the end of the typhoon season before proceeding north. We plan to commence our trip about the first part of April 1975, and then to cruise the Australian east coast to Thursday Island. From there we plan to enter Indonesian waters and visit several Indonesian ports. Upon our departure from Indonesia it is our intention to cross the Indian Ocean via Christmas Island, Cocos Keeling, and Mauritius to the South African port of Durban.

The United States Consulate in Auckland has advised us to contact you so that we may obtain visas for Indonesia prior to our leaving New Zealand. It is our understanding that we must obtain a clearance approval for Indonesian Territory before visas can be issued by the Indonesian Consulate in Wellington.

I append the following data for your consideration:
1. Name of yacht: *Starbound;* Port of Registry: Baltimore; Hailing port: Annapolis, Maryland; Documentation No. 261706.

2. Owners of yacht: Gordon G. Stuermer and Nina R. Stuermer.
3. Type of yacht: Auxiliary Ketch.
4. Displacement: 35 tons.
5. Net tonnage: 30; Gross tonnage: 31.
6. Radio call sign: WJ 5529.
7. Captain's name: Gordon G. Stuermer, United States citizen, Passport No. D2235549.
8. Crews' names: Nina R. Stuermer, United States citizen, Passport No. D2228314. Ernest G. Stuermer, United States citizen, Passport No. D2228315.
9. Last port before entering Indonesia: Dili, Portuguese Timor.
10. First port after leaving Indonesia: Christmas Island (Aust.).
11. Indonesian ports and dates of visit: It is very difficult for a sailing vessel to accurately predict its itinerary months in advance of a planned visit, but we expect to enter Indonesia at Kupang during the first half of August 1975. We intend to depart from Indonesia, probably from the island of Bali, during the first half of October 1975. We hope to visit ports on the islands of Roti, Timor, Savu, Flores, Sumbawa, Lombok, Bali, and Java.
12. Passengers' names and cargos: None.
13. Purpose of our visit to Indonesia: A desire to see the country and learn something of its peoples; to provision our vessel with food and water prior to our Indian Ocean crossing.

As we are planning to leave New Zealand by the end of March 1975, we would be grateful if this matter could receive your immediate attention.

Very truly yours,
Gordon G. Stuermer

It was ten weeks before we received an answer to the above letter. It came in the form of a single flimsy sheet which spelled out our itinerary and was signed and stamped with seals from the Indonesian Department of Foreign Affairs, the Directorate of Sea Transport, the Department of Defense and Security, and, finally, the Vice-Consul of the United States of America. I've already mentioned how Nina, armed with this Clearance Approval and our passports, took the night train from Durban to Wellington and obtained our visas from the Indonesian Consulate there.

What we would have liked to do was to sail north from Dili, around the island of Alor, then head west stopping at several small ports on the northern side of what are called the Lesser Sunda Islands. These include

Flores, Sumbawa, Lombok, and Bali. Then perhaps we might visit the two major ports of Java, Surabaja and Djakarta. But we were running late now and couldn't risk being trapped by the northwest monsoon. Once that cyclic system sets in, a yacht has a hard time making westing, and even a harder time if the occasional typhoon of that season shows up. The smart thing for a yachtie to do is move out of the monsoon area by the first week in October, and some people think even that is pushing their luck.

Since we were already committed to go to Kupang to drop off our "refugees," we were in somewhat of a quandary. Should we go north from there and sail up between the islands of Adonara and Flores? Or should we head northwest and make the passage between Flores and Sumbawa? Or should we head west for Bali, spend more time there, and then play it by ear?

Once again time and money directed our course. *Starbound* arrived in the harbor of Kupang at 1630 hours on August 13. If we stayed in Kupang for just one week, we'd only have five weeks left before we had to be on our way southwest out of the monsoon area. And Bali was about 600 nautical miles away, perhaps a week's sail. That would leave us only a month at the outside. We decided to sail directly to Bali; then we would see.

The small city of Kupang was built right to the water's edge and looked like a slightly soiled Arabian fantasy—probably because of the occasional minarets, slender lofty towers which were attached to mosques and surrounded by one or more balconies from which the Muslim faithful are summoned to prayer by the cries of the muezzin.

Small dhows carrying lateen rigs sailed back and forth past us as we anchored *Starbound*. Everyone gave us a wave and called greetings to us in Indonesian.

A government gunboat was anchored nearby and I took the launch over to ask their advice about entering. They asked me aboard and I met the captain, "Rudy" Sudarjo, and his chief engineer and executive officer, Darmawan. Darmawan had a little English and Rudy a little less, but we managed to get along fine. They let me know that we should wait until morning to go ashore and asked me to come over with my wife at about 0900 to have breakfast with them. After breakfast Darmawan would take us ashore and show us where to go. Very hospitable people.

We were all up at dawn listening to the muezzin. The Australian news broadcast mentioned that the refugee ship which had left Dili on the same day as we would get to Darwin late that afternoon. Our eight extra crew members were very happy that they were not aboard that ship!

Ernie took Nina and me over to the gunboat and we had a very nice fruit breakfast with Rudy and Darmawan. Then we went ashore in the gunboat's big launch and Darmawan took us to customs and immigration, then to the Navy office, where we had to present our Clearance Approval document to the commandant. I was glad that I had made many copies of it, because everybody wanted one. When the Navy finished with us we had to return to customs where two police officers met us and returned with us to *Starbound*. They searched the backpacks of all our refugees, then they searched the boat—very politely, though. Finally we had permission to go ashore. Ernie spent the next hour ferrying everyone into the beach. What a long involved procedure! It was late afternoon before we were finished with everything. Nina and I decided to stay on board until morning.

We spent a week in Kupang. Through Rudy and Darmawan we met Jim Arahman, a young business man who spoke beautiful English. He'd learned it from books, movies, and the radio. Jim was very smart and very ambitious. Evidently his father had died when he was quite young and although there were older children in the family his brains dictated that he become the head of the household. Nina and I were invited to his home for dinner and we became frequent guests. It was a lot of fun watching Nina learning how to cook Indonesian food in an Indonesian kitchen from Jim's tiny mama. We also learned some basics of the Indonesian language, which isn't as hard as it sounds. Within a few days we were able to shop around town and make ourselves understood without any trouble at all. The people were delighted when we spoke their language.

We decided to get under way on August 21. We said good-by to our Indonesian friends and cleared for Bali. The clearance procedure turned out to be a lot easier than entering; it took about one hour. Jim was practically in tears when we left and so was Nina.

Just half an hour before our anchor came up, the yacht *Moonbird* came in and anchored near us. We took Jim Arahman with us and went over and met the owners, Dennis and Nancy Bailey. They filled us in on the Dili situation; evidently full civil war had broken out between the various factions and all yachts were being cautioned to stay well clear of the place.

We left Jim with the Baileys, said good-by, and were motoring out of the harbor by 1500.

It only took us four and a half days to Bali, motor-sailing most of the way because of very light winds, which are a common occurrence at that time of the year. We sighted Bali at 0800 off the starboard bow and came close to running right on by. The westerly current runs strong, and during the night we couldn't tell how fast it was carrying us. The log was reading about 15 percent slow because of that current.

We turned up the center of Selat Badung, the straits between Bali and Penida, the small island to the east of Bali. We were heading for Benoa, the only good harbor on the island. It is located on the east side of the hammerhead-shaped peninsula which hangs down from Bali's south coast. We made good headway until Cape Mebulu, the southernmost tip of the peninsula, lay at 300 degrees bearing—and then we stopped. The square sail and raffee were both filled and pulling well. We started the diesel and ran it up to 1,500 RPM's. No progress. We upped it to 1,800, made about one mile, and stopped again. The current had to be about 7 knots! We couldn't believe it! Far to port we could see the Bali shore. We could even see the Benoa Cape we wanted to round. We pulled out the Sailing Directions and read them again. They are confusing in parts, but finally we found a paragraph which stated that the current was weaker near the Bali shore. We steered left and watched *Starbound* crab her way west.

Far off the bow we could see the fishing fleet come out of Benoa and head down toward us. At first all we could make out was that they were small boats with lateen-rigged sails of many colors. As we closed with the shore they appeared closer and we admired the slim hulls with double outriggers attached. Each carried a single sail which was indeed beautiful. Some of the sails were of one color and some were as multihued as the wings of giant butterflies. Soon they were zooming by us, and at speeds which had our mouths hanging open. They were really fast! There was one man or a man and a boy in each boat. They smiled and waved as they skimmed over the surface of the blue sea, climbing up the backs of the big swells and then surfing down their faces.

We turned our attention back to our progress and saw that the shoreline was finally going astern at a respectable rate. But it was 1400 before we rounded the Benoa Cape and started in toward the harbor.

The entrance to Benoa is tricky. After rounding the cape, while staying clear of its outlying coral reef, a boat must progress to the northwestward until the northern reef lies athwart the bow, then make a hard left and run down the line of the reef, which is about an uncomfortable 200 yards away. That's the easy part. Directly ahead lays the little projecting cape off Benoa village, which is by now visible. The buoy system is confusing because some are buoys, some are barrels, others are daymarkers of a type, and all of them seem to be out of place, something which we found later to be often true. However, there is a range on shore to guide on, and we steered in looking ahead at what seemed to be a whirlpool. It turned out to be just that! The reefs make the passage a dog-leg, and the strong current following the passage sets up a circular motion to the water which is truly nasty to behold. After turning to the right, which must be done just short of the whirlpool, the harbor opened up and we could see the rest of the passage clearly marked by a series of three big red nun buoys—and then we were in the harbor. Ernie came down from the crosstrees from where he had been calling out the dangers to me. We decided right then that when it came time to leave we would pick the stand of high tide to make our exit.

Ernie walked up onto the foredeck, then called back, "Hey, look! Isn't that *Topaz*?"

It was indeed she. The big, green-hulled Baltic schooner was anchored near the outer fringe of the anchorage area in which a dozen yachts swung on their hooks. We took a turn around her and greetings flew back and forth. The crew invited us to tie up outboard of them for the time being. We were happy to accept, since the anchorage looked fairly crowded. *Topaz* was the only "yacht" we could raft up to.

She had come in a week before us and already had Bali fairly well cased. It was really enjoyable to sit below in her big main saloon again with a drink in our hands again and get all the information the easy way. We renewed our friendships with Karen and Larry Cross, Cathy and John Carr, and Phyllis and Bob Brinkerhoff. We met Ginny and Jim Rooney for the first time; two of the original members of the Great Escape Sailing Company, they had rejoined *Topaz* since we had last seen her in New Zealand. And two of our favorite resident bachelors were on board, Peter Lenker and Carl Hartman.

It was too late in the afternoon to commence entrance formalities. Larry told us they were rather involved and the Balinese officials closed shop fairly early. So we had a few drinks and caught up on each other's adventures. When we all got hungry *Topaz*'s crew took us ashore, showing us where to land the launch, and introduced us to Kassie, an Indonesian lady who was the proprietress of one of a series of small kiosks lining the waterfront near the landing place. A plate of Indonesian rice or noodles with vegetables and bits of meat cost 100 rupiahs each, 25 cents U.S. At those prices we couldn't afford to open the canned food we had aboard. And the food was delicious.

Next morning at 0900 the harbor master came on board and very promptly charged us harbor fees for *Starbound* and ourselves: $5.00 for the boat and $1.75 for each person on board. Then he told us how to conclude our entrance procedure. It sounded complicated.

A young man named Wayan Kota had beat the harbor master aboard by one hour. We had met him briefly the afternoon before. Wayan was looking for work and since *Topaz* had hired him earlier to do a few jobs and recommended him highly, we had decided to hire him to paint the hull and house sides for us. But first we had to finish entering the country. So for a start I hired Wayan to help me with the procedure. His English was nearly perfect, while my Indonesian was shaky. As soon as the harbor master had departed, I gathered up our papers and, with Wayan as guide, went ashore and started on the rounds to the customs, police, and Navy offices, which were all located on the waterfront. Immigration was to be our last stop but Larry Cross had told me I'd need more rupiahs for immigration. So we had to take a bus 9 kilometers into the capital city of Denpasar and find a bank. The logistics worked out well because the immigration offices were located on the highway just south of Denpasar.

Our bus ride was fascinating. The buses are not the big silver behemoths

Americans are used to. They're small trucks, mostly Japanese, which have had the back roofed over and wooden seats installed down each side. They are called "bemos" (pronounced "bee-mohs"). One man drives the bemo and a helper stands on the step at the rear, takes fares (25 rupiahs per one way to Denpasar), and crams all the bodies aboard that he can manage plus all the packages the bodies are carrying.

The road to Denpasar is lined with Indonesian homes and Hindu temples. In front of them are flowering trees and behind, palm trees and rice paddies. I found the entire passing scene beautiful. In general the Balinese seemed much more affluent than the people we'd met in Kupang. More friendly too, with a certain sophisticated manner we found delightful. Wayan told me he thought this was because Bali was so rich agriculturally; everyone had enough to eat, therefore more leisure time was available to allow these traits to develop.

Denpasar was crowded, noisy, busy, dusty, and very interesting. I noticed quite a few tourists wandering around, but only a few of those were the "big hotel" type. Most were young and casually dressed, the backpacking kids we'd been meeting all around the world. Wayan told me that most of them stayed in Kuta Beach, "where the action is," located on the opposite side of the peninsula from Benoa. I decided that Nina and I would have to make a visit to Kuta Beach soon.

Wayan signaled the bemo driver to stop at *imigración.* They were located in a low modern building with a courtyard in front surrounded by trees. The officials spoke some English, but Wayan came in very handy. I had to fill out another sheaf of paper and turn over our passports to be stamped. They told me I should pick them up in a few days. In return I received three "shore passes" for which I had to pay a total of 675 rupiahs, U.S. $1.60. We were to carry these on our persons any time we went ashore and were to show them at the post office in order to receive our mail. To my chagrin I also found out that since we'd officially entered Indonesia at Kupang, our thirty-day visas would expire on September 12 and that on or before that date I must pay a 9,200 rupiah fee for each of us, a total of U.S. $66.60 for visa renewals. With all the charges I had a hunch that we were going to be broke by the time we left Indonesia.

We caught the bemo back to Benoa Harbor and since it was close to 1600 I let Wayan go for the rest of the day. He promised to be back aboard by 0800 next morning to start sanding and painting. We had found that an active tropical sailing agenda took its toll on our topsides about every six months, and they were really looking shabby. Wayan worked an eight-hour day for 750 rupiahs, or $1.85. I could not afford not to hire him. That very low price released me and Ernie to take care of the rest of the ship's work— Ernie doing the rigging and sails and I the machinery.

Nina, Ernie, and I had to make an important decision: to hurry our boat work in Bali and sail to Surabaja and Djakarta for a quick visit in each port, or to remain in Bali and see the country once the boat work was complete. I think all three of us really wanted to stay and relax, but we were disturbed by that old feeling that we might be missing something. That feeling was dispelled after talking to some of the other yachties in the harbor. They told us that we really should have stopped by some of the smaller ports to the east. Even though we would have had to pay something in each port, there are no tourists, so it's more like the old Indonesia. "But for a yacht," they said, "Bali is tops! Things we need are available and we can get work done at a decent price."

We were also told that Surabaja and Djakarta are the two worst places in Indonesia to visit with a yacht; that yachties must sleep topside on their boats with some kind of weapon handy, or even stand night watches to avoid being boarded and having gear stolen.

One yacht crew which had recently been to Surabaja reported having rocks thrown at them by Javanese standing on the waterfront. Pickpockets run rampant in the two big Javanese cities and muggings are frequent. "And that's not the worst!" we were told. "Wait'll the officials get through with you—a yachtsman is charged a fat fee every time he turns around! Just remember, Javanese are not Balinese, not by a long shot."

So we decided to stay in Bali. We could get *Starbound* in shape and see the country and relax. And I had writing to do. Around about the first part of October we would head for South Africa via Christmas Island, Cocos Keeling, and Mauritius.

Life aboard a yacht in Benoa Harbor is interesting. *Starbound* remained snuggled against *Topaz*'s tall green hull and we were grateful for her hospitality and the security she afforded. Her large crew set themselves "duty days"; two persons were always aboard on two days' rotating duty while the rest scattered. They took their shore leave in Denpasar and Kuta Beach. Some toured the whole island. A few took buses, ferries, and planes as far as Surabaja and Djakarta.

Our very limited budget wouldn't allow us anything so ambitious as a trip to Java, but Nina and I planned a modest four-day jaunt to the interior of Bali—as soon as the boat work was complete.

Wayan kept busy sanding and painting. When he finished the port side and transom I turned *Starbound* around so he could work on the starboard side.

Ernie alternated between working on the rigging, setting up the lanyards again, and going to Kuta Beach to swim and wander through the narrow streets. He traded an inexpensive wrist watch for the use of a 150cc motorbike and spent a week with a few recently found friends touring much of Bali. With his backpack and sleeping bag strapped on the bike, he managed to have a fine time on $3 a day. His biggest expense was the required driver's license, which cost $6.50.

Nina spent many of her early mornings in Denpasar wandering through the public market. She would check at the post office for mail and before noon the heat and humidity would drive her aboard a bemo for the return ride to Benoa. Afternoons were best spent relaxing in the shade—at least for a Westerner—and we took our salt tablets every day.

Ten days went by very quickly. I worked on the engines and wrote between monitoring Wayan's work. Nina and I spent a few evenings together in Denpasar and Kuta Beach. After the sun had dropped below the horizon the temperature was perfect for strolling. All the shops were open in the evening; true tropical hours.

On September 3 our water tanks ran dry. We had been carefully rationing our Thursday Island water, using it for drinking only, because Bali water had to be boiled for ten minutes to kill the "bugs" before it was drinkable. Now we had to put that water into our tanks—the hard way. Every drop for all the yachts in the harbor as well as the small businesses on the waterfront came from one slow-running tap located behind the police guard's shed at the entrance to the harbor area. We would wait in line with our jerry cans, sometimes as long as half an hour, then fill them while the little Indonesian ladies behind us watched with interest. Then we'd lug them the 300 yards to the waterfront, climb down the slanting stone seawall on an old, rusty steel ladder to the dirty beach, and put the cans in the launch. Aboard *Starbound* we'd spill them into the tanks, then repeat the process. Two trips would give us almost 40 gallons. We closed the two forward tanks valves and used only the two aft tanks to halve our pollution problem.

Wayan finished painting the hull and house sides. I put him to work on the bowsprit, catheads, and anchor winch. *Starbound* was looking classy again.

After those were finished, Wayan still wanted to work, but I only had one thing left for him to do: get fuel for *Starbound*. It took him a half day and was an interesting operation. First I gave him some money. He hired a bemo for 1,000R and drove to the fuel depot about one-third of the way to Denpasar. The fuel depot loaded four 200-liter drums of fuel in the bemo for 30R per liter and please return the drums—that'll be 24,000R. Also, 60 liters of gasoline for the outboard motor at 57R per liter. Then Wayan drove the load back to the waterfront and hired four men, always available, at 200R per man to help roll the 450-pound drums down the seawall and load them into a small sailing prahu. Several of these prahus were always available to carry people and goods to Benoa village and back. Wayan rented the prahu for 1200R. The prahu's skipper expertly sailed the lateen-rigged boat out to *Starbound,* came alongside beautifully, and, cushioned by our fenders, tied her up securely. Then, with a hand-crank pump and hose lent by the fuel depot, we all took turns pumping the fuel into *Starbound*'s tanks. When the drums were empty Wayan returned them to the fuel depot by way of prahu and bemo. When he came back to *Starbound* I paid him another half day's wage: 375R. Total cost for 220 U.S. gallons of diesel and 17 gallons of gas came to 30,795R or about $77. Not bad: about 33 cents per gallon. And that's the way a yacht gets fueled in Benoa, Bali.

Nina turned into a trader. Many canoes from Benoa village would come by *Topaz* and *Starbound* with articles to sell, mostly carvings: barong masks, reliefs, figurines—some of them beautifully done. We wanted to buy some but after paying for the extension on our visas and buying fuel, we were concerned about having enough money for stores. But Nina found out what "change-change" meant. She went through our lockers and foraged out all of our old clothes, as well as some not so old. She cleaned, mended when necessary, and made up her "change-change" bundle. Then when a canoe came by she would spend as much as two hours haggling over a carving she liked, showing one article at a time from her bundle. The Indonesians had met their match. But they loved the game and I think they admired Nina. They wanted clothes, so they kept coming back with more, and nicer, carvings. I got accustomed to seeing two or three small Balinese men sitting on their heels on the cabin top. They would puff away on their clove-scented "krackle" cigarettes and ·Nina would sit with them. They would talk in pidgin English and pidgin Indonesian about anything except what was uppermost in their minds and very deliberately ignore each other's wares. Somehow a trade was always consummated.

It was somewhat in this fashion that we acquired a beautiful "addition" to *Starbound.* We had admired the carving which had been worked on the teak of another yacht. Parts of the binnacle and the main hatchway had been beautifully carved with trees, flowers, and Balinese "dragons." We found out that a young man named Linggi from Benoa village had done the work. So Nina asked Wayan to bring Linggi to *Starbound* because she had some carving in mind: the entire after bulkhead in the main saloon! Linggi had no English at all but with the help of Wayan a deal was struck. I still am not sure what was involved; I remember one of my wrist watches and an old one of Nina's were part of it—and a small transistor radio—and a 1,000 rupiah bonus when he was through. Whatever it cost it was worth it! The carving measures 2 feet by 6 feet and is carved in relief about 1½ centimeters deep into the old butternut timbers. It depicts a traditional scene from the *Ramayana,* an epic of India which recounts the life and adventures of Rama and his wife, Sita.

Linggi worked for six days on the carving, from 0730 to 1600, and on the last day brought in a small floral offering and made a Balinese prayer in front of the panel. Wayan told us the prayer was to thank the gods because the carving had come out so well and to ask that the next one be as good. I hoped it would too. We were delighted with the beautiful piece of art, and more so because it was a part of our ship.

Our work was done on *Starbound* except for provisioning, which would be our last task in Bali. Nina and I took our packs and camera case and left for the high country. We couldn't afford to rent motorbikes, so we decided to take bemos to wherever we wanted to go. They were a very inexpensive mode of transportation and we could look at scenery while someone else did the driving.

We left early Saturday morning for Denpasar, where we caught a bemo for the town of Ubud, known as a center of Balinese painting. We stopped first at Mas, the woodcarving village, and visited the establishment of Ida Bagus Tillum. The series of buildings, housing workshops and the display museum were the finest example of modern architecture we had seen in Bali. The carvings were incredibly good and the prices matched the work—at least for Bali. One exquisite carved panel measuring about 2 by 3 feet was priced at U.S. $300.

After a few hours of looking, we caught a bemo to Ubud and met Peter Lenker as we disembarked. Peter guided us to a small Indonesian hotel or "losman," called Canderi's, located about 100 yards down the Monkey Forest path from the highway. Several young Europeans were staying there. A double room cost 650 rupiahs and included a private bath with "American" toilet. This meant that a tiled reservoir in the corner was full of water and a dipper hung alongside. The floor sloped to drain through a hole in the base of the wall. One stood in the middle of the floor and used the dipper to get wet, then soaped up and rinsed off, again with the dipper. The toilet was indeed "American"; a Crane bowl with no seat! The hopper led directly to the outside open drain and the toilet was flushed with—you guessed it—the dipper.

Having checked in, we went to the Monkey Forest, which is a haven for monkeys of all sorts. We fed them dried corn from cobs we had bought for the purpose. They're running loose, so we had monkeys on our shoulders right away. It was quite an experience for zoo-oriented Americans.

Dinner at Canderi's was really good. The tables were on a covered raised dais not far from the open kitchen. We had a meat "pizza." It was a very Indonesian pizza, but delicious. We also ate a fruit salad which was superb: melon, orange, pineapple, and nuts covered with grated coconut and a sprinkling of coarse raw sugar.

Next morning we checked out after a fine breakfast and caught a bemo back to Denpasar. Then we switched to another bemo which would take us to Bedugal, a peaceful resort beside the beautiful highland lake of Bratan.

The scenery along the way was worth the ride; there are many bare breasts in the country. The girls only cover up when they go to the market.

The lake was indeed beautiful. Located in the semi-extinct volcano crater of Mount Bratan, it was a picture of serenity. Best of all, we were over a mile above sea level and the air was cool and refreshing.

The hotel at the resort on the water's edge left us unimpressed. It was scroungy and expensive with no charm at all. We bargained with a young boy to row us across the end of the lake in his canoe to what appeared to be a pretty hotel located on the hill side above the lake. The hotel was named Lila Graha, meaning Beautiful Garden, and it was! The young manager, twenty-six-year-old Made Putra, made us welcome and after a certain amount of bargaining rented us a charming bungalow for 2,000 rupiahs a night—with a "Western style" bath. Except that all the water was carried to the rooms by little Balinese women and poured from the outside of the bungalow into the bath via a pipe in the wall. There was no electricity because the "Honda generator tidak bagus"! Oh, well, the bungalow was comfortable, the scenery was utterly magnificent, and we felt cool for the first time in two months.

We went to bed early, awoke early, and walked down the hill to the lake. Further along the lake shore we found the Temple of Ulu Danu, dedicated to the Goddess of the Waters, Dewi Danu. It was the most beautiful temple we'd ever seen anywhere.

Nina met a small boy about eight years old just outside a Buddhist shrine very near to Ulu Danu. He was selling old Chinese coins, three of them for 25 rupiahs. The fields were cultivated right up to the shrine and he told us he found the coins by digging in the dirt. Nina bought all of them he had.

We walked to the village of Candikuning and had breakfast at a market stall; a bowl of fried rice with a fried egg perched on top, some dried shredded meat which Nina called "tarantula hair," and some other unidentifiable but delicious goodies. We checked out the local market and found begonias, plump carrots, white rabbits, doves in cages, and, joy of joys, huge heads of lettuce. We bought five heads to take back with us because they didn't have any in Denpasar. We wanted to buy a cabbage too, but they were 3 feet across with the outer leaves on them.

It was time to return to *Starbound.* We checked out of our bungalow, took a last long look at the cool, still lake in the crater, and caught a bemo back to hot, dusty Denpasar.

It was time to leave Bali. *Topaz* planned to be on its way to Singapore on October 1 and we would head for Christmas Island October 2.

September 30 was a busy day. First we went to the university clinic to get our cholera shots renewed. We wouldn't get into South Africa without them. Most of *Topaz*'s crew went with us. We received prompt, polite treatment for the price of 50 rupiahs each.

Going in with *Topaz,* we leased a big bemo made from a converted weapons carrier and attacked the public market. We bought all the stores for both ships at once, making trip after trip to the bemo with boxes and sacks and cases and bags. Pete Lenker even bought two Java finches in a bamboo cage.

We were back aboard by 1200. Nina began stowing the stores while Ernie and I worked on the ship. We broke *Starbound* loose from *Topaz* in the afternoon, taking one of their anchor rodes with us, the nylon one, and left *Topaz* hanging on a single anchor. We hauled the nylon rode in with our winch, washing it down as it came aboard, then broke out their 200-pound "light" anchor and hosed the mud from it. Two of *Topaz*'s crew brought their big launch under our bows and we lowered the cleaned anchor into it, followed by the rode, which they flaked down in long loops. It was one way of paying our "rent" and would much expedite their getting under way in the morning.

We anchored *Starbound* in the now almost deserted anchorage and later that evening took the launch over to *Topaz* to say good-by. We had become very fond of that group.

At 0430 next morning we were up to see *Topaz* off. We made a launch run to collect their last-minute letters for mailing and take pictures of the big schooner going out the pass. We would miss them.

So now it was our last day in Bali. We went to the post office and checked our mail, dropped *Topaz*'s cards and letters in the box, and put in a change of address.

In the afternoon Ernie and I put 60 gallons of water in the after tanks to get us to Christmas Island where we could get drinkable stuff. We were ready to go.

In the morning on October 2, I went ashore and cleared with customs, immigration, the Navy boys, and the harbor master. So help me, the harbor master and customs tried for more rupiahs! I broke out my receipts and firmly told them that they already had my last rupiah. They shrugged their shoulders, stamped my papers, smiled, and said good-by.

Back on *Starbound* I found Nina doing some last-minute change-change. We were the last yacht in the harbor. The carvers wouldn't see any more boats for about six months and they sold cheap. Nina exhausted her goodie-bag and bought three beautiful teak panels carved in heavy relief and a very lovely figurine of a Balinese dancer carved from satinwood.

Wayan came out in a canoe to say good-by. He had tears in his eyes. We brought the launch aboard, then upped the hook and motored out the pass as we said we would, at the stand of high water.

PART IV

South Africa to Annapolis

The Indian and Atlantic Oceans

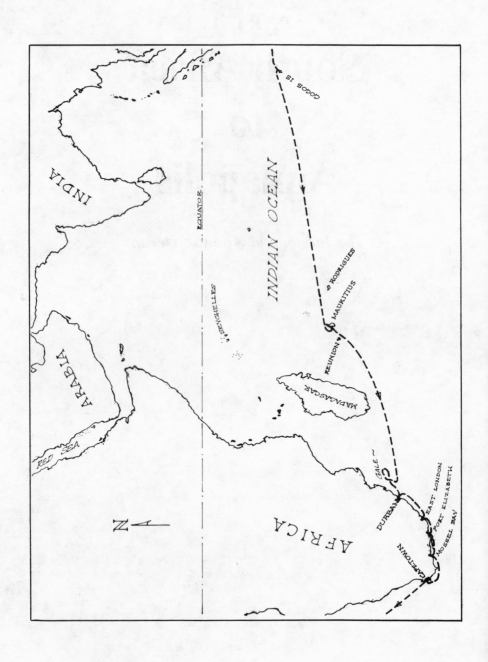

20

Across the Indian Ocean to South Africa

We were homeward bound! That was our general feeling as Bali faded away into the haze and approaching monsoon clouds off the starboard quarter. We'd passed the halfway mark of our voyage, as far as distance is concerned, when the strong trades drove *Starbound* around the top of Australia. But now we felt as if we were three-quarters through our great adventure. Only Indonesia and South Africa still lay ahead when we left Thursday Island—and now, so quickly, there was only South Africa left.

The delightful South Pacific was far behind us and we really weren't looking forward to the Indian Ocean, nor the South Atlantic. We knew the Indian Ocean could give us a rough trip because of its prevalent cross-swell. And the South Atlantic just looked like a lot of ocean to cross.

We couldn't dawdle any longer. Our time was running short and we didn't have much money left either. We had already decided to try to get back home in time for our country's Bicentennial celebration on July 4, 1976. Besides, we knew we should get around the Cape of Good Hope by the end of February to take advantage of the best weather the tip of South Africa can offer—a short-lived offer at best. And if we didn't get through the Caribbean area by the last of May, we might meet an early hurricane and have a bad time of it—no way to end a world cruise.

Our intention was to spend Christmas and New Year's Day in Durban. We had a lot of work to do on *Starbound* yet; her bottom had to be painted, and there were parts to buy which had not been available in Bali. Also, we wanted to see something of South Africa. With our limited funds we weren't sure how we were going to manage it but we had to try.

275

The four-day trip from Bali to Christmas Island was remarkable only for its constantly unsettled weather. Gray, gloomy days they were. At least the wind stayed generally behind us. We did our navigation through occasional holes in the cloud cover.

Starbound sailed into Flying Fish Bay at 1900 on October 7, just as the daylight faded completely. Two Australian sailors in a motor launch appeared out of the dark and hailed us, then led *Starbound* to a gigantic cylindrical buoy. They shackled our bow line to it and came aboard for a drink. The Aussies were from the *Diamontina,* a navy survey ship temporarily stationed at Christmas Island. They told us that we should go ashore in the morning to complete our entrance formalities, then shoved off for their ship. A huge swell was running, so the *Diamontina* was holding station off the harbor until the sea settled down. In fact, the harbor was closed to all large ships for the same reason.

With the gold-on-blue dawn we could see five ships out on the horizon, just waiting for the swell to subside so they could come in and pick up their loads of phosphate, the only export of Christmas Island.

Nice people, the Aussies, wherever they are. Nina and I were led through the entrance formalities with dispatch. It was a good thing, though, that we'd renewed our cholera shots in Bali. Our "shot cards" were the first items they wanted to check.

We went to the post office and mailed letters, then to the bank to change our last few American dollars to Australian. There was an honest-to-God supermarket in the tiny town, a real funhouse after being in Indonesia for so long. And the prices were low!

Our passports had been retained for a half day and we stopped by the police station to pick them up. The superintendent of police, Brian Schoobert, told us that we were the 175th yacht to sign the log in 1975. Not all of those yachts were cruising the world, of course. Many were Australian-owned boats going to, and coming from, Indonesia. Still, that's a lot of yachts. Brian mentioned that the number was increasing each year.

We stopped by the harbor master's office to see about getting fresh water on board and were told we'd have to wait for the swells to go down. Then we would pick up a small buoy which was moored about 100 yards off the head of the crane dock, a large concrete affair from which the big line-handling boats were put into the water and retrieved again when their job was complete. After we'd picked up the buoy, we were to carry a line to the dock head, pull our stern into a position near the dock, and span the water with a hose. Same old routine, except for a nearby coral reef which might make our position uncomfortable.

We spent the afternoon at the small, hospitable Christmas Island Boat Club doing our laundry in their washing machine and drinking the potent Aussie beer. When all our clothes were clean again we had the tough job of getting the launch off the rocky beach with the swell running like it was. There's no way to tie to the dock itself. The swell would smash a small boat up against the big steel pilings.

Next morning we were given a taste of the weather the Aussies at the club had warned us about. A squall came through about 0430 followed by more wind and swell from the north. Three-foot waves on top of the big swells carried right into the harbor. It was too rough to even go ashore. We battened down the ship, crawled into our bunks, and read the day away.

Next day was October 10, my forty-fifth birthday. The harbor was almost calm, so we unshackled *Starbound* from the big span buoy and nosed her around by the dock to pick up water. When we were in position and hooked up we flushed out our tanks to get rid of the last of Balinese water and filled them up with nice clean stuff. Now we could quit boiling all our drinking water. We were back on the big span buoy by 1000.

At 1230 we met Peter Barrett at the boat club. Peter is the geologist for the phosphate company and manager of the club. He'd offered to take us on a tour of the island in his Land Rover.

We bounced over bumpy dirt roads for miles. Millions of the small red crabs indigenous to the island were migrating to the sea for their annual mating ceremonies. We unavoidably crushed hundreds of them. Other vehicles had been doing the same for days and the odor of dead crabs rotting in the sun was almost visible. But the island was beautiful. Peter drove down a steep track through the jungle which ended at the southwest coast. The "beach" resembled a moonscape. The waves had undercut the whole coastline and there were hundreds of blowholes spraying salt water high into the air.

Back on the plateau again, the Land Rover carried us to one of the strip mines. We watched the scoops pick up loads of phosphate from between myriad limestone pinnacles and dump the stuff into trucks. We followed the trucks to the big plant on the high bluff above the harbor and saw the phosphate receive its simple processing, then be moved on a long conveyer to the storage area. Huge radial arm cranes swung out over ships berthed at the foot of the bluff and with more conveyers dumped the ore directly into the ship's holds. The ship that had come in that morning was filled with ore and was disappearing over the horizon before dark. Peter told us that the company could keep doing that for thirty-five more years before all of the top-grade phosphate was exhausted from the island's deposits.

We drove back to the boat club, stopping for our clearance papers at the shipping "clark's" office on the way. Then we checked out with Brian Schoobert and the harbor master, Bill Howell. We were ready to leave in the morning.

The evening was spent on board *Starbound* with Peter Barrett and American Charlie Burnett who was in the harbor with his trimaran *Typee*.

We ferried everyone ashore at 2100 and said good-by; we wanted to get away early.

At 0500 Ernie ran the launch over to the span buoy and let go our bow line. We hoisted the launch on board and motored out of the cove. The whole island looked still asleep.

With the square sail and raffee set we made good time all day. A rain squall would catch up and pass over us now and then, followed by fifteen minutes of light fluky air. Then our east wind would come back and *Starbound* would pick back up to 6 knots again. And so through the night.

We calculated we would raise Cocos Keeling in four days. We had wanted to arrive at daybreak, but instead we picked up the flash of the aerobeacon at 0200 Thursday morning, a few hours early. We'd averaged a little over 6 knots on the passage. And in spite of the mostly cloudy weather, our navigation was right on. We'd been shooting Canopus and Regulus in the mornings, the only two stars usually visible, then midmorning and afternoon sun lines, even though the sun usually appeared as a fuzzy ball. There was nothing to see at all in the evenings, as the clouds closed off every vestige of sky.

We hove to until daylight, not daring to approach the atoll in the dark, and listened closely for the sound of breakers. The current is strong near the Cocos Keeling group. It generally sets westward at about one knot. We stood a very tight watch.

At first light we could see the islands clearly, which meant, as low as the atoll is, that we were damn close. We started the diesel and powered for the pass into the lagoon. The pass lies between Direction Island and Howick Island, and it well behooves any boat unfamiliar with the water to make damn sure it's heading between the right two islands.

The weather was still cloudy and there were scattered rain showers all around. The transition from bouncing ocean waves to the smooth lagoon was as delightful as ever. One minute we were fighting the helm against the uneven motion of a mean cross-swell at the entrance to the pass, the next we were gliding across the placid waters of a lovely lagoon.

Ernie went aloft to guide us through the coral to the anchorage at Direction Island. It was beautiful and completely deserted. The island was thick with coconut palms and had a white sand beach rimming the lagoon side. It was truly the "desert island" of my childhood dreams.

Our chart showed some buoy symbols, supposedly for mooring aircraft, but no buoys were visible—none at all. A small concrete pier in good repair was the only sign of man's work. We anchored in 2 fathoms of water right off the pier, secured the engine and sat topside admiring the place.

Nina fixed breakfast, and by 0900 a big motor launch showed up and started working its way through the coral. It maneuvered alongside and George Kerr and Doctor John McCarthy came aboard, representing H. M.

Customs and Immigration, respectively. The tower on West Island had reported our arrival, so they'd come over to enter us. This was a standard procedure. Three Cocos Islanders were crewing the launch, so we invited them aboard too.

We were entered and cleared at the same time, so all we had to do when we wanted to leave was take up the anchor and shove off. Very handy.

We found out some interesting things about Cocos Keeling. It used to be that cruising yachts were given a big welcome at Home Island by the family owners of Cocos Keeling, the Clunies Rosses. Those days are long gone. Too many yachts are cruising nowadays and the Clunies Ross in current residence evidently feel that so many yachts constitute a severe ache in the derrière, which is probably true. So, all yachts are respectfully requested not to stop at Home Island.

Yachts can work their way through the reefs to West Island if they want, but it's a tricky passage for anyone not familiar with the water—and not very many yachties would be. West Island is where the Aussie government resides. The big drag about going to West Island is that the commissary there charges 150 percent duty on any purchase a yacht makes. The bite is to preclude the possibility of a series of visiting yachts cleaning out their stock before the next supply ship arrives. It's very effective; we decided we didn't need a damn thing. Besides, we had only $5 in the cash box until we got to Mauritius, our next stop.

Just as George and John finished with our papers and were saying good-by, a small sloop entered the pass and came sailing across the lagoon toward us. It turned out to be the Swiss yacht *Drakkor* with Alfred Sauser and Rolf Hubacher aboard. As soon as their anchor went down I ran over in the launch and brought them back to *Starbound* so they could go through their entrance formalities more easily. *Drakkor* was actually smaller than the government boat.

George and John told us a few more things. There was a big steel rainwater-collecting tank in the middle of Direction Island and we could take showers, wash clothes, and top off our tanks if we wanted to carry water jugs back and forth. Also, we could help ourselves to the coconuts. But we could not kill the chickens, of which there were about 200; they belonged to the natives on Home Island.

We asked about the weather, and George Kerr said he'd have the local radio station give us a forecast at about 1200 hours on 1400 kHz.

We said good-by and watched the government boat zigzag its way through the reefs back toward West Island. It was already past 1100, so we sat around the afterdeck and gassed with Alfred and Rolf while the Panasonic receiver sat on the house top tuned to the local station. At 1210 the announcer addressed *Starbound* and told us that the local weather was going to be just as we were getting it for the next few days, but that next day at 1630 hours the Cocos control tower would give an Indian Ocean area forecast on 2182 kHz.

We went ashore and played Robinson Crusoe. The water tank was there, a large, square steel job about 20 feet on a side and 10 feet high, located 100 yards from the beach just up from an old concrete marine railway ramp. We took baths, using the rubber hose attached near the bottom of the tank. There's a big concrete wash basin next to the hose connection, so next day was designated laundry day.

We picked some big green drinking nuts from the coconut trees, which were low enough to the ground to make it easy, then went back to *Starbound* feeling fine indeed. It was a restful anchorage, with unsurpassed natural beauty.

Next morning we did our laundry, taking turns rub-a-dubbing clothes on our small scrubboard. We hung them on clotheslines strung between main and mizzen shrouds to dry, then went back ashore to explore.

There is something very satisfying in tramping over a small, deserted coral island with a machete in hand, the sound of the wind and sea always present, our ship peacefully at anchor in the bay. We would always remember this place.

The promised weather forecast came through on time. The Cocos control tower told us that the weather was generally unsettled over the entire area because of the approaching monsoon. But the meteorologist explained that just 200 miles south of Cocos' latitude, clear weather was waiting for us. In any case the wind would generally hold southeasterly with occasional showers. Good enough! We decided to shove off in the morning.

Ernie, Rolf, and I spent the waning afternoon snorkeling on the reef. It's a very beautiful reef, but a lot of small sharks started getting entirely too nosy, so we didn't stay long. Rolf had done a lot of diving, all over the world, and he told us that many divers consider the smaller sharks more dangerous in many ways than the big ones. "They haven't grown up yet, and they're kind of dumb, so they're likely to take a bite just to see what you taste like."

We invited Rolf and Alfred to dinner. It was a good evening. We lounged around and listened to taped music, solved the problems of the world, and lubricated our vocal cords with the gin and tonic we'd acquired at Christmas Island.

In the morning Ernie and I made a last trip ashore for more drinking nuts. We also filled a few jugs with rainwater from the big tank to use in our batteries. The Christmas Island water in our tanks tasted good because it was full of minerals, but for the same reason it wasn't too good for the batteries.

The launch came on board and was lashed in place. We winched the anchor up, waved good-by to *Drakkor,* and were out of the pass by 1000.

Starbound rounded the north shoal and we put her onto her course of 253 degrees true for the great circle route to Mauritius.

Excerpts from the log.

20 October, Monday: Same old stuff! Two solid days of 10/10ths overcast. Everything is moldy! Rain squalls, winds 15 to 20 with gusts to 25 during squalls and no letup in sight. Still, can't bitch too much; the wind is still behind us. Grumpy doesn't hold course with the wind and sea combination. Ernie thinks the clutch is slipping but it's too wet to open up the lazarette and work on it. We steer all night, two on and four off. Lots of rain and waves slop on deck from nasty cross-seas.

22 October, Wednesday: Clearing at sunrise but it looks like more rain is on the way. We obtain a fix on Mars, Venus, and Canopus this morning which matches our deduced reckoning. This is our fourth day out at noon and we've averaged 150 miles per day. The wind switches to south by midday. We brace the yard hard up against the shrouds. It looks like the south wind is going to stick around. We brail up the square sail at 1700; a rough job! But a good thing because dark brings 25-knot winds with gusts to 35. We are being smacked with some very rough beam seas. We fix Grumpy's wiring and clean up the control circuit. It's good not to have to hold onto the wheel all night!

25 October, Saturday: Spend the morning watch, 0400 to 0700, working on the propeller shaft stuffing box and the condemned electric bilge pump. Am fast becoming a firm believer in manual bilge pumps; they don't fail just when they're needed most. Big waves slap the hull hard! We're still under jib and mizzen; wind gusts are reaching 25 to 30 in squalls, so we can't use the main, still we're making 6 knots with a solid beam reach. The sky is clear and sunny by 1030. What a relief! Our noon shots are good and the taffrail log reads 990. We should hit the halfway mark by tomorrow. Nina makes spaghetti for dinner and cookies for dessert; yummy!

26 October, Sunday: The damn bilge pump goes blooey this A.M. So much for "submersible" electric pumps. I set up the old prime-to-suction technique using the washdown pump. It works fine. It's turned into a beautiful day; sunny with beam trades. We put up the mainsail—finally. Our speed is up to 7 knots. Ernie and I work on Grumpy's clutch and fix it in about one hour. It's getting a big hazy by sunset, and cooler. The wind is backing a bit. No star shots again! The clouds won't cooperate.

31 October, Friday: Set the clocks back to the minus 4 time zone this morning. We have a 10/10 cloud cover again with more drizzle until 1100. Fuzzy noon sights put us far south of our rhumb line. We change course to 290 degrees magnetic and switch the rig to square sail and raffee. The new course will take us about 25 miles south of Rodrigues and on a line for Mauritius. The wind and sea are way down and we have very comfortable sailing. *Starbound* made 160 miles noon to noon this day! Lost our stainless

steel Charley Noble this morning; Damn! Colin Corbett made it for us
while we were in New Zealand and it was a beautiful piece of work. The jib
sheet caught under it and flipped it right over the side. We really feel bad
about that.

3 November, Monday: Another gorgeous day; our third in a row now.
We get a good fix at 0430. We're still a few miles south of our rhumb line,
probably due to the northeast current. We're sailing slower now and have
100 miles to go at 1700 today. Must crank up the mill if we want to get on
soundings north of Mauritius to take advantage of the west tide at noon.
The flow is about 4 knots and we don't want to fight it. We commence
"rock-crushing" at 1800 hours with the engine at 1,500 RPM. The sunset
looks squally and the wind is light and variable. Try to call Port Louis all
day with no luck. Got a fair fix from Jupiter and Achernar at 1830 which
puts us 90 miles off soundings. The wind is very light, so we douse the
square sail and raffee and make like a motor boat—one advantage of having
a big diesel and 300 gallons of fuel.

4 November, Tuesday: 35 miles to soundings. We can see clouds above
Mauritius but haze obscures the land. We sight Round Island at 1000 and
the mainland at 1100. We are on soundings at 1230 and the fair ebb tide
starts to carry us fast at 1330. We roar by Gunner's Quoin, turn left around
the northwest corner of the island, and admire the shoreline all the way
down to the entrance to Port Louis. We've crossed the Indian Ocean!

Port Louis is a deep, narrow harbor with ships moored in a fore and aft
line on either side of the main passage for nearly a mile. The town smelled
Indian, reminiscent of Suva. I could nearly taste the curry by sniffing the
harbor air.

We motored all the way into the harbor, just as far as we could go, and
turned right, around the stern of the last ship in line. A passage between the
ship and the shore led to a nice clear spot of water with a big rusty salvage
barge moored in the middle of it. We tied alongside the barge with all our
tire fenders hung out and secured snugly to her with two breast and two
spring lines.

A boatload of officials were alongside almost immediately. They were
friendly, efficient, and helpful. They cleared us within thirty minutes and
we liked Mauritius already. Dark was coming, so we stayed aboard and
went to bed early for a night's uninterrupted sleep.

In the morning Nina and I started the now routine circuit: post office,
telegraph office, bank, store, and vegetable market.

The post office delivered good news to us: a letter from our publisher
with the news that some money had been deposited to our bank account,
and a letter from my father with a money order for $500. Whee! We
declared a holiday—a Day of Solvency!

There was a telegram from Ray Kukulski asking if he could join us in Mauritius on November 15 for the trip to South Africa. We wired back a happy affirmative on the prepaid form. We hadn't planned to stay in Mauritius quite that long but we decided it would be a lot of fun to have "the hero of Papeete" with us again.

We changed our money order at the bank for American dollars, then walked back to the waterfront to find a money changer. A hole-in-the-wall shop right across the street from the post office gave us 6.40 rupiahs per dollar, a considerably better value than the official bank rate.

Nina and I prowled through the town and picked up a few goodies for an uncanned dinner. The main city market is a fascinating place. Almost every kind of vegetable and fruit is sold in stalls. Prices are more or less set, so bargaining isn't such a way of life as it is in Indonesia. Also, the market is much cleaner and more orderly. The prices were so low that we knew we'd be able to stock up the boat at low cost, at least as far as fresh foods were concerned. Canned goods are all imported and expensive, but we still had plenty aboard from our wholesale buys in Australia and New Zealand. Aboard *Starbound* we never open a can when fresh food is available.

At one end of the city market are the meat stores. Each type of meat has its own small shop, so the signs read in succession: Beef, Mutton, Pork, and Poultry and Eggs. A major pedestrian thoroughfare runs for two blocks right through the middle of the market and is the primary meeting place in town. A swarm of humanity mills about in all directions, speaking in several tongues. Everyone seems to be at least bilingual.

I took Nina back to *Starbound* with the groceries and with Ernie set out to find the drydock where we had been told several yachts were tied up. We met Eric Robinson on *Quetzal,* and Jim and Peggy Simpson aboard *Kalayanee.* Both boats were waiting to get into the drydock and in the meantime were doing what all yachties do—boat maintenance. We exchanged information and a few sea stories and arranged to meet later at the Merchant Seaman's Club, a very nice club indeed and a primary meeting place for yachties in Port Louis. We were told that a good drink could be obtained there for a fair price.

We had nine days to play with before Ray flew in to join us, so we became tourists for a while—in a yachtsman's kind of way; we took bus rides. Eric Robinson and I decided to check out the yacht club located in the small bay up on the northwest corner of the island. It is a beautiful bay and a nice little club, but very quiet. Three or four small yachts were moored out. There is a hotel there where we managed to buy a beer for an exorbitant price. The whole place seemed almost deserted—maybe it was the time of year. In any case, it was a half-hour bus ride to town, and town is where the action is, and the market, and the yachties.

Nina and I strolled all over town and found a good place to buy canned goods: the establishment of Lim Fat, located on Royal Street. They deliver to the quay and their prices are good. We also discovered M. C. Appavou and Company, who can supply duty-free liquor by the case and are located just two blocks from the post office.

Just 100 feet across the water from where *Starbound* was snuggled up to the big, steel salvage barge is a four-story brick building owned by Blythe Brothers. On the third floor I found Mr. Robert Huron, the Shell Oil Company representative, and arranged to take on fuel and water at their quay. Next day we moved *Starbound* all of 100 yards and pumped the fuel tanks full from a truck, topped off the water tanks, and moved back to the salvage barge.

Ray flew in on schedule and we spent three more days exploring Port Louis, one day at the beautiful Royal Botanical Gardens and one at the race track watching the last outing of the season.

Finally, on our last day at Mauritius, I took the bus alone to Vacoas, a small town on top of a mountain and talked to Her Majesty's meteorologists. The weather picture looked good. No typhoons were predicted and our winds would be fair for at least three days, perhaps more.

When the bus dropped me back in Port Louis, I walked directly to the port captain's office and cleared *Starbound* for South Africa. We would leave in the morning.

The Sailing Directions state that a yacht departing Mauritius and heading for Durban, South Africa, should sail out of Port Louis harbor and turn southwest. The course should be layed for a point in the ocean 100 nautical miles southeast of the most southeasterly point of Madagascar. From there a new course should be set directly for Durban. It must be remembered that the Agulhas current runs south through the Straits of Madagascar, sometimes achieving a maximum velocity of 5 knots. It is therefore wise to keep northing while crossing the straits. It's easy to fall off too far to the south, particularly for a sailing yacht, and very difficult to get back up north against the strong current.

The reason for crossing that watery point southeast of Madagascar is to avoid the nasty weather and possible countercurrents which that huge land mass can generate closer in to its coast.

Starbound hit that point right on the button at 1200 hours on November 24, 1975, six days out of Port Louis. We changed our course to 275 degrees magnetic and drove for the South African coast.

The sailing had been beautiful so far, mostly with a moderate southeast wind. But we were getting a little apprehensive. *Starbound* was well below the trade wind belt and the sky no longer contained those puffy little white ducks of clouds with flat bottoms. Instead we began to see stratus and cirrus, and the horizons looked greasy gray. Each night the wind started to lighten at dusk and would disappear completely by midnight. So we would start the diesel, not wanting to fool around in an area of unpredictable weather.

November 29 was another quiet, cloudy day until 1500 hours. Then a 15-knot wind sprang up from the northeast, a surprising direction. We set all fore and aft sail, but in spite of the 6 knots speed we made we were worried. Things didn't feel right. And we weren't sure if it was the wind from an unexpected quarter, or maybe because we were in the highest latitude we'd seen since leaving Annapolis, or maybe our sailor's sense telling us to watch out.

Excerpts from the log.

30 November, Sunday: The northeast wind drops off to nothing in the early hours, then comes back from the southwest. What the hell? The wind increases in strength all day long. We drop the mizzen at 0600, and the main by noon as 35-knot gusts start hitting us. The seas are lumpy. This day ends with the wind dropping somewhat to 18 knots from the south-southwest. Our 1900 fix puts us 20 miles north of our rhumb line, so we change course to 265 degrees.

1 December, Monday: Can we believe it? It's a lovely day under square rig. Clouds come back in with the evening. We dropped the raffee at 1400 and brail up the square sail at 1700 and put on the yankee. We start the diesel as lightning shows up off the bow at dark. The wind goes light and variable again and the lightning continues, but far off the bow.

2 December, Tuesday: We will be about 40 miles out of Durban by tonight. But in the early A.M. the wind switches from north to calm to south to southwest with showers. By 0245 we have a strong breeze and fall off to 030 magnetic to keep it comfortable. The seas are getting rough. By 0400 the southwest wind is up to 25 knots and the seas are very rough. I'm afraid we're in for it; this looks like one of those South African southwest "busters" which blows against the Agulhas current and puts up a very nasty sea. By 0700 the wind gusts are up to 35. The barometer is rising, which the Sailing Directions tell us is one indication of a southwester. It screams all day with sustained winds of 35 knots and gusts to 45, occasionally 55. The seas are big with square tops and a lot of water in them. We guess their height at 20 to 25 feet and that's being conservative. We sight the coast in the evening just before dark, thank God, and turn to the northeast and head back to sea with the wind and seas on our starboard quarter. We don't want to get too close in the dark. Now we know where we are, even though we can't make any headway against these seas. It is very rough and very cold.

3 December, Wednesday: We stay under bare poles with the engine running and heading mostly east northeast. We are quartering downwind and the troughs are canyons! We take a few big waves over the quarter.

One big one with heavy water in it curls over and drops tons on us—can't see the deck for many seconds, just water and foam. Good thing we have our safety harnesses on. Ray gets bounced into the mizzen mast and the weight of water hitting the dinghy puts enough stress on the davit's strongback to crack it along the grain. When morning comes we also find that the barrel of the binnacle is loose at the base. We are glad to see daylight. Some sun is out and the wind moderates by 1000 and allows us to turn to the west for the coast. The waves are still very big with a few breaking tops but only a little bit of slop comes aboard. As we approach the coast again the seas calm down. We are off Cape Saint Lucia according to our sights and the RDF. Nightfall brings a calm and a long swell from the south. We motor almost due southwest for Durban.

4 December, Thursday: A northeast wind comes up at daylight and blows 8 to 10. The sails are working again and helping us toward Durban. We sight land to starboard at first light and it sure looks good. The seas are smooth—thank God! Durban is sighted ahead at 1200. We crank up the diesel to hurry our arrival and try to raise Durban Harbor on the radio. No luck—we've got a hunch our transmitter is on the fritz. We motor into the harbor on a bright, sunny afternoon. A police launch intercepts us as soon as we are past the huge breakwater and signals us to follow them. We are most happy to do so.

21

The Dark Continent

It is obvious that there are two ways to take a yacht from the Indian Ocean to the Atlantic—other than heading back east. One way is the Red Sea–Suez Canal–Mediterranean route. The other way is to sail around the tip of South Africa. We would have loved to see the Mediterranean, but both our time and money were running low. If we were to go that way it would mean heavy fuel costs to get up the Red Sea and through Suez against prevailing winds and currents. That passage is not called the "thousand-mile blowtorch" for nothing. And once in the Med we wouldn't want to rush through. We'd like to visit the Greek Islands and the Yugoslavian coast which we'd heard is very beautiful. Next time around . . .

So South Africa lay before us. On the east coast there is the major city of Durban, the logical spot for a yacht to enter the continent now that the more northerly port of Mozambique's Lourenço Marques has been "liberated" from the Portuguese. We had been warned in Mauritius that we should not go there, because of the possibility of having our ship "nationalized." We were disappointed. The word was that it used to be a marvelous place for yachts, with a beautiful harbor.

We decided to stay in Durban through Christmas and New Year's Day, see as much as we could of the country, haul *Starbound* for a bottom scrub and paint job, then round Capes Agulhas and Good Hope. We would make a short stop at Capetown and get on our way back to the Caribbean with one stop at Saint Helena Island.

The entrance procedures are quite formal. The Durban harbor police launch which met us as we came through the breakwater escorted us to a nearby anchorage and asked us to stay there until they returned with the health authority to see us. They were back in less than an hour. The doctor examined us, the ship, and our papers, told us to haul down our Q flag, and turned us over to a harbor pilot who was by then standing by. The pilot had us raise our anchor and directed us to Mayden Wharf, about 2 miles into the harbor.

About an hour after we tied up, the customs and immigration people dropped in and proceeded to really check us out. We filled out about a dozen forms. Everyone was quite formal, but friendly.

We asked them about facilities at the Point Yacht Club, "the" yacht club in Durban where yachties can go with their boats. They told us we'd have to make our own arrangements and that as a first step we should telephone the harbor master.

We found out that the harbor master was at the yacht club for the day, so we walked along the waterfront walkway for about half a mile and found the club. We also found that space for boats was at a premium. For such a prestigious club the yacht accommodations are atrocious! A large breakwater projects far out into the bay to partly enclose the club's mooring area, which has an overly large share of sand bars and shoal spots. All boats are on fore and aft moorings, except those at the small and rather dilapidated "transient yachts" dock located on the opposite side of a large, concrete launching ramp from the club house. A second rickety dock on the far side of the club had a few small yachts tied up along one side and we could see the boats were already aground at only half tide. We wondered why the club didn't dredge out the whole place.

The transient dock was for yachties and there were a lot of them there: three rows of boats tied three abreast. We met several friends—Wayne and Carol Roberts on *Landfall*, Tony and Mary Brown on *Mystico,* and Al and Helene Gehrman on *Myonie.* We quickly made some new friends among the other yachtsmen tied up there, too. We were filled in on the Point Yacht Club drill. The club itself, we were told, is a fine place with a good dining room and an excellent men's bar. The officers and members of the club were very nice indeed and often went out of their way to help the cruising yachts in any way they could. However, the club secretary obviously disliked yachties and was not very friendly.

"You'll have to check in with him," someone else said, "then avoid him. Go see Bob Fraser—he's the club's liaison officer for the cruising boats and he's a real gentleman."

Everything was as advertised. We were happy to finish with the accurately described secretary, and really happy to make the acquaintance of Bob Fraser. Bob told us we'd have to stay at Mayden Wharf for a week at least. The transient dock was too crowded to put a boat as large as *Starbound* into it. The dockmaster would try to find a mooring for us but it would probably be out beyond the end of the breakwater.

The Capetown-to-Rio yacht race is the big event for South African yachtsmen and was about to get under way. Racing boats were shoving off to Capetown daily—although they weren't leaving any vacant berths at the club. The boats still in Durban were mostly foreign entries, including several American boats. Many of them were tied up near us at Mayden Wharf, including the famous *Ondine,* and *Sirocco,* notorious for once having belonged to Errol Flynn.

We had a good time at Mayden Wharf. Many of the South African yachts entered in the race were not really "racing" yachts, but cruisers. There is a reason for this; evidently South Africans are taxed heavily on the purchase of a boat. But if the boat enters in, and completes, the Capetown to Rio race, the tax bite is either partly or fully relieved.

Because there were several of these cruiser/racers near us we became good friends with a number of very nice people, like Charles Paice and his daughter Dianne, and Terry Ellis, a well-known photographer from Johannesburg, and his charming wife, Heather. We met Dan Wood, an American who was working for an organization called Guide Dogs for the Blind. Through Dan we met Katie Hawks, also American, who had been in Africa several years and was teaching at the Indian University in Durban.

We discussed our plans for touring South Africa and Rhodesia with Dan and Katie, with the result that Dan offered to let us use his Volkswagen "Kombi" van to make the trip, while he sailed from Durban to Capetown on the yacht *Camrita.* Meanwhile Katie was talked into coming along with us as guide.

The next week was spent working with the people at Point Yacht Club trying to obtain a mooring there for *Starbound.* We finally got permission to move her to the club on Saturday, December 13, just two days before we were to start our trip into the interior. We had to put her on four anchors, one of which I had to borrow from the club, well out beyond the big jetty and the protection it afforded. We snugged her into place solidly. Then we arranged with young John Brown from *Mystico,* Tony and Mary's son, to check her every day while we were gone.

Foreign visitors to Durban are not allowed to leave the vicinity of the city without permission from immigration. That was a task I had successfully taken care of the week before. So when Monday morning came we were ready to go, except that the dockmaster wanted me to come in and see him. I did, and to my surprise was charged a 30 rand deposit on the mooring, plus a 10 rand per month fee (payable in advance), and was notified that this was all on a thirty-day "probationary." I was also told that we were subject to move our boat within twenty-four hours upon notification. I paid the money, got a receipt, and left.

Five of us and our gear made a tight fit in Katie's little Japanese compact but we made it to Johannesburg O.K. and there picked up Dan's Kombi and headed for Rhodesia.

We had some trouble at the border because we did not have "multiple reentry" visas, but the problem was resolved and we were allowed through with the proviso that we come back through the border at the same place. We happily agreed.

We drove to Bulawayo, camped for the night in the prettiest camping ground any of us had ever seen, and in the morning continued north to impressive Victoria Falls. We camped near them for the night, took another look in the morning, and headed back south for Wankie Game Park.

That night while sleeping in our small nylon tent, Ernie and Ray were awakened by some hungry hyenas who tried to get in but gave up and ate a bar of soap instead. The signs posted around camp said to beware of hyenas—they will eat anything.

We spent the next day driving through the park taking picture after picture of wild animals who came quite close to the van. And if we were quiet and didn't move suddenly, they would go about their business while keeping a wary eye on us.

We headed for the border again and camped once more in Bulawayo. Next morning we were up early and on the road by 0800. Just before we reached the border we ran into a military checkpoint and got the once-over from a polite lieutenant who then waved us on around the barrier. There were a lot of soldiers standing by, dressed in multicolored jungle garb. They all carried automatic weapons.

We crossed back into South Africa and headed for Kruger National Game Park. We camped at the grounds near the town of Tzaneen and were entertained all night by a spectacular lightning storm. It rained a lot, causing some damage to the roads.

Next morning we passed through the Phalaborwa gates into Kruger Park, paid our fee of 9 rand, and were on our way. We spent three days and two nights in Kruger and loved it. It was a marvelous experience and we wished we could stay longer.

The climax came on our last day as we were on the road leading out of the park. We'd already seen nearly every animal we'd wanted to see, including elephants. But we hadn't seen a single lion. The rains had been so good lately that the animals were everywhere instead of congregating around the waterholes. That meant the lions were all back in the bush, instead of at the waterholes where we could see them. We came around a curve in the road and there was a huge lioness sitting right in the middle. We stopped, then slowly rolled the Kombi toward her until we were about 50 feet away. She just sat there and looked at us and we looked back at her, our cameras clicking. Then she yawned, got to her feet, and strolled off into the brush. She gave us a very impressive good-by to Kruger National Park.

We left the park about noon on the day before Christmas, and drove fast for Johannesburg, arriving there about 1930—and found that we couldn't get into Dan's apartment, where we'd planned to spend Christmas Eve. There was some kind of mixup and the apartment manager hadn't received word from Dan that we were to be let into the place, and he wasn't going to let us in, and that was bloody that. Our arguments and persuasions were of no avail.

We remembered that Terry and Heather Ellis lived somewhere in Johannesburg. I called Terry, explained the situation, and asked if we could camp in his yard for the night. He was delighted that we'd called. So our Christmas Eve was spent in a lovely warm living room in the company of good friends, singing Christmas carols.

We awoke in the morning to the sound of Terry and Heather's small children opening presents which had been left by "Father Christmas." Terry and Heather insisted we spend Christmas Day with them. It was only after we'd accepted that we were told the invitation included a drive out to Neil and Lilian Passet's country home for a dinner party. What gracious hospitality; we were welcomed like old friends. We swam in the big pool, played cricket on the lawn, and ate a delicious buffet supper.

We returned to Terry and Heather's for a quiet evening. In the morning Ray, Katie, and I drove the van across town and exchanged it for Katie's car. We loaded the compact back up, shoehorned ourselves in, said farewell to Terry and Heather, and headed back over the mountains for Durban.

We arrived back at the Point Yacht Club at 1700. A light drizzle was falling and our friends told us that it had rained every day since we'd left. *Starbound* was a mess. With all the weather she'd become very damp inside. In fact, she smelled like a swamp and was cold and clammy. I fired up the M.G., turned on the heating system, then helped Nina put away all the gear we'd carried. What we needed was a few warm days to dry out the entire belowdecks area.

In the morning we took a hard look around. *Starbound* was definitely not in the same position in which we'd left her. Then we discovered why; the port stern anchor line had been cut, obviously by the propeller of a boat that must have passed very close to her stern. Since it must have been a powerful engine in that boat for her prop to whack its way through a one-inch diameter line, we suspected the harbor tour boat, which insisted on roaring past our stern at a speed which effected a maximum wake.

It was time to start putting *Starbound* in shape for her Atlantic crossing. Originally it had been my plan to get some kind of a job in Durban and make a few bucks, but that was out now. To get a working permit in South Africa is about a four-month procedure and the law is very strict about it; no permit, no work. So we counted our few remaining dollars, then called the States and arranged to borrow enough money to see us through.

We were in the throes of making a major decision. When we started our trip we had planned to finish it in Honolulu, Hawaii, where I thought to work in Pearl Harbor Naval Shipyard. I had spent part of my childhood in Hawaii, two years more as a young man in the Navy, and two more years, with Nina and Ernie along too, working at Pearl Harbor as a naval architect. So we had thought to go back—now we were reconsidering. We planned to keep living aboard *Starbound* and we had heard from friends in the islands that the powers-that-be were trying to discourage boat owners from doing that. Also, after having traveled most of the way around the world at this point, we were beginning to realize that the Chesapeake Bay area of the United States has to be one of the few great places in the world where we could live in the life style to which we had become accustomed. We really missed the bay and now decided we would return to Annapolis.

We began scheduling. The Capetown-to-Rio race was to start on the 10th of January. The later we arrived in Capetown after that, the better. We'd heard that the huge influx of boats into the town had depleted the stores, boat supplies, and patience of the place. We thought it might be a good idea to let Capetown get partway back to normal before we blew in. It was decided to get away from Durban about the 10th of February, a good time to round Cape Agulhas according to the local yachtsmen. Then we'd have time to make the 850 miles at our leisure, avoiding the bad weather we might hit if we pushed it, and still be able to see a bit of Capetown before heading across the South Atlantic on about the 10th of March.

So the start of a major work period was initiated. To put it briefly, we checked out the entire boat. Once again Nina had charge of the storekeeping as well as doing most of my typing for me. Ernie went to work on the electronics and the rigging. I worked on the engines, both main and motor generator, and the other machinery. The anchor winch, drain pump, and main seawater strainers all needed work. I put in a new bilge pump, a manual job which wouldn't clog and would take all the water out of the bilge, not just part of it. The outboard motor needed an overhaul and I took care of that too. Parts by the dozen had to be found and bought and that was also my bailiwick. The pocket notebooks started getting filled up again.

Ernie and I dropped the square yard to the deck, sanded and painted all 40 feet of it, and refastened the hanger and swivel bails over lead liners so the yard would no longer have a tendency to rotate.

It wasn't all slavery. We had time to socialize in the evenings. We met many more people too. The South Africans were really helpful when I had to run down parts. Erwin Gebbers was one of those rare guys who knew where all the secret storehouses in town were. He was outfitting his new ferro-cement ketch for a world cruise while we were there. He lived right across the street from the yacht club in a very nice apartment, and his new boat was still in its building cradle just a few blocks down the street, so we saw a lot of him and his wife, Joan. Basil George gave us a lot of help too. Just a young guy, he had bought an older boat and was putting her in shape to go deep water. Basil's father-in-law was a real radio bug. He fixed our "ship to shore," then came down to *Starbound* and tuned it for us.

I made arrangements for *Starbound* to be hauled on the government slipway on February 4. They do none of the work at all; they only haul out the yacht and walk away. A waterhose is available and that's about all. We had to locate, then borrow or buy, scrapers, steel brushes with long handles, pans and paint rollers, and, most important, 5 gallons of bottom paint. The advantage of all this is, of course, price. The charge for the government slipway is 20 rand for the first day and 10 rand for each succeeding day. Advance payment must be made, so I arranged for a three-day affair and paid out 40 rand. I wish I could find an arrangement like that in the United States. The first step in hauling a boat in the Chesapeake is to find a cosigner for a bank loan.

Dan Wood came down from Johannesburg to see us and tell us all about the terrible trip he'd had from Durban to Capetown aboard *Camrita*. They'd been caught out in several bad blows. The yacht had lost a lot of gear and, worst of all, several crew members had been injured. We asked Dan if he'd like to see how a yachtie does it and go with us to Capetown. He must be a glutton for punishment because he accepted enthusiastically. He said he was thinking of going back to the U.S. anyway, so he would quit his job, make the trip with us, then close out his apartment in Jo'burg and head for North Africa to see some of the country before flying home. We agreed that he could join us on the 8th or 9th of February.

Our haul job was shorter than planned. We came out of the water at 1630 on the 4th, had the bottom clean by 2100, working with floodlights, and dropped into our bunks exhausted. Next morning I worked on the rudder while Nina and Ernie sanded and repainted the transom and quarters which are hard to do from the water. I managed to take the play out of the rudder which had been caused by a loose key in the upper coupling flange. By the time that was finished Ernie had half the bottom painted with the first coat. While I was helping him finish, the director of the facility came down and asked us if we might be ready to go in early the next day. He had a trawler with troubles which had to come out as soon as possible. We didn't see any reason why not. We got up next morning at 0400 and started to put the second coat on the bottom as soon as it was light enough to see. We slid back into the water at 0800 and were back at Mayden Wharf by 0900.

We liked Mayden Wharf better than being out on a mooring. It made it very handy for supplying the boat. Of course, the wharf is primarily for the fishing trawlers, and yachts are only there on sufferance. The fishermen, as always, were friendly. They gave us a lot of good advice concerning the route to Capetown, and they also loaded us up with goodies from the holds of their refrigerated ships, goodies like prawns and lobster tails.

Dan Wood joined us on the morning of the 9th. We figured to be out of the harbor on the morning of the 13th. A dozen last-minute jobs were taken care of each day and the evenings were spent with old, and new, friends—drinking and talking.

On the 11th the weather report looked good, so I started our clearance procedure. It's a good thing I started early. It took two full days to complete and must have been the most complicated wheel-spinning drill I'd ever had to go through. The Indonesians and French were models of simplicity by comparison. There's no use my going into detail about it; the procedure changes from year to year, but never gets any simpler.

The morning of the 13th dawned clear and quiet. A last-minute check with the weather boys told us that northeast winds would commence to blow later on in the day, so it was the perfect time to get out of Durban Harbor. A yacht must motor out almost directly to the northeast, then turn east when the bar is cleared and work out to about 2 miles off shore, turn to the southeast until the boat is in the flow of the Agulhas current, and finally change course to the southwest heading for East London. A strong northeaster makes it difficult for a yacht, with its relatively small power plant, to get across the bar of Durban Harbor. We started the diesel, took our lines aboard, and shoved off. A radio check with Port Control gave us clearance to proceed out of the harbor mouth, so we told them thanks and good-by, and advanced the engine revs to 1800.

The local yachtsmen had told us there was no way to round the tip of South Africa from Durban to Capetown without getting clobbered at least once by adverse weather. We were determined to be the first yacht to make the 850-mile trip without trouble of that kind.

Our sailing plan was to leave on the aforementioned northeasterly wind and run fast for East London, some 265 miles to the southwest, dive into port before a southwesterly could nail us, then sit tight and wait for the next northeasterly. Since the fair northeasterlies lasted only twenty-four to forty-eight hours and the foul southwesterlies blew for about the same length of time, we figured we could outsmart them.

After East London there was Port Elizabeth about 135 miles further along to the southwest. Then we'd turn almost due west for Mossel Bay and hop another 200 miles. After that there was really no place in which to duck. The last 255-mile leg from Mossel Bay to Capetown had to be timed to perfection. We'd have to round Cape Agulhas, the southernmost tip of the continent, then the Cape of Good Hope, and turn due north for the last 40 miles to the safe refuge of Table Bay. There is a big, beautiful bay called False Bay between Cape Hangklip and Cape Point, which looks like a good place to stop, and in an emergency I guess the phrase "any port in a storm" might be apt. But it's a shallow bay and a long way in before any shelter could be found, and a long way out again too. The worst thing about it is that it is wide open to any southerlies, the worst blows on the southern coast, and the chances of being embayed for quite a while are good.

Well, we made it! And we did it just as we'd planned—almost. We did encounter a few small difficulties.

First, a study of the charts and the notes appended thereon are enough to scare hell out of a sailor. Anyway, they scared hell out of us. Here is one of them:

CAUTIONS
1. Ships should maintain a safe distance off the coast owing to the possibility of sandbanks at river mouths having shifted or extended seaward.
2. Freak waves of up to 65 feet in height, preceded by a deep trough, may be encountered in the area between the edge of the continental shelf and 20 miles to seaward thereof. These can occur when a strong southwesterly is blowing, the sea is rough, and the barometric pressure is low.

And here is another:

CAUTION
Strong currents, whose influence may extend to 20 miles seaward, have been experienced along this coast setting directly onshore for no apparent cause. Great caution, therefore, should be exercised while navigating in this vicinity.

A yacht should play the Agulhas current for all it's worth, which is a lot. A good place to be is right on its edge all the way to East London and then to Port Elizabeth. That current can run 5 knots and, the fishermen told us, sometimes faster. *Starbound* made the 265-mile trip to East London in thirty-six hours, and then the 135-mile jump to Port Elizabeth in twenty hours. That means we averaged 7.2 knots, and that is moving right along. At one point Ernie and I took careful bearings on points ashore and clocked our speed at 10 knots for over three hours. We thought we'd made a mistake! The whole point is that the current must be used to get into port before the boat is slapped with an adverse wind running against that same current. We just made it in each case.

The edge of the current is easy to find. The water color turns from pea green to a pretty blue, as if it were painted on the sea. After we hit the blue we sailed *Starbound* a half-mile more into it, then followed the color southwest. If a yacht moves in too far toward shore and gets into the pea-green water, not only will the fair current be lost, but in many places a countercurrent will run, sometimes up to 2 knots. We kept *Starbound* in the blue until we had to slant off into port.

Every port in South Africa must be formally entered and cleared.

Clearance papers from the last port must be presented at the next, along with passports, visas, inoculation certificates, and anything else they ask for. It is an idiotic procedure but it's the law. Also, before entering each port, a yacht is required to contact the harbor authority by radio and get permission to enter. The entrance channels are narrow and a ship might be coming out or a dredge might be working and partially blocking the channel. Yachts without radios have a problem. We made our contacts on 2182 kHz, but VHF-FM would have been more handy. That is primarily what all the ports monitor.

Coming up to East London we began seeing a lot of cirrus and the barometer started to drop. We radioed the port and they forecast southwest winds at 20 knots. We fired up the diesel, put on all possible speed, and rolled in between the jetties at 2000 hours. We heard cheering from the north jetty as we rolled by it in the dark but put it down to some fishermen full of antifreeze. We motored up the Buffalo River for over a mile until we came to a fixed bridge, then tied up to an old wooden barge on the north bank. We were still adjusting the spring lines when a car pulled up and a nice gentleman from the East London Yacht Club called to us. He was a delegation of one sent by the other members to bring us to the club for a drink before closing time, and we should bring our towels and have a hot shower too. They had a very bouncy little club. It was the club members we had heard on the jetty, "just cheering in another boat ahead of the weather."

We stayed in East London through the next day and left for Port Elizabeth at 0800 on February 16 with a new northeasterly blowing. We entered Port Elizabeth at 0400 next morning just as the wind switched again. A dredge was working the entrance, so the harbor people sent out a small launch to lead us in. They directed us to the "fish jetty" and once again I was happy we'd kept the four old tires on the foredeck to use as fenders.

Now the southwesterly began to howl. We lay in Port Elizabeth for seven days. Dan Wood decided that we were going to get to Capetown too late for him, so after three days of weather watching he packed up his gear and caught a bus to Johannesburg, with a promise to visit us at Annapolis after we returned home.

The small yacht club at "P.E." is hospitable, with a nice little bar on a veranda overlooking the mooring area. The members filled us in on the town and suggested some sightseeing. We watched dolphin being trained at the sea aquarium. We visited the snake park and museum and we strolled through Happy Valley Park. Mostly we worked on *Starbound*, read books, and wrote.

An interesting trimaran named *Triad* had just been launched and was being outfitted just down the dock from us. I am personally not too fond of multihulls as cruising boats, but this one was a beauty. She was of cold-molded wood construction and put together with painstaking care. I've never seen better woodwork. The kids who built her were Ron Koopman, Roger Wood, Juliet Wood, Lynette Van Cittert, and Rupert Exton. We spent quite a few hours talking with them after the day's work was done. We could tell them something about the places we'd been but we couldn't tell them much about boats. South Africans grow up knowing the sea and ships.

A beautiful racing boat called *Golden Fleece* arrived from the west one day and tied up outboard of us for a few hours. We met Gordon Neil, her owner, who had flown to Port Elizabeth and was taking her back up to Durban. He had about enough time to admire *Starbound,* check the weather, and shove off. He told us that the westerly was going to keep up for a few more days and he would take advantage of it by staying close in to the coast and out of the mainstream of the current. I'm sure he would make Durban in record time. Anybody who can race a yacht off the South African coast is bound to be a fine seaman.

We finally had a respite on the 24th and lost no time in clearing port for Mossel Bay. It was a short-lived northeasterly. The wind fell light on the night of the 25th and we ended up powering in against a very light westerly, arriving in the small port at 1500 on the 26th. Visibility the night before had been terrible, with a lot of ship traffic coming against us, sometimes passing on either side of us at the same time. It was a bit nerve-racking. We turned on the sealed-beam spreader lights a few times just to make sure that we were visible.

Mossel Bay was a charming little town with an economy based primarily on fishing. We understood that it used to be a "hot" mining town in the old days and that some effort was being made to revive that industry. We enjoyed ourselves for a few days, constantly checking with the meteorologists in Port Elizabeth by telephone and listening to each report on the radio.

Finally on the 29th of February the Port Elizabeth boys told me that we had a good system coming up: about twenty-four hours of easterly wind, followed by a light, short-lived westerly, then some more easterly wind of dubious duration. After that they weren't sure what was going to happen.

We got under way at 1100, cleared Cape Saint Blaize under power, put on the square sail and raffee, and flew westward. On the 0100 to 0400 watch we sighted six ships; a very busy place! We ran into intermittent fog patches all night long. And then in the morning, off Cape Agulhas and just west of the Alphard Bank, the westerly wind came in at 20 to 25 knots. It had turned into a beautiful day with a clear blue sky and just a few cirrus clouds, but it was cold. And the waves grew very quickly until there were white caps on every one. It wasn't really bad, except that the wind was dead against us. We'd already secured the square rig, so now we put on the mizzen alone and hove to. *Starbound* liked it just fine and forereached quietly and without any fuss. When we got in too close to the coast for comfort, we put her on the other tack, and to try to make up a little ground we raised the jib and started the engine. In gear at 1,000 RPM and with the yankee strapped in tight, she started to make a little headway to the west, at the same time slipping off to the south and getting some offing for us.

By 2000 the wind had dropped to almost nothing and we were motoring due west with everything strapped in tight. At 2200 we dropped all sail since we were in a glass-flat calm. The swells were long and greasy and we were sliding through the water at 6 knots, 1,800 revolutions showing on the tachometer.

The 20th meridian went under our keel at 2300 and we found ourselves back in the Atlantic Ocean. Vast milky patches in the water gave us a fright when we first saw them. The boat going toward the back of a swell gave the optical illusion of *Starbound* driving right into a sandbank! Then we saw the shrimp boats coming out of False Bay and guessed what the milky patches were.

Rain and wind drove in from the south just as we had Cape Point light abeam. We carried on due west in zero visibility for two more hours to make sure we were well off the coast, then with great relief hung a right-hand turn and ran off before the mess.

Daylight illuminated a scene that should have been called "the birth of a continent." Squalls were all around us with a stroke of lightning here and there to keep things interesting. Fog roiled and swirled on the surface of huge gray waves. We could see the sky through clouds which ranged in color from purple to black, and once in a while we spied a chunk of rocky coast way off on the starboard beam. For comic relief there were seals in twos and threes popping up out of the water quite close to *Starbound,* wondering, we guessed, if they should play or run.

It was March 4, 1976. By 1130 we were out of the rain as if we'd shoved our way past a curtain. A bright blue sky was above us and Capetown sparkled in the sunlight well ahead off the starboard bow. We rounded Green Point at 1300 and headed across Table Bay. Table Mountain was very dramatic with a full cloud cover draped over it. That cloud cover is called the "Tablecloth" and usually heralds the arrival of a screaming southeaster, but it seemed relatively peaceful—until we started the approach to the inner harbor, and suddenly caught the full force of the wind coming around the eastern side of Table Mountain. It was blowing a full 40 knots!

We dumped the jib, which was still up, and tied it into the bow basket. I shoved the throttle up to 2,000 RPM, which is about as hard as we ever push the diesel, and worked our way up to the big jetties. A radio check with the harbor authority gave us clearance to come in, right after a departing ship cleared the jetties. There was no problem; we were only making about 2 knots against that wind.

A small tug came out to lead us to the yacht basin. We thought that was very nice of them. It was tight quarters in the yacht basin, though. In fact, when the tug yelled for us to tie up to the fuel dock, then pulled away and headed back, we couldn't see where the hell he was talking about until we made a quick study of our surroundings. And when I saw the "fuel dock" I nearly flipped. The dock itself was only about 20 feet long. It was an extremely tight spot. In fact, the only good thing about it was that the wind was blowing directly off the dock. If I made a bad approach, all I had to do was stop the ship dead in the water and let her blow off. I rammed her in full ahead, put the helm down hard to the left and went full reverse and layed her in perfectly. Ten sets of willing hands took our lines and socked them over pilings. Nina and Ernie took up the slack and there we were in Capetown, safe and sound, very happy to be there. We got a big hello from a bunch of friends. Colin Usmar was first aboard. This was his home port. He'd brought *White Horse of Kent* all the way around the world with no engine, and now he was equipping her to go again. Frankie and Jeff Clarkson from *Pilecap* helped with our lines too. It was like old times. I walked down the fuel dock and turned around to check how *Starbound* was situated. Her bowsprit overhung the deck of a small sailboat by 5 feet. Her transom planking cleared the club's launch by one foot.

The club secretary came down the dock to welcome us. We were only 50 feet from the front veranda of the Royal Cape Yacht Club and this was their fuel dock. It was rather obvious that we'd have to move *Starbound,* but the secretary told us not to worry about it until the southeaster blew itself out. If anybody just had to have fuel they could tie up to us and take the hose across our deck. Very nice people. A lot more casual than the club in Durban.

Customs and immigration had already been informed that we'd arrived and they were on their way over. While we were waiting for them I went into the clubhouse, found the offices upstairs, and filled in an arrival form. By the time I got back to *Starbound* the government men had arrived, so we got the paperwork out of the way very quickly. However, we were told that when it came time to clear, it was going to be the same old hassle. That meant I'd have to run all over town from office to office filling out all the same forms that a full-sized ship was charged with. We couldn't understand why they didn't simplify the procedures for yachts.

There was a satisfying stack of mail waiting for us at the Royal Cape Yacht Club, mostly letters from family and friends. And there was an intriguing note: "Welcome to Capetown. Don't fail to let me know if I can

do anything for you. I will be down to say hello within the next day or so."
It was signed Denzil Penny. Who in hell was Denzil Penny, we wondered?
We looked through our guest book, but the name didn't appear.

Next morning the wind had eased considerably, so the dockmaster
moved a few boats around at the club's floating docks and organized a
space for *Starbound*. We took on diesel fuel before we left the fuel dock, let
go our lines, and allowed *Starbound* to blow clear of the dock. We motored
in a big circle around the moored boats and finally nosed her in between
two big wooden pontoons, a secure berth for our stay. The bowsprit
projected over the afterdeck of the yacht in front of us, but we adjusted our
spring lines so that we wouldn't ride up on her. As a last "security" line, we
carried the anchor rode to the sea wall in front of the dock area and
shackled it to a big steel ringbolt. It would serve to take the strain when
another southeaster came along.

The shopping area of Capetown is about 2 miles from the yacht club.
Nina caught a ride in with one of the club members to do some shopping,
and I sat down at my desk to answer some of the more important mail.

An hour later I answered a knock on the hull and said hello to a tall,
well-dressed gentleman standing on the pontoon beside *Starbound*.

"Hello there," he said, "I'm Denzil Penny."

"I'm glad to meet you," I smiled. "We received your note but we can't
figure out who you are."

He laughed. "I thought you'd say that! I'm a friend of friends of yours
from Annapolis, Dan and Babs Bellinger. They were visiting here just a few
months ago and told me to be sure to look in on you when you came to
Capetown. Now, is there anything I can do for you? Do you need anything,
or to go anywhere?"

That was the start of a fine friendship. Denzil and his charming wife,
Jane, took us under their wing and made our visit to Capetown a
memorable experience. Denzil had just finished building a beautiful
cruising ketch which was to be launched in a few weeks, so we had much in
common. We spent a highly enjoyable day at their beautiful home, and
another touring the spectacular Cape area with them.

Our eleven days in Capetown went by too quickly. Charles Paice, whom
we had met in Durban, dropped down to the club and coaxed us away from
our work for a relaxing day at his home.

If it hadn't been for these gracious South African friends we wouldn't
really have seen much of the Cape area. They were excellent hosts and we
were very grateful to them for their kindnesses.

A few days after our arrival in Capetown a young Frenchman named
Michel Santander came to *Starbound* to see if we needed an extra crew
member to Martinique. Michel is a tall, personable guy with black, curly
hair and green eyes. He also has a lot of sailing experience, but we didn't

really feel that we needed an extra person along. He turned up every day, though, and asked if he could help me with the work on *Starbound.* I explained to Michel that for what I would charge him to come with us, he could probably fly to Martinique on a plane. But Michel said in his French-accented English, "But I do not want to fly! It is a terrible way to travel! I have gone everywhere in the world by sailboat and I would very much like to come with you to Martinique. I will pay my way with pleasure!"

I think Denzil Penny changed our minds about taking Michel with us. Denzil showed up one day while Michel was there and greeted him like an old friend. He knew Michel well, had sailed with him, and told me that he was a fine sailor and a good man to have on board any boat.

Nina and I reevaluated our thinking. We decided it would be nice to have four people on board to ease the watch-standing burden. Ernie brought up a good point too. He said, "It sure would be great to have an extra man—we could play cards again!" Michel played a good game of chess, too—one of Ernie's favorite pastimes. They had a board set up within an hour of meeting each other.

So our South African adventure was nearly over. We planned to leave on March 15, just two days away. I started the lengthy clearance procedure with Denzil's invaluable help. Even with my being driven around to the various offices in a luxurious Mercedes-Benz, the clearance procedure took two days to complete.

22

Home Are the Sailors

There is a lot of Atlantic Ocean to cross from Capetown to Martinique—around 5,200 nautical miles of it. Saint Helena Island is on the way, about one-third of that distance from Capetown. Ascension Island is out there too, about 700 miles northwest of Saint Helena. But that's about all—unless a yacht wants to go to Rio, then fight its way up around the hump of Brazil against prevailing wind and current.

Actually, our route was dictated by our remaining time and money. Of money we had none until we reached Martinique, where we were to meet our good friends Lyn and Dave Westergard. Of time: we wanted to be in the United States by July 4, just 110 days away. Assuming fifty days to cover the sea miles to the West Indies, we were left with only two months to hop up through the Leewards, the Virgins, and the Bahamas. We planned to touch Florida at West Palm Beach, a handy spot for fuel and water, then sail north with the Gulf Stream directly for Morehead City, North Carolina, and take the Inland Waterway to the Chesapeake Bay.

Our departure from Capetown was complicated by the first injury of our cruise. Ernie chopped a quarter-inch off the end of the middle finger of his right hand. He managed this painful accident by leaning one hand against the master stateroom door jamb and slamming the close-fitting door with the other. The small bone protrusion on the tip of the finger was splintered.

The doctors in Capetown are excellent. They repaired the finger with a small skin graft from Ernie's forearm and put his hand and arm in a cast to protect it against any movement. We asked the surgeon when we would be able to leave port and to our surprise he said we could leave immediately—as long as we stopped at Saint Helena Island and visited the hospital there for a checkup. He told us to remove the cast and take out the stitches ourselves, in one week. Then he loaded Ernie up with more antibiotics and gave him some salve and dressings to use on the finger after the stitches were removed.

We thought about it for a day while getting *Starbound* ready to go, then decided that we might as well carry on. The finger was giving Ernie some pain, but the doctor had said that it would, and we decided that it wouldn't hurt any worse at sea. He'd had so many shots of penicillin that the risk of infection was nil.

The weather systems were just right. A stiff southeast breeze was blowing just for us on our day of departure. It was March 15. The meteorologists told us the weather would hold for the next three days, and that would put *Starbound* back up to the latitudes of the southeast trades. We should have a following wind and sea all the way to Saint Helena. The south equatorial current would be with us too, and the Southern Atlantic was clear of storms.

Michel came aboard early in the morning with a group of his friends who had come along to say good-by. They cast our lines off for us and we backed *Starbound* out of her slip, calling good-bys to the dozens of yachts who had been our neighbors for the last two weeks. The Royal Cape Yacht Club members rang the ship's bell on the club veranda, everybody waved, and we steamed away between the rows of moored boats.

Clear of the harbor breakwater, we could feel the strong breeze bending around Table Mountain and pushing on the port quarter. We raised yankee jib and mizzen and set a course to take us between Robben Island and the mainland. By sunset the mainland was a thin gray line to starboard. The wind had backed fair, and square sail and raffee were set. Grumpy had the helm under his electronic control and *Starbound* flew northward, engaged in a game of tag with a few playful seals.

Excerpts from the ship's log.

20 March, 1976, Saturday: We've found the trades for sure! A beautiful day, the sky with puffy little flat-bottomed clouds. Square sail and raffee are really pulling. Nina makes an apple-chip cake to celebrate finding the trades.

22 March, Monday: The trades are just right for fast sailing. Noon ends the best six-day run we've ever had: 960 miles, an average of 160 miles per day. Nina won our daily game of Hearts and is cooking a great spaghetti dinner as consolation to the losers.

24 March, Wednesday: Still moving well, but slower. We make 115 miles noon to noon today. Took the cast off Ernie's arm and removed the stitches from his finger. It looks like hell, but we expected that. We dress the finger and carry on. We pass into West longitude today, so really feel as if we're heading home. We're ready for it, I guess, especially with time running out and our money mostly spent. A pay check will look good!

27 March, Saturday: The wind is falling off. By dawn we are down to about 3 knots. Saint Helena is about 80 miles away, so there is no point in motoring. We keep futzing along at 3 knots, since we'll never make it before dark anyway. A beautiful day and we're all relaxed. Ernie's finger looks O.K.

28 March, Sunday: We pick up lights from Saint Helena at 2400. We're still sailing very slowly. The island is in view at daybreak just off the port bow, which is as it should be. We crank up the diesel and round the eastern end. We sight the Jamestown anchorage at 0900 and start in; sure doesn't look like much of a harbor—no protection at all. The island looks like a big rugged chunk of brown rock from out at sea, but close up some green is visible in the narrow valleys and way up on top, too. We see *Myonie* and steer in on her. Al rows out to show us where to anchor. It's good seeing him and Helen again. *Frauchen* is here too—saw her in Durban. And a Swedish sloop with two brothers on board. Al tells us the holding ground is terrible, so we take a stern line over to one of the large buoys to which the local boats are moored.

The officials are aboard by 1100 to enter us. Health, customs, and immigration people are all very nice. They're all Saint Helena people and look like Polynesians except not as big physically. Three island girls paddle out to the boat in an old dinghy and Michel invites them aboard with my permission. They're a casual-looking crowd, but nice, just looking for fun. Al says all the girls here are very friendly because most of the men work on Ascension. The officials leave and Michel takes over the girls, while Nina and I socialize on the afterdeck with Al and Helen. One of the girls, a big ugly one, chases Ernie all over the boat, but he doesn't want anything to do with her. I don't blame him. Al says there are a lot of good-looking girls ashore. We decide to get some sleep and go ashore tomorrow. We stayed up most of the night and are really tired. The town will wait.

Saint Helena Island is unique. It is a British island located all by itself in the South Atlantic, 1,200 miles away from the coast of South Africa. The island contains just 47 square miles and a population of 4,600 people. It is one of the most isolated, populated islands in the world. Maybe that's why the British chose it as the site of Napoleon's exile. The estate of Longwood, located way up on top of the island, was his "prison" from 1815 to 1821, the year of his death.

There is only one way to land a dinghy at Saint Helena. A stone and concrete "landing place" is obvious from the anchorage. One motors or rows the dinghy to the landing steps and comes alongside carefully, since a big surge is usually running. Knotted lines hang within reach from a "strongback." One grabs a line in one hand and the dinghy painter in the other and disembarks handily, or not so handily, depending on one's agility. The bow of the dinghy is then swung into the bottom step of the landing and the dinghy is hauled up the steps onto the landing itself. The dinghy painter should be tied off to one of several handy railings.

The main street of Jamestown is about a quarter-mile walk away along the waterfront. Food supplies are usually available in any one of three or four stores, more so if a supply ship has been a recent visitor. Fresh vegetables should usually be ordered one day in advance.

There are a few nice little pubs in town. Yachties usually frequent the hotel bar and discothèque. The music in the "disco" is very loud and dated, about fifteen years old by U.S. standards—which means that Nina and I liked it and Ernie curled a lip at it.

Water is available on the dock, but there is a "dirty water" tap and a "clean water" tap. We were told which one to use by the local fishermen. Jerry cans have to be filled at the tap and dinghied out to the yacht, a time-consuming process.

Fuel can be obtained in 55-gallon drums. Diesel cost us about $1.05 per gallon. Gasoline is more. The local launches lighter it out and pump it into your tanks, for a fee.

Nina went with Ernie to the hospital located at the upper end of the little valley town, and the two excellent doctors in residence looked at his wounded finger. They took x-rays and found a loose bone chip which was causing an infection and retarding the healing of the finger. They were surprised that the Capetown doctors had fouled up. We were told that we must stay in Saint Helena at least ten more days or chance an infection which would cause Ernie to lose the tip of his finger down to the first joint. They wanted to see if the bone chip would spall off and come out by itself. If not, they would remove it surgically.

So what was intended as a four-day visit grew to two weeks. Each morning Ernie marched the mile up to the hospital and received another shot of antibiotics. Michel busied himself with the lonesome female contingent of the island. A very pretty girl named June came in for special attention. She was a frequent visitor aboard *Starbound.* Nina and I shopped and hiked and read and wrote. We took the square sail off the yard and overhauled the ancient piece of nylon. Nina sewed a big patch in the center of it to reinforce the badly worn area where the sail chafed against the mainstay.

One day we rented a small car at a very reasonable price, and the four of us drove over much of the island on the winding narrow roads. We toured Longwood and met the French consul in residence. We drove miles through the beautiful tropical rain forest which grows in the interior valley of the island. Then for a study in violent contrasts we drove to the Sandy Bay area on the south side of the island and admired the Gates of Chaos, a landscape that makes Death Valley look like a rose garden.

Michel and I topped off our fresh-water tanks jug by jug. It took a lot of trips. I bought a drum of fuel too, and had it pumped into our big plastic 17-gallon containers, then for a small price had it lightered out to *Starbound.*

Finally the doctors decided to remove the bone chip from Ernie's finger. They found three small chips instead of just the one they'd seen in the x-rays. The head surgeon removed them, dressed the finger, and told us we could leave in three days. Nina paid our bill with thanks. The charges for ten visits, x-rays, many penicillin shots, and extra medication and dressings to take with us came to U.S. $38. Hurray for socialized medical care!

Pilecap came in next day and we filled Frankie and Jeff in on everything we'd learned about the island. The small New Zealand sloop *Ben Gunn* arrived at the same time with Tony Ray and Kevin Oliver on board. We'd met them in Capetown.

On April 10, our wedding anniversary, we raised anchor at 1200 hours. We'd been at Saint Helena for fourteen days and as much as we liked the island we were very happy to get out of the rolly anchorage and head for home. Martinique was 3,900 miles to the northwest. The square sail and raffee were spread immediately and *Starbound* started making knots.

Excerpts from the log.

14 April, Wednesday: We do 6 knots all day. A sunny, lovely day. We catch a nice 15-pound mahi-mahi. The water pump on the M.G. blows out after about one hour of charging. I pull it apart and put in a new impeller.

20 April, Tuesday: The wind drops in the early A.M., so we motor-sail most of the day. Ernie splices the anchor line back into one piece again. We might need it in the West Indies. Rain squalls in the afternoon give us baths.

24 April, Saturday: Grumpy got screwed up last night. We finally fix it in the early morning. A wire to one of the mercury switches broke inside the insulation, a tough thing to find. We sight the *Southampton Castle* heading south. She came into Saint Helena while we were there. Made 122 miles from noon to noon today. I feel terrible today. Must have caught a virus in Saint Helena—it's just about the right time for it to go through incubation. We motor sail at 1,000 RPM all day. We are really getting into the Doldrums. The equator is just ahead.

25 April, Sunday: Slow, sunny, hot, and muggy! I spend the day changing the oil, oil filters, and fuel filters on the main engine and motor generator. We crank up the engine again at 1430.

26 April, Monday: We cross the equator shortly after midnight after spending two years in the southern latitudes! We have pizza and wine for dinner to celebrate.

27 April, Tuesday: We're sure as hell in the Doldrums. The wind is all

over the place. Rain squalls hit us often and hard. It is very hot and muggy. We pull the raffee and secure the square sail. The weather finally clears up, but it is flat calm. We are motoring at the most economical speed—1,200 RPM—but we are worried about fuel.

29 April, Thursday: Set fore and aft sail with vangs. The wind comes and goes. The engine has been going almost constantly for six days now. We are supposed to have a narrow band of trades at this longitude, but guess we can't have it lucky all the time. We experience an annular (95 percent) eclipse of the sun this morning. It gives off a strange light. We've never seen one at sea before. A light breeze from the southeast this afternoon, but small rain squalls are continuous.

1 May, Saturday: A clear day with a few rain squalls. Dolphin are playing all around the boat. We've never seen so many at the same time. It's a good sign that we're getting into the northern equatorial current. This afternoon the wind finally starts coming out of the northeast. Maybe we've found the trades.

2 May, Sunday: What a Sunday! The wind drops at midnight and we go onto the engine again. A squall hits hard and we drop the main and go on the port tack with jib and mizzen strapped in. At 0400 with a 10/10 drizzle, both fuel lines clog and have to be cleaned. We have very little fuel left. At 0630 the alternator belt comes apart. That belt also drives the fresh-water circulating pump for the main engine—a stupid arrangement. The replacement belt is too long and I have to change the alternator adjustment bracket to make it work. By 1000 we are running again. A salt water leak shows up in the elbow of the salt water line leading to the exhaust. I spend the rest of the afternoon fixing that. It turns out to be an electrolysis problem, but localized. Then we run out of propane! Ernie pulls our beat-up alcohol stove out of storage and he and Michel clean the burners. The bottom of the stove tank is rusty and leaking, so they fiberglass it. What a day!

3 May, Monday: Everything has to get better and today is the day. We make 128 miles to noon with an east-northeast wind blowing at 12 to 15 knots. These are real trades! Fiberglass and alcohol do not get along together. I should have known. We strip the fiberglass from the alcohol tank and try solder. Looks like we've got it now. We don't have much alcohol either, so Nina is fixing one-burner meals instead of her usual gourmet cooking.

7 May, Friday: More strong trades at about 18 knots. Great sailing; about 160 miles per day for the last four days! ETA at Martinique is the 12th, one week later than I told the Westergards. Sure hope they can wait for us. Oh, well—we can't do anything except enjoy the fast sailing. We have another 160-mile day today.

8 May, Saturday: Gray-green water! Where is our Caribbean blue? Maybe this is the discoloration from the Amazon River. I've heard that it stains the ocean for hundreds of miles to seaward, and we're not all that far away. The winds are tending east, which is good—that's what they're supposed to do at this latitude. We're well above South America now and approaching the West Indies.

11 May, Tuesday: We raise Martinique in the afternoon about 1400 hours. God, it is good to see land again after thirty-one days. The first since Saint Helena! A check on the fuel gives us 2 inches in the port tank and 4 in the starboard. Since the tanks are curved at the bottom, that ain't much!

All afternoon we sail, and watch Martinique rise further and further from the sea. The four of us are on deck constantly. After the long passage, the sight of land is wonderful!

The sun sets in splendid West Indies fashion and the island is silhouetted against the darkening orange-streaked sky long after the sun is gone. A bright three-quarter moon comes behind us, which means we'll have light for piloting into the harbor.

Our spirits are very high. We split the last of the vodka, make four drinks, and sit topside with our "sundowners." Then we pour the last of the stove alcohol into the beat-up little two-burner and Nina invents a passably good dinner. We clear the Ilet Cabrits at 1900, about 2 miles off, and enter Saint Lucia Channel.

Diamond Rock separates itself from the mainland ahead of us. We slowly approach it, still under full fore and aft sail, all of us fascinated by its presence—even Michel, to whom this evening means less than to Nina, Ernie, and me.

Then just at 2200 hours on May 11, 1976, the bearing on Diamond Rock matches the bearing we'd taken two years and five months before. We have sailed *Starbound* around the world! Memorable moments occur in everyone's life, but Nina and I consider this to be one of our finest. We stand on the deck of our little ship, congratulate each other with a kiss, and watch Diamond Rock slide past, its precipitous walls reflecting the moonlight.

Once Diamond Mountain on the mainland lay abeam, we turn *Starbound* to the north for the Bay of Fort-de-France. The sailing is slower now as we are getting in the lee of the high island. And then the wind disappears. I start the engine, praying that the fuel will hold out until we are on soundings. Even a depth of 100 feet will allow us to anchor if the engine stops.

Slowly we progress northward and then we open the bay! The lights of Fort-de-France cover the shoreline. And of course the northeast trades come across the saddle of Martinique and give us a fairly stiff headwind. We put the bowsprit into it and motor at 1,200 RPM, expecting the engine to choke on air and stop at any moment. But it doesn't. We roll right into the yacht anchorage, the wind and chop getting less as we approach the shore, and then we are there.

The anchor goes down at 0200 on May 12. Nina opens a bottle of wine she'd secreted away and pours four glasses full to the brim. We all sit on the edge of the house top, contemplate the shore, and talk about how good life is.

Our voyage back to the Chesapeake Bay is epilogue. But I want to hit the high spots so as to define the route which I found fast, fun, and trouble-free.

Dave and Lyn Westergard were still waiting for us in Martinique. Dave stuffed enough cash in our pockets to get us home in luxury and then some.

We stored up. The fuel tanks were bone-dry. I had to take a few jerry cans of diesel to *Starbound* in the launch before I dared start the engine to get her into the fuel dock. Our water tanks were quite low; about 20 gallons were left. The propane, of course, was gone. We were low on almost everything else.

But money can work wonders. Two days later we said good-by to Michel, who was very excited because his mother was flying in from Paris to see him. With Dave and Lyn on board we slashed north across the Martinique Passage and anchored that same evening in beautiful Prince Rupert Bay, on the northwestern coast of Dominica.

Dominica had changed. The people of the island were going through a "black power" drill and we ran into a few cases of downright nastiness. Two tourists had been shot and killed a few months previously and so tourists in general were avoiding the island. Many of the big hotels had closed. The situation reminded us of the way we found Grenada in 1973. We suppose that in the normal course of events the power structure on the island will "discover" that tourists are a primary source of income and will then clean out the dissidents. We hope so, since Dominica is a very beautiful island.

We leased a car and visited the Emerald Pool again. It's still very beautiful but its access has been modernized and so many more people visit it. Therefore there are "footprints on the sand" such as beer cans and film wrappers.

We spent a day cleaning the goose barnacles from *Starbound*'s bottom and on the morning of May 17 left for Guadeloupe.

Another bouncy trip across the Dominica Passage and a smooth sail up the coast in the lee of Guadeloupe put us at Anse Deshaies. The little bay makes a fine overnight anchorage—even an interesting place to spend a few days, but we were in a hurry.

Next morning we were away for English Harbor on Antigua. We made a fast passage and by early afternoon dropped the hook in a very crowded Nelson's Dockyard. We spent two days exploring the Dockyard again and two evenings at the Admiral's Inn. On May 20 we topped off our tanks with fuel and water, a good place in which to do it, and were off for an overnight sail to Saint Barthelemy, or Saint Barts, as everyone calls it.

We had easy sailing and dropped anchor about 1500 next day in the snug little bay at Saint Barts. It is a good island for food supplies and boat gear, as small as it is. And it's an especially good place to buy booze. Mount Gay Eclipse rum, my favorite, costs $14 per 12-bottle case. That's about as low a price as is available in the West Indies. The old days of 50 cents per bottle are gone forever.

We rented a "Moke" next morning and toured the island. It's a pretty place. Keeping the Moke running was an adventure in itself.

Dave and Lyn had to get rolling, so we left for Saint Maarten on May 23 at daybreak and dropped the anchor before noon in Great Bay just off the nice little town of Phillipsburg.

Dave and Lyn had to fly north next day. We tried to talk them into going as far as Saint Thomas with us, but they had to get home.

We spent the afternoon exploring Phillipsburg. I think we walked through every gift shop in town and had a drink in every bar in town. It's a good thing there were three shops for every bar.

I saw Dave and Lyn off next morning. After they'd gone I just stood around with my hands in my pockets, feeling rather out of sorts; a letdown, I guess, after the continual driving excitement of the last several days.

I snapped out of my blue funk as soon as I got back to the beach and saw our ship in the harbor tugging at her anchor chain. We decided to leave in the morning. It was still a long way home and we had less than six weeks before July 4 arrived. There was going to be a rip-roaring party at the Westergard's house on Kent Island in the Chesapeake Bay on that day. It was going to be a celebration of our country's Bicentennial and *Starbound's* arrival home. We were determined to be anchored off their beach well ahead of time.

When I tried to start the main engine next morning, I found a dead starting battery. It had been getting worse for the last few weeks and I knew enough about batteries not to fool with one that was four years old; I simply went and bought a new one. By the time it was installed the day was shot, so we relaxed for another night.

We left for Virgin Gorda on May 26, another overnight trip. We raised the island at daybreak, made a run around its eastern end, and ducked into Gorda Sound. At the eastern extremity of the sound is a hotel complex called the Bitter End. We picked up one of their moorings and relaxed for a day and night. The swimming was marvelous near the reef.

It was a four-hour sail to Coral Bay on the south coast of Saint John. We spent the night far up a hidden inlet and were under way in the morning for Saint Thomas.

Starbound sailed into Charlotte Amalie Harbor on May 30, a Sunday, and anchored off the Caribbean Harbor Club. It was our first American port since Pago Pago, American Samoa—but with a big difference: this port had a U.S. Coast Guard station and we could renew *Starbound*'s documentation.

On Sunday the customs offices are not open, but a customs officer is available on the commercial dock to enter and clear the interisland small craft. We were an American yacht entering an American port, so our entry procedure took about five minutes.

We liked Saint Thomas but it was expensive. We kept *Starbound* in the anchorage because the dockage rates at the marina were 30 cents per foot per day. And they charged us $3 per day to land our dinghy at their dock! For this our dinghy was secure and we could use the showers and coin-operated laundromat. We still had to take taxis into town to shop; it was too far to walk.

Starbound left Saint Thomas on June 5 and headed northwest through Virgin Passage. For the next five days we stayed on a nice fat reach and sailed northwest. We passed many islands to port: Grand Turk and the Caicos, Mayaguana and Samana Cay. We would have liked to visit Georgetown on Great Exuma Island but we didn't have proper charts. We decided to sail down to the Bahamas in a couple of years and explore them thoroughly.

We wanted to make a short stop at San Salvador Island. It was on our rhumb line and easy to get into. We anchored off Cockburn town in more beautiful water. Before we could put the launch over, a motor boat came around the northern corner of the little bay and asked us to follow them to the "marina." Our chart didn't show any facility like a marina, but the motor boat's black operator assured me that he was the port captain of the marina and that I would be able to get in.

Well—we were glad as hell it was high tide! Another couple of coats of paint and *Starbound* wouldn't have made it through that cut in the rock! Once into the small square basin, though, it was quite roomy. There was enough space for a dozen yachts of fair size.

We stayed three days. Tony Leicester, the manager of the place, took us under his wing and made us welcome. The hotel marina is called the Riding Rock Inn and its primary purpose seems to be to house and escort people on diving trips in the surrounding waters. And people were there in droves! For a little island it was a busy place. The bar at the inn was the favorite meeting spot. We made our pilgrimage to the place where Columbus is supposed to have landed on the island in 1492. A stone obelisk marks the location.

The weather looked good, so we decided to be on our way. I managed to borrow a chart from Tony which showed a much larger scale of the northern Bahamas than the old chart I had. We topped up our water tanks again. At high tide on June 14 we slid *Starbound* through the narrow cut and back into the Caribbean.

We sailed northwest and by morning of the 16th we were past Spanish Wells and swinging west into Northeast Providence Channel. The wind was right behind us and we moved fast with the current helping. At dusk Freeport on Grand Bahama was behind us, West End was abeam, and West Palm Beach, Florida, was dead ahead.

By midnight the loom of lights from the Florida coast stretched north and south as far as we could see. Nina stood with me on the deck, hugged me, and said, "Look at that! It's *our* country!"

At 0600 on June 17 we motored hard for the West Palm Beach jetties. The Gulf Stream tried to sweep up north and we had to quarter across it. Finally we rolled into quiet water, turned left down the Intercoastal Waterway, went about a mile, and tied up at a handy marina. We were back in the U.S.A.

Next day I found charts of the Intercoastal Waterway from Morehead City, North Carolina, to Norfolk, Virginia. We called the meteorologists and found out that the weather would get squally as we progressed north but the winds would stay generally southerly. That was fine! *Starbound* was in the Gulf Stream by 1600 heading north under square rig.

Exactly seventy-two hours later we were inside the breakwater at Morehead City. It had been a rainy trip with almost continuous squalls during the last day. But like the man told us, the winds stayed southerly, so we'd made good time—and the Gulf Stream had helped a lot.

We said good-by to the open ocean. For the next five days we motored up rivers and down creeks, through canals and in or out of locks, under fixed bridges and through swing bridges. We anchored each night in some out-of-the-way cove and caught up on the sleep we'd missed, while the wind blew a gale in the open ocean east of us.

On June 26 we arrived in Norfolk, Virginia, and went into Little Creek for fuel, water, and new alternator belts. We stopped at Cobb's Marina and it was like old times. Mrs. Cobb gave us a big welcome.

We called Dave and Lyn and let them know where we were and that we'd be at the big party for sure. We pulled out of Little Creek on June 29, very early, with Ray Kukulski back aboard to join our homecoming cruise up the bay.

About 1500 on July 1, 1976, we dropped our anchor in the 18-foot hole located in the bight of the shallow bay forming the foot of Kent Island. Annapolis was just across the Bay, but we'd sail over after the Bicentennial celebration. There weren't likely to be any slips or anchorage space available anywhere in Annapolis until the next Tuesday, five days away. And then we would have an open dock waiting for us at Mear's Marina on Back Creek, our old stand.

In the meantime we had our own celebration to attend. Looking toward shore we could see someone on the Westergard lawn shading his eyes with one arm and waving with the other. And looking across the water toward Bloody Point we noticed three familiar boats coming toward us.

Home were the sailors.

APPENDIX A

Food, Stores, and Galley Equipment

I once read that to determine the amount of food you need for a cruise you simply list the foods you use for one week, multiply by four to get one month's worth, then stock up for however many months you will be unable to buy provisions. In fact, you must first take the list, substitute preserved foods for fresh, then make up the food stores list. Simple—until I tried it. My experience has been that finding suitable, appetizing protein, in tins or in the dried state, is difficult. The crew soon becomes tired of beef stew, corned beef hash, spaghetti and meatballs, tuna, and sardines. You will be able to catch fish, but you can't always depend on it. Fish are generally caught near islands, in major oceanic currents, or near the continental shelves. The larger, pelagic fishes are sometimes caught in the open oceans, but not often from slow-moving yachts. So this leaves you mostly dependent on the stores on board.

At the outset of the cruise you will undoubtedly have many of the "luxury" items available from the local supermarket as provisions on board. However, these will gradually be used up and you will be faced with the prospect of replacing them with the not-so-luxurious items which are available. Also, you may find that many items which keep well in the kitchen at home tend to spoil rather quickly when stored aboard a boat. Especially vulnerable are items packaged in cardboard cartons, waxed paper containers, or plastic bags—even when stored in a dry locker.

Sooner or later you have to eliminate many luxury items from the stores simply because replacements are not available or are too expensive. A good example is paper towels. Granted they are great for cleaning up messes, but

315

they can't be washed and used repeatedly, as rags can. So take a supply of rags along. Also in this category are paper napkins. One is unlikely to find any to buy, except in large, well-populated cities—and that eliminates most of the places yachtsmen like to visit. We gave up on paper products after most of ours were ruined when water got into the "dry" stowage area. It's my opinion that there is no really dry stowage on a boat unless it is in lockers above the level of the cabin sole, necessarily limited space.

Galley equipment can be a problem if not selected carefully—with a view toward noncorrosive materials. And finding substitutes for fresh foods is always a problem, even if there is a refrigerator aboard.

Food
Things that keep well—and things that don't.

Real (not chemically) smoked meat will last several months if hung in a cool, dry, well-ventilated place. If kept in a refrigerator it will last indefinitely. Some Dak brand smoked salami we bought in Curaçao lasted for one year, hanging from the overhead in the galley. We kept freshly killed (not aged) beef for twenty-five days in our refrigerator (which maintains a temperature of 40 degrees F). Freshly killed beef is tough but is good in stews or when pressure-cooked, and after about a week the meat is tender enough to eat as steaks.

Tinned luncheon meats are available and can be cooked with eggs in the morning when the bacon is all gone, but they will not keep well after being opened, unless refrigerated. Whenever possible, buy tinned meats which contain no vegetables. Fresh potatoes, onions, carrots, and garlic can be added for a stew. The taste is much improved and the dish contains more vitamins.

Cheese keeps well if it is a good firm type such as cheddar or gouda. If not refrigerated, it must be kept as dry and cool as possible—not always easy in the tropics, but well worth the effort since cheese is a good source of protein. It is also very compact and thus makes for easy stowage.

Eggs should be bought fresh, unwashed, and *unrefrigerated*—generally directly from the farmer. Wipe the eggs carefully, then coat them liberally with petroleum jelly and store them in egg cartons. It is important to turn the cartons over each week to prevent the yolks from sticking to the side of the egg shells. For safety's sake, after three weeks break each egg into a cup and take a sniff before using it. Most of our eggs lasted for three months when preserved in this manner. If eggs have been refrigerated (chilled) they will last about two weeks, so go to the extra effort to get them fresh.

Dried eggs should be considered for use by anyone who intends to do extensive cruising. They come in tins and are available in "whole egg" mixture, "whites only," or "yolks only" and work well. We've used the whole egg mixture with good results in baking and for pancakes. Eggs are virtually impossible to obtain in French Polynesia (except in Tahiti), so take good care of them.

Bread is always a problem if one doesn't bake. However, salt water bread can be cooked on top of the stove and is satisfying, if not a gastronomic treat. Add a little corn meal to the mixture and it tastes a lot like English muffins. When ordering fresh bread on various islands, we always asked that it be baked twice. After initial baking remove from the oven and cool, then bake again for fifteen to twenty minutes. This makes a rather thick, dark crust which keeps the bread fresh for as long as a week. If the baker can't do it, it can be done on board.

Crackers and crispy snacks should be removed from cartons (even if sealed in plastic) and put in tins or jars. However, if purchased in the tropics, they may already be soggy, in which case crisp them in the oven if you have one. If not, use a skillet with low heat. Cool before stowing. This also prevents weevils by destroying any eggs which may be in them. This method also works well for pasta and rice.

Flour and cereals can be a real problem if not stored properly. The best method we've found is to empty the bags into large tins or jars and put a few bay leaves on top. The bay leaves keep weevils away. I don't know why—they just do. This may also work with pasta and rice, but we didn't try it. If you're really down on weevils, heat the filled tins or jars in the oven (without lids) at 200 degrees F for 1 hour, let cool, then seal with sterile lids. I treated some rice that way and it kept for two years. It is a lot of trouble, but it works.

Butter can be purchased in tins (outside the U.S.) but must be kept cool to prevent spoilage. We use fresh butter on *Starbound,* when available, and keep it refrigerated. It stays fresh and is good-tasting for six months or more, and is usually cheaper than tinned butter. Francine Clarkson, on the yacht *Pilecap,* packs her butter in salt with the same result. We also keep a supply of tinned vegetable shortening on hand for use in baking, and use vegetable oil for other cooking.

If vegetables are to be kept without refrigeration, they must not have been refrigerated prior to purchase. Once refrigerated, they spoil very quickly if kept at room temperature. Even if you buy them from a vendor, they may have been shipped in chilled containers, so be sure to ask. Be especially careful on the small dry islands in the Caribbean where most of the produce is shipped in from elsewhere. Fresh vegetables will keep well when stored in an open basket or hammock in a dry place out of direct sunlight. Potatoes and onions will keep for months in a dry, dark place if one sorts them carefully every week or so and removes any that have become soft or spoiled. We kept a supply of powdered potatoes to use when our fresh ones were gone, but found that they occasionally disagreed with some people—possibly because of the preservatives they contain. Carrots and cabbage should be kept cool and damp if possible to prevent shriveling. Don't wash vegetables until you're ready to use them, but be sure to check them carefully for bugs before bringing them aboard. Cockroaches are a terrible nuisance—and are almost impossible to get rid of once they are established on a boat.

Citrus fruit and apples keep well if not refrigerated prior to purchase. Green pineapple will last well too, but the smell of the ripening fruit sometimes causes problems for seasick-prone individuals.

We use dehydrated vegetables and fruit on *Starbound* whenever possible. The larger the package, the cheaper they are, so we buy restaurant-size packets and stow the unused portion in jars or tins after they have been opened. The directions for preparation can be put right in the container with the food. Our dried foods lasted over a year. We used peas, green beans, and sliced apples, reserving them for use when fresh items were not available. They cost less than like amounts in tins and take up far less stowage space, and you need not worry about tins rusting out and their contents spoiling.

We always check tins carefully before opening and never taste the contents of questionable ones. If we have any doubts—over the side they go! Botulism will kill you. It has no smell or taste, and usually doesn't change the appearance of tinned food. If the lid is puffed up or if there is a loud hiss when you open a tin, throw it away (except for vacuum-packed items, like coffee).

Dry milk keeps best if it is put in airtight containers. We have had boxes of dry milk spoil after only a few weeks at sea. Most countries have whole dry milk in tins available, but we've not been able to find any in the U.S. We use it for cooking and for drinking, and never use tinned milk aboard. Dry milk tastes better and takes much less stowage space.

Peanut butter is an old standby at sea. But it will turn rancid in the tropics if not kept refrigerated, so take small jars. They'll cost more, but it's worth it.

If you like honey, take a good supply with you. It's hard to find in the Pacific, and when available is very expensive. We use it on *Starbound* to prevent seasickness, or to stop vomiting caused by seasickness.

How to . . .

Roast coffee: Put several cups of green coffee beans in a heavy skillet on top of the stove. Stir as they brown to prevent scorching. The darker the roast, the richer the taste. Cool, then grind and store.

Bake breadfruit: Put breadfruit directly on stove burner. Turn as the outside becomes charred. When the outside is completely black, it is done. Cut open and use in place of potatoes or rice.

Make coconut cream: Grate coconut meat with a hand grater. Put grated meat in a clean cloth and squeeze to remove juice. Add about 2 tablespoons water and squeeze a second time. The result is a thick, lovely coconut cream. Add a little rum, lime juice, and ice for a great drink, or add sugar and thicken with cornstarch for a pudding.

Make poisson cru *(raw fish with lime):* Squeeze juice of several limes into a bowl. Add thinly sliced (strictly fresh) fish and let sit for about 5 minutes. Add coconut cream and serve. Minced onion can be added.

Pasteurize milk: Heat the milk at 145 degrees F (63 degrees C) for thirty minutes. Cool rapidly, then store below 50 degrees F (10 degrees C).

Principal Supply Ports

The most difficult task of the storekeeper on any boat is laying in stores at the outset of a voyage. The second most difficult task is keeping the boat stocked up once under way. Keeping in mind that situations tend to change from time to time, but with a view toward making this task as painless as possible, I have compiled a list of *principal* supply ports with my opinions about them. They follow in the order in which we visited them as we sailed around the world—except that I have listed the islands in the Caribbean in alphabetical order.

Castries, Saint Lucia. Moderate prices and good selection. English spoken. Stock up on New Zealand cheddar cheese and tinned butter. If you have a freezer, get frozen meat here. There is a big department store with excellent selection.

Fort-de-France, Martinique. Prices about 50 percent higher than in the U.S. and slightly higher than those in Saint Thomas. Plan to spend about two hours each day marketing, unless you want to take a taxi to one of the supermarkets. Buy fresh fruit, vegetables, fresh spices, live chickens, and eggs at the open market, but be prepared to bargain for each item (in French). Fish is sold in the open fish market near the vegetable market. Don't be put off by the smell. The fish is good. Meat can be bought in the butcher shops in town but is very expensive. This is the place to stock up on all those French goodies. They are available in Tahiti—but expensive! Fresh milk is available. Clothing is expensive. Liquor is available at moderate prices. It can be purchased and put in bond—duty free. Good docks for landing in a dinghy.

Philipsburg, Saint Maarten. Best food prices I found in the West Indies. Friendly people. English spoken. Fresh milk, eggs (chilled), cheese, smoked sausage, and variety meats. Frozen meat, good variety of tinned goods.

Good selection of liquor at excellent prices—and no hassle with bonding. Fresh vegetables did not seem to be plentiful—probably imported from Florida. There is a supermarket in town. The people were friendly, and even changed U.S. dollars into the local currency. Take a taxi from the market to the waterfront. There is a good dock for landing in a dinghy.

Charlotte Amalie, Saint Thomas. Prices slightly higher than in Saint Maarten, but less than the other islands. Several supermarkets, but if you stay at the Caribbean Harbor Club it is a long walk, and you'll need a taxi to bring stores back to the boat. The other marina along the waterfront is noisy because of low-flying aircraft but is certainly closer to town. Fresh, unrefrigerated vegetables are available from market boats along the waterfront and are about the same price as in the supermarkets. American brands are available, as are many of the luxury items not found on other islands. Meat is frozen. Fresh milk is available. Good dinghy dock.

Willemstad, Curaçao. Good prices and good selection. All fresh items available. Purchase fresh produce from South American sailing boats along the quay downtown. This is the last chance to stock up on tinned goods, and there are several ship's chandlers who can supply stores by the case. We used Henderson (Curaçao) Ltd. Telephone them first. They'll let you go into the warehouse to check out items you're not sure about, will put your order together, and will deliver to the waterfront. Fresh eggs, milk, and meat are available. Stock up on Curaçao liqueur, good Dutch cheese, and Dak smoked sausage (the hard type).

Cartagena, Colombia. Cheap prices. Lots of fresh meat, eggs, and produce are available. Buy coffee beans and roast your own. Beer is about 9 cents per bottle, Pepsi and Coke 3 cents per bottle. Stock up here. When you get to Tahiti beer and soft drinks cost as much as liquor. And liquor costs are shocking! Eat in restaurants while here. It is cheaper than using your ship's stores.

Papeete, Tahiti. The most expensive place we visited in the Pacific. Many French goodies are available, but be prepared to pay through the nose. Fresh eggs, milk, fruit, and vegetables are plentiful. Buy them at the open market from the lovely Tahitian women. Get there no later than 0700 for a good selection. Fresh fish is sold in the same place in the afternoon. You can sometimes buy fish right off the fishing boats on the waterfront. Cheese is imported from New Zealand and France. All meat is frozen and very expensive (ground beef from N.Z. cost us U.S. $3 per pound). We found two supermarkets in town: Donald's of Tahiti and Bon Marché, both right on the waterfront. We preferred Bon Marché because it was closer and slightly cheaper, but bought our cheese and meat at Donald's. There are many small Chinese-owned grocery stores in town if you care to shop around for the very best prices. They always have at least one person who speaks English, and are polite and helpful—not always the case in French-owned stores. If your boat is tied up near the park, dinghy landing is not easy because you must negotiate the riprap which lines the shore—a slippery operation at low tide.

Pago Pago, American Samoa. Good prices. Many U.S. items available at Burns, Philp & Company supermarket and wholesale store right on the waterfront near town. Toko Groceries Distributors, located outside town, is also a good source. Telephone them first to see if they have what you want, then take a cab and stock up while there. If you have a large order, they may deliver. Fresh eggs (refrigerated) can be bought in the stores, but check at the government office in the public market and order unrefrigerated eggs from them. All fresh produce is sold in the public market. Stock up on liquor and U.S. wines at the government liquor store in town. Liquor prices in New Zealand and Australia are almost as bad as in Tahiti, and their local wines are awful. Stock up on tinned tuna while here. Buy it by the case from one of the canneries. If you have cockroaches on board, ask the cannery people if they still provide free pest extermination service for yachts. Good dinghy landing near the public market.

Suva, Fiji. Good supply port, but inconvenient. If you're going straight to New Zealand, stock up only on fresh produce and sugar. Eggs, meat, and vegetables are plentiful, but no fresh milk available. Duty-free shopping here. Good place to have hand work such as watch repairs done. We had a stopwatch and wrist watch both worked over for about U.S. $6. You will be far from town, so ride the bus for about 10 cents each way. Good dinghy landing.

New Zealand. Good prices and everything is available. Dairy products are especially cheap. Good fresh meat of all kinds is available and is also cheap. Stock up on fresh or tinned cheese, butter, and meat. Tinned goods cost about the same as in the U.S. The tides run about 12 feet, so dinghy landings can be a problem.

Australia. Everything is available and good. Prices are comparable with those in New Zealand, except that meat is a little higher and dairy products are quite a bit higher. If you coast-hop, the farther north you go from Brisbane, the more expensive supplies become. Unless you're tied up in a river, dinghy landing is a real problem.

Denpasar, Bali. Excellent fresh produce is available (except large cooking onions) and is very cheap. Buy green coffee beans for U.S. $1 per kilo and roast them yourself. Eggs cost about 90 cents a dozen. Fresh meat is sold in the open market near the vegetable market, but is never refrigerated. Go early in the morning while it is still fairly cool, check the meat carefully, then if you decide to buy some get it to your boat as quickly as possible. We ate mostly fresh vegetables while there, and depended on our breakfast eggs for protein. Food is so cheap here that many yachties eat ashore instead of using ship's stores. This is not a good place to buy tinned goods of any kind because of the high cost. Take a basket or box when going shopping. One of the little "carry" girls who hang around the market will put it on her head, follow you around while you fill it up, translate for you when necessary, then carry it to the Bemo station for you. All for 25 rupiahs (about 6 cents).

Christmas Island. Almost everything is available. Liquor is duty free and there is a good selection. Produce and eggs are all chilled, and the meat is frozen. But this is a good place to stock up on tinned goods. Landing a dinghy here can be downright dangerous because of the large swells.

Port Louis, Mauritius. Good prices. Get fresh meat and eggs at the open meat market, and fresh vegetables, spices, and fruit at the vegetable market nearby. Across the street from the vegetable market is an ice cream parlor, and next door is a pharmacy. We stocked up on tinned goods at Lim Fat & Sons Ltd. They are located at 34 Royal Street, and will deliver to the quay if you ask them. Dinghy landing is no problem.

Durban, South Africa. This is a big city with lots of supermarkets. Everything is available including some good South African wines. Take on all the stores needed to get to Capetown. Yacht harbors in South Africa are always located on railroad land, so are generally a long way from towns, where the stores are. The Point Yacht Club in Durban is an exception. It is only four blocks from town and has a good dinghy dock.

Capetown, South Africa. Same as Durban, but the yacht club is 2 miles from town. This is a good place to stock up on oranges and apples for the long haul to the Caribbean. Try the light white wine called Fleur du Cap, which is cheap and good. Smoked meat is readily available and is good, but fairly expensive. Your boat will most likely be tied up at a dock here.

Galley Equipment

Yachts making long passages never seem to have enough fresh water on board, so galley equipment and dishes are washed in sea water. Because sea water is so corrosive each item in our galley was checked with a magnet prior to purchase to ensure that it was stainless steel—except for a cast iron skillet that was used for "baking" biscuits on top of the stove, roasting coffee beans, etc., an aluminum colander (which barely survived our cruise), and a rotary egg beater. The beater was stainless, but one of its fittings was plain steel. It rusted out and broke halfway across the Pacific. It was a year before a replacement could be found. Aluminum doesn't rust but needs to be rinsed in fresh water to prevent deterioration.

A list of the galley equipment on *Starbound* follows. It is all stainless steel except where noted. The only things we wanted that we didn't have were a freezer, and a pressure cooker large enough to use for canning.

Propane stove (4 burner w/oven and broiler; porcelain)
Refrigerator (7.5 cu. ft. w/6-tray capacity freezer across top)
Electric blender
Pressure cooker (4-quart capacity)
Skillets (2 porcelain-covered cast iron, 1 cast iron)
Pots and pans (7 assorted sizes w/ lids)
Grater
Knives (4 assorted sizes)
Dish pan and dish rack (plastic)
Cooking spoons (4 assorted sizes; wood)
Can openers (several sizes and types)
Cork screws (2)
Kitchen tools (1 set plus 1 extra spatula)
Hand rotary egg beater (1 with nylon gears)
Whisk (1)
Baking pans (2 cake, 1 muffin, 2 pie, 2 loaf, 1 roaster)
Mixing bowls (2 sets, also used for serving food)
Flatware (service for 8)
Colander (aluminum)
Tongs (2)
Tea kettle (1)

Tea pot (1)
Coffee pot (1)
Flour sifter (1 2-cup capacity)
Measuring spoons (1 set)
Cheese slicer (2)
Measuring cups (1 set)
Ice pick (2)
Salt and pepper shakers (1 set)
Sugar bowl and creamer (1 set)
Dinner plates (8 restaurant-type heavy china)
Mugs (6 heavy plastic and 8 ceramic)
Glasses (12 heavy plastic nesting-type and assorted heavy glass)
Spice rack (1 wooden wall-type)
Cooking thermometer (1 stainless steel and glass)
Fishing gear (300 ft. of line, stainless leader wire, assorted hooks and lures, assorted weights)
Clothesline and clothespins
Washboard
String bags for carrying groceries
Nutrition books
Cookbooks
Rolling pin
Vacuum cleaner
Broom
Steam iron (with stainless steel shoe plate)

APPENDIX B

Tools

A cruising yacht must carry a lot of tools. They are almost as important as food and water in that basic survival can, and does, depend on them.

Tools are heavy and bulky. They take up a. lot of prime stowage space, space which is dry and handy.

Spare parts can be wrapped against dampness and stowed almost anywhere, but not so tools. Tools must be readily available. The weight of a full complement of tools such as *Starbound* carries precludes a single stowage area unless the area is located amidships. The weight of a load of heavy tools carried to one side of the centerline can induce a sizable list, even to a yacht as beamy and heavy as *Starbound.*

We considered every stowage area on our boat, then shrugged our shoulders and selected the driest, most accessible area available—excluding the galley; this was under the forward settee in the main saloon. We compensated for their slightly off-center-line weight by stowing spare parts on the opposite side of the boat under the port quarter berth.

Power Tools

Power tools are nice to have if there is a motor-generator set aboard or some other way to generate a sufficient supply of alternating current. *Starbound* has a 3-kilowatt Onan diesel M.G. which does a good job; it charges the battery banks, runs the hot water heater for the domestic supply and the heating system when we feel the need for it—and we can use power tools at the same time. Listed in order of importance:

1. Drill motor, ⅜ inch with bits
2. Grinder/sander, 3,600 rpm with discs and soft pad
3. Saber saw, with assorted blades

4. Flat bed sander, with plenty of sandpaper
5. Circular saw, with assorted blades

Hand Tools

The items on this list might seem to be obvious, but at only one time did *Starbound* have to borrow a tool: a swaging device for "Nicopress" fittings. On the other hand, we've loaned various tools out several times to yachts which were not so well equipped and/or considered themselves too small to carry a more complete tool inventory.

Hand tools, machine
1. Hammers, ball-peen (2)
2. Screwdrivers, all types and several sizes
3. Pliers, all types and several sizes including vice grips
4. Vises, one large bolt-down type and one small vacuum base type
5. Fixed-size wrenches (spanners), ¼ inch to 1 inch, box and open end combinations (metric if required)
6. Adjustable wrenches, 6-, 8-, 10-, and 12-inch sizes
7. Torque wrench, ½ inch drive, 150 foot-pound capacity
8. Socket sets, 2 complete w/¼ inch and ½ inch drives
9. Allen wrenches, complete set
10. Files, several sizes and cuts, triangular, flat, and round
11. Punches, one set
12. Cold chisels, one set
13. Micrometer, one inch
14. Feeler gauge, two sets (hide one in your clothes drawer)
15. Tubing tools, cutter, vice, and flanger
16. Hacksaws, two holders and various gauge blades
17. Tape measures and scales, 12-foot, 50-foot and 1-foot (straightedge)
*18. Taps and dies, complete set

Hand tools, wood working
1. Hammers, claw (2)
2. Hand saws, cross-cut, rip, back (with holder), piping
3. Framing square, small and large
4. Folding rule, 6-foot
5. High-speed wood bits, for use with electric drill
6. Wood planes, three sizes
7. Surform planes, complete set
8. Draw knife
9. Wood chisels, set from ¼ inch to 2 inches
10. Circular saw bits for use with electric drill
11. Brace, complete with wood bits, including expansion bit and screwdriver bits

12. C-clamps, various sizes
13. Counter bores and countersinks for use with electric drill
14. Tapered bits and countersink combinations for use with electric drill

Electrical Tools

1. Soldering gun
2. Soldering pencil
3. Wire strippers
4. Terminal crimpers
*5. Multitester (buy a good one—ours was too small)
6. Solder, solid core, resin core, and acid core

Plumbing tools

1. Stillson wrenches, three sizes
2. Propane torch, with various tips, bar solder, and soldering paste. Don't forget an extra tank of gas.

Not-so-obvious tools

1. Single bit ax
2. Crowbar
3. 5-pound sledgehammer
4. Short-handled shovel
5. Wire swaging tools
6. Sheet metal shears
*7. Small, flat hydraulic jack
*8. Ratchet hoist (3-ton capacity)
*9. Cable cutters
10. Propeller puller
11. Magnet, 5-pound capacity (stow far from the compass)
12. Garden hose, 350 feet, with spare fittings

* Indicates tools we didn't have and wished we did.

APPENDIX C

Spares

If a yachtie carried every spare item he really wanted to have aboard, he'd sink the yacht. Discretion is necessary. Weight, available space, and money are important limiting factors. But these factors balance as nothing against the overwhelming factor of safety. A yachtie must ask himself, "What items on my yacht will, in failing, prevent or seriously hamper my ship from making it safely to the next or nearest port, which might be 1,500 nautical miles away?" Those items are first-priority!

While planning our voyage we spent many hours making lists of everything we wanted to carry. Then we categorized and assigned priorities to each item. By the time we balanced what we could spend on spares against the available space to carry them, only the first-priority items were seriously considered—with a few exceptions.

Second-priority items were considered to be those spares which, while not mandatory for safety at sea, were not likely to be found at any except the largest, most modern ports.

Our spares categories are kept broad: Bosun's spares, machinery spares, and electrical/electronics spares.

The following lists are not intended to be agonizingly complete. They include all first-priority spares and some second-priority items. And since the lists are applicable only to our vessel, they are intended simply as a guide for other yachtsmen.

Bosun's Spares

1. Sails: main, jib, storm jib, storm trysail
2. Line: 600' ⅝" dia., 300' ½" dia., assorted small stuff. (Note that virtually all running rigging on *Starbound* is restricted to two sizes of line.)

329

3. Wire (enough for a spare shroud or two and a headstay).
4. Line and wire rope fittings: wire terminals, turnbuckles, padeyes, shackles, thimbles, etc. (i.e., everything needed to make up new standing rigging).
5. Paint: enough for three complete paint jobs (with plenty of thinner and good-quality brushes).
6. Fiberglass and resin.
7. Nails, screws, and other fasteners.

Machinery Spares

Main engine and generator

1. Zinc pencils for heat exchangers (10)
2. Sea water pump impellers and seals (4 sets)
3. V belts (2 sets)
4. Oil and fuel filters (enough to change on schedule)
5. Oil and transmission fluid
6. Alternator and voltage regulator (complete spare set)
7. Starter motor brushes and starter motor relay (the motor itself is easy to overhaul, but the relay is difficult).
8. Complete set of spare hoses for all systems (fresh water, salt water, exhaust, oil, fuel, and hydraulics).
9. Gaskets for heads, manifolds, pump bodies, etc. (a complete set is best).
10. Piping fitting tubing
11. Fuel injectors (a full set is desirable). I recommend diesel engines for cruising boats, but if you've got gasoline you'll need several sets of spark plugs and points, and at least two repair kits for the carburator and fuel pump.
12. Water temperature and oil pressure gauges and a spare ignition switch (if in exposed location).
13. Steering cables (if used)

Electrical/Electronics Spares

1. Hydrometer
2. Transistors for auto-pilot, chargers, radio-telephone, radio direction finder
3. Spare fuses for above
4. Wire and terminal devices for all uses including batteries
5. Spare diodes for charger and radio-telephone
6. Light bulbs for everything
7. Switches (various)

8. D-Cell batteries—available almost anywhere, but keep a store of 'em.
9. Spare refrigerator switch and freon charging kit
10. Brushes for all electric motors
11. 6-volt batteries for flashlights

APPENDIX D

Passages

From	PASSAGE To	DISTANCE (N.M.) Rhumb	Actual	DATES Left	Arrived	GENERAL WEATHER
Norfolk	Bermuda	583	710	10/27/73	11/5	Gale, storm, squalls, rough seas
Bermuda	Antigua	910	965	11/18/73	11/26	Calm at start, E trades finish
Antigua	Granada	—345—				Beautiful sailing
Granada	Curaçao	423	425	1/7/74	1/10	Strong E trades
Curaçao	Cartagena	445	451	1/22/74	1/24	Strong E trades
Cartagena	San Blas	190	193	2/5/74	2/7	Mod. trades, choppy cross-sea
San Blas	Panama	90	96			Moderate trades
	Panama Canal		—46—			Beautiful and hot
Balboa	Galapagos	905	938	2/26/74	3/5	Light trades, doldrums, hot
Wreck Bay	Academy Bay	42	45			Calm, hot, hot-hot
Galapagos	Marquesas	3143	3253	3/15/74	4/10	Calm first 3 days, trades
Hiva Oa	Nuku Hiva	95	95			Moderate trades
Nuku Hiva	Ahé	478	495	4/27/74	5/2	Calm, slow, and hot
Ahé	Papeete	266	273	5/6/74	5/10	Calm, slow, and hot
Papeete	Bora Bora	—180—				Good trades, warm
Bora Bora	Pago Pago	1070	1088	8/15/74	8/27	Gentle trades and calms
Pago Pago	Tonga	320	325	9/7/74	9/9	Strong trades
Tonga	Suva (Viti Levu)	438	455	9/19/74	9/23	Moderate trades
Suva	New Zealand	1020	1160	10/12/74	10/24	Gale, adverse winds near N.Z.
New Zealand	Mooloolaba	1236	1248	4/27/75	5/8	Calm, strong trades
Mooloolaba	Thursday Island (Barrier Reef)	—2400—				Strong trades, choppy seas
Thursday Is.	Timor (Dili)	—1050—		7/31/75	8/8	Unpredictable winds, slow, hot
Dili	Kupang	—166—				Motor boat ride, hot
Kupang	Bali	518	527	8/21/75	8/26	Gentle trades, land breezes, hot
Bali	Christmas Island	583	590	10/2/75	10/7	Light winds, clouds, rough cross-swell
Christmas Island	Cocos Keeling	532	544	10/11/75	10/16	Same as above

| PASSAGE | | DISTANCE (N.M.) | | DATES | | GENERAL WEATHER |
From	To	Rhumb	Actual	Left	Arrived	
Cocos Keeling	Mauritius	2360	2444	10/18/75	11/4	Unsettled clouds, rough cross-swell
Mauritius	Durban	1546	1710	11/18/75	12/4	Good trades, gale off Durban
Durban	Capetown	–847–				Unpredictable, gale in Capetown
Capetown	Saint Helena	1658	1716	3/15/76	3/28	Strong trades, fast passage, cold
Saint Helena	Martinique	3753	3878	4/10/76	5/11	Mod. and gentle trades S of equator, calms 2° S–4° N with squalls. Trades N of doldrums
Martinique	Saint Thomas	–380–		5/11/76	5/15	Trades and sunny
Saint Thomas	San Salvadore	–660–		6/5/76	6/10	Trades and sunny
San Salvadore	West Palm Beach	–360–		6/14/76	6/17	Trades and sunny
West Palm Beach	Morehead City	–530–		6/18/76	6/21	Squalls and S winds
Morehead City	Annapolis	–350–		6/22/76	July 1	Sunny, calm, hot
		TOTAL 30,892				

Glossary of Nautical Terms

Aft. Toward the stern.

Amidships. Usually the line of the keel, but sometimes midway between the bow and stern.

Anchor rode. A line attached to the anchor of a small boat.

Baggy-wrinkle. Bushy-appearing chafing gear made from old rope and wound around a stay to prevent wear on a sail at a potential point of chafe.

Belaying pin. A device of brass, iron, or wood which is set in the "pinrails" and is used for securing the running rigging.

Bilge. The turn of the hull below the water line.

Binnacle. A box or nonmagnetic metallic container for the compass.

Bobstay. Chains or heavy wire rigging running from the end of the bowsprit to the vessel's stem to support the bowsprit from beneath.

Boom. A spar to which the foot of a fore-and-aft sail is attached.

Brail. A rope of a fore-and-aft sail, leading in from the leech to the mast.

Bulwark. A vessel's topside above the deck.

Cathead. A heavy timber projecting horizontally from the bow of an old-fashioned vessel through which the fall of the "cat" tackle is rove, the sheaves being set in the cat head. This tackle heaves the anchor to the cat head. This process is called *catting the anchor.*

Caulking. The material used to fill a seam to make it watertight.

Chain plate. Metal strips bolted to the side of a ship or yacht to which the standing rigging is attached.

Chronometer. A very accurate clock.

Clew. In a fore-and-aft sail, the lower corner aft; in a square sail, the two lower corners.

Cockbill. To trim the yards by the lifts in a diagonal manner. One end of the yard is tilted up, the other end down.

Companionway. Steps or stairs leading below from the deck.

Copper sheathing. The covering of copper sheets on a vessel's bottom to protect the wood from marine borers.

Crosstrees. Comparatively light timbers thwartships on a mast which support the tops and spread the rigging.

Davits. Small cranes used to hoist a boat aboard.

Deadeyes. A round block of lignum vitae with several holes through it and a groove around the edge to receive the lower eye of a shroud or the strap of a chain plate.

Downhaul. A tackle or rope by which a sail is hauled down.

Draft. The depth of water necessary to float a vessel.

Fiddles. A coaming around the edge of a table or shelf to prevent things from falling in a seaway.

Fife rail. A pin rail in a semicircle around a mast.

Fore-staysail. A jib-shaped sail setting from the fore stay.

Futtock shroud. Iron rods which support the tops and topmast rigging.

Gammon iron. The ring which holds the bowsprit to the stemhead.

Gaff. The spar upon which the head, or upper edge of a fore-and-aft rectangular sail, is extended.

Gaff jaws. The fitting on the inboard end of the gaff which slides on the mast.

Halyard. Ropes and tackles for hoisting sail and yards.

Hand (sails). To furl a sail.

Hawse. Holes or slots in the bulwarks through which mooring lines are passed.

Head. The compartment with toilet facilities.

Heave to. To lay the vessel on the wind with the helm to lee so the vessel will come to and fall off but always out of the trough of the waves.

Lazy jack. Small ropes leading down vertically from the topping lifts to the boom to hold a fore-and-aft sail when taking it in. Applies to gaff-rigged and lug-rigged vessels.

Leeway. The amount a vessel is carried to leeward by force of the wind or current.

Mainstay. A piece of rigging, usually wire rope, that serves to stay a mast from forward.

Marconi (Bermuda rig). A mast from which is set a leg-of-mutton (triangular) mainsail.

Martingale (Dolphin striker). A small spar beneath the bowsprit which forms a truss for the support of the jib boom with the martingale guys and martingale stays.

Parrel. A band with revolving balls of lignum vitae that goes around a mast and holds a yard close to it, and allows the yard to be hoisted and lowered.

Pratique. Permission to hold intercourse with a port, given to a ship that has satisfied health regulations.

Quarter. The after part of a vessel's side.

Raffee. The triangular sail usually flown above a square sail, set from the mast truck and the yardarms of the yard.

Ratlines. Rope rungs seized to the shrouds which form a rope ladder.

Reef. To reduce sail area.

Rhumb line. A straight line on a Mercator chart.

Riprap. A wall of stones thrown together without order so as to strengthen a breakwater.

Rove. To pass a rope through a block or a hole.

Saloon. A large cabin on shipboard.

Scupper. A hole in the bulwarks to allow water to drain from the deck.

Shackle. A U-shaped metal fitting with an eye in each of its arms through which a pin is screwed or driven.

Sheerstrake. The uppermost plank of the topside.

Sheet. A rope by means of which a sail is trimmed.

Shroud. A wire rope giving athwartships support to a mast, bowsprit, or boomkin.

Sole. The saloon or cabin floor.

Square sail. A sail which sets from a yard slung athwartships on the fore side of a mast.

Stay. A wire rope giving fore-and-aft support to a mast.

Sprit shrouds. The shrouds used to stay the bowsprit.

Taffrail. The aftermost rail on a vessel.

Tang. Broad bands on the mast to which shrouds and stays are attached.

Topmast. The next mast above any lower spar.

Transom. A flat stern on most vessels.

Variation. The difference between true and magnetic north at any place.

Wood down. To remove paint down to bare wood.

Yankee jib. A large triangular headsail set on the fore-topmast stay. It does not fill the whole fore triangle area.

Yard. A spar crossing a mast horizontally, from which a square sail is set.

Zincs. Plates of zinc placed at points where dissimilar metals come into contact with steel in order to prevent electrolytic action.